LETTERS OF ENGAGEMENT

1884-1888

Marie-Jaqueline Lancaster

To my late mother

Jaqueline Hope-Nicholson

who always hoped these letters would be published one day

LETTERS OF

ENGAGEMENT

1884–1888

The Love Letters of

Adrian Hope and Laura Troubridge

Edited by their granddaughter
Marie-Jaqueline Lancaster

TITE STREET PRESS

First published in Great Britain in 2002 by Tite Street Press
11 Winchester Court, Vicarage Gate, London W8 4AB
Copyright © 2002 by Jean Baptiste Hugo for the estate of
Laura (Troubridge) Hope
Editing, narrative and annotations © 2002 by Marie-Jaqueline Lancaster

Distributed by Gazelle Book Services Limited
Falcon House, Queen Square
Lancaster, England LA1 1RN

British Library Cataloguing in Publication Data
A catalogue record for this book is available from the British Library

ISBN 0-9534746-1-5

Typeset by Amolibros, Watchet, Somerset
This book production has been managed by Amolibros
Printed and bound by T J International Ltd, Padstow, England

CONTENTS

Year Two 1885/86

Year Three 1886/87

Year Four 1887/88

ACKNOWLEDGEMENTS

I would like to thank my second cousin, Richard Gurney (grandson of Laura's middle sister 'Vi' Troubridge and Walter Gurney) and his wife, Clarice, for their unstinting help and encouragement in every way, not least for the gift of one of Vi's marvellous family photograph albums and the loan of another one, without which I would not have been able to include such an interesting selection of photographs. Sadly, Laura's numerous family photograph albums were inaccessible.

My thanks are also due to Brenda Kirby for her invaluable editorial advice and to Richard Unthank for his clear presentation of the family trees. I also owe a great debt of thanks to my publishing manager, Jane Tatam of Amolibros, who has provided invaluable guidance through the various publishing stages of preparing the reprint of *Life Amongst the Troubridges* (1999) and this volume, its sequel, under my own imprint of the Tite Street Press.

HOPE Family Tree with HOPETOUN/LINLITHGOW connection

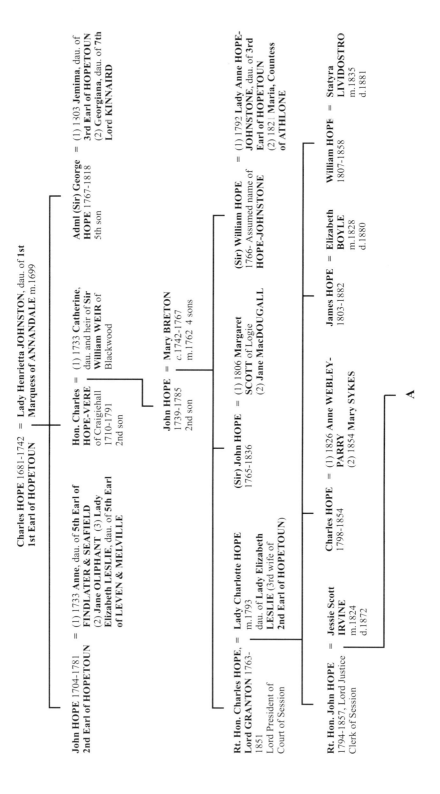

Charles HOPE 1681-1742 = Lady Henrietta JOHNSTON, dau. of 1st
1st Earl of HOPETOUN   Marquess of ANNANDALE m.1699

John HOPE 1704-1781 = (1) 1733 Anne, dau. of 5th Earl of
2nd Earl of HOPETOUN   FINDLATER & SEAFIELD
                         (2) Jane OLIPHANT (3) Lady
                         Elizabeth LESLIE, dau. of 5th Earl
                         of LEVEN & MELVILLE

Hon. Charles = (1) 1733 Catherine,
HOPE-VERE   dau. and heir of Sir
of Craigiehall William WEIR of
1710-1791   Blackwood
2nd son

Adml (Sir) George = (1) 1303 Jemima, dau. of
HOPE 1767-1818   3rd Earl of HOPETOUN
5th son   (2) Georgiana, dau. of 7th
                   Lord KINNAIRD

John HOPE = Mary BRETON
1739-1785   c.1742-1767
2nd son   m.1762 4 sons

(Sir) William HOPE = (1) 1792 Lady Anne HOPE-
1766- Assumed name of   JOHNSTONE, dau. of 3rd
HOPE-JOHNSTONE   Earl of HOPETOUN
                       (2) 182 Maria, Countess
                       of ATHLONE

Rt. Hon. Charles HOPE, = Lady Charlotte HOPE
Lord GRANTON 1763-   m.1793
1851   dau. of Lady Elizabeth
Lord President of   LESLIE (3rd wife of
Court of Session   2nd Earl of HOPETOUN)

(Sir) John HOPE = (1) 1806 Margaret
1765-1836   SCOTT of Logie
                  (2) Jane MacDOUGALL

Charles HOPE = (1) 1826 Anne WEBLEY-
1798-1854   PARRY
                 (2) 1854 Mary SYKES

James HOPE = Elizabeth
1803-1882   BOYLE
             m.1828
             d.1880

William HOPE = Statyra
1807-1858   LIVIDOSTRO
               m.1835
               d.1881

Rt. Hon. John HOPE = Jessie Scott
1794-1857, Lord Justice   IRVINE
Clerk of Session   m.1824
                          d.1872

A

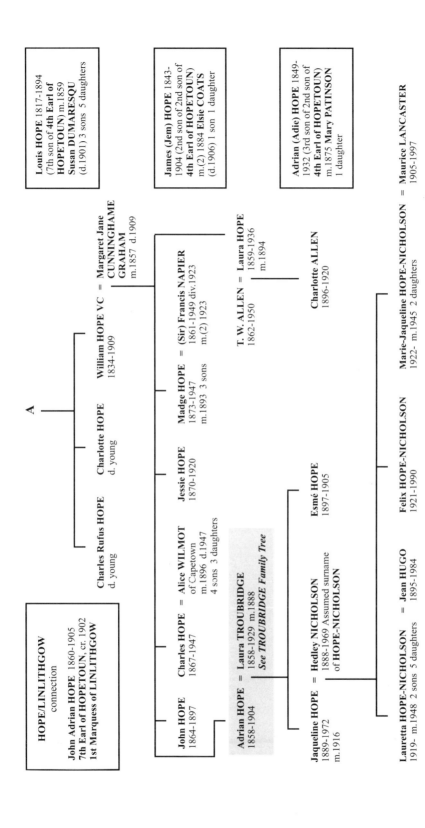

HOPE/LINLITHGOW connection

John Adrian HOPE 1860-1905
7th Earl of HOPETOUN, cr. 1902
1st Marquess of LINLITHGOW

A

Louis HOPE 1817-1894
(7th son of 4th Earl of HOPETOUN) m.1859
Susan DUMARESQU
(d.1901) 3 sons 5 daughters

James (Jem) HOPE 1843-1904 (2nd son of 2nd son of 4th Earl of HOPETOUN)
m.(2) 1884 Elsie COATS
(d.1906) 1 son 1 daughter

Adrian (Adie) HOPE 1849-1932 (3rd son of 2nd son of 4th Earl of HOPETOUN)
m.1875 Mary PATINSON
1 daughter

Charles Rufus HOPE
d. young

Charlotte HOPE
d. young

William HOPE VC
1834-1909
= Margaret Jane CUNNINGHAME GRAHAM m.1857 d.1909

Jessie HOPE
1870-1920

Madge HOPE
1873-1947
m.1893 3 sons
= (Sir) Francis NAPIER 1861-1949 div.1923 m.(2) 1923

T. W. ALLEN
1862-1950
= Laura HOPE 1859-1936 m.1894

Charlotte ALLEN
1896-1920

Marie-Jacqueline HOPE-NICHOLSON 1922- m.1945 2 daughters
= Maurice LANCASTER 1905-1997

John HOPE
1864-1897

Charles HOPE
1867-1947
= Alice WILMOT of Capetown m.1896 d.1947 4 sons 3 daughters

Adrian HOPE
1858-1904
= Laura TROUBRIDGE 1858-1929 m.1888 *See TROUBRIDGE Family Tree*

Esmé HOPE
1897-1905

Felix HOPE-NICHOLSON
1921-1990

Jaqueline HOPE
1889-1972
m.1916
= Hedley NICHOLSON 1888-1969 Assumed surname of HOPE-NICHOLSON

Lauretta HOPE-NICHOLSON
1919- m.1948 2 sons 5 daughters
= Jean HUGO
1895-1984

CUNNINGHAME GRAHAM connection

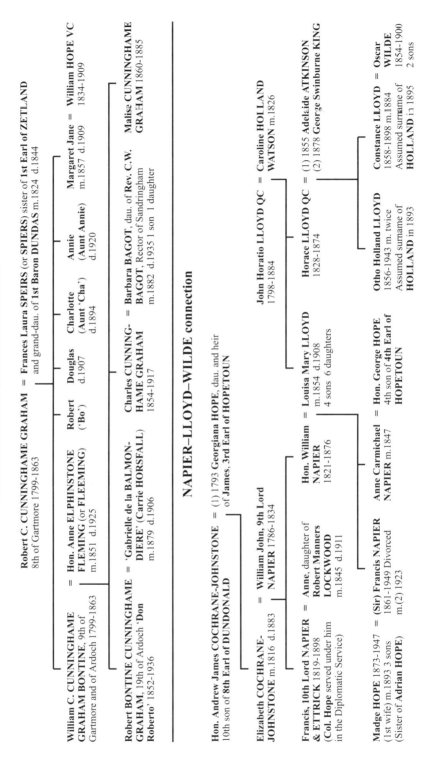

Robert C. CUNNINGHAME GRAHAM = Frances Laura SPEIRS (or SPIERS) sister of **1st Earl of ZETLAND**
8th of Gartmore 1799-1863   and grand-dau. of **1st Baron DUNDAS** m.1824 d.1844

William C. CUNNINGHAME = Hon. **Anne ELPHINSTONE** | Robert | Douglas | Charlotte | Annie | Margaret Jane = **William HOPE VC**
GRAHAM BONTINE, 9th of | **FLEMING** (or **FLEEMING**) | (**'Bo'**) | d.1907 | (Aunt 'Cha') | (**Aunt Annie**) | m.1857 d.1909 | 1834-1909
Gartmore and of Ardoch 1799-1863 | m.1851 d.1925 | | | d.1894 | d.1920

Robert BONTINE CUNNINGHAME = 'Gabrielle de la BALMON- | Charles CUNNING- = **Barbara BAGOT**, dau. of Rev. C.W. | Malise CUNNINGHAME
GRAHAM, 19th of Ardoch 'Don | **DIERE**' (**Carrie HORSFALL**) | **HAME GRAHAM** | **BAGOT**, Rector of Sandringham | **GRAHAM** 1860-1885
Roberto' 1852-1936 | m.1879 d.1906 | 1854-1917 | m.1882 d.1935 1 son 1 daughter

---

NAPIER–LLOYD–WILDE connection

Hon. **Andrew James COCHRANE-JOHNSTONE** = (1) 1793 Georgiana HOPE, dau. and heir
10th son of **8th Earl of DUNDONALD**   of **James, 3rd Earl of HOPETOUN**

= William John, **9th Lord** | **John Horatio LLOYD QC** = Caroline **HOLLAND**
NAPIER 1786-1834 | 1798-1884 | **WATSON** m.1826

Elizabeth COCHRANE- = Anne, daughter of | Hon. **William** = Louisa Mary **LLOYD** | **Horace LLOYD QC** = (1) 1855 Adelaide **ATKINSON**
JOHNSTONE m.1816 d.1883 | Robert Manners | **NAPIER** | m.1854 d.1908 | 1828-1874 | (2) 1878 George Swinburne **KING**
 | **LOCKWOOD** | 1821-1876 | 4 sons 6 daughters
 | m.1845 d.1911

Francis, 10th Lord NAPIER = Anne Carmichael = Hon. **George HOPE** | **Otho Holland LLOYD** | Constance **LLOYD** = Oscar
& ETTRICK 1819-1898 | **NAPIER** m.1847 | 4th son of **4th Earl of** | 1856-1943 m. twice | 1858-1898 m.1884 | **WILDE**
(**Col. Hope** served under him | | **HOPETOUN** | Assumed surname of | Assumed surname of | 1854-1900
in the Diplomatic Service) | | | **HOLLAND** in 1893 | **HOLLAND** in 1895 | 2 sons

Madge HOPE 1873-1947 = **(Sir) Francis NAPIER**
(1st wife) m.1893 3 sons | 1861-1949 Divorced
(Sister of **Adrian HOPE**) | m.(2) 1923

TROUBRIDGE Family Tree

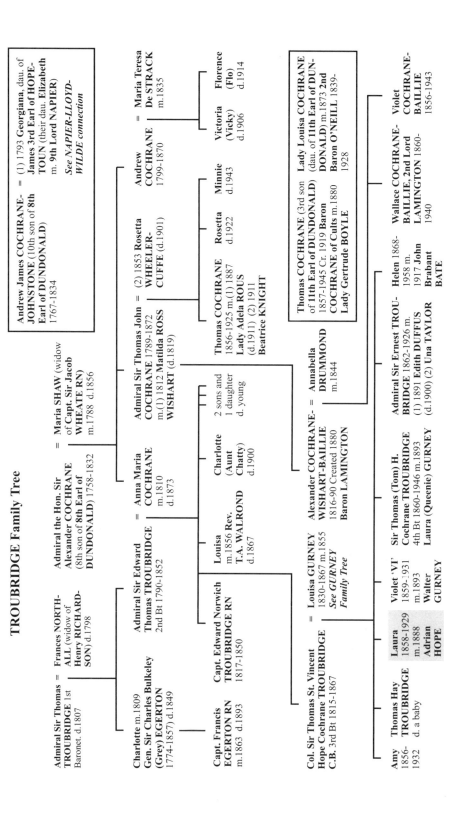

GURNEY Family Tree

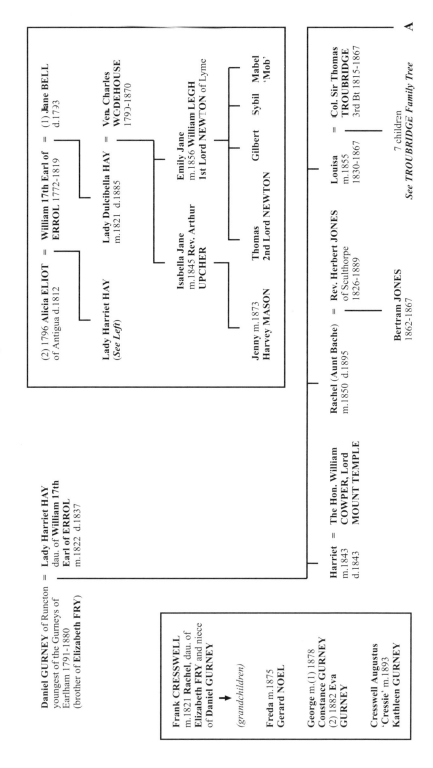

Daniel GURNEY of Runcton youngest of the Gurneys of Earlham 1791-1880 (brother of **Elizabeth FRY**) = **Lady Harriet HAY** dau. of **William 17th Earl of ERROL** m.1822 d.1837

(2) 1796 **Alicia ELIOT** of Antigua d.1812 = **William 17th Earl of ERROL** 1772-1819 = (1) **Jane BELL** d.1793

Lady Harriet HAY (*See Left*)

Lady Dulcibella HAY m.1821 d.1885 = **Ven. Charles WODEHOUSE** 1790-1870

Isabella Jane m.1845 **Rev. Arthur UPCHER**

Emily Jane m.1856 **William LEGH 1st Lord NEWTON** of Lyme

Jenny m.1873 **Harvey MASON**

Thomas 2nd Lord NEWTON

Gilbert   **Sybil**   **Mabel 'Mob'**

Harriet m.1843 d.1843 = **The Hon. William COWPER, Lord MOUNT TEMPLE**

Rachel (Aunt Bache) m.1850 d.1895 = **Rev. Herbert JONES** of Sculthorpe 1826-1889

Louisa m.1855 1830-1867 = **Col. Sir Thomas TROUBRIDGE** 3rd Bt 1815-1867

Bertram JONES 1862-1867

7 children
See TROUBRIDGE Family Tree

A

Frank CRESSWELL m.1821 **Rachel**, dau. of **Elizabeth FRY** and niece of **Daniel GURNEY**

(grandchildren)

Freda m.1875 **Gerard NOEL**

George m.(1) 1878 **Constance GURNEY** (2) 1882 **Eva GURNEY**

Cresswell Augustus 'Cressie' m.1893 **Kathleen GURNEY**

A

Francis Hay GURNEY of Keswick 1826-1890 m.1847 = **Margaret FFOLKES** (Aunt **Minnie**) d.1899

Rev. William GURNEY of Runcton Rectory 1827-1898 = **Anna BOILEAU** (Aunt **Amy**) m.1852 d.1897

Charles GURNEY 1833-1899 m.1861 divorced = **Alice PRINSEP** m.(2) 1897 Col. Stracey-Clitherow

Somerville GURNEY (Uncle **Tum**) of Valleyfield, later of Runcton 1835-1917 = **Katherine HAMOND** (Aunt **Kitty**) m.1857 d.1917

Margaret (Aunt **Maggie**) m.1856 d.1901 = **James ORDE** of Hopton 1830-1880

13 children including

8 children including

4 children

10 children including

8 children including

Reginald (Puny)
Lewis (Dor)
Cecil
Lovel
Edward
Hudson

Rachel (Tivo)
Helen (Ape)
Constance m.1878 George CRESSWELL d.1879
Beatrice (Bea)

Mortimer
Geoffrey (Gee)

Eva (Beaver) m.1882 (2nd wife) George CRESSWELL
Winifred
Kathleen m.1893 'Cressie' CRESSWELL
Richenda

Henry Edward
Thomas Claud

Laura (Queenie) m.1893 Sir Thomas (Tom) TROUBRIDGE 4th Bt
Rachel m.1891 2nd Earl of DUDLEY

Walter m.1893 Violet (Vi) TROUBRIDGE
Anthony
Philip

Rose m.1883 John BIRKBECK
Lily
Ruth
Mabel m.1887 Sir William CURTIS d.1888
Audrey
Muriel

Charles (Tardy)
Lancelot
Julian (Doonie) m.1885 Alice ARCHDALE

Evelyn
Sybil
Margaret (Daisy)
Betty

ABOUT THE
ILLUSTRATIONS

Facing page 132

1 Knocklofty House, Clonmel, in Co Tipperary

Tom Troubridge and brother officers of the 60th Rifles stationed at Limerick had rented Knocklofty House for the fishing. Tom's sisters came to 'keep house' for them in August and September, 1884. Seen in the photograph from left to right: Edward 'Bean' St Aubyn, Amy, Helen, the newly engaged pair, Laura, and Adrian Hope, Vi and Tom. Ernest was away at sea.

(Tite Street Archive/Vi Troubridge's first Album)

2 East front of North Runcton Hall, near King's Lynn, Norfolk

Home of Daniel Gurney where his young Troubridge grandchildren spent their childhood after the death of their parents. This watercolour, by the eldest daughter of Daniel's eldest sister Elizabeth Fry, is one of the many illustrations in her remarkable 'Katharine Fry's Book'(1878), a 600-page folio album measuring ten by fifteen inches, chronicling the history of the extended Quaker Gurney and Fry families. The handwritten text, illustrations, portraits and caricatures are all her own work. Katharine stayed with her Uncle Daniel Gurney at Runcton in 1830 to help him finish his equally large folio album, the *Record of the House of Gurney,* making fair copies of all the documents and coats of arms. Eventually 250 quarto copies were privately printed in 1848, and alluded to as 'The Apochryphal Book of Dan' by his more sceptical relations.

(Courtesy of Henry Buxton [of Easenye branch], Ware, Herts)

3 'The Castle ' at Hunstanton

At their grandfather Daniel's death in 1880, the young Troubridges had to make the move from the then forty-three-room North Runcton Hall to this very ordinary seaside house in nearby Hunstanton – pronounced Hunston – which they instantly christened 'The Castle'.
(Richard Gurney/Vi Troubridge's second Album)

4 'The Castle' dining room

The conventional interior is here enlivened by such ideas as the dining table sprouting a large Japanese parasol shading a vase of peacock feathers, bad luck notwithstanding.
(Richard Gurney/Vi Troubridge's second Album)

5 The Hunstanton Jazz Band

The Troubridge sisters kept their spirits up by forming their own Band, which consisted entirely of first cousins, playing here in 1887. *Left to right, standing:* the unmusical Laura relegated to the tambourine, Kat and Winny Gurney (of the Runcton Rectory) and Vi Troubridge. *Seated:* Chen (another 'Runcton Rec' sister) and Amy Troubridge, the real musician among them.
(Richard Gurney/Vi Troubridge's second Album)

6 Dandies of the opposite kind

Charles Orde in close-buttoned riding trousers, and Adrian Hope (*see* 8). Laura once described Charlie, despite him being her favourite cousin, as *un peu neutre* (neuter) compared to Adrian who was so obviously the reverse.
(Richard Gurney/Vi Troubridge's second Album)

7 Evelyn, 'E', the handsome eldest Orde sister

'E' was a great friend of Laura's. Even Augustus Hare was susceptible to her good looks when he first visited Hopton in 1887 and recorded his admiration in his *The Story of My Life* (Vol 6, 1900).
(Richard Gurney/Vi Troubridge's second Album)

8 Adrian Hope, elegant as ever

Photographed at Yarmouth while staying at Hopton St Margaret with Laura and the Orde cousins. Adrian lived in a permanently impecunious state, yet managed to dress impeccably and run to a new tam o'shanter when called for by Laura.

(Tite Street Archive)

9 Summer in the garden at Hopton

Laura loved staying with her Aunt Maggie Orde at Hopton, and was eventually to be married from there. *Left to right*: Charlie on the banjo, his sisters Betty and 'E', Laura next to Aunt Maggie, Sybil, and Daisy wielding the ubiquitous parasol.

(Tite Street Archive/Vi Troubridge's first Album)

10 Royal Naval Lunch menu

The Royal Naval Lunch at Goodwood on 31st July 1884 was a splendid occasion with a 'very swagger' picnic lunch that did much to help Adrian and Laura to recover from their late-night dancing of the night before – which had kept them up until 3.30 a.m. This colourful menu card was tucked away with other nostalgic mementoes amongst Laura's 'engagement' letters.

(Tite Street Archive)

11 Roland Le Strange, of Hunstanton Hall

Roland, was growing up fast and 'not so conceited and *masherish* as he used to be' according to Laura, with whom he flirted outrageously despite being ten years younger. He found her 'ripping' as Schéhérazade in the Runcton Tableaux of 1887.

(Tite Street Archive/Vi Troubridge's first Album)

12 Eva Gurney of Runcton Rectory

Eva had married the young widower George Cresswell in 1882. She frequently invited Laura and Adrian, during their long engagement, to stay with them in King's Lynn or at their holiday house in Hunstanton where George kept his yacht, the *Wild Duck*.

(Tite Street Archive/Vi Troubridge's first Album)

13 Rosy Gurney of North Runcton Hall

Seen here in 1882, a year before her marriage to the eccentric and highly musical Johnny Birkbeck who she often accompanied on the harp when he played the organ or violoncello. She, too, arranged many meetings between Laura and Adrian at their Thurloe Square house in London.
(Tite Street Archive/Vi Troubridge's first Album)

14 & 15 Lieutenant Hope saving the Powder Magazine

Contemporary engraving of this episode in the Crimean War on 15th November, 1855, when William Hope VC *(see inset)* with his band of Volunteers climbed 'The Windmill', as it was known, and covered the exposed powder boxes stored there with wet tarpaulin and blankets to protect them from the surrounding flames, exploding shells and burning wood flying through the air. For this act of bravery, Lt Hope was awarded the Sardinian Medal for Military Valour, conferred by Victor Emmanuel. Some people thought he should have received a bar to his VC won some five months earlier for another conspicuous act of bravery when he tried, under heavy fire, to save the life of his Adjutant left wounded in the field after the attack on the Redan fort, Sebastopol. *(See p34 , footnote 7.)*
(14—Courtesy of Mrs Arthur [Muriel] Hope, source of engraving unknown; 15—inset photo from VC and DSO complete record ..., Ed by Creagh and Humphris, Vol 1 [The Standard Art Book Co, London EC4, 3 vol edn, 1924])

Facing page 324

16 The newly married Oscar Wilde

Wilde married Constance Lloyd in the spring of 1884 and it was while on honeymoon in Paris that he had made notes for 'Le Jardin des Tuileries'. This photograph, taken of him in the following autumn when he was lecturing on the Isle of Wight, almost makes him look the settled, married man.
(Courtesy of Merlin Holland)

17 Wilde's poem illustrated by Laura Troubridge

Adrian asked Wilde, with whom he was friendly, to contribute a poem to Mrs Tyssen-Amherst's anthology *In a Good Cause* (1885) in aid of the Children's Hospital in Hackney. He agreed, provided Laura Troubridge illustrate it. She managed this pen-and-ink sketch but found the small space allocated daunting

and the last verse's reference to *blue* blossoms in the Tuileries Gardens made her comment to Adrian that she thought 'Oscar's Muse was out of town' at the time, to which Adrian wrote back agreeing that the poem was 'twaddle'! ...
(In a Good Cause, *Wells-Gardner Darton & Co, 1885*)

18 Robert Cunninghame Graham

Adrian was able to help Robert Cunnnghame Graham (his first cousin) after Robert's immediate arrest for his actions on behalf of the unemployed in the Battle of Trafalgar Square on 'Bloody Sunday' (13th November 1887), while Adrian's father Col Hope VC went bail for his wife's nephew. 'Don Roberto', as he was known, was equally at home as a socialist MP, a Scottish laird or a gaucho in Latin America, and was a much admired writer of distinctive tales, essays and biographies.
(Courtesy of Lady Polwarth)

19 & 20 The engaged couple

Adrian and Laura agreed to differ on the subject of Robert and his part in the Trafalgar Square riot – Adrian supporting his action at all times and Laura taking a somewhat dour (as she admits) and thoroughly disapproving view.
(19 – Richard Gurney/Vi Troubridge's second Album; 20 – Tite Street Archive/Vi Troubridge's first Album)

21 'Bloody Sunday' riot in and around Trafalgar Square

Contemporary engraving showing 'FIGHT AT THE BOTTOM OF PARLIAMENT STREET BETWEEN THE POLICE AND CONTINGENT FROM SOUTH LONDON AND BATTERSEA', one of many depicting different aspects of the 'Bloody Sunday' riot in Trafalgar Square and surrounding streets on 13th November, 1887, by the unemployed and their sympathisers (including Robert Cunninghame Graham, who for his pains was sent to prison for six weeks). The riot was a very confused affair as the mounted police would prevent the mob from entering the square by one side street only to find that they had infiltrated through another one. Here the mounted police at the bottom of Parliament Street fight off the mob which had started from West Battersea, gathering contingents from Vauxhall and Westminster, and debouched from Old Palace Yard into New Palace Yard. The battle raged from Westminster Bridge almost to Birdcage Walk and the mob only gave way when the Life Guards arrived out of the darkness in Whitehall Place.
(The Graphic, *19th November, 1887)*

22 Sir Tom Troubridge Bt

Despite wearing mufti, Tom has a military air about him. He was a captain in the King's Royal Rifle Corps when he married, in 1893, his first cousin Laura 'Queenie', daughter of Charles Gurney and Alice née Prinsep. 'Uncle Charles', who for some time had been estranged from his wife, did not attend the wedding and 'Queenie' was given away by her brother-in-law, the 2nd Earl of Dudley. (Her younger sister Rachel had married Lord Dudley some two years earlier.)
(Richard Gurney/Vi Troubridge's second Album)

23 Lady Troubridge – Laura 'Queenie' née Gurney

Portrait of 'Queenie' at the time of her marriage (1893) by Tom's sister Laura, by then married to Adrian Hope. Lady Troubridge became famous for her The Book of Etiquette – the complete standard work of reference on social usages *(1926, last reprint 1988). Her* Memories and Reflections *had been published the year before and gave a surprisingly happy account of her and her sister Rachel's unconventional upbringing.*

(Courtesy of Robin Mackenzie, grandson of Tom and 'Queenie' Troubridge)

24 Ernest Troubridge, aged nineteen

Ernest, the younger Troubridge brother, had already been at sea for four and a half years by the time he came home on leave in 1881, aged nineteen. He was appointed to the Royal Yacht some three years later, then travelled all over the world and by his next leave, in 1887, he had grown black, mutton chop whiskers – much to Laura's indignation. The following year he was awarded the Silver Medal of the Royal Humane Society for jumping overboard to save the life of sailor who had fallen from a torpedo boat in Suda Bay, Northern Crete.
(Tite Street Archive/Vi Troubridge's first Album)

25 'Dodsie' Wright, everyone's favourite

'Dodsie' (Ernest, b 1878) only child of the Troubridge governess Clemence (Vleminck) and Willy Wright, the steward at North Runcton Hall when the young Troubridges went to live with their grandfather Daniel Gurney. 'Dodsie' was loved by everyone but especially by Laura to whom he was a page at her wedding.
(Richard Gurney/Vi Troubridge's second Album)

26 Helen, the youngest of the Troubridge sisters

Helen, always the baby of the family, had a surprising talent for looking sultry in fancy dress, especially as the Sultana Nourmahal, 'the Light of the Haram' from *Lalla Rookh* (1817). This was a very popular series of Oriental tales in verse linked by a story in prose by the poet and musician Thomas Moore.

(Tite Street Archive/Vi Troubridge's first Album)

27 Laura's Christmas Card

The Troubridge sisters had been designing decorative tiles since 1874 and selling them first to numerous relations and later to Mortlock's shop in London. Then Mansell's, the art publishers, asked for Christmas and New Year Cards for 1879 and Laura produced many colourful one-offs of fairies and 'fancies' with much gold detail.

(Tite Street Archive)

28 'The Queen of Hearts' set

One of Laura's six watercolour illustrations (8.5 by 8 inches) to the nursery rhyme 'The Queen of Hearts, she made some tarts ...' with the words handwritten below each scene. The Italianate background here is in a delicate sepia line that contrasts well with the highly coloured playing-card characters. The heart shape is set on a repeat pattern in gold. Laura had also designed a cover and three decorative preliminary pages for this book project when Adrian's friend Jack Scott Gatty set it to music in 1887. Sadly, it did not find a publisher with, or without, accompanying music.

(Tite Street Archive)

29 'The Little Mermaid'

For Hans Andersen's fairy story, 'The Little Mermaid', Laura produced front and back covers and ten large-page line illustrations. She had hoped to get this published as a children's book (10 by 8 inches) in the style of her *Little Thumb* (1883) but without any success. Finally the story with the ten illustrations was published, very much reduced in size, in the *English Illustrated Magazine* (Christmas, 1891).

(Tite Street Archive)

"]

30 Frontispiece of Mrs Molesworth's The Old Pincushion

In 1887 Adrian asked his friend Mrs Molesworth, the children's book writer, if his fiancée could illustrate her next book but this had already been commissioned so Laura was asked to do the one after, *The Old Pincushion* (Griffiths, Farran, Okeden & Welsh, 1889) of which this is the frontispiece. She was disappointed that it was not a fairy book and that the illustrations were to be in wash and not line, which was her speciality.

(Tite Street Archive)

31 & 32 On board the honeymoon house boat

At last Adrian and Laura's four-year engagement came to an end and his cousin Jem Hope lent them his luxurious house boat, the *Crocodile*, for their honeymoon in August 1888. The mooring on the Thames at Pangbourne in Berkshire was not exactly like Bellagio on Lake Como which had been their impossible dream but in her Journal of the time Laura called it 'a heavenly idle life', and they were able to visit Bellagio much later on in life.

(Richard Gurney/Vi Troubridge's second Album)

EDITOR'S FOREWORD

The archives of the Hope-Troubridge alliance are endless and to me—Adrian and Laura's granddaughter—fascinating. Laura Troubridge's early journals dating from 1873 up to her engagement to Adrian Hope in 1884 have already been published as *Life Amongst the Troubridges—Journals of a Young Victorian 1873–1884,* and now these letters between Adrian and Laura during their long engagement from 2nd August, 1884 to exactly four years later—2nd August, 1888, continue the story up to their marriage. They give a very personal view of the period and were not intended for publication but I do not feel that either of them would object to their unveiling over a century later.

Laura collected their 'engagement letters' and arranged them in date order to form a continuous running dialogue. They used to think of their letters as being the next best thing to talking face-to-face, and, the daily posts being considerably faster and more frequent than those of today, their answers or comments on exchanges of news are near enough to the original questions to make this 'conversational' aspect ring true. At the start of their engagement, Adrian was living, reluctantly, at his family home of the time in Battersea, when not away for social weekends or being put up in central London by his closer relations with whom he is a favourite house guest, while Laura was largely confined to the little seaside house in Hunstanton, Norfolk, that she shared with her three sisters—Amy, Violet and Helen, and their two brothers—Tom and Ernest—when on leave from the army and the navy respectively. However, she managed to leaven the bracing winds of Hunstanton with numerous visits to the large country houses of her Norfolk relations and other friends.

The six young Troubridges had been orphaned when their parents—Col Sir Thomas Troubridge 3rd Bt and Louisa née Gurney died within a few weeks of each other in 1867. They were then brought up in Norfolk by their elderly grandfather, Daniel Gurney, until his death in 1880 after which, determined to stay together, they moved to a modest house in Hunstanton.

Adrian Hope was the eldest of six: three sons—Adrian, John and Charles, and three daughters—Laura, Jessie and Madge, the children of Lt-Col William Hope VC and Margaret Jane née Cunninghame Graham. Colonel Hope began his married life in the diplomatic service but relinquished that world, first for the uncertain one of experimental agriculture and then to develop his design for a revolutionary gun. Their family fortunes sank to zero, to the detriment of their children's education, let alone their happiness.

During the first year of their engagement, Adrian is appointed Secretary to the Great Ormond Street Hospital for Sick Children where, apart from administrative duties, his work consists largely of fundraising for which he develops a talent. He has a love-hate relationship with the hospital and this, together with the vicissitudes of the projected Hope gun of his very unstable father, provides a tragic thread to his comparatively short life. (He dies at forty-six.) Laura, already a talented amateur artist with one successful illustrated children's book to her name, concentrates on developing her facility for achieving a likeness in portraiture and her skills as a book illustrator.

Their love letters over this engagement period of four years are equal in length to four average novels and massive cuts were necessary to arrive at a readable package. In editing them I have aimed at retaining a combination of personal narrative with their comments on contemporary events and anecdotes involving the personalities of the time, such as Sir Charles Dilke and other Liberal politicians from whom Adrian hoped to get a more congenial job, the Oscar Wildes (to whose children, Cyril and Vyvyan Holland, Adrian eventually becomes guardian), and the artists and writers who express admiration for Laura's work—Kate Greenaway, 'Lewis Carroll', Sir John Millais, Mrs Molesworth. The manners and morals of the time, the way of life in large country houses, the vagaries of ladies' fashions and so on are mercilessly exposed. As a result of condensing the letters, much of the 'love dialogues' and the minutiae of everyday life are lost, so that the reader must make allowances for the sometimes abrupt shifts in continuity necessitated. I have not translated the innumerable endearments in French at the end of many of their letters.

Laura's letters tend to be happy-go-lucky and full of her daily round in Norfolk: regular painting and drawing sessions followed by the statutory walks along the seashore despite blazing sun, torrential downpour or freezing snowstorm. The weather is an endless source of interest and in nearly every letter she gives vivid descriptions of the state of the sky, the flowers in the garden and the mixed blessing of living in bracing Hunstanton. These 'word paintings' delight Adrian but would pall if constantly repeated here. Sometimes her emotions take over and she spills out her love for him and the agony of their separation. More usually, she views their relationship in a haze of delight as being the prelude to an everlasting and wonderful life 'till death us do part'.

Adrian, although also fired with romantic love, is overwhelmed by his consuming *physical* desire for Laura and frustration at his lack of a well-paid job, which prevents their immediate marriage. He pours out his love almost daily as a threnody on the infinite aspect of their engagement that he finds almost unbearable. Often the sentiment turns to sentimentality and appears quite uncharacteristic of the sophisticated man of the world that he presents to his friends. The juxtaposition of these fraught declarations of love and desire with the graphic day-to-day accounts of his doings makes his letters read most oddly at times. Adrian's anti-Jewish sentiments, when expressed, are highly regrettable but very much of his period when the 'Jew' was so often treated in a socially patronising manner or equated with the worst type of money-lender.

The 'mutual' friend, Jo Jolliffe, whom Adrian sees several times a week, is often his companion in melancholia as well as continual interrupter during Adrian's letter-writing which frequently takes place in Jo's rooms at the Bachelors' Club where he lives in as secretary. He is, it seems, by nature bad-tempered, often depressed, and has a tendency to drink too much, besides which he bestows his greatest affection on his white rats who provide their own share of distractions. The references to 'poor dear Jo' are greatly reduced in the editing but his presence is never far away and in the end he earns his place as Adrian's 'best man'.

Where my brief explanations do not hold up the flow of the letters, they appear in the text within square brackets, otherwise further information is confined to endnotes placed at the end of each month. Basic 'family trees' of the families concerned—Hopes and Cunninghame Grahams, Troubridges and Gurneys—include only the names relevant to the correspondence. The biographical notes that follow on the end of the text provide background details of the young Hopes and Troubridges and their parents.

PRELUDE TO LOVE

FROM LAURA'S MEMOIRS

AND JOURNALS

SUMMER OF

1880, 1881, 1883 & 1884

'Looking back through a long spell of time I find this scene but nothing is distinct—no whisper was heard in my heart to tell me that it was HE—like any other stranger I saw him. In perfect innocence I forged the first link in the chain that was to bind us one to another. I took the first step, and that in self defence to escape from an Egyptian Prince who had begged to be introduced to me, and for whom I immediately felt an aversion. I turned, and saw someone more to my taste standing nonchalantly in the doorway—a tall slight man with a handsome foreign looking face, pale and wasted looking as if after a long and severe illness. He was an amused spectator of the little scene with the swarthy Egyptian and I suggested, looking over my shoulder at him in rather an off-hand manner, that we should go into the garden. We sat together in an arbour and he offered me a cigarette, which I smoked and enjoyed, and his white poodle Fosco did tricks for our amusement. But all the while I watched the entrance gate by which I hoped and expected an older friend would appear. He came not and, in my pride, I was glad that should he come he would not see me wearing the willow.'

It was not love at first sight, according to Laura's *memoirs* quoted above which were written several years after this first meeting between Adrian Hope and Laura Troubridge in the summer of 1880 when he was twenty-two years old and she a few months younger. The occasion was one of the Sunday At Homes of her cousins, the de Bunsens, at their famously hospitable 'Abbey Lodge' in Regent's Park but it did not even rate a mention in her journal for 1880. Their next brief meeting was a year later, also at Abbey Lodge, when Laura's sparse entry in her journal for 22nd May, 1881 merely mentions three of the day's guests as: 'an artist—most cracked, a Romanian Prince, & Mr Hope to tea', without further comment.

Soon after this last meeting, Adrian, who was recovering from rheumatic fever, had been told to live abroad in a hot climate and he obtained the post of Private Secretary to Sir James Longden, Governor of Ceylon (Sri Lanka). He was a great success there and would have stayed on in the colonial service had Sir James not fallen ill and decided to come home and retire. So within three years Adrian returned with him and after spending a few months with his sister Laura and their Cunninghame Graham great aunt in Paris, where he was known as *'le beau anglais'*, he found himself once more at a loose end in London. Lack of family funds had prevented him from going to university or studying for the Bar, and without any of the usual qualifications—political patronage being what it was at that time—he depended on his social contacts to recommend him for any suitable government or diplomatic post on offer. Amongst these were Sir Julian Goldsmid, whom he had met in Ceylon, and his elegant Italian wife—'Milady' (Virginia) for whom Adrian was to become a favourite confidant and companion. At this third sighting, Adrian appeared to be the more smitten of the two. Laura was staying at Penshurst Place with the de L'Isle daughter, Minnie Sidney, and noted in her journal for 1883:

> *10th September* ... I painted alone in the State Room—it was a public day & the British public simply poured in with creaky boots & muffled idiotic remarks, but presently a change & I had rather a romantic meeting much to my surprise with one Adrian Hope—a pal of Jo's who used to be a pal of mine years ago. He had come to see the house with some friends. So we chatted and walked over the house & garden—it was odd and pleasant.

Adrian had come over in a party that included Lady Goldsmid and Laura persuaded them to stay to tea. Adrian told her after they were engaged that as they drove away Lady Goldsmid looked at him and said, 'Hum, either you have been in love with that girl—or you are—or you will be,' all of which he basely denied! As for the 'Jo' mentioned above [Hon Spencer Hylton Jolliffe], it was only *one* year earlier, in the summer of 1882, that Laura first met Jo: 'a new man—who wears an eye glass & was cheery' at the Batemans. Lee Bateman was an admirer of her elder sister, Amy, and they went about as a happy foursome. By Christmas time of that year Jo was inviting Laura: 'to come to anything or everything! at the Bachelors' Club', where he was the resident secretary.

Jo was a difficult young man and still a little in love with Laura—insofar as he loved anyone—as he was to show unmistakable signs of jealousy after Adrian and Laura's next meeting. This was a year later, in June 1884, when Laura and Amy were spending a hectic week in London with the de Bunsens at Abbey Lodge. One afternoon, six girls of the house party set off to meet several friends at the great attraction, the newly-opened International Health Exhibition, colloquially known as 'the Healtheries', in the Horticultural Gardens [then in Queen's Gate]. Only two others turned up and Laura thought it was going to be 'awfully flat' but her 1884 journal recorded otherwise:

> *5th June* ... As Amy and I were buying chocolates at the most delicious place, Mr Jolliffe and Mr Hope appeared. They had been chasing us all over the exhibition. It was impossible to remain in a bunch in such a crowd so Mr Hope and I went off to see the Old London St. & lots of the show. It is much more amusing than the 'Fish' ['the Fisheries', another part of the exhibition] and I want to go lots of times. Mr Hope and I went & drank milk and ate brown biscuits at the Dairy. When he and Mr Jolliffe were looking for us Mr Hope had suggested that we would be at some highbrow part of the Exhibition—looking at pictures I think, but Jo had said firmly: 'If I know the Troubridges they will be at the Chocolate Stall', and we were! Amy and Mr Jolliffe went off and had Indian coffee in a tent. [Laura added later: 'I was rather agreeably surprised—as I thought Mr Hope so very smart and Londony—that he liked drinking milk.']

Within ten days of leaving London, Amy and Laura were back again for a 'glorious' seven-week stay at No 45 Gloucester Street, Warwick Square, entirely due to a happy exchange of houses with two elderly Miss Gemmells (nicknamed 'the Gemmidges') who liked to spend these summer months at the seaside 'Troubridge Castle' at Hunstanton. The two brothers Tom and Ernest were away in the army and the navy respectively, while the two younger sisters, Violet and Helen, were paying family visits and would join them later.

Their first Sunday morning, 21st June, was a disappointment, as the two sisters wanted to follow the fashionable promenade in Hyde Park but failed to find the necessary chaperon. However, they were expected at the de Bunsens' regular At Home in the afternoon and set out on foot for Regent's Park when, as luck would have it, they came across Mr Hope at Marble Arch, but sadly *not* on his way to the same place and at Abbey Lodge they were disappointed to find 'nothing but Germans'. 'The Healtheries' proved irresistible and Laura and Amy visited it with a married cousin as chaperon, Rosy Birkbeck (née Gurney, of Runcton): '…the whole place looks like fairyland with millions of twinkling lights, the *lovely* music & coloured fountains playing sky high…but you really want a man to take care of you in that huge crowd.' Within the week Laura's favourite brother, Ernest, newly appointed to the Royal Yacht, arrived from South America. Entertaining and chaperonage problems rapidly receded with Ernest in the house and they gave an instant tea party to which Jo Jolliffe and Mr Hope were invited and the day ended, of course, with another visit to 'the Healtheries'. Laura was to have four meetings in June, however brief, with Adrian and some twenty more before she left London in early August when their whirlwind romance was sealed by their engagement.

Her journal for July 1884 showed increasing, if discreet, interest in the occasions when Mr Hope was present. One such was a visit to the Howard-Vyses, Jo's nephew and his wife, at Stoke Place in Buckinghamshire:

> *1st July* Very late we set off for Paddington Station and went down to Slough in a comfy Saloon, Mr Jolliffe, Mr Hope & ourselves, had an amusing journey. Spent a long, lovely summer's day there. Heaps of people to lunch. I sat next to Mr Hope—poor Jo was on duty. In the afternoon loads more people came & the Blues Band played under the cedar trees. We wandered about the garden, which is simply lovely, went in a boat on the lake, sat in the strawberry beds, played tennis, dined—Mr Hope sat by me—

& we talked. After dinner we had our coffee on the terrace by moonlight. ...

3rd July Rather a hurry to get off to Henley in time. Wore my lilac cotton frock with satin ribbons, & a sailor hat trimmed with white daisies. Felt very happy. At Paddington Mr Jolliffe & Mr Hope appeared & the Ordes [cousins]. A nice journey, & down to the enclosure in a fly. Ernest & I & Jo & Mr Hope spent a delightful day—listening to the Hungarian Band playing most beautifully. Had lunch in a huge tent, sat on the Barge moored alongside, then Mr Hope, Jo & I went off in a boat. We sat together in the stern, with 2 boatmen to row us. The whole scene was so gay & pretty, the day lovely...with the river crowded with boats full of people all looking smart & amused. ...

8th July ... We had some people to tea. Mr & Mrs Oscar Wilde, she dressed for the part in drimp white muslin with absolutely no bustle, saffron coloured silk swathed about her shoulders, a huge cartwheel Gainsborough hat, white, & bright yellow stockings & shoes. She looked too hopeless, he was amusing of course. Mr Hope came & lots more but I forget the rest.

The young Troubridges had met Wilde through their cousins Charlie Orde, and Cresswell Augustus Cresswell (known as 'Cressie' or 'Cripps' and sometimes 'Gussy') who was at Magdalen with Wilde. Cressie had wanted to meet Sarah Bernhardt and Wilde promised to arrange this if Cressie in turn introduced him to the Troubridge sisters. In 1877, while at Oxford, Wilde wrote to a graduate friend of his: 'My greatest chum, except of course the Kitten [Reginald Harding], is Gussy who is charming though not educated well: however he is *psychological* and we have long chats and walks.'[1] It seems that 'Cressie'/'Gussy' went in for psychologising—making interpretations of behaviour, motives and mental processes. Laura's comments in her journals do not appear to appreciate this aspect of her cousin!

As Secretary to the Bachelors' Club, Jo had sometimes to return to his duties there whereas 'Mr Hope' was free to escort Laura to lunch, meet her at the de Bunsens, walk her back to Gloucester Street or wherever else she chose to go. In a party at 'the Fisheries' they still managed to roam about *à deux* before returning to Gloucester Street for tea and dinner and another theatre party:

> *11th July* ... Went off to see *Chilpéric* at the New Empire Theatre, a spectacular thing with any amount of ballets, glittering tights, bad jokes, & an electric light ballet [which Toulouse Lautrec had recorded with his 'Marcelle Lender dancing the Bolero in *Chilpéric*']. Then on to the Salisbury Club where Mr Hope was waiting for us & we had an amusing supper in a private room— quite a failure as to the menu—but most cheery & amusing all the same, & stayed late.

> *Sunday, 13th July* I went by myself to a little Church near at hand and thought. ...

There was no let up in her social round—she went to the zoo in a hansom with Jo Jolliffe but drove back with Adrian. The following night there was a ball where all her friends came (except for Jo who was ill) and they danced 'to that most perfect of dance music—the Hungarian Band—till the sun was shining'. She kept the little dance card all her life, tucked in with Adrian's letters of the period. Mr Hope was her first partner and out of the eighteen dances listed, his name appeared against six valses, three polkas, a *tempête*, the all-important 'supper dances' and the proverbial 'Sir Roger de Coverley' at the end— or as truthfully noted in pencil 'sat out with A. *most* of the evening'. It would not have been considered good manners to dance too often, or remain, with the same partner, but the stuffier conventions never bothered Laura or her sisters too much and there were no parents hovering in the background to upbraid them for such comparatively minor social infringements. There was the occasional day without a glimpse of Adrian about which Laura was philosophical, as when the Orde family came to lunch and to 'do the Healtheries' in the afternoon. Laura drove there with her favourite cousin, Charlie Orde:

16th July... Had tea in the Chinese place, rather pretty but the
Chinese Band making the most dreadful noise all the time—a
wild sort of bag pipes, excruciatingly loud & a brutal drum. We
roamed about & thoroughly did the Exhib., dined & stayed till
10. listening to the bands, one from Versailles and the Grenadiers.
Thousands of people, & to think of meeting one particular soul
out of all that multitude was so obviously out of the question that
I did not even think of it but loved being with dear Aunt Maggie
[Orde] & the others.

17th July A letter that pleased me very much was put into my
hand this morning when I woke—and a basket of roses—from
Adrian Hope. He arrived at four and brought me two beautiful
stuffed peacocks from Ceylon—one he had shot there and the
other had been his tame peacock, and ill luck or not they gave me
great pleasure.

This precious letter from Adrian confirmed what she had hoped
about his affection for her. He *had* been looking for her the night before
at 'the Flesheries', as he called it, which he had visited with Sir Julian
Goldsmid, and thinking of the dance a few days earlier and the
forthcoming Bunsen Ball: 'how nice it would be to have another valse
with you'. Laura's journal continued:

18th July ... Off about 11. for the de Bunsen dance. We knew it
was pre-doomed to failure—for they had chosen the only night
in the week when there happened to be several good balls on, &
so of course no one came! Still I could not possibly imagine
anything so really *deadly* as it turned out. We danced all the
time—but still I was not happy. I did not enjoy in the smallest &
most infinitesimal degree any single minute of this evening & no
one was there who I would have walked across a room to see.

Laura was very hurt that Adrian did not appear at the de Bunsens
(he failed to extricate himself in time from his many other dances that
night), and after enduring four whole days without seeing him she
was reduced to writing a stiff little note inviting him to dine later in

the week in a party at her great friends the Wallscourts—Lord 'Wally' and Jane 'Midget'—before going on to a big fête at 'the Healtheries', finishing with a request for him to take away the peacocks: 'if something nice doesn't happen soon. We have had nothing but bad luck since they were in the house,' and a pained reference to the de Bunsen Ball: 'the de B. entertainment was deadly indeed—you were quite right not to come—so far as your own amusement was concerned.'

> *23rd July* ... We lost our party directly and wandered about 'the Healtheries' together listening to the lovely music. I felt very happy—Mr Hope & I sat together in a quiet corner under a fir tree & had a long talk & later we went to 'Ceylon' for coffee. I shall always remember this evening. Mr H. took me home about 1 o'clock—hush, Journal, hush.

> *24th July* Rather demoralized & down very late. ... After dinner we all, including Adrian, collected & went off to see Madame Tussaud's new wax works show—a band played & the whole place was lit & rather amusing. Some of them dreadfully lifelike—went downstairs & gloated over the horrors, but the place shut up at 10, which was rather flat.

Another whole day without Adrian was helped by the arrival of brother Tom who was able to accompany them to the Marlborough House Garden Party, for which they had bought new frocks—white nunscloth with white satin ribbons and lace hats. Vi's dress did not fit so she wouldn't go. 'Found heaps of people we knew. Vagued about & talked with our friends. The Chinese Band was banging away in a corner & the Coldstream in another.'

Adrian wrote to tell Laura of his dinner with Jo, who had been unable to join them at a recent party:

> 'He was simply unbearable, too rude & cross. Today he is a little better for I keep on assuring him that all our pleasure was

spoilt, that the whole thing without him was a fiasco, etc. etc. In fact I have lied like a trooper until he now feels better & is prepared to meet you tomorrow & to sympathize with you on your wasted evening …'.

26th July … We 5 [Amy, Laura, Vi, Tom and Ernest] set off for the Gaiety to see Sarah Bernhardt in *Adrienne Lecouvreur*. Mr Hope met us there. A good play, very tragic & horrible. Afterwards all went on to the Salisbury—where Mr Jolliffe met us & we had a most successful supper party. Mr Hope is a very good host & the whole thing was amusing. Left at 2. with a lovely bouquet of carnations for each of us.

30th July … Arrived at the New Club ball at 11.30 to meet the Duffs who never appeared till past 12.—however, we had the 2 Hoares [cousins] and young Wal [Gurney] & Mr Hope to take care of us. Amy was furious with old Duff who danced 6 times with her, bored her to extinction & gave us nothing nice for supper & no champagne—but *we* two had a very happy time & soared far above all these pin pricks! with such a floor, such music, & *such* a partner—home about 3.30.

31st July Called at 8. & told several times by Tanner [their lady's maid] that I was going to Goodwood, so got up, collected my scattered senses, breakfasted off strawberry jam & bread & milk & started myself off in good time. Mr Jolliffe & Mr Hope met me at Victoria—& Mrs Yorke Bevan—& we went off to Chichester by special train. It was *such* a hot day. I was nearly asleep & Mr Hope *quite*. The day is a very mixed one to look back on—I mean as far as the pleasure went. Crowds of people & the whole thing a *very* pretty sight but the party would *not* sort itself aright. Mr Hope & I were a prey to the unremitting attentions of Mrs Bevan and Jo! & nothing short of downright rudeness could have rescued us from their clutches. The part I liked best was lunching with dearest Ernest at the Naval Lunch—a very swagger picnic spread under the trees. We left at 5. but missed the special by 5 minutes & had to wait ages for another. A long journey home—tired but happy—talking in a corner with A.H. while Jo slept & Mrs Bevan sulked!!!

Amongst Laura's letters was the Royal Naval Lunch Menu decorated with the Royal Yacht and racing scene for this Goodwood Cup Day:

ROAST BEEF. CORNED BEEF
Salmon. Mayonnaise of Chicken.
Roast Boned Capon.
Braised York Ham. Roast Chicken.
Pigeon Pies. Braised Ox Tongues.
Aspics of Foie Gras. Aspics of Prawns.
Vanilla Cream, Cherry and Currant Tarts.
Greengage Tart. Gooseberry Tart.
Raspberry and Currant Tarts.
Lemon Jelly. Maraschino Jelly.
Macédoines of Fruits.
Savoy Biscuits and Philberts and Cakes.

ICES
Pine Apple Cream. Strawberry Cream.
Lemon Water.

DESSERT
Grapes. Pine Apples. Gooseberries.
Cherries. Greengages. Raspberries. Plums.

---

1   *8th July* Wilde's letter, from Oxford, was sent to William Ward ('Bouncer') during the week ending 3rd March, 1877. (Cf *The Complete Letters of Oscar Wilde*, ed by Merlin Holland and Rupert Hart-Davis, 2000)

YEAR ONE 1884–85

ENGAGEMENT & HOLIDAY IN IRELAND

2ND AUGUST

TO

4TH OCTOBER 1884

At 45 Gloucester Street, Warwick Square

2nd August The day of my life—but quite unconscious of it. I rose, breakfasted, talked & laughed—as on any ordinary day. Afterwards, feeling rather in a fright, I went off all by myself to interview a strange Mr Cooper, an engraver in the Strand, about my book. He turned out to be a most harmless civil old chap— who having had a letter from Caldecott [Randolph, the artist and illustrator] praising my 'Little Mermaid' drawings, is anxious to do what he can about them.

… About 4. drove with Amy to the Grosvenor Gallery—Mr Hope met us there & we looked at the pictures together. Then Vi joined us & we all went to Charbonnels next door for iced coffee and *petit fours*. Said au revoir, not goodbye, walked partly home to dinner, we three sisters. Then Amy dressed up the strangest & most fantastic dummy & called it 'Aunt Chatty' [Troubridge] to preside at the 'drum' [party] as sundry cousins had failed as chaperon. Mr St Leger came—& was funny—but I was not in tune with fooling & remained on the balcony until Adrian came late.

I had faithfully promised to play games with the others & *not* spend a tête-à-tête evening but all such promises were thrown to the winds. We only came in & danced for a few minutes with the rest. We sat together all the evening & when the moon had risen above the housetops & looked down on us, we knew that we loved each other—till death us do part—and we were very happy.

So this was their *unofficial* engagement day. From then on events passed quickly as the young Troubridges had arranged to spend much of August and September in Ireland and Laura had to connive at Adrian joining them for some of the time. Her elder brother, Tom, and a group of brother officers of the 60th Rifles stationed at Limerick, including their old friend Edward 'Bean' St Aubyn, had taken a house – 'Knocklofty' – in Co Tipperary, for the fishing and asked the four Troubridge sisters to keep house for them.

At 45 Gloucester Street, Warwick Square

Sunday, 3rd August So strange to wake & remember last night. If it had not been for the little gold chain, I should have thought it all a dream. I drove to St Anne's [Soho] by myself & Mr Hope was waiting at the Gate—he looked pale & ill. We sat together in church—but it did not feel restful to me. We walked together in the park and then Amy, Vi and I came back here. After lunch put on a white frock for I felt too happy to wear black, and at 4. He came. We had tea later, rejoicing that Mrs Grundy had left town, we got a good hansom & drove down to the Prince's Gate & spent a very happy time in the Kensington Garden of Eden. ...

5th August ... After 4. Mr Hope arrived. It seemed to be about 3 weeks since we had met but I believe it was not quite so long really. ... I still call him Mr Hope but I am trying to get used to the other in my mind.

6th August ... About 4.30 we drove to Westminster Abbey to see some monuments—his great-grandmother, Mary Breton, who had a sad & romantic story which he told me, & his godfather, Brig. Hon. Adrian Hope C.B., who was shot in the Indian Mutiny of 1857/68. Mary Breton married John Hope in 1762 and had 3 sons in 3 years. By all accounts she was very happy, despite her parents' disapproval of the marriage, but she killed herself within a year of the last son's birth [possibly due to a form of postnatal depression]. We strolled about the great church together & felt as if we were abroad. ... Dressed to dine with Mrs Bevan. Amy & Vi's men had failed them so they would not come & I had to go alone which I hated. It was a dreadful party & *so* long, only Mr Jolliffe, Adrian, myself & Mrs Bevan, & all at X purposes more or less!

7th August ...Met Adrian quite by chance walking down Jermyn Street with his 2 brothers [John, nearly twenty, and Charlie, seventeen]. He introduced them to us—they are not in the *least* like him. ... Dear Limps [Helen] arrived from staying with the Gurneys at Keswick. I told her about us—she was intensely surprised—glad in a way I think—yet she cried & we went off to her room to talk it over. Adrian came to dinner to make her acquaintance—& for a farewell occasion in dear Gloucester St. After a cheery dinner all together, Cressie and a friend came for a mild 'drum'—but we did not know much about them. We were very happy out on the balcony with the moonlight—only it was the very last evening together ... .

8th August A lovely hot day, too much rather for London. Found Adrian waiting for me in the Grosvenor Gallery & we went together to Charbonnels, where we drank iced lemonade through straws & felt better. Then walked to Scott Adies to choose him a cap for Knocklofty...went to lunch at Blanchards—defying the world & Mrs Grundy together. After shopping...visits to the dressmaker...letter-writing...sending off parcels and packing up & more last-minute shopping arrived home at 7. at the same time as Adrian—who had come to take me to the Station—& I had not even dined & I was so tired, with thousands of things to think of—but somehow they finished up in a desperate way—& we drove off together, Adrian & I, waving goodbye to Gloucester Street.

Such a drive, almost too happy to feel how near the parting was. Adrian fastened on the chain he had given me with a tiny gold padlock, & as we passed the Abbey put on my finger the most *lovely* sapphire ring. Our horse fell down but we scarcely noticed it! Arrived dreadfully soon at Euston. Then Adrian took the tickets, did the accounts, got us a carriage, newspapers, & took care of us all, & saw the very last of us—having done everything he could for our comfort on the journey, And the train went so *very* soon—& we had to say our first goodbye although we called it 'au revoir'.

IN IRELAND, 1884

Knocklofty House, Clonmel, Co. Tipperary 9th August

Dearest Adrian…I was wide awake all the way to Holyhead, there was so much to think of—and to look at, for me to sleep. Then whenever I looked up from my corner I saw this word 'Engaged' on the window pane, so I could not forget it if I would—and outside *our* moon was shining down all the time. … Tom could not get leave till the afternoon so at Clonmel we four sisters mounted an Irish Car and drove off to Knocklofty. Have you ever tried an Irish car?—they are really too vague and funny—I don't know how *we* shall get on at all for we shall have to sit *back to back* to balance! and *I* found it necessary to hold on tight with *both* hands—but perhaps this will improve with practice. The house has lots of rooms & long rambling passages full of nooks, & quiet corners for tête-à-têtes, and old pictures, and books. The garden is rather wild & deserted—but very picturesque, with big forest trees & shady walks—& stiff flower gardens & borders—& the river close to the house through a valley with the ruined Castle—Kilmanahan—just the other side. …

At 8. Tom arrived—and we went for a little stroll together through a wood—and Adrian I told him then—and he kissed me, and told me he was very glad for he thought directly he saw you you were 'a thundering good chap'. This is Tom's *highest* praise. I do not mind telling you now, that it was *rather* a relief to my mind—and he is going to write to you tomorrow about your coming—and I think we shall be *very happy* here—and you will be welcomed by them all now. … We never finished about telling your sister. I hope you *will*, for I know if 'twas Ernest I should feel sad about it if he had not told me first. I do hope we shall be friends some day—she and I—and that she will *forgive* me! Yrs ever, Laura

Adrian's eldest sister—another Laura—was a year younger than Adrian and unnaturally possessive of her favourite brother. From then until his departure for Ireland a week later, Adrian wrote every day from his club.

Vine Club, 8 St James' Square 9th August

My Darling Laura, It is only today that I have begun to realize your absence. When the Irish Mail bore off your sweet face last night I was too stunned to grasp the fact that you were gone from me. … You are my last thought at night & my first in the morning. … I have been reading your dear letter over again & when the old man opposite me turned away his head I kissed the signature. Ever your lover, Adrian Hope

13th August

My Darling, Today I had a long talk with my Father about his Gun [Colonel Hope's revolutionary new design]...after lunch I took an Artillery General to see my Father & talk about the Gun again. Then—Guess! I dined with the Hubbards & went to the 'the Healtheries' with Clemency H. who taxed me with being engaged to you? She said that she had been told so by a man at Abbey Lodge. Clemency told me that she had promptly denied the truth of this statement, but that she had afterwards heard so much of my being constantly with you that she now began to believe. I did not deny it but at the same time I chaffed her into not believing a word I said. She evidently was only making a guess. ... I was lectured for being a male flirt. Fancy being lectured by Clemency for flirting. ... Poor Clem, she spoke very nicely of you once or twice and I gave her a lot of good advice about her own love affairs. We agreed that we would be good friends. I cannot make out whether she guessed anything or not.

Did I tell you that on Sunday during Church I sat with those two dear little hearts in my hands & pressed them to my lips as I thought of you, my own darling Laura. ... So we made a mistake as to the [engagement] finger! That shows want of practice in both of us, does it not! Goodnight my darling Laura, Your Adrian

There were, of course, no letters while they were together at Knocklofty and Laura's journal remained blank except for the briefest of entries recording Adrian's arrival there the day after her twenty-sixth birthday:

> *16th August* I went down the avenue on to the old bridge to meet him—no *Him*, waited—and presently—he came.
> [A discreet blank space follows.]

> There turned out to be no difficulty about Adrian staying at the Hotel at Knocklofty—which did not exist—as this good Irishman, our next door neighbour, had asked Mr Hope to stay at Marlfield though he only met him on the train by chance coming

from Dublin. We spent the afternoon sitting under the trees at Kilmanahan Castle, with soft rain falling all the time—collecting a store of rheumatism for our old age. ... We had a very cheery dinner all together, and after Amy sang to us till Adrian had to go at *half past 10*. I saw him set off for his lonely walk, with a lantern, & in his pocket a loaded pistol! [It was the time of 'Moonrakers' during the wild Agrarian disturbances in Ireland.]

Sunday, 17th August ... If I had golden ink I would use it ...

Laura's later memoirs recounted that after their engagement had appeared in the *Morning Post* it was considered all right for Adrian to stay in the house with them, and that when the faithful Tanner unpacked for him she shed salt tears all over his shirts, saying: 'If only it hadn't been Miss Laura!'

2nd October All the days here have been happy days. I have been too happy to write of our doings for words are too dull & cold to describe it all—at least the words that I could use here—where any eye may read what I write. ... Adrian & I will keep the memory of them in our hearts for ever—'*The happiest brightest summer that we shall ever know*' [the refrain of a popular song of 1884] for we have never been so happy in our lives—whatever the future may have in store for us.

4th October Such a long day, beginning at Holyhead—an endless [overnight] journey to London, arriving about 6 o'clock at Euston. ... Despatched the maids home (from St Pancras) to Norfolk with all the luggage, Logie [Amy's collie], the Jackdaw & the blackberry jam!

[*Later*] Adrian came to St Pancras to say goodbye—the end of our long delightful summer time. We were going back to Hunstanton after 4 months' absence. ... To bed early & did not require rocking to sleep.

After both their parents died within weeks of each other in 1867, the six young Troubridges went to live with their maternal grandfather, Daniel Gurney, at his forty-three-room North Runcton Hall, near King's Lynn, but when he died in 1880 they had to leave 'Runcton', as they called their beloved home for the past twelve years, for a small house in nearby Hunstanton which they named ironically 'The Troubridge Castle', or just 'The Castle'. Laura was alone in not liking this joke name and she rarely referred to it as such, heading her letters with a plain 'Hunstanton'.

The four sisters started life there on a total combined income of £600 a year, out of which they paid an *annual* wage bill of £43.12 shillings. Of this sum, the faithful lady's maid Tanner received £20.4 shillings, two others—presumably to undertake the cooking and cleaning—£12 and £6 respectively. 'The boy', who did much of the hard work, rated £5.12 shillings. Their guardian, Somerville Gurney ('Uncle Sommy'), paid the taxes and rates, etc. It was he who took over Runcton in 1880 on the death of his father—Daniel Gurney—as his elder brother Hay Gurney, who inherited it, did not wish to move his family from their home at Keswick. The brothers Tom and Ernest were only in residence at 'The Castle' during their leaves.

While looking for a job, Adrian lived with his parents and the two younger sisters, Jessie and Madge, in an inexpensive house temporarily rented by Colonel Hope who was in considerable financial difficulties—Warwick House, No 39 Albert Road (renamed Albert Bridge Road in 1897), in Battersea, or 'Bitter-sea' as Adrian called it.

The 'letters of engagement' proper can be said to start from then on, when Laura began to receive early—little did she know how premature—wedding presents.

LETTERS OF ENGAGEMENT
ADRIAN—LAURA

4TH OCTOBER 1884

TO

21ST JUNE 1885

Hunstanton   4th October

My darling Adrian, … Found a present awaiting me from Mr Hebbert, that funny old bachelor we told you of. I think you will like it—it is an enormous square of stuff—a portière I suppose, of light white satin worked all round with a deep border of high art embroidery, in gold & copper colour and brown. It is lovely I think & I was so surprised at his sending it to me. … Goodnight darling. I hope you will rest in peace tonight with no disturbing *dreams*. Once more goodnight with a soft kiss from your loving L.

[CONTINUED]   Sunday, 5th October

… It is so curious to be here again looking out on quite one of the most hideous views possible, a row of odd little yellow lodging houses and a grey wintry sky—instead of those lovely woods. … Longing to hear from you, ever your Laura

Vine Club, 8 St James' Square   4th October

My own darling, … I found my Mother looking very ill and pale—her state of health distresses me dreadfully. Today I have spent talking business with my Father until my head felt as if several guns had burst inside it. … Wasn't it nice getting to bed last night! though I did not sleep for a long time for I kept thinking of the night before when a certain little head was very near me. Goodnight my Love, A.

Hunstanton   6th October

Darling Adrian, … I miss you dearest very much—and yet alas! you have no past in my life here—and it seems almost as if it was a curious vivid dream, sometimes, that we spent all those delightful days together. It takes all the blueness & the depth of the sapphires to bring their reality of it back to me. … I have dreamt of you every night since Knocklofty. It is so *odd* to take up my everyday life here again, feeling it is all so different to me really—so empty & poor—without you to talk to, heart to heart, & *then* I miss you—Oh so much—and the love & sympathy that I always feel sure of with you darling—All this, you may be certain I keep to myself. Tonight I have been making them all laugh—with Irish stories! though my real thoughts were all with you …

[CONTINUED]   7TH OCTOBER

… What a vague mind I was in last night. Today I know quite well that you *are* a *stern reality*!!! Ever your Laura

VINE CLUB, 8 ST JAMES' SQUARE   7TH OCTOBER

My sweetest Laura, I have been to see Mrs Hubbard's man about Zanzibar & I think from what I gathered afterwards at the Foreign Office, that only a Naval Officer will be appointed [to the Secretaryship]. At the F.O. they were as civil & nice as they always are. A striking contrast with the Colonial Office which is usually rude. Tomorrow I lunch with Lady Goldsmid & shall probably meet Dilke. This may be of use to me. I saw Austin Lee at the F.O. & we had a long talk.[2] …

Oh! My Darling how I miss you & how terrible it is to write instead of talk to you. Ireland seems like the most beautiful dream (Oh let me dream again). Love conquers all things, let us take that as our motto darling—*Amor vincit omnia*.[3] I am full of anxiety as to the future but try to feel a confidence in an all-loving & all-wise Father. But it is hard. *My* poor Father drives me all but frantic with his visionary dreams which he pours out to me, for, Alas! I am the one member of this family with whom he is on decent terms. My sweetheart what can I say more than that I love you so. Goodnight & happy dreams sweet love, Your Adrian

8TH OCTOBER

My Laura, … Jo & I met today. His oldest & most vicious rat is dead (thank heaven)…My lunch today was nice but not a success as regards Dilke for he came not. … Goodnight, from your Adrian

NORTH RUNCTON HALL, KING'S LYNN   9TH OCTOBER
[WITH UNCLE SOMMY & AUNT KITTY GURNEY]

Dearest Adrian,…I like *our* new motto *very much indeed*. I cannot help feeling glad—and ever so much relieved that Mrs Hubbard's idea of Zanzibar seems falling through. I ought not to say this if you are disappointed about it darling—*mais enfin c'est ainsi que je suis!* [but after all that's how I feel!] I love you so—I cannot think what life would be without you for years. It must be awfully trying to have to listen to so much from your father that you cannot *possibly* really sympathize with—or believe in—& the whole thing must be so depressing. …

Uncle Sommy chaffs me awfully about you of course. He reads ridiculous paragraphs out of the newspapers—supposed to be about you—the latest at breakfast this morning was that you had *eloped* with the Baroness Burdett Coutts [the philanthropist]! He read quite gravely about a column, describing it, beginning: 'We regret to hear etc.' Of course we were all dying with laughter! He is really *too bad*. ... Always your Laura

VINE CLUB, 8 ST JAMES' SQUARE   9TH OCTOBER

My own dear *Laure*, ... Jo dines here with me tonight and we do a play together after which supper at the Bachelors'. He looks so much better, he smokes no more & has kept steadily to Claret which is a comfort. If you & I were going alone to the play Darling how I should look forward to it & the Supper by our own fireside after!!! Good afternoon Miss Troubridge, your Adrian

P.S. I have had quite a civil letter from my sister which is a blessing. I am glad that you prevented me from writing what I intended.[4]

SCULTHORPE RECTORY, NR FAKENHAM   11.30 P.M. 10TH OCTOBER [WITH UNCLE HERB & AUNT BACHE JONES]

My darling Adrian, everyone has gone to bed at this not very dissipated hour. ... I simply died with laughter over your postscript ['Who lives at Sculthorpe Rectory? I am wildly jealous & demand an instant reply'.] You have not much cause for jealousy here! Don't you remember this is where my old Uncle & Aunt live, the Herbert Jones. I can not even pretend that the house is full of gay curates! A very early love of mine has been dining here tonight [Sir Lawrence Jones, Uncle Herb's nephew]. However even that will not give you much cause for those *wicked feelings* to rise – for he came with his wife and after congratulating me, he talked mostly about his baby son and daughter! He is nice and good looking. I think you would like him – but he is dreadfully in love with his wife.

I suppose Lady Goldsmid still had hopes of Dilke's Secretaryship for you. Have you heard anything more of the Paris thing? Yesterday I had a long letter from your mother, it seemed to me so sad – and I am afraid it must have been a great effort to her to write it. She told me all the history of her married life—& your father's – at least a sort of outline sketch of it all. Of course it was very interesting to me – how strange it is that ill luck seems to have followed whatever he undertook – and quite unconsciously her own devotion to him shows all through the letter. Still I am almost sorry she wrote it – it *must* have been rather harrowing recording every failure in black and white! What disappointments they have gone through. Oh darling I trust the future holds something better in store for us.

Tomorrow we shall find the dear Rough Seaman (brother Ernest) at Hunstanton. Amy has written a long letter from Llanarth (staying with her friend Poppy Herbert) and says: 'A youth is staying here—but I forget his name, he is quite devoid of interest!' Rather crushing isn't it? He must be very remiss with his attentions & have absolutely *no* leanings towards 'le sport !' [flirting]. Your sister has written again from Paris and nicely. My eyes are tired so I shall finish this little pen & ink talk. If I could see you – I think *perhaps* I should kiss you. *Bonsoir, toute à toi, Laure*

This long extract from Mrs Hope's letter to her prospective daughter-in-law (received on 9th October) does much to shed light on the character of the colonel as well as to explain the family worries that haunted Adrian throughout these engagement years—and after.

'... From all Adrian has told me I feel much drawn to you in sympathy, and believe that as far as an old woman and a young one can be congenial, we should be so to one another, especially when we have one connecting link so dear to us both. I am not however going to write a mere commonplace letter, but to ask you to use your very bright intelligence to follow me in a long story which I prefer telling you myself to having it given you by others in a more or less distorted version. Things have gone so contrary with us, and our position is so anomalous, that I cannot bear your remaining in the dark, on points which you are entitled to know the truth and the *whole truth*. I think that you will appreciate my motives in thus writing to make you quite *au fait* to the position of affairs.

'To go back a long way when Adie was a tiny mite at the Hague, *'l'enfant polytone'* of the Legation, sending everyone into fits with his funny little Babel of language, a mixture of French, German, Dutch & Italian, my husband and I found out that much as we liked it, diplomacy was no profession for poor people.[5] He had not expected to be poor for when we married, my father-in-law[6] seemed well & hearty, and as second Judge in the Scotch Courts had a large salary. But the fates were against us, he died suddenly, his affairs were very involved, & we found our income very small. At that time Lord Napier's [the minister] brother William came to the Hague on a visit. We will say no harm of the dead, but I will only remark that I, unused to business, felt an instinctive dread of a man so full of projects.

'Among others he was deeply interested in a scheme which seemed very fine, practical, philanthropic & national—viz. to purify the Thames, and make what is a disgrace to us, a profit. My husband threw himself into this scheme, with the same ardour with which he had led a Forlorn Hope[7] in the Crimea. To my own selfish regret we gave up diplomacy & came to London, that my husband might help to carry out this work. At first things went well. My husband had other work, went to Russia and negotiated & obtained a concession for the largest railway ever contemplated at that time in Russia. It was to connect Moscow & Sebastopol,—Sebastopol was to be a free town. Mr Hubbard[8] & several other Directors of the Bank of England were the Concessionaires. My husband telegraphed to them, "I have got all you want but one thing, answer yes or no, for the Emperor leaves to-morrow." They met, authorized Mr Hubbard to telegraph "Accepted". What demon possessed that staid little church builder who can tell! but he went & telegraphed the reverse.

'That was disaster No 1. Then Mr Henry Hucks Gibbs,[9] also a Director of the Bank of England, who had entered into the Thames purification scheme, shelved it most selfishly, leaving my husband after many years of exertion out in the cold. He was determined (my husband I mean) to prove his theories right. I fully sympathized with him, and giving up all society— even friends, we buried ourselves in an old place in Essex [Parsloes].[10] I gave up every other occupation to teach my children, while my husband took a farm to illustrate his agricultural principles. All he did is recorded in the *British Association Report* from 1870-1876.

'... He still fought on, hoping to recover the damages he was entitled to in the great Thames scheme—also so far that has been a failure. Now there remains his invention of the Gun, it has been tested & not found wanting in France, and if circumstances had not been so cruelly adverse to us hitherto, we might reckon with certainty on a happy future—but who can battle against the uncertainties which attend the launching of a novelty.

'You see the life of a clever, hardworking man, disappointed & baffled at every turn, is thus laid out to your view. You need never fear to hear him accused of aught mean or dishonourable, only of want of success. … You will I think feel what pleasure it has been to me, at my long sacrifice to stand by my husband in his difficult way of life. It is only when I see the consequences that fall on my dear children that my courage gives way.

'You will help me to animate my Adrian with faith & hope in the future, believing that God must sooner or later give even in this world, some reward for such hard strife in the good cause. Have you tired of all this? Still I am glad to put in your hands a statement of facts I have lived through, as doubtless in your new relation to us, many things will be said to you and which without the knowledge of the truth may mystify and wound you. Were my own daughter placed as you are, I should wish her to be so dealt with …'.

What Mrs Hope did not say was that as an adolescent Adrian was taken away from school—ruining any chance in the future to go up to Cambridge as he wished—in order to help with the interesting if unprofitable agricultural experiments. He was left to learn what he could from a series of feckless tutors, while his sister Laura was virtually adopted by their Aunt Annie Cunninghame Graham and lived abroad with her. His two brothers, John and Charles, were largely farmed out to various aunts for their school holidays so that only the two younger daughters remained at home, Jessie (for years a semi-invalid with a malformed leg, possibly a tubercular hip) and Madge. From his gun and gunpowder inventions the colonel expected quite unrealistically to become a millionaire so that in effect he never provided for his family but relied on handouts from his in-laws and such advances as he could obtain on his inheritance. As a consequence, Mrs Hope's health broke down but her loyalty to her husband lasted until her death in 1909 which he survived for less than a week. Laura did not seem unduly overcome by all these Hope revelations.

HUNSTANTON   SUNDAY, 12TH OCTOBER

Dearest Adrian, … I send you a letter I had a day or two ago from my cousin Tom Legh in Paris:

> '… I should never have chosen such an ignobly common gift as salt cellars, but was overruled. If anyone else give you salt cellars please do not hesitate but swap mine for anything you may fancy. … If you choose to come over here I would marry you myself, i.e., give you in marriage, and would save you any amount of bother. Meanwhile if I were you I would set a new example, and instead of all the veil and white clothes humbug, be married in travelling clothes …'.

It amused me. Fancy his forgetting the good wishes & stuffing them into a postscript & his offering to marry me himself is rather startling! … Really darling we shall soon be able to set up house—with our portière, pair of Dresden Jars from Otway Cuffe, a coral set from Mrs Cuckoo Wickstead—*and* salt cellars!! … Goodnight for tonight, Ever your loving L

[CONTINUED]   13TH OCTOBER

… I should be awfully glad if you would go and see Mr Cooper, the engraver who lives at 100 Strand. I left my 'Little Mermaid' drawings with him and he said he would show them to the firm of Macmillan & Co. I said I would sell the drawings in outline as they are—to be coloured or etched by anyone who bought them, if they liked. Ever your loving Laura

HUNSTANTON   15TH OCTOBER

Dearest Adrian, … Do come to Hopton on the 22nd if you possibly can [to meet her Orde cousins]. … The Tom Leghs' present came this morning—4 pretty little silver things—and whether we go north or south I suppose we shall always eat salt—so they are really useful to us. I am afraid it would be *very disappointing* to hear we were not to meet for so long—till December, but I know you will come unless it is really against your—I mean *our* interests for you to leave London then. Ever your Laura

SALISBURY CLUB, 10 ST JAMES' SQUARE   15TH OCTOBER

My darling Laura, I was grieved that my poor Mother should have written such a sad letter. It has done her good I think to write to you, for she rather feared that I had been unwilling to talk to you of my Father. My darling, do not be frightened at this sad story for I think that though I am not clever like my Father that I have more common sense to carry through the business of life. I do so long to see you again sweet love & I do miss you more & more every day. I cannot get used to the loss of your dear companionship. What it will be if I have to go abroad God knows! ... Every one of the plans for Secretaryships I spoke to you about has been upset—Siam, Paris, Zanzibar etc. I hope to have an appointment with Dilke tomorrow or next day when something will be fixed about me. Goodbye now darling Laura, Your Adrian

HUNSTANTON   17TH OCTOBER

Dearest Adrian, ... *How delightful* to see you again, *dear, darling, lover of mine*. Did you see the account of Ld Lytton's love letters just published, they were reviewed & quoted in the *Pall Mall* October 7th. They *are* a warning to lovers! the most arrant rubbish—I should think even his dust would blush to know that they are printed. ... Ever your loving Laura

HOPTON HOUSE, GREAT YARMOUTH   SUNDAY, 19TH OCTOBER
[WITH AUNT MAGGIE ORDE]

Dearest Adrian, ... Moritz de Bunsen[11] is staying here and wants to make your acquaintance before he leaves. He wants to talk *shop* with you—so *perhaps* I shall allow you half an hour with the eminent Diplomatist! He might have something to suggest—for he is in with all sorts of people—& *very* interested in the service. I feel I am become quite worldly! We are just off to Church— I shall try not to think of you all the time there. Ever yours, Laura

SALISBURY CLUB, 10 ST JAMES' SQUARE   20TH OCTOBER

My darling, This time tomorrow (6 p.m.) you shall give me a kiss if you will? The thought makes me wild with delight. I long to rush up & down the room. Today I went & told my Tailor all about you. Don't laugh, he is a very sympathetic man indeed & has lent me a fur coat to travel in as my own will not be ready for me. I had to have a new outside put to the fur lining. The 12 o'clock train tomorrow will bring down one very happy passenger. ... Your lover, Adrian

There was a short interlude in their daily correspondence when Adrian spent two weeks with Laura to be introduced to some of her Norfolk relations, known collectively by where they lived. Uncle Hay Gurney and Aunt Minnie (née Ffolkes) of Keswick Hall, Norwich and their eleven surviving children were the 'Kes' Gurneys and remained so even after they moved to Thickthorn House nearby; (the Rev.) Uncle Willie Gurney & Aunt Amy (née Boileau) of the Runcton Rectory, King's Lynn and their seven surviving children were the 'Recs'; Uncle Sommy Gurney and Aunt Kitty (née Hamond) of North Runcton Hall, King's Lynn and their ten children were the 'Valls', from the time they lived at Valleyfield close by, or 'the Runctoners'. Another Reverend, Uncle Herb Jones, and Aunt Bache (née Rachel Gurney) whose only child was long since dead, lived at Sculthorpe Rectory, near Fakenham, known as 'Scully'. Aunt Maggie Orde (née Gurney) of Hopton House—later called Hopton St Margaret, Great Yarmouth (whose husband, James Orde, died in 1880) and her seven surviving children needed no distinguishing sobriquet.

It was Vi and Helen, the two younger sisters, who spent long periods staying with their 'Kes' and 'Rec' cousins while Amy and Laura much preferred the life at Runcton, where Uncle Sommy was their favourite uncle, and at Hopton, where Aunt Maggie was their favourite aunt. Of the thirty-nine *first* cousins they had on the Gurney side alone, Laura's favourites were: Eva of the 'Recs', married to her cousin, George Cresswell, and living in King's Lynn; Rosy of the 'Valls', married to Johnny Birkbeck and living in London; and the two eldest Ordes—Charlie ('Tardy'), at Barclays Bank in Yarmouth, and Evelyn (E.) who, although some five years younger than Laura, was considered to be, 'almost the prettiest, nicest, & dearest girl I know'.

There was a fourth Gurney uncle, Charles and his wife, Aunt Alice (née Prinsep)[12] but they were no longer included in the family circle, although old Daniel Gurney remained very fond of this son, Charles, who was a banker and one of those implicated in the financial crash of the Overend, Gurney Bank in 1866. He feared he might go to prison for this and other Gurney partners' business negligence and voluntarily exiled himself to Bordeaux for a time. When they started a public issue all the partners, including Laura's grandfather, Daniel, personally guaranteed to make up any bad debts—which eventually amounted to some £18,000,000—a huge sum for those days. Family homes were sold up, old Daniel Gurney virtually bankrupted himself and only survived because his sister Hannah (Lady Fowell Buxton) allowed him £2,000 a year to continue living at Runcton and to provide a home for the six orphaned Troubridges.

Charles and Alice Gurney were in the Marlborough House Set, although later she was spoken of as being an invalid and of having 'withdrawn from Society'. They had two daughters and two much younger sons, and at some stage were divorced and she remarried in 1897. It was the elder daughter, Laura ('Queenie'), who was to marry Laura's brother, Tom, in 1893.

Adrian and Laura returned to Hunstanton for the last few days of this holiday for Adrian to be introduced to 'The Castle'. When they had to say goodbye: 'we could not even say au revoir for our next meeting is uncertain unless it is Christmas.'

---

2   *7th Oct* Sir Charles Dilke, Under-Secretary of State for Foreign Affairs under Gladstone (1880/82), since then President of the Local Government Board (LBG). Austin Lee was his PS at the Foreign Office.

3   *7th Oct* Laura later noted on Adrian's letter that he had this motto *Amor vincit omnia* (Love conquers all things) engraved inside her wedding ring.

4   *9th Oct* Laura Hope, Adrian's eldest sister, had written very unpleasant letters to both Adrian and Laura on their engagement. She thought her brother could do better than marry Laura who had little money of her own and no expectations.

5   *9th Oct* Col Hope was for five years Military Attaché in Washington and afterwards at The Hague (1857/61) under the 10th Lord Napier & Ettrick, then Minister Plenipotentiary.

His fairly tenuous kinship with Lord Napier was through the latter's mother Elizabeth, only daughter of Hon Andrew James Cochrane-Johnstone (10th son of 8th Earl of Dundonald) and his first wife Georgiana, daughter and co-heir of James, 3rd Earl of Hopetoun. Adrian was descended directly from the 1st Earl of Hopetoun through his 2nd son's second son, John Hope (1739-85) who married Mary Breton— Adrian's gt gt grandparents.

6   *9th Oct* John Hope (1794-1857) Lord Chief Justice of the Scottish Court of Session, and son of Charles Hope, Lord Granton (1765-8151) who had been its Lord President.

7   *9th Oct* 'Forlorn Hope' was the term given to advance storming parties in the Crimea. Col (then Lt) Hope, aged twenty-two, had volunteered to lead one such on the Redan fort—and did so successfully, only for it to fail due to lack of planned reinforcements. On his return to the forward trenches, he was told that his adjutant was missing so he went back under very heavy fire from the Russians to look for him. He found the adjutant too badly wounded to be carried and so Lt Hope returned, again under very heavy fire, to collect a stretcher party. It was for this bravery on 18th June, 1855 that he was awarded the VC. Some months later there was a great explosion in camp and Lt Hope was again to show his courage by volunteering with twenty-five men to climb on top of a windmill being used as an ammunition dump and to cover the exposed powder boxes with wet blankets to prevent an even worse explosion. For this act on 15th November he received the Sardinian Medal for Military Valour, conferred by Victor Emmanuel. The colonel's VC remained in the Hope family until 1997 when it was sold at auction to the Tower of London, to be on view in their armouries.

8   *9th Oct* J G Hubbard, later 1st Lord Addington, was also an MP, and Chairman of the Public Works Loan Committee.

9   *9th Oct* H H Gibbs, later 1st Lord Aldenham, was also an MP.

10   *9th Oct* Col Hope had very advanced views on agriculture and the use of sewage and to that end in the late 1860s he rented Breton's Farm (known as 'Parsloes' after its owners), near Romford, Essex, where he carried on a market garden business while experimenting with his agricultural theories. He was a member of the Committee on the 'Treatment and Utilization of Sewage' which body decided to make use of his Breton's Farm for its observations. They appointed a specialist to live and work on the farm and a Dr Russell at St Mary's Hospital, London, to make the necessary analyses. Highly detailed accounts, with graphs, of the experimental work undertaken at Breton's Farm were published annually in *The Report of the British Association for the Advancement of Science*, 1870-76 inclusive. As with all the colonel's enterprises, this one did not bring him any riches but the references to his work in these reports make fascinating reading, especially in the light of present-day sewage problems and the interest in organic agriculture.

11   *19th Oct* Moritz (later Sir Maurice) de Bunsen, then Minister at the British Embassy in Madrid, son of Chevalier Ernest de Bunsen of Abbey Lodge, Regent's Park, and Bette née Gurney of Earlham, a niece of Laura's grandfather Daniel Gurney. Amy Troubridge remained half in love with Moritz for all her life.

12   *19th Oct* For more about Charles and Alice Gurney and their family, *see also* 3rd July, and 11th Nov, 1886 and footnotes 89 and 91, pp 249 and 271.

NOVEMBER 1884

Hunstanton   4th November

Darling Adrian … I could not wait this morning to see the very last of you for I did not want you to see how unhappy it made me to say goodbye. … Vi is so easy going when we are alone here & we drift along together very well. She is really much jollier in home life than when she has to help amuse people & make things go off. Tonight after dinner I am going to look over a great many old letters & burn what I do not wish to look at again. … I feel so grave I can not smile at all this evening—& there are no little tunes hummed now. …

[Continued] 11.30 p.m.

I have looked through so many old letters & passed through ever so many different moods—such long letters from Jo! after all I suppose there must have been a *grain* of truth in what you have often said to me—letters from Lee Bateman that have been sent flying into the fire—and oh such a funny packet of queer boy love letters from Douglas Grant.[13] I have really been laughing over them, quite by myself, it is a shame, but they are so funny. I had quite forgotten he had written so fervently & so often. … Now I have come to the packet of letters I was really looking for & that it has been in my heart to burn [from Lawrence Jones]—a packet tied across with white satin ribbon with a big seal to fasten it—& so it has been for nearly 4 years—& tonight I am going to break the seal & burn each & every letter. I have finished with them all. I have not a shadow of regret for anything or anyone in the world—only a great wish & longing for you. … I am tired & rather sad. Ever your own love, *Laure*

5th November

My darling Adrian, … I want you to direct your letters to Hunstanton—as you used to do—not Troubridge Castle—because I do not like the name. I hope you don't mind but somehow I don't like it. I tried to stop the nickname at first but public opinion was against me, so I believe I talk of the 'Castle' sometimes myself—but it annoys me to see it written. … Darling, I have read your letter again. I should like to scold you a little for something you have written. If it is your 'fault' that yesterday I felt sad & lonely without you—it is also your 'fault' that I have spent some of the *very* happiest hours of my life since I have learnt to love you—so darling please do not have any more thoughts like that—I feel so sure that we were meant to make one another happy. It is not given to everyone to love as *we* do—and I could *never* have one *shadow* of regret that we have met and it is so—even though we are parted now. Ever your Laura

Sir Charles Dilke as president of the Local Government Board (LGB) made an offer to Adrian (through his private secretary, Mr Bodley)[14] that if Adrian were to work in the office of a Poor Law Auditor for nothing to gain experience, then he would be considered a candidate for a Poor Law Auditorship when one fell vacant. There were only two people above him so he might not have to wait long. The posts were worth from £500 to £700 per annum. Adrian's name was also on Foreign Secretary Lord Granville's private list for a consulship, which was not worth much according to Adrian but would serve to keep his name before those who had places to give away.

HUNSTANTON   7TH NOVEMBER

Darling Adrian, I can not make out what you yourself think of Mr Bodley's offer. Is it work that you would like or dislike? I suppose it would be better not to refuse it—as it might lead to something—& anyhow would be better than doing nothing which I know you are tired of. *I don't want you darling to take anything for my sake that you feel you could not care about*—or feel any interest in—*unless* it was purely *pour passer le temps* until something better turned up. If you were to get this appt. at £700 a year, with my two pence we should feel quite rich. .... I suppose it is a good thing to have your name on Lord Granville's private list—but if you leave me alone in England & take my heart away with you there will be no happiness left in life for either of us dearest, will there— I did not mean to write this, but writing on just what was in my heart it came.

[*Later*] I have weakly promised to go out with Mimi Fenwick tomorrow driving tandem donkeys! to take luncheon to their shooting party. I shall probably be very much bored, besides the chance of being brought home on a shutter! ... I should so love to see you for a minute tonight and to rest my head—where it loves to lie. *Avec trois petits baisers—Bonsoir, ta Laure*

P.S. I am glad you are comfy at the Club. Have they provided you with a nice hard mat., [mattress] not too wide?

WARWICK HOUSE, ALBERT ROAD,   SUNDAY, 9TH NOVEMBER
BATTERSEA

My darling Laura, About this offer of Dilke, I mean to accept it in any case, for it will give me work & enable me to show that I will work & can. Then I shall not be bound in any way if anything better offers. Sweet Love, I wish that I had been there to kiss you the night you burnt your letters, they must have made you feel so sad. Nothing I think makes one feel so (pleasantly or unpleasantly) sad as to read old letters over again. … For the time adieu from your Adrian

VINE CLUB, 8 ST JAMES' SQUARE   10TH NOVEMBER

My Sweet Love Laura, Yesterday I went to see Mrs Napier[15] at Lancaster Gate. Oscar Wilde & his wife came in while I was there. He dressed quite like anyone else, she in mouse-coloured velvet with a toque to match looking horrid. Oscar was as amusing as ever & waxed quite tender over the Orde Family & Hay Gurney. He talked tremendously but was always funny. She never opened her lips but seemed in a state of silent sulky adoration. … This afternoon I am going to call on a friend, Lewis McIver, who has just married Claude (Goldsmid) Montefiore's sister!! Lots of money, the Jews are furious, but the deed is done.

[*Continued* 12 p.m.] … McIver who is living in a dear little house in Norfolk St seems perfectly happy with his Jewish bride who is dark & sallow but with such a sweet smile. After that I went to call on my cousin Jem Hope, Lady Mary's son [grandson of 4th Earl of Hopetoun], who is also just married to old Sir Peter Coats' daughter, Elsie. They long to welcome their new cousin. … Here is a kiss which I send to you—Goodnight my Love, from Adrian

Laura stopped off one night with her cousins, the Leghs of Lyme, where Amy and Tom Troubridge were staying, and then all three went on to the Cochrane-Baillie [Lamington] cousins in Scotland for ten days where they found the youngest daughter, Violet, who was two years older than Laura, and Wallace, the Lamington heir who was two years younger.[16]

LAMINGTON, LANARKSHIRE   12TH NOVEMBER
[WITH LORD & LADY LAMINGTON]

Darling Adrian, … It was a long journey to Lyme, changing 6 times—and I missed one & had to wait 3 mortal hours at Buxton, not getting to Lyme till 9 o'clock instead of 6. At Lyme I found only the Legh girls, Sybil & Mob [Mabel], & Katy Bagot—a very jolly girl, with our Tom as 'Jack among the ladies'— and he was in the midst of a violent fl———n with Sybil. Next morning Amy, Tom and I started off for this place. They stopped the Express for us at Lamington to the rage & disgust of most of the other passengers. One old chap hung out of the window all the time we were there, pouring out volumes of abuse at the guard in the broadest Scotch to our intense delight & amusement! ...

The garden here as far as I can see looks very new & painfully artificial—full of stiff flower beds, little terraces & young trees, but backed up with great hills—which I love. ... There are only 2 people here besides ourselves—Lady Nina Macdonnell, an Irish girl, rather amusing, with a plain face & *any* amount of assurance [her journal notes: 'took a dislike to Lady Nina, she has wild spirits & laughs incessantly about nothing which is very depressing to me.'] and a most *delightful* & *fascinating* young man who took me to dinner last night—& banked with me at Loo in the evening. I am sure we will be *great* friends—You won't mind will you darling because you know you are *not* jealous! What a shame—how you would punish me if you were here—especially if you saw this *ugly, uninteresting*, dull reality! His name is Carmichael.

This morning what do you think I did—entirely for love of you & your country? I distinguished myself at breakfast by eating a bowl of porridge with cream. There was a little table in the corner of the dining-room spread with little wooden bowls full of it. I eat one of these & Wallace Cochrane-Baillie managed *three*—while everyone else laughed at us. It was really very good but I am told it is *very* fattening so I don't think I shall repeat the experiment *very* often. Violet Cochrane is singing so prettily, love songs of course. ... There is just a *chance* Adrian of our meeting in London before Christmas. I think if you were to call on the Birkbecks at 30 Thurloe Sq. [in South Kensington] it might remind Rosy [née Gurney, late of Runcton] of her duty. I wrote to her a day or two ago. ... Goodbye darling, *je t'aime toujours*, Always your Laura

Vine Club, 8 St James' Square   12th November

My Love, ... My Father has just patented a new gun powder & a new cartridge for sporting guns!! He is quite as pleased as if someone had left him a fortune & is at present full of what he will do for me in the future. How gladly I would give the future to anyone who would assure the present. ... How hateful the want of money is. Your Adrian

13th November

My dearest Laura, This day I have been to & fro like a dog. I have seen the Auditor of a London District whom I am to work under for nothing. The work seems hard but how the thought of you will make that work a pleasure. My Father, with whom I lunched today, had great hopes of his new powder. Curtis & Harvey the powder-makers are enthusiastic according to him. … Is your 'Carmichael' a punishment for my 'Goldsmid'. I go down tomorrow with her to Somerhill. Darling how I long to give you one (or more than one) kiss just behind your pretty ear. Don't turn the head of your Carmichael! Does the new maid button boots well? As well as someone whose chief wish it is always to button your boots, darling? If you come across Jefferies' new novel *The Dewy Morn*[17] mind you read a most amusing lover's speech in which he declares his admiration & love for her knee!! … Today I cannot write, my Soul is weary within me. Darling I send you kisses, Your Adrian

LAMINGTON, LANARKSHIRE 13TH NOVEMBER
[WITH LORD & LADY LAMINGTON]

My own darling Adrian, … We had a very nice day yesterday in spite of the rain & the mist. We went up to a dear little chalet in a pine wood among the hills, a little cottage room lined with wood, with lattice windows. There was a huge hamper of *gobbets* waiting for us. These were unpacked & then Violet Cochrane-Baillie cooked the luncheon, & Lady Nina, Amy & I were the kitchen maids, & laid the table & held the dishes—it was great fun. There were no tiresome servants, only ourselves. She really did cook, not make believe—fried eggs & bacon—and all sorts of things. You would have loved to be there & messing with us I know. Violet offered to lend *us* the chalet for our *lune de miel*! Then Tom & Mr Carmichael & Wallace arrived to lunch & we had the most cheery occasion ending with speeches & toasts & songs with chorus! As we were Irish, Scotch, and English gathered in that little hut, there was a great deal of chaff & quarrelling over our respective countries. After lunch we left a vague boy to struggle with the untidyness we had left, & went for a long walk across the hills, entirely ignoring the pouring rain & the wind, till 5. Then rather an amusing School room tea—for they have still an old fossil French Mademoiselle lurking upstairs—& then wild dancing in an empty room till dressing time, so you see we manage to amuse ourselves somehow, not badly.

Lady Nina improves on acquaintance but I think she is rather too much of a good thing—I like Violet C.B. ever so much the best. … I don't care for Lady L. & though *most* correct in her conversation, there is a reckless abandon about her evening toilettes that I am convinced eclipse even Mrs W.F. [one of Adrian's elderly, widowed admirers of whom Laura pretends to be jealous] in her most demoralized Parisian days! I have been quite shocked & I *hope* you would have been so too, although I doubt it! Is Sir Charles Dilke to be at Somerhill? I wish he was—that you might shove him into a pond, & then save his life, and earn his everlasting gratitude, & the very best plum he has to dispose of. ... Goodbye darling—take care of yourself, & think always lovingly of your Laura

VINE CLUB, 8 ST JAMES' SQUARE   14TH NOVEMBER

My own Sweet Love, My brother John is making up his mind to join the Regiment of Mounted Infantry being raised for service at the Cape by Paul Methuen [later Field Marshal and 3rd Baron, who had fought in the Crimea with Col. Hope]. Of course he will have to go as Non commissioned officer at first but he would I think get his commission after a bit. Two old friends of mine are going out & it will be rather fun. How nice the Chalet sounds, you must have delighted in it. But for a habitation for a month? rather cold even though warmed with love. ... Believe me ever your lover, Adrian

LAMINGTON, LANARKSHIRE   14TH NOVEMBER
[WITH LORD & LADY LAMINGTON]

My dearest Adrian, ... The rage here seems to be to picnic about in the house. Last night Wallace gave a tea party in his bedroom! a most cheery occasion ending up with a general introduction to our old friend 'the Muffin Man'[18] led by Tom with great success. Tonight we picnic in the old Schoolroom.

[*Continued* twelve p.m.] We have been dancing tonight in rather a quaint hall—with a tartan carpet—to the strains of the Lamington village band— not *quite* so appalling as those drum & pipe discords that used to haunt Knocklofty—but *still* a village band—fortunately stationed at the end of a conservatory so they had the benefit of the distance & looked very picturesque in tartan among the plants while we danced merrily in the hall—not *quite* true of all of us that last remark. ... I had a letter from my cousin Rosy Birkbeck this morning —'Could not you come and stay with us in Thurloe Square on your way back from Scotland? ... Will Mr Hope be in town then? if so you could see a great deal of him—*or perhaps he could come & stay with us too*'—so after all we have something to look forward to before Christmas. ... Of course you will be able to *audit* as much as you wish all day. Johnny Birkbeck spends all his days studying at the College of Music, but then when you come back what delightful times we might have—& what delightful evenings for Johnny plays for *hours* & *hours* the organ—and the violoncello—& his faithful little wife accompanies always on the piano, or the harp. So you & I ought to be able to have a few tête-à-têtes, and we can play & make believe they are not there at all. What an appreciative audience we shall be! ... The new maid is an excellent boot-buttoner—but she omits some of the ceremonies sometimes observed on these occasions! & she is very quick. Goodnight, ever your *Laure*

SOMERHILL, TONBRIDGE   [A.M.] 15TH NOVEMBER
[WITH SIR JULIAN & LADY GOLDSMID]

My darling Laura, I got down yesterday [Friday] and Goldsmid & I played billiards together from the time I arrived till dinner time. She came & watched us at first but soon retired with a pain vulgarly called stomach ache I believe!! We had a very quiet dinner all by our three selves. The only excitement was caused by the butler giving me claret & Champagne mixed which made me think of you Love. After dinner Julian had a long talk with me, he was very kind about my engagement but evidently thinks we are curious fools. Then Lady G. went to bed & we went to the small smoking room. ...

Do you know that I was awfully tempted to join the force yesterday which is going off to Bechuanaland. But don't worry about it for I have discovered that the very idea of leaving England without you is horrible to me. ... It makes one sick to think of all the money being wasted every day by rich people on folly which would enable us to marry & live quite happily together somewhere. How I long for that time when we shall have our home together ... Oh Darling, we shall never tire of each other's company shall we? Your faithful lover, Adrian

LAMINGTON, LANARKSHIRE   16TH NOVEMBER
[WITH LORD & LADY LAMINGTON]

My darling Adrian, I *felt* what had been in your mind...I think it is only a sacrifice of your inclinations, *not at all of* your interests, for supposing I had never existed—or we had never met—although it is all very well for a boy like your brother to join an expedition like that, & a good thing for him to see something of the world, & perhaps win his spurs, it seems to me a different thing altogether for a man of 26 *unless* he has been a *failure* at other things & wants to get out of the way—especially for *you* as I don't think you would care for a soldier's life or career—but I understand it must sound very tempting to you with your love of adventure, & the work of next week must seem *very dull* by comparison. ... I feel sure you are meant for something better than this—I cannot fancy you as a mere *unit* in a large body of men, with no voice of your own about anything, which is practically the condition of a private soldier. Now I shall think no more about it—as you told me not to worry.

I had a long tête-à-tête quite by chance yesterday after tea, with the new man here whose name I find is Stirling Stuart. He is ugly beyond description, very good natured, sporting, vulgar and original—& goes everywhere, seems to know everybody & cannot even dance! He is enormously rich as his uncle—Mr Stirling Crawfurd—left him all his fortune. He appeared at dinner with a masker's collar 4 inches high & his shirt fastened with *one* black safety pin! which it appears is a mania of his, and alternates with a *gigantic* midas of pearls & diamonds! He arrived here from the Hope-Veres,[19] at Blackwood, & when I found that out I gently drew him about them. In his opinion they are devoted to one another. He told me a good deal about the house & also that the first wife is buried *in the approach*!!!—rather awkward now—there is no church yard but he had a small piece of ground consecrated, in front of the dining room windows—& there is her grace enclosed with handles.

Amy & Tom go tomorrow to the Monteiths at Carstairs for a shooting party—Amy forgot to tell Poppy Herbert (Flo Monteith's sister) I was with her—so of course I am not asked—but Violet C.B. was delighted that I could stay on here so I don't mind. I really like her—she often talks to me about you & what we mean to do. *Unlike Sir Julian*, I believe *she* thinks we are much to be envied. I have heard she once loved someone who was not rich but Lady L. who is a *tremendous* matchmaker—would not *hear* of it—so it had to die out. I can see it is in her mind sometimes. I suppose she will be arranged for with some rich old man—as her sisters were.[20] Lady Lamington asked me if it would be any good if she should write to Lord Derby [then Colonial Secretary under Gladstone] about you as she knows him very well.

Last night I took a French novel to my room, & though I did not like it at all I could not put it down. The whole story was of love—really passionate love, gradually *fading* away to ennui—& then to *intense dislike*—it is an old novel & very cleverly written, but I hate it. ... I do not fear that we shall ever tire of each other, even when it has become quite natural to us to spend our lives together...Ever your Laura

SOMERHILL, TONBRIDGE   SUNDAY AFTERNOON, 16TH NOVEMBER [WITH SIR JULIAN & LADY GOLDSMID]

My darling Laura ... Yesterday the first detachment of guests came in time for tea—Mr & Mrs Childers whom I like very much. He is overcome by the cares of the Exchequer [of which he is then Chancellor], Mr & Mrs Collier [later 2nd Lord Monkswell], the Roches [Sir David and Lady Roche 2nd Bt]— she is a beautiful American, Count Münster [the German Ambassador] who is a jolly fat German as you know, and Colonel & Mrs Inigo Jones—she says her mother knew you at Hunstanton, he is in the Guards. After a bit arrived the McIvers who are my very particular friends. At dinner I sat between Mrs Childers and a Mr Cartwright who is a Radical M.P. of great ability. Mrs Childers & I had a great talk about all manner of things, finally about what I am always thinking & dreaming of—yes you my heart's darling.

Dinner over we had a dull time in the great Saloon upstairs. Milady sang & then all the women went downstairs & upstairs to bed. We bolted to the Smoking & Billiards room where I had some great games with [Robert] Collier. They did not keep it up late but I sat up in my own room for hours smoking & thinking of you & of a time when we may be here together. Seeing McIver here with his wife had set me off on this train of thought. They are so happy. She bade me tell you that they waited five years for a happiness which she says has obliterated the memory of their long waiting & made it seem but a few days. Ah! may we not have to wait so long as that for ours.

Breakfast this morning at 9. was funny for hardly anyone came down until 10. which made Julian quite furious. I went to Church do you know!! A queer little ugly tumble down place it was. We went a party in the Bus. The Sermon was too funny. First of all the parson read us the dedication prayer of the Temple of Solomon & then quite sharply in the same tone of voice said: 'Mildewed damp walls are unfavourable to the growth of a devout spirit therefore I propose to cover the walls of the Church with Minton's Encaustic Tiles.' He further described a young girl, beautiful as an Angel, called the Destroying Angel from her power over men's hearts, sitting before her mirror combing her long black hair & feeling that, though she had the World the flesh & the devil, she wanted something more. A gluttonous girl you will agree with me in thinking her. This extraordinary person was represented as craving after religion but too weak minded to give up the World for the sake of her salvation. Altogether, so far from falling asleep I sat & laughed till the seat shook & I woke Childers who cried 'Hear Hear' under the impression that he was in the House again. Mrs. Collier, McIver & I walked home & I ate a huge lunch after which I went out & played a capital set of tennis. ...

So you go about having tea in young men's bedrooms!!! ... By the by I don't like Mrs Roche much, she is too thin & I more than suspect that her figure has to be arranged in front by the aid of those——?? Oh!... Tell the Mother [Lady Lamington] not to scent her letter paper as it is abominable to do so...Adieu Sweetheart

Little did Adrian know at the time that he and Laura would eventually live in the Chelsea studio house at 34 Tite Street [later renumbered as 52] built in 1882 for the artist, John Collier (brother of Robert Collier above). In her current journal, Mrs Collier wrote of a certain fellow guest at this Goldsmid house party: 'An exceedingly handsome Mr Adrian Hope…the best looking man I have ever seen for a very long time, tall, splendid dark eyes & hair & a beautiful face, & very nice manners & ways.'[21]

Lamington, Lanarkshire   18th November
[with Lord & Lady Lamington]

My darling Adrian, … Lady L. told me to tell you that the Consulship for Cannes was vacant & she thought it might be worth while your trying to get it. She is very much interested in you & I—and has just been giving me *volumes* of good advice—all of which I knew quite well. However it apparently pleases her to give it & it did not hurt me to be told what I knew already—that we should wait till we had enough to live comfortably on before we marry etc. etc.! so I allowed her to run on—she is a very agreeable woman. I think you would like her.

Yesterday that odd creature Mr Stirling Stuart departed. I walked with him to the Shepherd's hut on Sunday afternoon—he kept me in fits of laughter the whole way. I think he is certainly cracked. Afterwards I was made to draw Mr S.S., his profile on the wall. He is quite *hideous* with a nose like a snipe, so they all laughed the whole time at his *extraordinary* shadow profile. … Yesterday we had a tea-party in Lady L's boudoir called the 'Bower of Bliss'. There is a notice written up in the hall every day to say where tea is to be— isn't it nice and vague?

Amy & Tom have left for Carstairs so we were a very small party at dinner—Only Lady L. & Violet & Wallace & myself. In the evening I played billiards with the latter, who I like, but think he is rather smitten with Lady N. MacDonnell—who left on Saturday—which is a pity if true for he is far too nice for her. Afterwards I had a delightful time in my own room over the fire—reading *The Light of Asia* [a very popular long poem in blank verse about Buddha by Sir Edwin Arnold, 1879] which I have often heard you speak of. It is *quite beautiful*—& fascinates me. … Ever your loving Laura

Paddington Workhouse, Harrow Road   18th November

Amour de ma vie, When I got home last night I found my brother John in a great state of excitement. He is to sail on the 26th of this month which is sharp work. My Father came home late in time to have a painfully violent scene with John & myself as to this scheme which he entirely disapproves of. However that does not matter much.

I breakfasted at 8. & came to the Royal Oak Underground Station thence walking up here & finding no one at all. I wonder how long I shall have to wait for the Poor Law Auditor. Another time I shall not be so punctual. This seems to be a huge building. I am sitting in a large room with the windows looking out on a garden. The sun is shining brightly, there is a good fire. Big ledgers are ostentatiously placed about. But still no Auditor. ... I do hope that this is going to turn out really an opening for me & one which will make me independent.

[CONTINUED]
(from Wandsworth & Clapham Union, St John's Hill)

In came Mr Roberts the Auditor who set me to work. The work I found myself quite able to do & though mechanical not entirely uninteresting. About ½ past one we had finished the work to be done & walked down to the Paddington Station Restaurant Bar where we had an abominable lunch. We walked to Victoria & took train to Clapham when we got out & walked to this place. Then I worked away till ½ past 5. when I came back home to finish my letter to you. I found my brother here in a dreadful state of mind. The Doctor has refused to pass him!! But we hope to get John through somehow. I am off to see Jack Napier [second son of 10th Lord Napier & Ettrick] on this subject— he was with the Gordon Highlanders in South Africa in 1881—& show him the report of an excellent Doctor to whom John went immediately after being rejected. Our Doctor gives the lie to the other of course as they all do. The fact is the boy was upset with last night's row with my Father—as I was myself. ... Your Adrian

P.S. You see that Hardinge Cameron[22] is to marry again, a Miss Adelina Blake of Thurston, Suffolk. Do you know her at all?

Wandsworth & Clapham Union, St John's Hill   19th November

Ma bien aimée Laure, ... Mr Roberts the Auditor who is a little fiery Welshman has been slanging some people like mad over their sins in account keeping. He is not a bad little man with red whiskers & a hard face. Mr Lilley the Assistant Auditor is a timid little man very anxious to show me what he can & nervously fussy about little details. I forgot to say I was the first again this morning which evidently pleased Roberts who begins to think that I may be fit for something after all. Another violent scene has just occurred. Really these people seem to be too stupid for words. I quite pity Roberts who is now crimson with rage, three Overseers are quaking in their shoes before his righteous wrath. I wonder whether Mrs R. rules him at home.

[*Later*] I found a letter from John at the Vine Club. It is all right & he is going. Methuen has been awfully kind. Now I am going to try & get John made Special Correspondent for the *Morning Post* or some other daily paper. I am afraid that the Cannes Consulate is an unpaid one & already filled up by the appointment of the principal House Agent there. I do dread your being beset with worldly advice to give me up because of my poverty. From what I hear I hope that the Liberals are safe for yet another year, in which case I shall be pretty certain of my appointment. ... Oh, Darling when shall we meet again.

[CONTINUED]
(FROM WARWICK HOUSE, ALBERT ROAD, BATTERSEA)

... My love, no work is dull to me now that I feel I am working for *you*. Though I confess I have cast rather longing glances to South Africa. Will you tell Lady L. that I am very much obliged to her for her kind offer. If she really will write to Lord Derby I think it might do me good. She should say that I have been P.S. to the late Gov. Sir J. Longden (of Ceylon) and that I am now working under the Poor Law Auditor for London in hopes of an appointment, but that I should prefer an appointment in the Colonies as they are better paid. If she really knows Lord D. well she should ask him to see me *personally*. That is my only real chance of getting anything out of the C.O. [Colonial Office]. Mr Goschen[23] has written a very kind letter offering to see me & I shall certainly go & urge him as an old friend of my Father's to do something for me. My letters must read so selfishly darling with this continually recurring 'me' & 'I'. But I think they always stand for 'us' & 'we'. ...

John sails on Wednesday morning from Gravesend. Do you know I feel his going alone dreadfully & I shall miss him very much poor dear boy. ... I am very low tonight & wish that someone could put her dear arms round my neck & let me rest my head on her shoulder.

Your Adrian

Lamington, Lanarkshire
[with Lord & Lady Lamington]

20th November

Darling, … Wallace wears a grey kilt & looks very well in it. I should like to see you in a kilt some day if we have anything to do with Scotland again, but I don't think you are so *Esau* like as Wallace—& it rather suits the dress! We have a little talk sometimes but I feel very like the lady in the song, who said 'All men are to me as shadows *now*'. Are you pleased darling? It is perfectly true. … I hope you will be able to get out of town often for Sundays. I am sure it will be good for you after your Workhouse days. Lunch at Refreshment rooms sounds very uncomfy. Do you eat those stale sandwiches & ancient currant buns? I *hope* not—how fortunate it is darling that you are one of those men who do not *care* about luncheon!!!! … Goodbye *dearest dearest* Adrian. Take care of yourself for my sake—Ever yours, Laura

St Pancras, Guardians of the Poor,
Pancras Road

21st November

My darling, … It would be of course the best thing that could happen were Lord Derby to give me some Colonial Appointment, for if well paid it might darling, yes it might enable us to marry very shortly. This however is only a dream I fear (I mean the Colonial Appointment). … After working till 3. I went out to St Pancras & had some lunch there, not that I felt hungry but I was tired out & sick with the smell of the people whom I had been worrying all the morning. St Pancras made me think of the morning we had breakfast together after you had used me as a pillow all the way from Chester, my love. I send you one long kiss darling, from your Adrian

Westminster Union, Poland Street

22nd November

My darling Laura, Lady Goldsmid saw my brother John yesterday & was quite delightful to him. She gave him a letter to Sir Algernon Borthwick, the proprietor of the *Morning Post* who was very kind & sent John down at once to the Office where he found that another man had been arranged with. I hope to get him another Correspondency if it is possible. … I go every day to the [Vine] Club now on my way to the Workhouses in order to get my day's supply of happiness & courage. Your letters are my greatest joy. I get quite cross & peevish if by chance I fail to get one.

My Father & I are slowly making friends again but it is really a bore to have such a very theatrical relative. So you would like to see me in a kilt like

48

Wallace C.B. Well some day it may be given to you to see me in one though it has always seemed to me a draughty style of dress. How would you like it if your clothes were cut off short above the knee. For indoors I think that (with *only* us two present) it would suit admirably. But for outdoors? ... I should like to know what picture you have copied at Lamington. I fear none & that the delights of—!!! with Wallace C.B. were too much for your good intentions of making a copy in every house you go to. I feel jealous of W.C.B. Your Adrian

LYME PARK, DISLEY, CHESHIRE   SUNDAY, 23RD NOVEMBER
[WITH MR & MRS WILLIAM LEGH 'COUSIN MILLY')

Good morning Darling Adrian, ... We had a long journey to get here—10 hours. Wallace carefully looked out our trains from Manchester & chose one for us that ran *every* day in the week *except* Saturday! so we were stranded at that wretched place for 2 hours—and arrived here just before 10 p.m. ... Tom [Legh][24] talked about Paris & a little about you—he told me you were immensely admired by the Parisian ladies!!! especially by a Madame Gustave (I think he said) Rothschild. What is the meaning of *this* darling. I must say I don't think Tom shares the enmity you have for him.

I rather regret the dear little room I had at Lamington, all blue & white & spangled with daisies. Here Amy and I have 2 large rooms opening into each other, called the mahogany rooms, very high & panelled to the ceiling with dark mahogany, with *gigantic* furniture of the same. The only picture is a huge & ghastly representation of St John the Baptist's head on a charger, a pale green face looking up, with a half shut fishy eye that follows me about the room & only rests when I am lying in bed as it is exactly opposite to my couch! However I am not given to nightmares and custom has robbed that fixed *wink* of most of its terrors, but Mrs Herodias who is carrying it off in triumph is so very buxom & yellow & the horrible little daughter looking on, with a huge brawny copper coloured soldier showing every known muscle, supporting the head, make up altogether *not* a very pleasing group [probably a copy of a painting by Peter Hendriks Schut, *c.* 1618-60]. ... I am just going off to tea in Cousin Milly's boudoir entirely covered with the most lovely carvings by [Grinling] Gibbons. He was for years here, doing this room. ... Sometimes I miss you oh so much. Keep up your courage darling. Ever your own Laura

VINE CLUB, 8 ST JAMES' SQUARE   24TH NOVEMBER

My dearest darling Laura, … I found my way down to Shoreditch Workhouse this morning with some difficulty. It was snowing when I started & I found a thick fog in the City. … You have certainly crushing luck whenever you travel about. Do you think darling that we shall miss our way to Bellagio some day on our honeymoon? I wish Tom Legh were not at Lyme. He seems to be full of malice. However I forgive him. Because I trust you so, love, that I don't think you will attach too much importance to my Paris Amourettes? … How I long to see you again my own love, Your Adrian

LYME PARK, DISLEY, CHESHIRE   24TH NOVEMBER
[WITH MR & MRS WILLIAM LEGH 'COUSIN MILLY']

My own darling Adrian, in a month it will be Christmas Eve—and we may be at Runcton again together. I do hope we shall have that happiness. A Mr Carew arrived this afternoon, an attaché from Paris & a friend of Tom's but as different as possible. He seems rather nice. They told me he was engaged to a girl for a long time—for years—before he was able to marry, and then she died when they had only been married a year. He has a little daughter of 3 years old. I should not have guessed he had such a sad story, he seems just like any other young man, not particularly interesting, but agreeable as I think attachés usually are.

We have all been playing the Word game—everyone snapping up the words & fighting for them. The first game I nearly won, then the next we played I forgot all about the wretched game & my thoughts wandered away & rested on *quite* a different subject, so when we finished I had only *3 words*, little tiny words—and they all laughed at me—& somebody else had *Hope*! Wasn't it silly. *Laura* it must *not* occur again but it really was quite Mr Legh's fault for he began *wrangling* over some stupid word with Cousin Milly and their voices became *so* X & I began thinking how horrid it was, & how I hoped the time would *never* come when you & I would talk to each other in that sort of way and forget to be gentle and loving—and so my thoughts roamed on, and dwelt on you, and there they felt so happy & at home, I could scarcely bring them back to our noisy game, for curiously, *that* seemed to become *unreal* & like a dream—though I was actually taking part in it, & *I* seemed to be living another life entirely, in my own vivid thoughts. Do you know that odd feeling? Goodnight dearest, Yr L.

WARWICK HOUSE, ALBERT ROAD, BATTERSEA
LATE, 24TH NOVEMBER

My dearest Love, As it was my little sister Madge's eleventh birthday I went & bought her a copy of your *Little Thumb*[25] with which she was delighted indeed. My Mother says that it is a revelation as to your genius & has scolded me for not having said enough to her in praise of your drawings and paintings. ... Yes my Sweet I would prefer to live with you in England. I think that until I get this Auditorship nothing can be done unless by a person knowing Dilke or [Joseph] Chamberlain[26] well. Such a person could ask for an Inspectorship for me as a personal favour but once I get the Auditorship there can be no question as to my being a fit man to promote. ... Darling goodnight. Your Adrian

LYME PARK, DISLEY CHESHIRE
[WITH MR & MRS WILLIAM LEGH 'COUSIN MILLY']
25TH NOVEMBER

Darling Adrian, You dear silly old Adrian, you don't suppose I cared 2 pins for Tom Legh's remarks. They only amused me—& I thought I would tease you a little! & really Tom only meant them as the mildest chaff. Before the 2nd August [their engagement day], darling, I cannot quarrel with you for amourettes as you call them!! & thank heaven we have perfect trust in each other for without it I, for one, could not love you as I do, with *all* my heart— so think no more of what I said. Really I rather *like* Tom, & he makes himself very agreeable and tells me about Paris life—which I like to hear of. I have been sent into dinner with him both nights. The first we talked of Sarah Bernhardt & the plays etc. & last night he amused me describing weddings at the Embassy, and ours—& then we discussed married life in France, about which I of course know very little. ...

What do you think of this invitation from Ethel Chapman to take the lead again in *Sweethearts* at Sandringham with Mr Lambart, a new young man? I have accepted the very good looking man!! I hope you don't mind. Joking apart, darling, if I thought my acting would annoy you *in the least* I would *at once refuse* but I remember our talk on the subject and that you gave me special dispensation to do so. Always to the end, your Laura

WARWICK HOUSE, ALBERT ROAD, BATTERSEA
12 MIDNIGHT 25TH NOVEMBER

My darling, I have just finished packing John's clothes & things for him— into a tin box wondrous small. Poor dear fellow, when one can do so little for him it is a comfort to do that & you know I pride myself on packing well.

[CONTINUED]   26TH NOVEMBER

John & I went down this morning to Fenchurch St. He begged me to tell you that his only regret at leaving England was at not having seen you again, though he said: 'hers is not a face you can ever forget'. When we got to the station we were told that the Special for Tilbury could not start as the vessel had been delayed by the fog on the river & was stuck in the Docks. So we took a train down to Blackwall & there found the *Pembroke Castle*.

Getting down as we did before the rush, John was able to stow away his luggage without any bother. The sight was a very curious one indeed as first one & then another & then a crowd of these Gentlemen Volunteers made their appearance. Some were in patent leather boots with such smart coats & such neat luggage. It made me feel so sad for them, they evidently had no idea of how they were going to rough it. I fortunately was able to introduce my brother to some nice fellows going out & he found that he knew 3 or 4 so he will not feel so lonely. They are to sleep in hammocks slung where the Cabins *were*. The decks have been cleared from side to side which makes it light & airy. There were rows of plain deal tables to seat 12 & when I left at one o'clock dinner was being served out. It looked good & wholesome. Troop A, which consists entirely of Gentlemen, struck me as having a fair lot of nice men. They are separated from Troop B, which consists of old soldiers & others. These are a rough looking lot. I fancy Methuen will have a time of it keeping order as until they get to Cape Town he has no power or authority, the men not having been yet sworn in as Soldiers.

About your acting. Dearest, I shall always love you to do what you like & I take a pride in the thought that you are so clever. ... The Xmas invitation to Runcton is delightfully kind—of course I will come though it may be only for a very few days. Here is a letter from Mr Cooper [telling Laura that Macmillan's had turned down her 'Little Mermaid' drawings as a book]. When I bought *Little Thumb* they told me it had had a great sale & had been very successful. Your Adrian

27TH NOVEMBER

My darling, ... How I should love to see you act. Oh that handsome young man whom you have accepted by telegraph. ... I am going to see Mrs Childers tomorrow & shall flirt desperately with her or anyone else who may be there to drown my feelings of agony. First Tom Legh. Then Carew. Now a stranger. And yet you wonder that Clemency [Hubbard] called you a f——?? Darling I love to hear of you amusing yourself & your letters tell me you think sometimes of me in the intervals between the victims? My Love, my love, Goodnight, Adrian

Lyme Park, Disley Cheshire   27th November
[with Mr & Mrs William Legh 'Cousin Milly']

Darling Adrian, I have been reading a *History of Ceylon* I found in the library here by Sir James Tennant. His description of the *insect world* in that favoured spot nearly made me sick, with pictures of the leeches taking their walks abroad—just as you described them to me. I have been having a talk with Mr Francis Carew & I felt *so* sorry for him, when he was asking about our future, darling—& what we meant to do—and he said several times—'Don't wait too long—believe me it is better to marry soon, than to wait for years for each other—as we did' & he looked so *miserable*, poor fellow. Last night Gil [the younger Legh brother] gave me my first lesson in picquet. Perhaps we shall amuse ourselves with it in the winter evenings on our *settle* in the corner by the fireside. Evy, Tom's wife, arrived today looking very pretty but mourning is not really becoming to her. [Her father had just died.]

It is rather disappointing about Macmillan—not that I really built on the vague chance. When I am in London I am going to find out what it would cost to publish my 'Little Mermaid'—as Mrs Legh wants to do it for me—or with me—as a spec, if it seems at all possible to manage *lucratively*. It is nearly a month since we parted darling, and it seems to me like 6. ... Ever yours L.

Greenwich Union, Greenwich   28th November

My sweet Love, I have been working away without a break trying to get the accounts of a very stupid old man in order for him. He grunts & says Oh Lord whenever I show him a mistake. No chance of a fish lunch as I had hoped for we are far from the Greenwich hotels. Tennant's *History of Ceylon* is still the standard book of reference. It is well written by a great blackguard who behaved very treacherously to all with whom he worked. ... Your lover ever, Adrian

Jo's Room, Bachelors' Club,   Sunday, 30th November
8 Hamilton Place

My Darling Laura, ... I shall only get a few days off at Xmas, we leave off work the day before & Mr Roberts wants me to come back on the Monday after [29th]. But I do so want to see my dearest love tread the boards. Do you know I am rather glad the very handsome young man for *Sweethearts* has been discarded. I felt quite ready to be very jealous of him. ... I do love you so Laura mine. Dearest, I could write I love you on & on for ever. Now goodnight, Your Adrian

---

13 *4th Nov* Douglas (Beech) Grant, a young American who played the lead opposite Laura in W S Gilbert's *Sweethearts* for two amateur performances in 1882.

14 *7th Nov* J E C Bodley, Oxford graduate who became Dilke's PS at the Foreign Office in 1880. At first he tended to stay up all night, dancing and flirting, but gradually he came to use his considerable intellect and wide social contacts. (Cf *Sir Charles Dilke* by Roy Jenkins, 1965.)

15 *10th Nov* Louisa Mary née Lloyd, widow of Hon. William Napier (d. 1876), younger brother of 10th Lord Napier & Ettrick (who had employed Adrian's father in the diplomatic service). Mrs Napier's niece, Constance Lloyd, married Oscar Wilde in May, 1884, and her son Francis Napier was to marry Adrian's youngest sister, Madge, in 1893.

16 *10th Nov* The Lamington (Cochrane-Baillie) kinship was through Laura's paternal grandmother, Anna Maria Troubridge née Cochrane, who was Violet and Wallace Cochrane-Baillie's great aunt.

17 *13th Nov* Richard Jefferies (1848-87), acclaimed as a nature writer but also author of a few novels. *The Dewy Morn* (1884) included several hymns of praise to the heroine's knees, such as: 'Before those beautiful knees he could have bowed his forehead in the grass, in the purest worship of beauty. They were sacred, a sense of reverence possessed him ...'. (Cf Ch XIV, one-vol edn.)

18 *14th Nov* 'Oh do you know the Muffin Man who lives in Crumpet Lane?', the game song where each participant has to sing two repeats of the tune solo until all join in at the end with: 'We all know the Muffin Man.' (Cf *Within the Family Circle* by Violet Powell, p215, 1976.)

19 *16th Nov* James Charles Hope-Vere of Blackwood, Lanark (three times gt grandson of 1st Earl of Hopetoun) whose first wife had died in 1882. He then married Marie Elizabeth Françoise Guillemin, granddaughter of the Duc de Montebello.

20 *16th Nov* Laura later noted here, 'She was! ['arranged for with some rich old man']. Seven years later Violet Cochrane-Baillie married fifty-six-year old Henry Dundas, 5th Viscount Melville. The eldest sister, Constance, was already married to the 7th Earl de la Warr (b 1817), and the second, Amy, to the Italian statesman, Marquese Francesco Nobili Vitelleschi (b 1829).

21 *16th Nov* This journal was edited by her third son and published in 1964 as: *A Victorian Diarist—Extracts from the Journals of Mary, Lady Monkswell* Vol I, 1873-95, ed Hon E C F Collier (Cf 15th November, 1884).

22 *18th Nov* Hardinge Cameron, Julia Margaret Cameron's second son had been PS to the then Governor of Ceylon (Sri Lanka) a few years before Adrian was to hold the same post. Julia Margaret's niece, Alice Prinsep, was married to Laura's Uncle Charles Gurney.

23 *19th Nov* George Goschen, later 1st Viscount, one-time Director of the Bank of England and President of the Poor Law Board.

24 *23rd Nov* Tom Legh (later 2nd Lord Newton) of Lyme Park, Disley, Cheshire, was then in the diplomatic service as Attaché at the British Embassy in Paris. He and Laura shared a gt grandfather, the 17th Earl of Errol, whose daughter Lady Dulcibella Jane Hay (by his 1st wife) married Tom's maternal grandfather, the Ven Charles Wodehouse, archdeacon of Norfolk, and his next daughter Lady Harriet Jemima Hay (by his second wife) married Laura's maternal grandfather Daniel Gurney of Runcton, Norfolk. For an evocative small book on a childhood spent at Lyme a generation later by Tom Legh's daughter, Phyllis (Hon Mrs Gerald Sandeman), *see Treasure on Earth* by 'P.E.S.', illustrated by the author (Herbert Jenkins, 1952); later reprinted under the auspices of Lyme Park Joint Committee as by Phyllis Sandeman (1971, 1972, 1981). Some names are disguised but clearly recognisable is: '... Cousin Amy, a great favourite without whom no Christmas party was complete ...'. She always played the piano to great effect for the annual Christmas production and, of course, both before and after.

25 *24th Nov* Little Thumb—a Fairy Story by Hans Andersen, illustrated by Laura Troubridge. Text as translated by Miss Peachey (W A Mansell, 1883).

26 *24th Nov* Joseph Chamberlain took over Sir Charles Dilke's post of President of the Local Government Board for a short time in 1886.

DECEMBER 1884

POPLAR UNION, HIGH STREET, POPLAR 1ST DECEMBER

My darling, I have received two such nice letters from my Aunt Annie [Cunninghame Graham] & from my sister Laura. Laura hopes that you have forgotten & forgiven the stupid letter which she wrote to you in Ireland [when their engagement was announced]. My Aunt for the first time talks in a friendly way of you. It was beastly difficult to get down here & I had to walk & go by Underground & Bus & Railway to the docks. ... Freddie Gore told me he was going to act in the other piece at Sandringham & asked me whether I would understudy the part of the gardener 'Wilcox' in *Sweethearts*. I think *not* for I should not like to *act* with you. Freddie told me that Lambart will act with you after all. Notwithstanding, I don't feel *very* jealous from what he told me. ... I long to see you Love so much, Your Adrian

LYME PARK, DISLEY CHESHIRE 2ND DECEMBER
[WITH MR & MRS WILLIAM LEGH 'COUSIN MILLY']

My dearest, I don't think you made quite such an impression, Darling, on Mrs Edwardes [a new house guest] when you met—as she seems to have made in your mind, for when Sybil Legh asked if she remembered you—she said: 'Oh yes, she remembered you quite well—you were such a *nice little man*'!! ... You cannot think how glad I am of your Laura's message and that they have written nicely to you—after all silence was much the best & most peacemaking way we could take Laura's letters. I will try that it shall make no difference when we meet & of course forgive the letters—but somehow it is more difficult to forget—isn't it? Goodbye darling Adrian, Ever your Laura

3RD DECEMBER

Darling Adrian, Gil has been begging me to stay till Friday. He says no one will care! Shall I??? [Both the married Leghs had left Lyme.] ... Pray don't play the Gardener's part in *Sweethearts*. It would be too horrid to have you for my stupid Gardener and someone else for my 'Sweetheart'—what a *nightmare*. I am simply longing to see your *dear* face again. Ever your *Laure qui t'aime.*

POPLAR UNION, HIGH STREET, POPLAR 3RD DECEMBER

My Sweet, ... Oh! how cruel to call me 'a nice little man'. Well I heard you described the other day as 'a great big girl'. I hope you are pleased with the description. It made me think of young elephants. ... My head is full of a

Buzzing sound which says 'She is coming tomorrow, tomorrow, tomorrow'. … My Love, my own, Your Adrian

At 30 Thurloe Square, South Kensington [with Johnny & Rosy Birkbeck]

5th December Adrian had to leave at 10. for Stepney Workhouse…A. Did not get back from that horrid place till 7.30.

6th December Adrian to Bethnal Green Workhouse—& it was nearly 7. before he arrived quite tired out with the work. …

Sunday, 7th December … To Battersea to see Mrs Hope and Adrian's two little sisters, Jessie and Madge.

8th December … Adrian & I to the South Kensington Museum together, & looked at pictures & pretty things. The whole place was lit with electric light.

9th December … We had a delightful evening seeing *Romeo & Juliet* at the Lyceum, just the play for us.

10th December Adrian off to another outlandish place— Plumstead Marshes. … To my surprise found a very pretty little Madeira ring of 2 clasped hands, at Minipris—if it fits dear Adrian I will give it to him for Xmas.

11th December … Wore my long white dress, with the Parma violets Adrian brought me, to the Tyssen-Amhersts' party. Heard some lovely violin playing & some good singing. The whole thing was amusing & nice. Drove back *à deux* in a hansom. Talked a little in the den—our last evening.

12th December Adrian had to work at Camberwell miles away & could not even come to St Pancras to see me off. …

HUNSTANTON   13TH DECEMBER

My own darling Adrian. … I spent my last morning at Gorringes [department store] & there I met amongst others Mr & Mrs Edwardes with their little child, buying her some toys in the bazaar—I did not know husbands ever went to *Gorringes!* Before I left the Birkbecks, to my surprise they suddenly presented me with a wedding present, a very pretty one—a locket—a little painting of cupids, set in pearls, with a bow at the top. I like it so much. ... I travelled quite alone to Lynn, in a through carriage. Next door were 2 people who tipped the guard *not* to let me in with them—I had that fellow feeling which makes us wondrous kind. Goodbye Sweetheart, your own *Laure*

St Giles, Camberwell,   13th December
Board of Guardians, Peckham Road

Ma Laurette, ... My dear Mother is quite in love with your sweet face, and said how she felt sure of always getting on with you & loving you. ... My two old Graham [great] aunts in Leamington are I fear dying. Poor old things, I do hope they will live over the Sandringham Ball. ... I am kissing your photograph darling. I fear below *le collier de Vénus* ['the necklace of Venus' is the desirable area of the neck where a choker would be worn]——Goodbye dear Love, Your Adrian

St Mary Abbotts, Kensington,   15th December
Guardians Offices, Marloes Road

My own sweet love, When do rehearsals begin for *Sweethearts?* I long to hear what you think of Mr Lambart's acting. My mind is divided between hoping that he will act well for your sake & fearing that he may act too well for my peace of mind. There is a nice selfish sentiment for you to read. ... All day I have been suffering intensely from a forewarning of coming trouble to you or to myself. I cannot fight it off & it has sent my spirits down to zero. ... Tuesday week you shall give me a kiss & a pinch for being foolishly superstitious. ... In imagination I kiss your dark hair as it hangs over your neck. Your Adrian

Hunstanton   15th December

My darling Adrian, ... I am so glad you have accepted to stay with the Le Stranges [at Hunstanton Hall] for the Sandringham Ball on the 8th. Will you beg, borrow or steal a Court dress for the occasion? ... Oh your poor aunts. How I hope they will live on a bit, but if they *should* die before Christmas you will come to me darling all the same, won't you, because there will be no party—only relations—and you are *almost* a relation too now. It's quite different from a ball, isn't it? and after all they are only great-aunts. ... How I do miss you & the pleasure of being together, it is like starving to be without you now. ...

How glad I am that your mother was not disappointed with our visit to her. It would have been such a bore for you if they had disliked me. She was so kind and easy. ... Ever yours only, Laura

16TH DECEMBER

My own dearest Adrian, I had such a nice letter from Rosy about our coming again. Could we not manage some sort of vague *telephone* next time in our own sky high suite of apartments? Something like the advertisement:

'How are you dear?'

'Quite well thanks to Nubian blacking'

(or) ... to Eno's fruit salt (or) ... to Parrs life Pills

only we would not say anything so dreadfully *terre à terre* [down to earth] ... then we need not talk so late downstairs.

We begin to rehearse on Saturday when Ethel Chapman who is in charge of the theatricals is going to bring over the fascinating *jeune premier* to be introduced to—his Sweetheart! ... Goodnight dear dear Adrian, Ever your Laura

GREENWICH UNION, GREENWICH   17TH DECEMBER

My dearest Love, After finishing our work at Lewisham (which is a very nice, pretty place), I was fortunate enough to escape in time to go & see old Cooper. Read his letter (enclosed) & digest its criticism. Then I went to Sampson Low & Co. the publishers and saw Mr Marston who spoke very highly of the 'Little Mermaid' drawings. He wishes to have permission to try doing one as a Specimen. ...

No mortality among my Great-Aunts shall prevent my coming down to Xmas to you, not if they all were taken at once. But I fear that if they die between now & the Sandringham Ball I may have to give that up. Darling, if I go I must go in Colonial Office uniform, much uglier than a Court dress, but still alas! the proper thing for me which the other would not be. ... I went to bed with my Laura lying so quietly on my heart. She did not seem to mind a bit. ... Goodbye dear love, Your Adrian

HUNSTANTON   19TH DECEMBER

My poor Adrian, ... I have just had such a nice cheery letter from your Mother. She advises me never to keep any old letters! but I have bought such a nice little old oak corner cupboard with brass hinges—for a few shillings—to keep the letters I love best—*all* from the same person, and some few of my wedding presents. Everyone I see talks about the theatricals. The room in the Sandringham Club [at West Newton] will not hold more than 150 but I think that is quite enough. I am getting rather frightened about it. ... As for 'going through passionate love scenes with another'—you know *Lambart's* thoughts will be somewhere else all the time, as well as mine. ... We are going to dance at Runcton on Boxing night but I don't think we shall get up a play this year. ... Rather disappointing about the Court dress, is your uniform a policeman's—like the diplomatists wear? or something nicer? I am having a new frock for the Ball. I hope you won't quarrel with it, it is a sort of peach colour, quite pale, the sort of shade one sees in a French 'Journal de Mode' called '*Jambe de Nymphe*' but that is *simply horrid*. ...

By the by, bring a gun if you like, because Tom says they will be shooting at Runcton. I hope we shall be able to have some times alone together—we shall be 18 or 19 in the house. ... Ever your own *Laure*

VINE CLUB, 8 ST JAMES' SQUARE   20TH DECEMBER

My own dearest Love, Your new dress should look very pretty & the name of the colour sounds quite delightfully gauzy. I will bring you *Autour du Mariage* which will make you laugh I think only I want to watch your face as you read it for some of it is sure to make you furious. Only three days now to our next meeting. ... What a good thing that we are to have a Dance at Runcton for I fancy Sandringham will be dull & a crush & I do long for a good valse with you, sweet heart of mine. ... You will all think me a dreadful being I fear because Xmas really only makes me think of my bills & I have never ever tried to look jolly. Is the [church] service at Runcton very appalling & do they ever have such a thing as an early service to which perhaps you & I might go together over snowy fields. I have not seen snow for years & years. Good afternoon, my darling love, Your Adrian

WARWICK HOUSE, ALBERT ROAD,   SUNDAY, 21ST DECEMBER
BATTERSEA

My dear Love, ... By the by, nothing shall induce me to shoot at Runcton. I am not going to waste hours when we might be together, shooting!! ... I feel that my only excuse for daring to propose to you is that I do love you with my whole heart & that my love being so great may perhaps make up for want of wealth. How I long to press you to my heart & never to let you go again. ... How I will take care of you darling when I get you all to myself. Not even Tanner shall take as much care of you as I will. Then perhaps someone will let me button on her boots, for which I have a natural talent, as I have for all *sorts* of lady's maid work. I am a capital Dresser as you will find some day if you allow me the privilege of being useful to you as well as—ornamental? ... I go to Upper Holloway tomorrow, to Lambeth on Tuesday morning, & My Laura's Arms that evening. Goodnight from *Adrian* who is simply wild to kiss you again on the mouth, sweet Love

At Congham Lodge, Hillington, W. Norfolk
[with Mr & Mrs Godfrey Chapman]

> *22nd December* The party is Mr & Mrs Chapman, daughters Ethel & Maude, & Col. Gore, a funny little thing, brother to Lady Errol [wife of 19th Earl]—too odd to look at—with a wild admiration for Adrian, a Mr Mainwaring Dunstan—like a professional, & Mr Alfred Lambart my 'Sweetheart' who I rather liked. [To Adrian she writes: 'Mr L. Is not dangerous but rather "a nice little man"!'] Rehearsed *Sweethearts*, drove over to the Sandringham Club—the stage is simply tiny, & the arrangement vague in the extreme. The other play, *A Comical Countess* [by W. Brough], is a costume farce & rather amusing. Ethel Chapman acts very well. ...

Adrian joined the Runcton house-party for a week over Christmas and managed to see Laura as 'Jenny' in the first performance of *Sweethearts* on the 29th for the 'Club' audience before going back to his Workhouses. This was followed by the Royal performance on the 30th and the last one on New Year's Eve for a 'village' audience.

At North Runcton Hall, King's Lynn
[with Uncle Sommy & Aunt Kitty Gurney]

> *26th December* ... The children's charades were good & amusing & then they recited. The Runcton Recs came, Vi & Helen with them, rather disconsolate for not having been invited to stay here. Dinner was amusing & the evening—dancing wildly. Eva &

George & Gerard Noel came. George was in the best of spirits because his wife was there & Gerard because his wife [Freda, George Cresswell's sister] was not. Tom sang songs & we finished with a wild cotillion & polkaing in procession all over the house, it was very jolly.

29th December ... A sort of scrambling rehearsal at West Newton when everything in the wildest confusion. After tea off to dress. I wore a fresh white frock with pink ribbons, my gardening gloves & a basket of flowers. I felt nervous. A. was there in the front row. ...

Congham Lodge, Hillington, W. Norfolk   31st December
[with Mr & Mrs Godfrey Chapman]

My *darling* Adrian, I think you would have been very pleased, it went off so well last night. It seems to be such a toss up with theatricals for last night after all it was the first play that everyone seemed to like the best & they laughed & applauded all the time and did *not* laugh when poor 'Jenny' cried! I did not feel in the least nervous—and exactly in the vein for acting. It was odd but I was so *far* more nervous on Tuesday when you were in the audience. About 30 people came from Sandringham & they did not keep us waiting at all, only 5 minutes. Yes darling, Lambart was *much* warmer in his love-making—I can't think why!! H.R.H. [later Edward VII] did not agitate us with talking on irrelevant subjects, he only said, 'Ah very good', or 'very well done' occasionally & led the applause which was most encouraging. Prince Victor & Prince George ['Eddy' Duke of Clarence and the future George V] were there, & the 'rest of the Royal family' as the prayer book says. After the play when I came round to the back of the room I *did* want you so. The Prince came & shook hands with me—& paid me compliments about my acting!! He said he had enjoyed it & liked the play so much—he hoped we did not find it very draughty on the stage etc. etc. & was nice & civil about it.

A Comical Countess did not go nearly so well as on Monday for they were all so nervous...and the footman [? Mr Dunstan] made so many mistakes that it rather frightened poor Ethel who acted very well, & he was *very piano* afterwards & disconsolate for H.R.H. had *not* smiled upon him—or taken any notice in any way!! much to our amusement.

I am sorry '84 is so nearly passed away. I have felt such happiness ever since I have known & loved you dear Adrian. What will the New Year bring to us? Last night I read some Essays by Hamerton called *Human Intercourse* [published earlier in the year]. One of them, 'Companionship in marriage', I am sure you would like … for the happiness it describes is just what I feel in my heart may be ours some day. … I have just been trying on my frock for the Sandringham Ball—the body I think will be pretty but it is rather décolletée & I have ordered an extra Tucker!!! on *purpose to please you*! A happy New Year to you my own darling true lover. Ever yours, Laura

At North Runcton Hall, King's Lynn
[with Uncle Sommy & Aunt Kitty Gurney]

> *31st December* After returning here to see the New Year in after the last performance of *Sweethearts* I felt so funny with my powdered hair & my white frock—the first & second act of *Sweethearts* blended—but in my life it is only the first that we have played yet—& even that is not finished. Thinking much of him tonight—& of the year—when the room was dark & quiet, & I alone with my thoughts.

The local Lynn newspaper reviewed at length the performance in front of royalty of the two plays, which raised over £75 for the Wolferton Church restoration fund. Both royal audience and cast were meticulously listed and the players individually praised. Due credit was also given to the interval pianist and local scenic artist, with an inordinately detailed description of the set:

> '… Mr [Charles] Orde played the old gardener Wilcox with genuine humour, his dialect was admirably sustained…In the two maid-servants' parts Miss [Amy] Troubridge acted exceedingly well; the tearful English maiden and the sprightly French attendant being cleverly sketched…Miss Laura Troubridge acted with much feeling and finish. As the young girl in the first act she was bright and arch…in the second act, when after the supposed lapse of many years she meets her lover of days gone by…perhaps the actress was at her best: the grey hair and graceful draperies adding to rather than taking from her personal charms, and the calm sadness and the tender thought for others portrayed being most sweetly and cleverly rendered. Mr Lambart in the very difficult part of the young lover, acted well, and [later] as the somewhat cynical old man into which he develops, both in manner and make up, he was capital. …

'… In the farce which followed, *A Comical Countess*, Miss Ethel Chapman played the 'Countess' with great vivacity. Her rapid changes of voice and expression, and a certain quaintness and piquancy of style suiting the character perfectly. It is one which requires clever handling and great variety…from first to last she held her audience in a way that would have done credit to any professional. Mr Mainwaring Dunstan played 'The Chevalier' with the quietness and ease of an old hand; and Col. Gore, as 'The Baron de Bergonce' was irresistibly droll, provoking much laughter. …'.

It was Amy who wrote to tell Adrian of the minor disaster that befell Mr Lambart during the last performance of *Sweethearts*:

'I saw a 3-vol letter addressed to you yesterday on Laura's bureau so I suppose you know all the details of our Congham doings. Perhaps, though, you were not told how *awfully* well Laura acted on Tuesday. She really distinguished herself, and looked so well. The Royalties were far more appreciative than the Club men and *Sweethearts* went far better than on Monday. Did L. tell you of the slight contretemps which luckily did not occur till Wednesday? Sir Henry Spreadbrows' moustache *came off* at the end of the 2nd act—just as the serious interest was beginning. Mr Lambart not only lost his moustache but also his presence of mind, and went off into weak fits of laughter! Laura kept her countenance perfectly—and carried it through—but it was *most* dreadful. … My *best* wishes to you for 1885. L. does not send her love, she is entirely absorbed in eating bread and butter … .'

52 Green Street, Park Lane [with Jem & Elsie Hope]

31st December

My sweetest Treasure, On this, the last day of that year which has brought me my greatest happiness & joy on earth, how can I think of anything but you, my love, my life. … How I long to hear what was your feeling at acting last night before all those Royalties. … I wish you a New Year full of joy & happiness—Oh! darling love how I hope that you & I will be one before the next year has come & gone. … Au revoir, *ma bien aimée*, Adrian

JANUARY 1885

SAINT GEORGE'S UNION, MIDDLESEX, SOUTH AUDLEY STREET

NEW YEAR'S DAY, 1885

My own Sweet Darling Laura, … So the Prince came and congratulated you. Charlie, who also wrote me a long letter, tells me that H.R.H. was very nice to you indeed. Do you know I am delighted that the pompous vulgar footman failed so for he richly deserved to fail, the man's conceit was just appalling. … I lament the tucker!!! Poor Jessie [almost fifteen years old] is very ill again. Her leg gives her constant pain & she is obliged to stop in bed altogether which makes her spirits very low. … I have just been to lunch in Green St when I gave one of those silver bracelets to Mrs Jem [Hope]. … Till Wednesday, Your faithful lover, Adrian

HUNSTANTON

2ND JANUARY

My own dear Adrian, Colonel Gore sent me a copy of *St Stephen's Review* with an account of the theatricals which has amused Amy and me very much. It was written by Col. Gore and Mr Dunstan—chiefly the latter—*Sweethearts* is dismissed as a mere *lever du rideau* [curtain-raiser]! and every point in *A Comical Countess* dwelt on most fondly. … Mr Dunstan is called '*delightful*'!!! Remembering how crestfallen he was that night and poor Ethel frankly said it had not been a success and very naturally blamed the boastful Dunstan—who said beforehand nothing ever made him nervous on the stage—& then was trembling all over & making all sorts of mistakes!—and then to read his own glowing description of the whole thing!

Yesterday I had a long letter from your Father. It was a nice clever letter but…rather a warning to us *not* to marry in haste—& repent at our leisure— for the usual reason—£.s.d. Colonel Hope says he: 'imagines from my note that it would be useless to try & persuade me to break off our engagement.' So he only advises most strongly our waiting, if necessary for years—in order that we may be comfortably off when we do marry—and he ends by hoping that: 'God will bless & prosper you *whether* you ever marry Adrian or not.' However…he is very complimentary to me, a good deal of jam to take with the truths that after all are no news to us…and since you asked me darling (5 months ago tonight) to be your own wife some day not one smallest *regret* has crossed my mind. …

What I am going to say sounds so like *sour grapes* that I could only say it to you because you know I am not jealous in *that* way, but I think there must be some want in my nature for I don't *care* much for silver bracelets—unless they are little bangles. I think if one was dusky brown all over & not troubled with much, or any other attire, those wide silver bracelets would look nice perhaps round one's ankles but that is scarcely how they are intended to be worn in this country—so I do not grudge the present! It is lovely in itself as silver work. Goodbye—for ever yours only, *Laure*

BERMONDSEY WORKHOUSE, RUSSELL STREET, BERMONDSEY

2ND JANUARY

My own sweet love, This place is a most un-get-at-able one, & I had to find my way through the slums of Bermondsey which reek of Tanning. ... By the by, is it a fact that H.R.H. said: 'What devilish neat ankles' referring to a young & flirty actress whom we both know intimately? ... *Bon soir ma chérie, mon âme*, Adrian

FULHAM UNION, HAMMERSMITH

3RD JANUARY

My own darling, ... My mind is a little disturbed with the philosophical way in which you refer to our marriage as such a very remote contingency. ... Has Tanner learnt the way of doing your hair powdered [as in the second act of *Sweethearts*], & will Amy allow you to go to the Ball like that? ... Your lover, Adrian

52 GREEN STREET, PARK LANE [WITH JEM & ELSIE HOPE]

SUNDAY, 4TH JANUARY

My darling Laura, ... So you think that it requires a brown skin to go clothed in bangles only. The effect would be striking on a white skin, more so perhaps. ... Does the joy of meeting at all make up for the pain of parting? What say you? If only we could see before us a fixed end to our period of waiting it would be perhaps less trying. ... I have been reading such a queer mystical book called *The Perfect Way; or the Finding of Christ* by Edward Maitland and Mrs Anna Kingsford, 1882. It is very nice & I love some of the things in it. ... Kiss your arm for me—Adrian

HUNSTANTON

5TH JANUARY

My own darling Adrian, ... We four sisters are just in from a long brisk walk along about the dullest road in England, a grey sky—and raining all the time! Still we amused each other—but I *long* to be swinging in a hammock under the trees in some lovely warm country, with flowers—and you by my side—& perhaps a few strawberries pour *varier les plaisirs*!

Oh that I were, where I would be—
Then would I be, where I am not
But where I am, there I must be
And where I would be, I can not—[27]

… A long letter from Ernest today, from Malta. He thinks they will be going on to China after all. He did not have a 'Merry Christmas' as it was beastly hot & pouring with rain all day & the Cook got drunk so even the dinner was a failure! Ever yours, *Laure* who loves you dearly

At Hunstanton

7th January Adrian arrived at 20 to 8 a.m.! We went for a turn on a sociable tricycle. … Dined at the Hall, where Adrian was staying with the Le Stranges. …

8th January All 4 of us sisters went to the Sandringham Ball. Prince Edward came of age & everyone was in Court dress— Adrian in Diplomatic uniform [his letter of 17th December stipulated Colonial Office uniform ?], with white breeches & silk stockings. He looked very well. I enjoyed it but not so much as I hoped to. …

9th January Caught an awful cold at the ball last night. Adrian came to take me to the Tenants' ball at Sandringham. Enjoyed it more than last night in spite of my cold. …

HOLBORN UNION, GRAY'S INN ROAD   13TH JANUARY

My dearest Love, … When I got to Lynn I purchased some candles to make darkness visible in the carriage so that I might read your present to me. Into the St Pancras train I got & settled myself very comfortably with all my luggage piled up round me & kept warm by my rugs & coats. I stuck one of the candles onto my portmanteau by melting the end of the candle. I began to read away, all the time thinking of you through my reading if you know what I mean to express…until I became aware of the fact that we had stopped & had evidently done so perforce as there was a chorus of angry passengers demanding to know why we were only 6½ miles outside Lynn instead of being well on our way to Ely. I was very unwilling to move or open the windows & so let in the cold wind. While I was debating in my mind whether I should be any worse off supposing I did nothing, a brutal Guard opened wide the door & telling me that the line was hopelessly blocked bade me get out. So out I had to get, first pocketing my cherished candle. I found myself at a little wayside shed of a station. Here we waited in the bitter driving hail while the Railway people were discussing how we were to be got rid of. After a bit we were put into a train & hustled off somewhere where we caught an express to Liverpool Street. I got to Green Street about 9.30, where Elsie Hope was fearing lest my dinner should be spoilt. ... She went into raptures over the 'Inspiration' sketch by L.T. So did Jem who at once offered his help in getting something of yours into the Grosvenor [Gallery].

Goodbye dear love of my whole existence, Sun round whose glory I turn, miserable when suffering under an eclipse of waiting longingly for the next turn which shall bring me within sight of you again. Au revoir, from planet Adrian

Mile End Old Town, Middlesex, Guardians' Offices, Bancroft Road

14th January

My Love, My Life, My Laura, Jem & I went to Sampson Low & gave Marston leave to take a proof of one of your 'Little Mermaid' drawings—with which Jem is in raptures. We chose the picture of the Prince finding the dear little Mermaid tailless by the water side. Jem suggests you go in for a 10/6 [ten shillings & sixpence] book & make it an 'edition de luxe'. ... On Friday Lady G. [Goldsmid] has her first Evening & I go with the hope that Dilke will be there & that he may say something nice to me about my chances of getting an appointment. How pleasant it would be to begin saving & buying little things for that house of ours when we mean to be so happy in the future. Today I see through my rose-coloured spectacles & regret that I had left them behind at Sandringham— will you forget my Gloom & I will try not to let you see it again? Goodbye, Adrian—your slave

Hunstanton

15th January

My *dearest*, ... I am delighted about Jem's idea of the Grosvenor Gallery. I have thought of trying a small panel picture of the illustration in my *Little Thumb* of him on the swallow's tail flying back to Fairyland, with a dark bird and a yellow sunset sky, but my drawing of the bird was entirely wrong. Do you think you could get me a stuffed swallow to draw from? ... Ever your love, Laura

Fulham Union, Hammersmith   17th January

My darling Laura, … Your 'Character' I quite long to see [Laura had found an old one done from her handwriting]. I heard the other day a story of two lovers who each wrote the other's characteristics down as they thought they really saw them. Alas! they quarrelled over their estimates of each other. I should never fear that result with you & me. … I did not see Dilke at Lady G's. Jo & I went home together & I am sorry to say that I sat up & expounded my views on politics to poor Jo till past three. He kicked horridly against some of my radical sentiments, others he swallowed like a lamb. We both felt as friendly as before & quite agreed to hold opposite views. …

At *The Private Secretary* [a 'smash hit' adapted from a German farce by actor-manager Charles Hawtrey] on Thursday with Elsie & her nephews & niece, how we laughed at it all. I never enjoyed such a laugh before, though I have been far happier when someone's black head was next [to] mine. Miss Maud Millett who does the young girl, the friend, maketh wondrous eyes for an 'Ingenue'. When we got back to Green St. we ate some delicious Oysters on toast Sandwiches. Quite a choice dish & one to be approved of.

[*Continued*] I had a satisfactory interview with Bodley who told me that he thought I should not have to wait long for my Auditorship appointment. … Good night my dearest Love & Life, Adrian

Hunstanton   Sunday, 18th January

My own darling Adrian, … Tardy [Charlie Orde] is here and hopes we will both come to Hopton for Easter—he is very keen about a play he wants us all to get up and act then. It is a long sort of serious farce by [W.S.] Gilbert—called *Engaged*. They acted it in London a few years ago. I am to send you a copy tomorrow to see what you think of it & whether you would take the part he proposes for you. I feel sure you could do it—in the first act you elope with me!!! but in the *end* darling—I *throw you over for Tardy*! …

Every morning I paint till lunch. In the bow window in the dining room I arrange my painting table, as it is small work & does not require an easel or oblige me to go to the studio which is cold & damp. … By the by, we will never draw out *maps* of each other's characters will we darling? not that we think each other *perfect*, that would be rather fatal but we will take warning from the other lovers' quarrel. … My dear dear lover, ever yours very dearly, *Laure*

Saint Saviour's Union (Surrey), Blackfriars Road

19th January

My Laura, On Saturday the Jem Hopes insisted on my dining with them at the Criterion where there was a Glee dinner. There was a good deal too much Glee & not enough dinner, in fact we set the whole thing down as a failure. ... I took off all my goods & chattels back to Battersea where I found Mother looking very worn out but they have had a sister to help in the nursing of poor little Jessie who is delighted with the Lilies of the Valley sent by you, and your letter is always under her pillow. To me it seems that unless Jessie gets away to Rhyl[28] soon she will die after having worn out my Mother & Nurse with weary watching. By the by, my old Great-Aunt Mrs Woodmass (Charlotte, sister of my grandfather Graham) died on the Saturday before the Sandringham Ball & my Mother was good enough not to tell me—though my being at balls has given great offence to some of the relations for which I do not care a snap. ... Goodnight my own dear love, Adrian

Hunstanton

19th January

Dearest Adrian, Here is the *Engaged* play book. There is really *too much* kissing in all 3 acts! Evelyn Orde [Charlie's very handsome sister] is *longing* with a feverish longing to paint her nose bright red & wear pillow stuffing & side curls as the old scotch widow! Charlie is dying to play Cheviot Hill and thinks nothing of learning the enormously long part. Belvawney (your part) is not *quite* so talkative—and an easier part all together. Then he has only to embrace *one* young lady instead of half a dozen! which perhaps will not be very difficult after a few rehearsals (private)! ... Tonight Limpet and I are going to patronize a 'Dramatic Entertainment' given by some amateur Ladies & Gentlemen of Hunstanton. They are going to play *Beauty & the Beast*. We have taken 2 stalls front row price 1/- [one shilling] each so we are not ruined by this little treat. I know the people who are going to act by sight but am rather puzzled to find a *Beauty* amongst them. Ever darling, Your *Laure*

Saint Saviour's Union (Surrey), Blackfriars Road

20th January

My dearest, On Sunday the McIvers gave me tea & sympathy—she longs to make your acquaintance and I fancy you would like them both for they are quite original & out of the common run of ordinary humdrum folk. ... My brother Charlie goes back to school this afternoon, burning to get his scholarship to Cambridge to make his fortune. I have got very fond of him these last few days. ...

How I long for my appointment that I may begin getting ready the home to which one day we shall come after our dream of heaven at Bellagio. For you really *shall* recant your opinion as to not enjoying a honeymoon my sweet love. ... Goodnight dearest, only a fortnight till we meet again—Your Adrian

WARWICK HOUSE, ALBERT ROAD, BATTERSEA   20TH JANUARY

My own dear Love, The Play will suit admirably I think. I have been chuckling over it at dinner. I cannot see Belvawney yet in my mind's eye. Is he to be a mysterious villain, a sort of skit on Hamlet & Iago. The traditional person with a single gleaming eye. Or what? ... Yesterday was foggy & we had to work all day by gas. Today I breakfasted by candle light & have seen no other than artificial light all day. Here is a letter of congratulation from one Price, a Ceylon Civil Servant, who has just heard of my engagement. I am rather glad to send you so flattering an account of your future Lord & Master as it is I fear the only one I ever received. The good man gets a little mixed for he apparently would like the position of my wife himself which would I fear be a little too hard a post for him & very unsatisfying to me. However I suppose one must make allowances for the hot sun of India. It also announces my *only* present. Well if I am to have you I do not want any single other thing in this world. Your loving Adrian

P.S. Goodnight. I kiss that white shoulder in my imagination (rather low down I fear) Oh!

HUNSTANTON   21ST JANUARY

My own dearest Adrian, ... I am glad to hear you approve of the play. Belvawney I should think was rather 'intense' a Greenery-Yallery Grosvenor Gallery sort of young man—but rather tragic too, for he has some very high flown speeches to make. ... Darling if you were near I would punish you somehow for what you say—how *horrid* of you to call yourself my 'future L- and M-'—a good hard *pinch* is what you deserve. You know you said it on purpose to tease me didn't you? and I am afraid you have succeeded!

Mr Cuffe and my friend Lily St Aubyn[29] are really to be married this year— it will be 6 years this summer since they have cared for each other & since he first proposed—should we have so much patience? I am glad to hear Charlie is ambitious & means to get his scholarship, so few boys that I know care about that sort of thing. ... You always—and for ever—*Laure*

HOLBORN UNION, GRAY'S INN ROAD   21ST JANUARY

Ma Laure chérie de mon coeur, ... I have had a letter from Graham Bower, the Private Secretary at the Cape who has promised to see what may be done for John [his middle brother] after the end of the Campaign against the Boers. Bower says that these estimable gentry are as cowardly as they are cruel & will give way without a blow. I devoutly trust that they will fight on the contrary as that must give John a chance.

I read *Engaged* over again & thought it very amusing but it depends for success on our powers of comic acting without laughing at our own absurdities. I much fear that Amy will be on the laugh all through. ... Your true lover, Adrian

HUNSTANTON   22ND JANUARY

My own dearest Adrian, The stuffed swallow is so pretty—and if an outline drawing *could* blush my *Little Thumb* swallow would be *crimson* by this time, for I have been comparing them! Thank you so much for sending it. ... I have just been reading a long account of Van Beers' pictures on view now in Bond Street at the Gallery they call the Salon Parisien. They are run down in the paper but I think *I* should like them. I have only seen one or two of his, & I was rather taken with the vivid colouring & clever effects. If he could make his women look like *ladies* it would be a great improvement. If it would not bore you I wish you would go & see them & tell me your impressions. Helen has a birthday on Monday—& we are beating up the neighbourhood for a hockey meeting to celebrate the occasion with much clashing of sticks and many bruises—she will be 19!! I wonder, will she ever develop into a young lady!

In this week's *Punch* 'To an Amateur Actress' is a snub that I feel I have not deserved, the cap does not fit at all. Even *supposing* I could act well enough & had *not* had the misfortune to be born a lady!—I could *never* have stood the *ennui* of acting the same thing night after night. I cannot think how anyone can have the courage to do it! because acting is so peculiar—I don't suppose it could *ever* become even sort of mechanical work, like most things that are repeated very often, as if it were no longer emotional—it would be a failure—I have been moralizing for a whole page—how vague of me—tear it up if it is dull. I have no time before the post to read it over. Adieu, *toujours toute à toi,* Laure

Lambeth Board of Guardians, Brook St, Kennington Rd   22nd January

My dearest, Mrs Adie Hope [Jem Hope's sister-in-law] told me she had seen *Engaged* 8 times & that my idea of Belvawney as an Operatic Villain was what had been acted on. Your part is very good & you ought to make a great hit. Mrs Adie says that Marion Terry did the part when you walk about talking and eating the tarts very effectively indeed, dressed in a *very* tight fitting cashmere dress of black, quite plain. She walked with long strides making little pounces on the tarts. … The news last night from Egypt was pretty exciting. We seem to have had fearful losses, 10 per cent of killed & wounded is very much out of such a small force. [The Mahdi is about to take Khartoum and Gen. Gordon to die]. … From fond lover, Adrian

Vine Club, 8 St James' Square   23rd January

My own Love, Last night I dined with Jo to meet his brother and sister-in-law Ld & Lady Hylton. I took a great fancy to Lord H. Arthur Sebright had his fiancée Miss Scott, her mother & Queensberry dining with him. Miss Scott looked very pretty but I was rather astonished at her dress. Ruby velvet body which did not come higher than her stays & a sort of lace tucker and two tiny epaulettes. Arms were perfectly bare & the very shoulder blades showed when she moved at all. It was rather too strong for a young girl. Not the faintest trace of a rudimentary sleeve & the dress *cut away* all round the arm hole which was very unnecessarily large. She could have put her head through as well as her arm. The effect was startling I can assure you. Our party went on to see *Romeo & Juliet*. Romeo had a bad cold poor fellow but struggled with it manfully. Juliet [Mary Anderson] was as charming as ever. I am quite certain that she must love him for she gives him such a down right kiss no stage embrace. We were in the second row darling & I discovered that that peculiar garment which Juliet wears as a nightgown is as transparent as the shirts of flannel that I have known some people play tennis in. Jo was very virtuous about this afterwards & declared himself to have been much shocked by the young lady's dress or rather want of it. When dear old Jo becomes a prude he is always intensely funny.

I must tell you about Price. He is a Welshman who is a Ceylon Civil Servant & who had an attack of madness once which began in my house in Kandy. He went out & walked along the road without any clothes on which was a great delight to all the native population. The cause of his illness was kind of jungle fever I fancy. It was to him and Burrows, a great friend of mine, that I entrusted my Kandyan Art Association. …

Fancy Limpet being 19. Why she will be getting engaged to be married soon. I wish that I were coming down to play hockey with you all on Monday. I have had a nice letter from Aunt Cha [Cunninghame Graham] at Rhyl but no sign of an offer to take Jessie yet. About the Guns & powder I hear nothing. You see I am not one of the faithful & my Father views with suspicion & dislike my extraordinary craze, as it seems to him, for an Auditorship. His idea is that I should wait patiently for my share of the enormous fortune which he will shortly realize & then I could choose for myself any career I liked to adopt.

... I looked at *Punch* when I found there was something in it which you deemed worthy of your attention and what amused me most was the way in which you fired up about the 'Lines to an Amateur Actress'. Confess dearest that you were drawn very successfully.

How I wish there were a telephone between London & Hunstanton for our especial benefit. Jo talked to his Cigar Merchant at Brighton through the telephone & that is not much nearer him than you are. [Telephones had been on sale to the public since 1877.] ... I kiss your sweet fair hands in which you hold my life & destiny—Adrian

HUNSTANTON   23RD JANUARY

My own darling Adrian, Your letter this morning was the first I heard of the news from Egypt. We are always faithful to the *Globe* so news is always a little ancient by the time it reaches us in this remote place. Certainly we paid very dearly for our victory. ... I am getting rather keen about *Engaged* but how shall you like that very public kiss! I think perhaps we might Bowdlerize the scene and shake hands instead—or even bow! I long to see you looking a stage villain—it will *just* suit you. (You see I am a little ruffled still—.)

My dearest one—after all there is no fear in my heart for the time of 'bondage' that you speak of—Ah! I always think I see nothing but happiness for us—in the future, but still—with my lips—I shall *never* say those *odious words*—you know what I mean—& what you called yourself! ['Lord & Master']. Ever your own, *à toi, et à toi seule, Laure*

CHELSEA GUARDIANS OF THE POOR,   26TH JANUARY
ARTHUR STREET

Ma Bien aimée, Jo & I went to see the Van Beers Pictures of which I send you the Catalogue marked with our impressions. Van Beers cannot paint anything but Cocottes, who throw themselves into the most impossible & indecent attitudes. His colouring is bad & coarse. ... I was amused watching dear old Jo, his face was a study as he inspected (*narrowly*) leg after leg in its varied hose!! Goodnight my darling, Your Adrian

HUNSTANTON   27TH JANUARY

My own dearest Adrian, We have been in fits of laughter over the Catalogue & yours & Jo's remarks thereon but I am *dreadfully* shocked to think that it was at *my* suggestion that you visited the Gallery. The critique that I read in the *Morning Post* gave a whole column of most interesting description of these works of art—but said nothing of the eccentricities you and Jo discovered there! Your account of it all is so funny that though I *am* of course awfully shocked—and feel perfectly satisfied that I should *not* admire these pictures— still I wish you two would continue to visits the sights of the metropolis—for our benefit & amusement. I cannot think of anything just now that I should like to hear of unless it is the 'Japs' at Knightsbridge, but I see by the papers that a party of *Nomad Fins* whatever that may be is shortly expected at the Alexandra Park Palace—and I may possibly feel some curiosity about them. ... Today came a letter from Ernest—halfway through the Suez Canal. He is rather amusing about the efforts to get the huge ship through.

> 'We have succeeded after 4 days journeying in getting through 30 miles of the Canal about 4 hours of every day being spent on shore—(not by me—but by the ship!). at this moment there are 15 ships waiting for us at different parts of the Canal— some to go one way, some the other. We have a tail of 8 ships behind us waiting for the "Hag" [*Agamemnon*] to move and she is hopelessly aground and has been so for about 2 hours. The air behind is quite *sulphureous* with the language being used on board the 8 steamers. We fondly hope to get to Ismalia tomorrow.'

He has grown long, black, mutton chop whiskers!! Fancy how horrid— but he will never dare appear in England disfigured in this way! ... Always to the end of the story, Your Laura

VINE CLUB, 8 ST JAMES' SQUARE   28TH JANUARY

Darling, When I went back to Battersea I found my dear Mother very ill again in bed, while Jessie lies helplessly in the next room. So that you imagine what a sad house this makes. … My brother John writes from his Camp at Langford on the Orange River:

> 'The Camp is the most arid spot not actually marked *desert*— we are literally ankle deep in sand…however the climate is splendid & we have no real hardships whatever.'

John looks forward longingly to their first brush with the Enemy. I do hope he will distinguish himself even if he is killed…Dear old John I do so long to hear of him as having done something gallant in action. That would do more to reconcile his father than anything I shall ever be able to do myself. Of course as I had a cold & did not go to Lady G's last Friday, Dilke was there & asked where I was. Most unfortunate. My Father has just given birth to a new Gun. Yet another invention. How I wish he would coin sovereigns instead. Goodnight Sweet, Adrian thy lover

HUNSTANTON   30TH JANUARY

Dearest, … Everything about Bechuanaland in the papers yesterday looks like fighting so I expect John will have his chance. I have been looking at the *Pall Mall* you sent about George Eliot. Are you a great admirer of hers? I have not any *great* enthusiasm about her books, although they are so clever. I like Charlotte Bronte's better, especially *Jane Eyre* because it is imaginative & mysterious. … I cannot settle about the little painting I am going to try for the Grosvenor. I have tried several drawings with the little swallow but they do not please me somehow. I don't think my star is in the ascendant just now—or whatever it is that presides over my modest artistic efforts. You cannot think how *exigeant* [demanding] art is—even a feeble disciple like myself is not allowed to offer half-hearted homage and attention—if I would reap *any* reward. Farewell, ever yours, *Laure*

---

27 *5th Jan* 'Oh that I were, where I would be— …'. This version was adapted from an American Revolutionary Army song, 'Katy Cruel'. *See* Alan Lomax's *Penguin Book of American Folk Songs* (1964).

28 *19th Jan* The Royal Alexandra Hospital, for children, at Rhyl in North Wales, where Adrian's Aunt Charlotte 'Cha' Cunninghame Graham had for many years been helping to run the hospital as matron—and much more. The Children's Convalescent Home at Rhyl, with twelve beds for patients, was started by 'two ladies' who had trained at Great Ormond Street: Miss Vizard, responsible for finance, general policy and discipline, and Miss Graham in charge of actual nursing and treatment under a visiting doctor 'who did not interfere much'.

Aunt Cha believed passionately in two things in the treatment of long-standing 'chronic' cases, especially cripples: fresh air and happiness. The hospital, which was something of a pioneer in this fresh-air treatment, was renamed, with permission, The Royal Alexandra Hospital in 1882, with facilities for 200 beds. The planned new hospital was not in fact built until ten years later and meanwhile Aunt Cha was to have a stroke in 1886 after which she resigned from the hospital to go and live with her sister Aunt Annie Cunninghame Graham and their niece Laura Hope in Cambridge. For further details of this pioneering hospital—and of Aunt Cha's influence—by a highly intelligent and very lame probationer nurse there in 1887, *see* *Reminiscences* by Agnes Hunt DBE, RRC [1867-1933/34], printed for the Derwen Cripples Training College by Wilding and Son, Shrewsbury (1935).

29   *21st Jan* On this letter Laura had later noted of Otway Cuffe and Lily St Aubyn: 'They did not marry then—they waited 12 years for each other—too long, for both had changed by then.'

FEBRUARY 1885

HUNSTANTON   1ST FEBRUARY

Darling Adrian, … Already I am so distrait at the thought of our near meeting at the Tyssen-Amhersts[30] that I simply can not give my mind *really* to anything. *Oh what a confession* though you are 100 miles away I find I am blushing—but it is true nevertheless—and *you* I suppose will be delighted! … All my thoughts of you are full of that *one* little word LOVE that means *so much*—and that *you* have really taught me to understand the *full* meaning of. *Au revoir mon bien aimé, Toujours ta Laure*

VINE CLUB, 8 ST JAMES' SQUARE   2ND FEBRUARY

Darling Laura, … Yesterday I lunched with Trevanion and his wife Florence & inwardly hoped that we should never make such fools of ourselves in public, they are always bickering & saying spiteful things to each other & against Matrimony, for which institution I have always felt a secret reverence. She took me up to see the baby—but babies of that age are only nice in their baths. … When I got home, strange to say my Father made his appearance & dined. After dinner he tuned up my violoncello for me & would have me sing to him which I did. Altogether he was quite in a good mind, I think he *must* be ill. Goodbye, your lover, Adrian

METROPOLITAN ASYLUMS BOARD,   4TH FEBRUARY
NORFOLK ST, STRAND

Chérie de ma Coeur, Yesterday I was very busy at Marylebone W.H. [Workhouse]…

Here the sun shines in on me as I sit listening to an argument on the price of scrubbing brushes which bids fair to wax warm & angry. … I don't like George Eliot's later novels at all and I am inclined to agree with you that poor Charlotte Bronte was the greater of the two. *Jane Eyre* was a masterpiece which was beyond George Eliot who was too bourgeois to know or to describe passion well. … Goodbye sweet Love, Adrian

At Buckenham-Tofts, Mundford, Norfolk [with Mr & Mrs Tyssen-Amherst]

> *3rd February* … A good big house, 6 Miss Amhersts & Miss Mimi Macdonald & her mother—no stiffness in the house or people. …

4th February Uncle Tum [Sommy Gurney] & Aunt Kitty with Lill & Ruth [their second & third daughters] arrived & others. In the evening danced & dumb acting [charades] in the hall.

5th February Adrian came at 3. Played billiards & the Racy game which I won. A little tête-à-tête with A., then dressed for the ball at Swaffham. I wore my black dress with scarlet feathers. (My pink ball gown is my smartest but one ought not to wear pink at a Hunt Ball because of the pink coats.) ... Enjoyed the ball very much & we drove home together afterwards.

6th February After dinner playing the most romping games. Came to the conclusion it was delightful staying about together.

7th February Alice Amherst photographed Adrian & I together—profiles—like William & Mary on a shilling. ...

At King Street, Lynn [with George & Eva Cresswell]

7th February ... After dinner Adrian & I sat in the boudoir with George & Eva [who is pregnant with her second child]. They went off to bed about 10. & left us to talk—very happy.

10th February I wore my pink ball gown to the Lynn Ball. Had a most delightful ball—lots of nice people there. ...

HUNSTANTON   13TH FEBRUARY

My own dearest Adrian, ... Amy was complimented on *our* behaviour at the balls! The Elwes'[31] said they had all noticed how happy we looked—and *yet* we could dance & amuse ourselves with others, instead of moping & sulking together the whole evening—as it appears Captain Follett & his fiancée Miss Fountaine were doing at Swaffham. He is so furiously jealous that he will not *allow* her to dance and so they sat side by side the whole evening perfectly silent & looking dull—not even dancing themselves. I don't care the least about what they choose to do—but I was pleased about what was said of us. ... *Toujours ta petite Laure—qui t'aime*

VINE CLUB, 8 ST JAMES' SQUARE   13TH FEBRUARY

My Dearest, Last night, as I came in at the door at Battersea, I met my father going off in his war paint for the ball of his Regiment. He was in the best of spirits, asked after you, & told me he was going to the War Office today to have an agreement signed & drawn up about his Gun.

[*Continued*] I have just been over to the Rag [Army & Navy Club] & seen my father who has had a very satisfactory meeting at the W.O. & with the Solicitor to the Treasury. ... Darling, will you be my Valentine this year? ...

(FROM JO'S ROOM, BACHELORS' CLUB, 8 HAMILTON PLACE) [*LATER*]

After dining I went to 105 Piccadilly [the Goldsmids] & found it had been hailing Pasha's. There was old Ismail the Ex Khedive & his attendant Pasha, Hobart Pasha & his pretty second wife, Fehmi Pasha the Special Envoy from the Sultan, Blum Pasha the Egyptian Finance Minister & another Pasha whose name I have quite forgot. Such a lot of red Fezzes was quite curious to see. Miss Winslow asked after you & said quite loud that she thought Jo & I had been running you hard. Jo was standing there but I hope he did not hear. We came on here and I am now writing to you through his conversation & in spite of a large white rat who will sit beside me to watch what I say to you. Sir Frederick Leighton was there, the handsomest man in the room. ... My love to the three Graces of Hunstanton, from Adrian

HUNSTANTON   SUNDAY, 15TH FEBRUARY

My own darling Adrian, Last night, we four girls and Evelyn [Orde] who is staying with us had a party in costume. There were present a soldier, a sailor, and a masher, and two of the most eccentric ladies, who danced, sang, laughed and eat oranges & chocolate till midnight! That is—E., Vi, Myself, Amy & Helen. Amy was a foreign Countess of great distinction—who sang wonderful Italian & French patois songs. I donned my disguise—a *redingote* would be best but I only had a Sandhurst patrol jacket & black knickerbockers of Tom's. I am quite tired with laughing today.

Yesterday afternoon it simply poured but the undaunted ones—Amy & Evelyn—procured a tandem with 2 immense horses & a very small dog cart & drove over to Sandringham, Vi clinging on by her eyelids to the back seat, blowing mighty blasts on a huge tandem horn!! I had somehow lost my pretty rose-coloured glasses and found it a great effort to *pretend* to be quite happy so

I was quite happy to be alone for a few hours and could arrange the chaos of thoughts in my mind. ... This is what I read in a letter this morning?

> 'Should Laura have any attention to give to the unimportant affairs of her cousin, you may tell her he has just risen from his couch with all the pleasant recollections of her most charming appearance to him in his dreams, still filling his mind.'

Isn't it *too* bad?—it makes me quite angry that I can appear to anyone without my knowledge, or leave—or yours! This is Wallace [Cochrane-Baillie] if you please—& I should like to know what business he has to dream about me. He is just starting on a tour in Asia Minor & if he stays away long enough perhaps I may forgive him. ... *Ta petite Laure*

PUMP COURT, TEMPLE [MR ROBERTS' LOCAL GOVERNMENT BOARD OFFICES]   16TH FEBRUARY

My Sweet Darling Laura, ... Jem & I collected the proof from your 'Little Mermaid' drawing from Sampson Low. Marston wants to know whether you are satisfied with the process which costs under £3 otherwise there is nothing but wood engraving which will cost about £7. What about a border round the prints, & what do you say to Jem's suggestion of tinting? ... I hope to see the book make a great sensation this Autumn. We will have it properly cried & advertised. My idea is to tie Sampson Low & Co. down to a fixed number of copies, say 1000, making them put down on paper that the sale of 1000 copies will produce such & such a profit. Then we will make a list of all the people who must & shall buy copies. Elsie has several brothers settled in America & she will make them buy copies & ask for copies & puff it no end. You must present a copy to the Princess Beatrice through your Cousin Minnie Cochrane[32] (don't you think so?). ... Marston said he thought the print was beautiful.

On Friday I dine with Jem & Elsie to meet her father, Sir Peter Coats [of Coats cotton, a generous patron of the Liberals] whom I shall make fierce love to as I want him to go down to the Patronage Sec. & ask for something for me. This will keep Dilke up to the collar & might perhaps get me a better post. ... No news as yet except that the govt. has accepted the offer of troops from Australia which is a great thing, the moral effect will be so good & will tend to bind our Colonies closer to us I hope. ... Adieu, *ma Laure, ton amant pour la vie*, Adrian

Adrian darling, ... We heard from the St Aubyns. Lill is in the 7th heaven for Dot [Otway Cuffe, her long-time fiancé] is staying with them for a long visit—& you & I know what a happy place a 7th heaven is. Her sisters say she is very happy but worn to a shadow. When will they be able to say that of me I wonder! Never I am afraid—for I laugh too much—I am convinced that must be the reason that however much I care for you I do not waste away. Dot has taken a very good cast of Lill's head—Dearest I am glad your affection for me has never taken that turn. It would be a severe test for me to sit for hours with a quill in my mouth & my face crusted with plaster of Paris. In our case you are more likely to be the victim!! You wouldn't mind would you darling? *Je te donnerais de temps en temps un petit baiser—à travers la plume d'oie* [From time to time I will give you a little kiss—via the goose-feather quill]! ...

Fired by the success of the bal masqué on Saturday night we are going to give another this evening—a bachelor's party—ahem, no ladies invited. You will think we are so babyish—but you know *really* it is only to amuse Helen!! *of course.* ... I am so glad Aunt Kitty [Gurney] was nice to you, for she is generally so entirely indifferent to people that she will not take the *trouble* to be nice but I *knew* she liked you dearest—& I have always been rather a favourite of hers. ... *Toujours ta petite Laure*

My dearest one, ... The 'Mermaiden' proof is certainly good. Now I want to see a proof printed in *brown* outline on *good* toned paper before deciding. ... If they cannot manage to print the background lines *really* softly in this process it will spoil some of the designs entirely. Before tinting, which could add a lot to the expense of printing, I want to see it done like *Little Thumb* with a brown margin, perhaps a lighter shade. I have been trying *coloured* margins & they look hideous & inartistic. Will you ask why it was reduced, it is a ½ an inch smaller. I can not help thinking if a good book can be managed costing £3 for each picture, it would be better than the risk of an expensive process. ... It is delightful of you to take so much trouble about my book, but it is just *like* you darling—.

We kept carnival at the Castle last night & had the queerest sort of *variety* entertainment—with 'the haughty beauty' [Evelyn Orde] as Midshipman (Free &) Easy, & Limpet [Helen] as a regular old salt in a huge red admiral's uniform & cocked hat & telescope as long as herself. A singularly active Highland Chieftain suddenly appeared in the middle of the evening—also a Greek peasant—and a Persian Prince—who everyone said looked as if he had walked straight out of the Arabian Nights—would you have recognized in this distinguished stranger anyone you knew? Do you know I think you would rather have *liked* it. I am afraid so—!!! *Je t'aime comme toujours, tu as mon Coeur—Toujours à toi, Laure*

METROPOLITAN ASYLUMS BOARD, NORFOLK ST, STRAND

18TH FEBRUARY

Ma Laure, ... Oh! how I should have enjoyed being there along with you. Before I had this large beard I used always to make such nice looking old women. Once I was introduced by my Aunts to some strangers who came into the drawing-room while I was there, as the Dowager Lady Napier & they quite took it all in & were so nice & civil to me. I fancy you were the Persian Prince Charming. Do, do make a little sketch of the fine costumes for me. ... Today the streets have been crowded near the Barracks. The mob cheering every bit of scarlet that appeared. For myself I cannot bear to see the fellows going off, for much as I ought to love being near you I feel quite wretched at being out of the row in Egypt. You won't be angry with me for telling you the truth, will you dearest love of mine?

I feel quite sure that your book will be a success and that it will lead to your coming to the front as a real artist. I love to think this for then, should we be condemned to a long engagement, you will have something to take your mind completely away from me. ... I had a most orthodox lunch today [Ash Wednesday] of salt fish, parsnips & egg sauce. Did you? ... Good morning my love, Adrian

HUNSTANTON

18TH FEBRUARY

My darling Adrian, ... Did you see or hear anything of the scrimmage on Monday [16th]—or have the papers exaggerated it. I mean the unemployed who sent a deputation to Dilke? Poor things, I am rather sorry for them. They certainly gave them a stone for bread at the L.G.B. [Local Government Board] but I suppose it was the wrong place to go to. What do you think about it? It seems hard lines if they wish to work & there really is nothing for them to do. *Je t'envoie un petit baiser de ta petite Laure*

19TH FEBRUARY

My own darling Adrian, ... so dearest you feel sad because you are not going away? I suppose if I were a man, I should feel much as you do, seeing all the excitement of the soldiers leaving for Egypt and knowing what stirring times they will have, and how much there is to be done there. I feel something of my father's spirit in me & I sympathize with you dearest—doomed to remain at home, but *I thank God* with all my *heart* that it is so. After all it is not only the risks of battle that they will run—but the hardships, and the climate, are all on the side of the Mahdi & will probably kill more men than the arab guns—in the end. ... [The last four pages are written in French—which Laura resorts to in times of great emotion—the gist of which follows.]

... If I only wanted to reign in your heart as your mistress, I might perhaps be cross at your admission, but as I want also to be your true *camarade* for life—then everything can be said between us without fear of offence. I believe that did you not love me so much you would not have this great desire to shine in the battle of life by one means or other. Am I right? But if I am mistaken, I want to ask whether you have truly considered that in marrying me you lose for ever your chance to take part in expeditions to foreign parts. You are not a soldier but there are ways for people like you to go as a correspondent or anything else. ... When we are married, will you always regret staying behind instead of going off to the wars? If I believed this, darling, I would rather say goodbye to you now before it is too late, even if it breaks my heart. *Ta petite Laure*

On the same day that Laura wrote the above letter, Adrian was penning a sixteen-page letter to her, six pages of which were taken up with an affirmation of his everlasting love. The following is a small extract:

WARWICK HOUSE,   AFTER DINNER, 19TH FEBRUARY
ALBERT ROAD, BATTERSEA

My own darling Laura, Your letter to Sampson Low & Co. was really admirable. You are as good a woman of business as you are good at everything else. ... Darling I think no one who ever saw you could help being more or less in love with your charming self so I can only pity Wallace Baillie & be thankful that to me has been given that greatest of all gifts—your loving heart. When I get low I take out your last letters, read them & look at your face which always rests on my heart. Then I know & feel that all else is nothing to me for you possess me entirely...I feel that I have no right to grumble at anything having won your precious love, which it will be my life's endeavour to prove worthy of unto the end. ...

I did not see the angry crowd that besieged the L.G.B. It was one of the most dangerous Mobs we have had for years. It is curious how ready we are to spend Millions in the Soudan & how we grudge the few thousands, which properly applied would relieve the unhappy men who are starving from the want of work. Surely an awful day of reckoning will come on a Nation which allows its successive Governments to shirk the fearful responsibility entailed by the chronic condition of the East End of London. The news from Ireland is very bad & men mutter that when the W.O. tried to take troops from there, Ld Spencer (Lord Lieutenant of Ireland) refused permission giving as his reason that he feared a rising of that unhappy people. Tonight Northcote[33] has given notice of a vote of Censure for Monday next [23rd] & it is a distinct possibility that Govt may be defeated. A certainty should the M.P.s Forster & Goschen join the Conservatives. I trust that this may not happen. ...

Tomorrow evening I have my usual trial of going to the Goldsmids & trying to look as if I cared for nothing on earth but to talk & pretend to be jolly. Sometimes I feel the mask almost slipping off as I look at all those people who talk & laugh away as if all life were a bed of roses. Then I remember that they all have their own love to hide & their own mask to keep on tight. ... If my letter to Vi with the photographs she wanted should prove incoherent, tell her it was written at the Bachelors' under such difficulties with Jo keeping up a flow of dull talk about the new house which they (the Bachelors') have taken & of his plans for a ladies lavatory. Also those white rats have now got to know me so well that they come & interfere with my beard as I write or sit on my head besides taking other liberties which I approve not of. ... *Ton amoureux qui t'aime plus que tout au monde*, Adrian

HUNSTANTON   20TH FEBRUARY

Darling Adrian, By the by, Jo seems to me a little *exigeant* as a friend. *I* want you to write—Jo becomes rampant when you *do*. Why darling it is almost as bad as having *2 fiancées* to please—no wonder your dear cheeks are thin! I suppose it is rather a bore for the hermit crab Jo when he wants to air his remarks and you are scribbling away to me and perhaps he has several fervent correspondences—but I doubt it—& there would not be elbow room for you both at that smart red table of his. I remember one night when I was amusing myself there making hay amongst Jo's most precious papers I opened a drawer which I think was locked & found ever so many little notes of—mine, put carefully away. I tore up several before Jo saw what I was about—& he was rather angry!!! ...

Uncle Sommy & Aunt Kitty are going to meet the Holdens. I was told dearest it was *our* bad example in appearing so happy together this Christmas time that induced Wally [the eldest Gurney son] to make up his mind to take this desperate step of proposing to Lucy Holden. How interesting the papers are now. I feel so sorry for Sir Redvers [Buller] having to *begin* retreating,[34] how he must have *longed* for more troops to fight instead…everything seems so disastrous now. The Conservatives cannot really wish to take the reins now when everything is in such confusion. 'Uneasy lies the head' that wears that high pointed collar just now I should think [Gladstone]. When I read about the vote of censure & the chances of the [Liberal] government going out— my thoughts fled to you—& your appointment & what would become of it all. I wonder if *we* (girls I mean) had the franchise—if one could rise superior to our private interests. I don't much think it but then *heaps* of men & all the poor people are the same! As an old Norfolker said: 'It were a bad thing to vote *agin* your daily bread'—which simply meant he did what his landlord told him to do! Yours always, come what may, *Ta Laure*

21st February

Darling, I have had the answer to my letter of Thursday [19th] in the long letter you wrote me on the same night. For you *could* not have written it had there been any regret in your heart and I feel very happy. … Doubts had risen in my mind, *not* as to whether you loved me darling, I would as soon doubt my own heart, but whether it was the best for you—I could not help fearing I might be to you what we have often said laughingly—*your serious burden*! … Ever dear Adrian, your *Laure*

Vine Club, 8 St James' Square 21st February

My dearest Love, … My own Laura it is just because I am not with you, by your side, that I sometimes have such a restless fit. When I am with you I never feel any spark of a wish to leave your side. … There was a large crowd last night at the Goldsmids. Much excited talk about the crisis but a sort of feeling that the Conservatives are not strong enough to hold office even though they might gain a triumph in a division. Gladstone's speech has produced a very bad impression on his own party. He sat down amidst a dead & ominous silence. … Your faithful lover, Adrian

HUNSTANTON   SUNDAY, 22ND FEBRUARY

My dearest Lover Adrian, ... I wonder what Charlie [Orde] thought of that particular costume—the 'transparent flannel gown' of 'Juliet'. It is just the sort of thing he would admire immensely, and *say so* to everyone! I think he is always rather gushing about Mary Anderson, but he never would be introduced to any actress he admired because he told me once it would destroy the illusion & he preferred to imagine them to be really the beautiful beings they appeared to be on the stage. I remember him saying that when Oscar (the Dress Improver) wanted him to meet Ellen Terry. What do *you* think of this? You must not chaff him about it, please dear—for that was a long time ago—he *may* have changed his mind. In the innocence of his heart he said something of the sort to a French actor whom he met somewhere—& who apparently took him for a harmless lunatic! and was rather offended besides! *Un peu neutre de lui, n'est ce pas? mais voilà ce que j'aime tu sais bien!* [A bit neuter of him, don't you think, but that is what I like as you know well]. ...

I was rather amused with a letter from Mimi Fenwick to Vi this morning— she is a typical modern sporting (*not* fast) boy-girl. She writes to say her father at last forbids her having anything more to do with the man she has been engaged to vaguely since the summer. *His* father won't give him any money to marry on & has been disagreeable so it is put a stop to. Mimi's comment on it is: 'I think it is *beastly hard lines*'!!! Ever your own *petite Laure*

VINE CLUB, 8 ST JAMES' SQUARE   23RD FEBRUARY

Ma petite Laure chérie, ... Laura (my sister) is much pleased with *Little Thumb* which she calls: 'very charming. How very graceful and quaint the drawings are, so suited to the fanciful imaginings of the Northern Poet. Your Laura must have a great deal of talent. I can understand how proud you must be of her.' I like Charlie Orde very much though he is *un peu neutre* as you say. But darling if *that* is why you like him so, tell me why you like me for I am sure I am not *that*. ... Goodbye dearest, Your Adrian

HUNSTANTON   24TH FEBRUARY

My darling Adrian, ... I am so glad you have got over your Pleurisy for I know it is very painful. Do you *really* take care of yourself, darling? ... I think I can explain the *apparent* inconsistency about *neutre*—it is very deep reasoning! I *like* Charlie—but *I don't like* you!! No—for I LOVE you—*voilà la différence*!! If a friend is *un peu neutre*, it doesn't matter, but a lover—no! Have I explained myself? ... Ever your *petite Laure*

Laura sent a note, undated, to Adrian enclosing a drawing of their two profiles in the style of a Roman emperor and empress on a medal, inscribed 'Adrian and Laura MDCCCLXXXV': 'What do you think of this curious old medal, darling? Would there be Peace or War in this reign? It might do for a bookplate. Salutations from the Empress Laura.'

Warwick House, Albert Road, Battersea   24th February

My Darling Laura, The first sight of the old coin & of your note banished my gloom. How excellent the likenesses are … and what a delightful bookplate it will make for us two. … I went to enquire after Elsie who is anything but well and has been in bed now for some days past. After I lunched there the other day I went up to see her in bed. She had such a pretty pink flannel Bed gown on. The bed was a large French one with a canopy thus [a very odd sketch]. Elsie confessed that *she* had wished for an old four poster but that Jim persuaded her of the superior healthiness of this Brass Bed. Is that a better view of it [he produced a second sketch]?

I feel happier as to the fate of the Ministry for badly as the present lot have floundered the others have not the courage to assume office now. The worst sign is that Gladstone has lost his nerve very much of late. Even if the Liberals go out, I hope to keep my place on the list for an Auditorship or perhaps get something better from the Tories. … By the by, the Vine has become the York Club & will under that name flourish I hope better than it has hitherto done. … Goodbye by my sweet Laura, Empress of my heart's love & devotion, Adrian. *Ton august époux*

Hunstanton   25th February

Darling, … I am *so glad* you liked my little drawing. … What a swagger visiting card of Ismail you enclosed [the ex-Khedive of Egypt, who inaugurated the Suez Canal in 1869]. To live up to our medallion I think we ought to be entitled to have some printed like that—'Laura' & then a Crown— and 'Adrian' would look much nicer than Ismail who is, I suppose, father to the fascinating youth I met a few years ago at the de Bunsens—a day that I have good reason to remember—*et toi aussi Chéri!* … *Toujours ta Laure*

27th February

Dearest, … The two proofs of the 'Little Mermaid' are a great improvement on the first. … As you suggested, we should keep some check on them about the number of copies printed & the proportionate profits one might expect...as if it is left vague we can do nothing to prevent them sending the usual 'publisher's bill'—which are well known humbugs. ... I rather wish they had used better paper—this is a good colour but very thin for such a large leaf. ...

I am very busy drawing—my head is cram full of drawings. The last would make you laugh, it is rather mad and illustrates this peculiar scene:

> Six shrivelled sisters
> Sifting shrivelled thistles
> With a shrivelled thistle sifter

I have long had an idea of making a queer picture book illustrating all those odd sayings that are hard to say—some French & some English. This is the first—six horrid old hags whirling round on a hilltop & looking most unholy altogether. *Toujours ta petite Laure*

YORK CLUB, 8 ST JAMES' SQUARE   27TH FEBRUARY

Ma petite Laure, ... The Goldsmids were full of nice & amiable remarks about your book *Little Thumb*. He said that he wanted much to see what so much talent could do in colour & said also that he was struck with the *power* shown in the drawings. ... They seemed to think that though the Ministry had got their death blow yet that they would gather together sufficient votes to carry on the Govt. The utmost majority the Govt hope for now is 15. I do not expect the Division will take place before 5. or 6. tomorrow morning. If only I were not so queer I would stay in town for it, but I am only fit to crawl back to Battersea & go to bed. My Mother is a trifle better. If she could only get strong enough to be moved it would be a great thing for her. Rhyl, with her sister Cha at the Hospital there, is the only place that will really pull her together. ... I send you a tender kiss, Sweetheart mine, from Adrian

(FROM WARWICK HOUSE, ALBERT ROAD, BATTERSEA)   [*LATER*]

My Laura, After writing to you from the Club, I wandered up Bond St & passing the Exhibition of Bouguereau's Pictures[35] I thought of you & went in to fulfil your wish that I might report on them. Here is the Catalogue with my remarks [of which the following are typical].

> 'Flesh superb. The women look as if they had limbs, nr violet powder.'—'Angels fiddling to a naked Saviour in a blue

Virgin's arms, both asleep sharing bad dreams'—'An idiot child fully clothed though *not* in its right mind. Dull'—'Legs & thighs a marvel of modelling'.

The women's limbs strike me as being well drawn & there is an air of reality about the flesh colouring without any of that offensive suggestiveness which so often spoils the nudities of a French picture. No 7 'Byblis' is the one that took my fancy most of all. A Nymph lying on her side beside a little running brooklet. Attitude very graceful, line of back & legs quite beautiful—hips not violently thrown into relief. But one thing struck me in all the pictures—what bad legs all his models seem to have. From the hip to the knee some of them are good, but they are all bad—very bad, below the knee. The arms again seem too thin for such very well developed bodies & the necks are poor. … Goodnight, I go to dream of thee—*Ton* Adrian *qui t'adore*

---

30 *1st Feb* William and Margaret Tyssen-Amherst (later 1st Baron Amherst of Hackney). Their elder daughter Mary, wife of Col William Cecil, was to succeed as Baroness Amherst of Hackney in 1909.

31 *13th Feb* The Elwes family of Colesbourne, Glos, and of Congham, Norfolk, are endlessly connected through marriage with Laura's relations and friends, including the Hamonds of Westacre, Norfolk (Aunt Kitty Gurney's family), the Ffolkes of Hillington, Norfolk (Aunt Minnie Gurney's family), the Birkbecks of Thorpe, Norwich and of Stoke Holy Cross, and later of Westacre, Norfolk (Rosy née Gurney's husband Johnny Birkbeck's family), the Chapmans of Congham Lodge, Norfolk etc.

32 *16th Feb* Minnie Cochrane, daughter of Laura's great-uncle Sir Thomas Cochrane (by his 2nd wife Rosetta Wheeler-Cuffe), was lady-in-waiting to Princess Beatrice of Battenberg, Queen Victoria's youngest daughter.

33 *19th Feb* Sir Stafford Northcote, then 1st Lord of the Treasury and leader of the Conservatives since 1881.

34 *20th Feb* Gen Sir Redvers Buller VC had been sent out to Egypt as chief of staff to join the expedition for the Relief of Khartoum. When the news of the fall of Khartoum and the death of Gen Gordon was received, his instructions to advance on Metemmeh were cancelled and he had to withdraw his desert column in the face of a much larger and active enemy force. This he accomplished successfully and he returned home to a hero's welcome.

In 1882 Sir Redvers had married Lady Audrey Howard née Townshend, widow of Hon G T Howard whose marriage Laura had attended with great excitement in 1873. Lady Audrey's sister, Lady Elizabeth (née Townshend) St Aubyn, later Lady St Leven—and known as 'Lady Booba' by the young Troubridges—was one of Laura's godmothers.

35 *27th Feb* William Adolphe Bouguereau (1825-1905). The exhibition of his works opened in December 1884 at Boussod Valadon, successors to Goupil, 116/117 New Bond Street. The small (5.5 x 4.5 inch) catalogue was printed at the Chiswick Press on cream handmade paper with a grey soft cover and allowed a page for each title of the seven paintings listed. Decora-

tive initials were printed in red and the Gothic style type in a very heavy black. The main reason for this elaborate little catalogue was to obtain orders for engravings of the artist's earlier works, which were also on view. The artist Auguste Renoir's reaction to his style just after he, Renoir, had been fitted with spectacles for myopia was to throw them on the floor, exclaiming: '*Bon Dieu, je vois comme Bouguereau*'! [Good God, I'm seeing as if I were Bouguereau!]

MARCH 1885

HUNSTANTON   SUNDAY, 1ST MARCH

My own darling Adrian, … I rejoice silently and against my [Conservative] principles when I read of the majority in the House of Commons. Dilke is not quick to fulfil his promise—is he? … I am very interested in Ld Durham's suit, I cannot help hoping he will get his divorce. It is such a *dreadful* fate for a young man to be tied to a wife who is hopelessly mad—'as long as they both shall live.' It is quite possible that the Milners [her parents] might not have known she was deficient if it came on gradually. Certainly Durham's evidence seemed to prove her mad, & one thought he must have been *madly* in love not to find it out before he married her. It is very sad altogether. I remember seeing her at a ball at Lord Zetland's & thinking her so lovely, & we noticed that she never spoke. … Adieu, *ta Laure qui t'aime 'un peu beaucoup' et tendrement*

WARWICK HOUSE, ALBERT ROAD, BATTERSEA   SUNDAY, 1ST MARCH

My Darling, I have been to Abbey Lodge [where Amy is visiting the de Bunsens]. Amy was quite delightful to me but every time she called me Adrian I looked round nervously at the old de B's to see whether they were not shocked by the familiarity. In fact dear love I felt quite silly & timid. There is a confession for a bearded man to make to his Mistress. … Goodbye my Sweetheart, your Adrian

HUNSTANTON   2ND MARCH

My darling, … What will become of all our blissful plans for the future—all our bright castles in the air if you do not take care of yourself—and starve yourself as you are doing now…you have been growing steadily paler, thinner & more delicate looking ever since we have been engaged—*it breaks my heart.* I feel that my great love for you gives me a right to ask you to go and see a really good, clever, Doctor. … I was reading Tennyson's 'Maud' and I came across these lines which are meant for you, don't you think? for God knows you are dear to me.

> But if *I* be dear to someone else
> Then should I be to myself more dear.
> Shall I not take care of all that I think,
> Yea e'en of wretched meat and drink,
> If I be dear,
> If I be dear to someone else.

For ever, your Laura

WARWICK HOUSE, ALBERT ROAD, BATTERSEA   2ND MARCH

My own Sweetheart, Jem told me there was no doubt that Elsie had got Typhoid fever, only in a mild form. Of course he is dreadfully anxious as his first wife died of it, & they expect the baby in three weeks. I much fear it will go hard with poor little Elsie then for she is as weak as a cat. …

A little artist protégée of my Mother's had been to see her & described how Mr Dodgson of *Alice in Wonderland* fame had dilated upon the beauties of the illustrations to one of Hans Andersen's stories done by a certain Miss? He had forgotten the name, but he said that of all the modern work which he saw, this had pleased him the most. He told the Artist Girl to get them & study them well. She, who had seen these praised illustrations to *Little Thumb*, then told him they were done by L.T. Was not that nice to hear of you from a stranger? …[36]

That sad Durham suit still drags along. It seems to me that Durham, if he says truly, when he declared he had suspicions of her sanity on their wedding day acted very wickedly in going into the nuptial chamber that same evening. Of course it is a very delicate question to argue on. Still if the poor girl was mad he condoned the madness then & it seems hard that he should *now* try to cast her off. Her first cousin 'Granny' [Alfred Milner] used to talk to me about it a great deal & from what he said I gathered that Durham certainly was guilty of overturning what was perhaps never a very stable intellect. …

Jo is off to a series of lectures at Lady Brassey's on 'Aid to the Wounded'. I think if anything could make me laugh, even if badly hurt, it would be the sight of Jo trying vainly to see his way to bandage the proper leg or arm for me. Goodnight, *ton* Adrian

HUNSTANTON   3RD MARCH

Darling Adrian, … The poor little 'Rose buds' [Rosy Birkbeck's stillborn twin daughters], Johnny must have been *so* disappointed for he wished for 10 descendants to speak with him—with his enemies at the Gate! However it is as well not to mock. … How amusing about Lewis Carroll & *Little Thumb*. I always am pleased when a stranger likes my drawings because I think *sometimes* one's friends may be prejudiced—in their judgement. … *Ta petite Laure*

4TH MARCH

My darling lonely Adrian, Your letter is *reassuring* but it has not *satisfied* me quite. … I hoped if you would see a Doctor—as I asked you to—he would order you to take more nourishing food. I mean fattening things. I have not the slightest ambition for you to take a prize at a show like a fat pig! on the contrary, you know I have an *envious* admiration for *flatness*, i.e. thinness, but I think if you were not so dreadfully thin you would not feel the cold so much, and would be less liable to catch cold. ... Darling, I shall *not* sit on your knee next week—you will *not* be strong enough to endure me! but we shall each have our *own* chair—not too near! If we were married it would be very simple, I would not eat any dinner unless you eat with me. And you could not let your wife starve—whom you had promised to cherish—could you? You know I am not given to croaking, but I think you have treated my letter lightly—as though it were the letter of a child or a silly fanciful girl, but you know I am neither & I did not write so without very good cause...I did not think you would refuse—your *Laure*

105 PICCADILLY   12TH MARCH
(WRITTEN AT LADY G'S ABOUT 5 P.M. WHILST SHE IS PUTTING ON HER *TEA GOWN!*)

My own Darling, ... I came here to lunch & have been driving about ever since with Milady. ...

[CONTINUED]   13TH MARCH
(FROM 52 GREEN STREET, PARK LANE, WITH JEM & ELSIE HOPE)

My dearest Love, I left Lady G., came on here & dined & slept. My lunch at the Goldsmids yesterday was very pleasant. Stewart of the *Morning Post* who is a friend of mine was there. In the afternoon I went to the Grosvenor Gallery with Lady G. to see the Gainsboroughs which were very soothing to my eyes. Poor Elsie is as thin as a lathe, I dread the ordeal which she will have to go through in less than three weeks from now.

(FROM WARWICK HOUSE, ALBERT ROAD, BATTERSEA)   [*LATER*]

My poor Mother is back in bed which is very sad. My Father is in great spirits for Whitworth's firm have signed the Contract to make one of his small guns & it will be taken to Shoeburyness where I hope to see it fired soon after Easter. If only his Guns turn out a success it will smooth the way for my Mother so much, & in a remoter degree for us two. How nice it would be to have a little money after all. Though in any case I shall take up Govt employment as I never mean to count on my Father for necessaries, though of course if he were able to help me to marry you sooner I should just jump at the help. ...

George [Cresswell] will never be half as madly fond a husband as I shall be to you—though I shall not go in for such public exhibitions of Love? ... *ma tendre petite Laure, croyez en mon amour,* Adrian

HUNSTANTON   13TH MARCH

Dearest Adrian, ... Have you read the accounts of Mrs Anna M. Longshore Potts M.N. and her lecture on 'Love, Courtship, & Marriage'? She says it is not sufficient to marry naturally, 'One should marry *consistently, physiologically, mentally,* and *magnetically*'!! Do you think we have properly considered all this Darling? She goes on to say: 'Long engagements are not to be recommended, *one or two years* solid courtship is enough.' I wonder what she would consider a long engagement. I suppose nothing less than what your Father calls the *Scriptural Period* of 14 years. Then she is a very severe about *corsets,* though I don't see the connection with the subject of her lecture. She suggests a *Crusade* against them—tight lacing is to be put down by a society of young men who are to wear a badge of white satin and refuse to *court* or speak to any girls who wear corsets! Isn't it nonsense—you won't become a member of it, will you darling?

Bea Gurney [of Keswick] is here—I never heard anyone talk so incessantly. I do wonder what was the particular type of perfection that Mr [Claude] Montefiore found realized in B. It quite haunts me. She showed me presents he had sent her quite lately—so he still gives her tangible proofs of his admiration—an immense solid silver *zone* [belt], worked with cupids, really rather a handsome offering but necessarily rather huge! Perhaps it is another of my *dour* ideas, but I think it is bad form to accept presents from a man you dislike, especially when they are offered in a lover-like spirit. ... Your own *Petite Laure*

YORK CLUB, 8 ST JAMES' SQUARE   14TH MARCH

My Darling, That dear Mrs Potts how she and I agree about corsets, we must be kindred souls. I yearn to meet her & admire her form untrammelled by Art. Does Bea G. go in for this too? I am sure that she had one on when I danced with her at Lynn. How fortunate that Montefiore is rich enough to encircle that beauteous & very rounded form in silver bands. Seriously, I believe she might marry him if she liked. It would be splendid. Fancy a piebald race of cousins with strange Quaker yearnings & odd Jewish tastes. I long to help this on if only to study the 'results'. Would that your waist was less or my purse bigger & then you too should have that attribute of Venus. ...

I left my foils I fancy at some Gymnasium before I went to Ceylon. Have you thought of a fencing Costume yet? These colours would look well. Black satin breeches on those pretty legs & black stockings. A yellow leather cuirass & a crimson shawl sash round your waist. How nice you would look. Au revoir *ma petite Laure*

HUNSTANTON   SUNDAY, 15TH MARCH

My own Darling, ... Bea made me laugh last night with her descriptions of this unfortunate man [Claude Montefiore] spouting page after page from George Eliot's works varied with extracts from Ruskin. To Bea of all people, who has not read a single thing written by one or the other, who never reads a book at *all* of any sort or kind if she can possibly help it! and was bored to extinction. However he went on to tell her that he intended becoming a *Rabbi* so he cannot exactly mean to marry a Xtian too—can he? He is so rich that his idea is if he was a Rabbi he would be, unlike most of them—entirely independent of his Congregation, and so he could preach the broader doctrines that he wishes to become universal among the Jews. Meanwhile he passes his time in writing endless & voluminous letters to his Beatrice! & the bestowing of zones & other offerings at his shrine.

Darling I don't believe it is *absolutely* necessary to wear black satin breeches & silk stockings for the *lessons* in fencing, though I am sure if we are to meet on equal terms & really *fight*—(which I am simply longing to be able to do) it could not be fair unless I had a costume as you suggest—for our mimic battles. ... I think I shall have some lessons on my own hook too if we are in London this summer. You would be agreeably surprised to find you were able to 'tell *all* my bones' as David expresses it, next time we meet. ... Always your own *Laure*

WARWICK HOUSE, ALBERT ROAD, BATTERSEA   SUNDAY, 15TH MARCH

My sweet Truelove, I have been lunching with the Oscar Wildes who both asked to be remembered to you & Amy. Through a thick fog I found my way to Tite St & looked for a *white door* which being opened let me into a very ordinary Hall Passage painted white. Going up a staircase also white & covered with a whitish sort of matting I found the angle of the landing cut off by a dark curtain from the stair case leaving just room to turn round if you were going higher. I however went through the Curtain & found a room to the right & left of the little Anteroom thus formed. The little man servant showed me into the room on the left looking out across Tite St on to the Garden of the Victoria Hospital for Children. No fire & a look as if the furniture had been cleared out for a dance for which the matting did not look inviting. The walls all white, the ceiling like yours a little but with two lovely dragons painted in the opposite corners of it. On either side of the fireplace filling up the corners of the room were two three-cornered divans, very low, with cushions, one tiny round Chippendale table, one Arm chair & three stiff (other) chairs, all covered with a sort of white lacquer. The Arm chair was a sort of curule chair & very uncomfy to sit on. This is the Summer Parlour. Nothing on the walls, so as not to break the lines. Certainly a cool-looking room & ought to be seen in the Dog days. Effect on the whole better than it sounds.

All the white paint (as indeed all the paint used about the house) has a high polish like Japanese Lacquerwork, which has a great charm for one who hates paper on walls as I do. The room at the back has a very distinctly Turkish note. No chairs at all. A Divan on two sides of the room, very low, with those queer little Eastern inlaid tables in front. A Dark Dado, but of what colour I know not, as, the window looking on a slum [Paradise Walk], they have entirely covered with a wooden grating on the inside copied from a Cairo pattern which considerably reduced the little light there was today. A gorgeous ceiling & a fire quite made me fall in love with this room as I thought how very lovely some one would look sitting with her legs crossed on the divan & with a faithful slave kissing her pretty bare feet. Here Oscar joined me & presently appeared Constance with her brother & his wife.

Lunch was in the Dining-room at the back on the ground floor, the room in front they have not as yet fitted up. A cream coloured room with what Oscar assured me was the only Sideboard in England, viz: A board running the whole length of the room & about 9 inches wide at the height of the top of the wainscoting. Table of a dirty brown with a strange device. Maroon napkins like rough bathtowels with deep fringes. Quaint glass & nice food made up a singularly picturesque table. After lunch we went upstairs to see where the Great O. sleeps. His room had nothing particular but hers was too delightful. You open the door of her room only to find yourself about to walk through the opening in a wall apparently 3 ft thick. When you get into the room you find that on the one side of the door forming a side of the doorway is an ideal wardrobe with every kind of drawer & hanging cupboard for dresses. Next to this again & between it & the corner of the room is the wash hand stand with curtains cutting it off. On the opposite side of the door is a book case & a writing table. All this is white & delightfully clean & fresh besides taking up little room. I must try my hand at a sketch again for you. Here is the key below:

I   Wardrobe

II   Washing place curtained off

III   Writing table fixed to Book Case

        with kneehole, solid part, drawers

How do you approve of that my pet? The bed looked very, very soft & nice.

Upstairs again Oscar had knocked two garrets into one delightful Bookroom for himself in which he had his bath as well. The doors & woodwork of this room were vermilion with a dado of gold leaves on a vermilion ground giving a delicious effect of colour which I revelled in.[37] Here I sat talking till ½ past six & listening to Oscar who, dressed in a grey velvet Norfolk jacket & looking fatter than ever, harangued away in a most amusing way. To *ma petite Laure que j'adore*, Adrian

P.S. I find that I have written of nothing but Oscar. Would that I had time to add more.

HUNSTANTON   16TH MARCH

Darling Adrian, … I was so interested in the Wildes' house & all the new ideas but I don't think we could live in a room without pictures or books, do you? and all white too & shiny, like living *inside* a jam pot—with the jam! Very well for a poet—but I should like the Turkish room the best—for very idle times. Her room sounds charming & the whole thing is not nearly so fantastic & outré as one would expect. You do not say if Mrs Oscar was dressed to live up to her husband's lectures, or was she still swathed in limp white muslin & lilies? Darling I have noticed when you go out to lunch—they always make you stay *all* the rest of the day—*so should I* if you would come & lunch with me, but it just shows what I have known for quite a long time now! & *how* different to most luncheon guests who depart with a sigh of relief all round about 3.—or 3.30. *Toujours ta petite Laure*

19TH MARCH

My darling Adrian, … So you are going to play 'Blue Beard' [to Mrs Adie Hope's—Jem's sister-in-law—'Fatima' in a musical charade]. Will you powder your beard with Reckitt's blue for the occasion? Anything like blue dye *I entirely forbid*, darling—because, awful thought *it might come off*! and leave tell tale marks when we meet again. Where!? ... never mind but *it would be embarrassing*. Gerard Noel brought me a long paper of your Father's about the guns as he is very interested in the subject and rather sceptical. ... Gerard was almost *rapid* for him—and showed us girls how to wear a sarong—a very *degagé* [casual] costume, I imagine first cousin to a *cummerbund*. Gerard said quite gravely a *sarong* was a very comfortable garment to *sleep* in—Oh! Oh!— Ever your own *petite Laure*

York Club, 8 St James' Square   20th March

My darling Laura, Tonight I am going to call on my Father at the Rag, a work of some difficulty as my Uncle Douglas [Cunninghame] Graham who is also a member has just returned from India and as they are not on speaking terms I have to cut them alternately.

Last night, after dinner with the Uniackes, a man called Cundy, a barrister, made *me* turn scarlet with his stories, the foul beast. ... *Adieu ma petite Laure bien bien aimée, de ton* Adrian

Hunstanton   23rd March

My darling Adrian, ... Last night I read your Father's paper called 'A Revolution in Gunnery'. I thought it *very* interesting indeed. It is so clearly & forcefully written that I could grasp the general principles of his invention. ... It must be wildly exciting for him that at last all these theories are to be put to the proof. I shall be *tremendously* keen to hear all about the trial of the Gun but I hope to goodness *you* dearest will not be there to witness it for it seems really *extremely* probable it should all bust up with the enormous quantity of quick powder he is going to fire it with. Seriously it would be a most crushing disappointment for your Father if all these cherished theories failed—only I suppose no inventor would acknowledge or believe it *really* was a failure. They would always explain it away somehow. ...

Vi & Helen enjoyed their visit to the Fountaines at Narford Hall for the ball but I don't think the latter was a brilliant success. The chief incident was that a Mr Bailey—another soldier from Norwich, got frightfully drunk and after behaving like a madman & frightening all the girls & making a great row, he was finally sent back to Marham *miles* off—with poor Mrs Fuller and Nessie F. *In a brougham*! Miss Fuller said nothing would induce her to have him inside the carriage so she made the footman get in & a lot of men tried to hoist this charming Mr Bailey on to the box—but he was so tipsy he could not stick on—so poor Miss F. had to give in—but they cannot have had a very nice drive. Captain Follett was there with his bride the others said she looked *perfectly miserable* & he was very X & sulky & dull. They are just back from their honeymoon. They went to Paris but were so fearfully *bored* there as neither of them could speak French that they left and retired to finish their honeymoon at Margate!!! ... Adieu *avec doux baiser de ta petite Laure*

24TH MARCH

My dearest, ... Poor Roland Le Strange has been awfully C.D. with jaundice & was in bed a fortnight. He said it was like a rough passage across the Atlantic all the time. He has *landed* looking very thin and yellow—& grown far taller. It must be quite heart-breaking for Mrs Le S. to have such a great big son [aged fifteen] in attendance. She will really have to knock off five years of his age & dress him in sailor suits like they do in [Pinero's] *The Magistrate* at the Court Theatre. ... Little more than a week to pass before we meet. To amuse ourselves at Hopton we will certainly race with the canoes if it does not *snow* & there is no skating. ... Always your loving *Laure*

100 LANCASTER GATE, HYDE PARK   24TH MARCH
[STAYING WITH HON MRS WILLIAM NAPIER WHILE ACTING IN THE BLUE BEARD CHARADE]

My darling Laura, Well the acting went off very successfully though the audience was terribly wooden. Everybody was pleased but there was not that feeling of being in rapport with them which helps on the actors. 'Fatima' looked very pretty in a green silk jacket with gauze sleeves over a chemisette, a pair of pink trousers with frills over the ankles were half smothered by a sort of tunic of brocade kept in at the waist by a gold sash—to me there was too much decidedly. 'Sister Anne' was not so bundled up, but neither of their figures are good enough for such a pretty style of dress. They sang their songs very well but 'Fatima' suffered a bit from stage fright & though she got through her repartees with me pretty well forgot the cues which put me out a good bit. The stage was mighty small to tumble down on & when I was stabbed I had to curl up a bit to get my long legs out of the way of the avenging brother. After we had songs & banjos, food & drink till about 1.45.

I have at last succeeded in persuading my Mother to send my little sister Madge to school—to Weymouth, one which my Aunt Cha praises highly. ... How dreadful for Miss Fuller & how piggish of every body who managed it at the Narford Ball. Why did they not shut the tipsy brute up in an outhouse & leave him till the next morning on some straw. I must say that Norwich seems to have a bad effect on the fellows quartered there. Still, you know, women are very much to blame in these matters, for they forgive them too easily. I have no doubt that this fellow will be forgiven & danced with & asked to dinner again as if nothing had happened. … Mrs Adie says that she must warn you that I have all the makings of a brutal husband from the relish which I seemed to have for the part of 'Blue Beard'. *Qu'en pense tu, ma petite Laure?* From Adrian

HUNSTANTON   26TH MARCH

My own darling Adrian, … I had another charming and beautifully and most elaborately worded note from your Father. This time he does not write of 'farinaceous food'—or 'exposed triangles' but sends me a copy of his lecture, with the discussion which followed printed at the end. Now I shall be expected to hold learned discourses with him on the science of *Ballistics* when we meet! … I think he loves his youngest child Madge best on the whole. … [no signature]

27TH MARCH

Dearest, About my book, if the publisher will not see buying it outright for £50 as we thought, rather than take 'The Little Mermaid' out of Sampson & Low's hands I would resign myself to taking whatever profit comes—*whenever* it comes—as the great thing is to get it published *à tout prix*. Nothing would encourage me so much as that, & if it was successful I should feel fresh & keen to begin new work. It is disheartening to feel that nothing is really settled yet about the drawings that I worked so hard to finish last spring. … Always your *Laure*

WARWICK HOUSE, ALBERT ROAD, BATTERSEA   28TH MARCH

My own dearest Love, … Last night you came to me in my dreams, dressed as if you were going to Court. I went & kissed you where I have never kissed you since Knocklofty. Is that a good omen? At all events it shows that we were married (in my dream). For that is a forbidden joy till then. … I thought it would be diplomatic to lunch in Piccadilly with Lady G. (as I have not been there for ten days at least) when I was received with open arms & rapturously kissed by —— !!! You may guess Darling. After lunch I stayed & helped to amuse some people who came. Then in sailed Mrs Sydney Jolliffe [Jo's unpopular sister-in-law] who laughed her horse laugh & said to me? 'You are always here Mr Hope' which brought down Milady from the other end of the room to say furiously that I was 'her best friend' etc., etc.

Afterwards I went to the S.K. [South Kensington] Museum to see Sir Cunliffe-Owen, the director. My business was this. I want to be made Commissioner for Ceylon at the Exhibition of '86. Owen very friendly & quite impressed with my own idea that I should be the best man for the post. It would be worth no money but to me it would be a labour of love & I really know a good deal about it. I rather covet the post which I could hold as well as the Auditorship one which seems so *very* long in coming. Above all, though it sounds cruel, I long to get away from here. This place—Warwick House—I loathe & so does my poor Mother. She was brightened up by a long visit from Lady N. [Napier & Ettrick], and one from Mrs Oscar Wilde. Lady N. & E. knew your Father when he was lying wounded at Constantinople, where My Lord used to go & see him every day. She longs to make your acquaintance. She says that next to my Mother she has known me the longest of anyone, which is true.[38]

[CONTINUED]   29TH MARCH

At the Goldsmids the Russian Attaché Stöeckl told me a good thing which Dolgorouki said to the Prince [of Wales] at Berlin.[39] It was in answer to a question by the Prince as to the likelihood of war. 'Monseigneur, if you lend *us* the money & we lend *you* the men it may come about, not unless.' ... Your true lover, Adrian

HUNSTANTON   SUNDAY, 29TH MARCH

My own dearest Adrian, ... I have just been killing off poor George Eliot & have finished the last huge volume of her *Life*. It is a pity Cross [her widower] has put in so much that is almost twaddle, it ought to be *sternly* weeded down to one volume. ... She acknowledges herself that her nature is 'more prone to live in *past* pain—than in the prospect of pleasure.' I suppose her bad health had something to do with it—but the fact was her spirits were crushed and weighed down by her marvellous brain '*for a woman*' so she became as *ponderous* in her moods as most clever men! ...

I wish I could write you a funny letter but my sort of throat makes me feel rather dull. If I was a bird I should go & sit in the depths of a hollow tree and ruffle my feathers all round me and shut my eyes all day—till I heard you chirping outside with a tender worm on a holly berry you had brought me for lunch. Then I think I should wake to give you a loving peck!! Oh I do so long to hear you say 'my darling' again. I have seen it written often by your hand but it is your *voice* that I long to hear, for I do not think you know—even *you*

how *very, very* dearly I love you, Adie, and how I long for your companionship—and sympathy. Every day—when we are apart, my letters will
not tell you that for I nearly always write you trivialities. I *dare* not allow
myself to dwell in my letters, or even for long in my thoughts, on the love that
we have for each other—because it would only make our long separations
harder to bear. ... I am happy here—in a way I have often told you—feeling
sure of our love—happy I suppose because after Dr Watts—'*It is my nature
to*'!! ... At Easter we will find all the happiness possible in the few days that we
shall spend together. Always your own *petite Laure*

---

36 *12th Mar* Charles Dodgson subsequently wrote to the artist 'Miss Troubridge' to ask if
she would do him a great favour and let him see the originals of the model she used for *Little
Thumb*. Nothing could be refused the author of *Alice* but the originals had gone to the printer
and she had not used any models. It was not until 1896/97 that Laura actually met Dodgson
when she and her seven-year old daughter, Jaqueline, were taken by Oxford relations to tea
with him in his rooms there. Laura asked if he remembered her book *Little Thumb* at which
the fifty-three-year old writer 'doddered' (according to Jaqueline's recollection) across the
room to a bookshelf, saying 'Do I remember, do I remember?', and picked out his copy—
which he had had specially bound—to show her. At the sale of his books after his death in
1898 Adrian was able to buy this copy to give to Laura.

37 *15th Mar* The interior decoration scheme for the Wildes' house at No 16 (since renumbered as No 34) Tite Street, Chelsea, was by the architect and designer E W Godwin (1835-
86) who had already built other houses in the street, including the controversial White House
for Whistler at No 35 some seven years earlier.

38 *29th Mar* Adrian was born in Washington (1858) when his father, Col Hope, was military
attaché there.

39 *29th Mar* The Prince of Wales was attending the eighty-eighth birthday celebrations of
William I, King of Prussia (1861-71) and German Emperor (1871-88).

APRIL 1885

At Hopton House, Great Yarmouth
[with Aunt Maggie Orde]

Easter Monday, 6th April … A little dance in the evening & a cotillion & games. After we 2 talked & A. spoilt my white frock by saying goodnight with a scarlet geranium in his button-hole!

7th April Helped arrange 'The World's Fair—a show of horrors' I was a mummy, Adrian the head of Holofernes cut off in a dish. …

HUNSTANTON   14TH APRIL

My *own* Darling Adrian, … I have been so energetic working with charcoal pencils, on Mr Jem's [Hope] studies of life models. I have not the black board or slate, but a huge roll of rough drawing paper. One can dust off the untrue lines with a handkerchief. I shall keep the sketches to see if my efforts improve. … Always yours, *Laure*

15TH APRIL

My Darling, I do miss you dreadfully. … A new maid has just arrived and I have to *interview* her. It bores me—but I must try to feign some slight interest in the subject of wages and *beer*, but really new servants give us little or no trouble because that good soul Tanner revels in training them up in the way they should go. … I have been thinking over one of our last talks—about the painting lessons. I was so carried away by my love of art that I did not sufficiently realize what the sisters would feel if I was to leave them all now (I mean before our marriage) for so long. Of course if lessons could be found in London it would be different—but I fear the other idea of going to Paris would be a *great* grievance. … I love you, Adie darling, from your *Laure*

P.S. I hope you had a satisfactory call on Sir Peter Coats about an appointment from the Liberals. I find our frocks are *always* sewn with Coats Cotton. *You know* how strong it is! The seams *never* part do they? or reveal odd little white holes in the sleeves! Tanner, to whom I spoke rather severely on the subject lately—showed me the cotton she used with the name on it— she swears not *by* it—but *at* it!! However no one else has invented a cotton to be used with a sewing machine.

17TH APRIL

My Dearest, … I am afraid studies from the nude are an acquired taste, *afraid* because I fear I am *rapidly acquiring it.* When Amy is home I am going to *sound* her about the painting lessons that we thought of but I am not very hopeful—there seem to be difficulties enough even if Mlle Ourliac[40] *would* consent to teach me. The more I think of it, the more I *long* to go to Paris, and the more dissatisfied I feel with the *play* work I do here and how I waste my time over things I really do not care two straws about. Meanwhile the love of Art that I have is slowly starving to death. Ever your loving *petite Laure*

YORK CLUB, 8 ST JAMES' SQUARE 18TH APRIL

My darling Laura, … Long's[41] two pictures of Xerxes choosing the models for Venus ['In Search of Beauty'] are fine but they seem to me too coldly classical, wanting in what the French would call the *pointe de volupté* needed to make them seem real. … Next we went to see Cosway's[42] miniatures which are really delightful. One of Mrs Fitzherbert's eye was really beautiful…then to see the picture of the greatest master since Rubens. Before Makart's[43] pictures the vile daubs of the modern school sink into the insignificance which befits them, poor worms who dare not handle Colour lest it should overcome them. The splendid richness of colouring & lavishness of decoration in Makart's last picture 'Summer' I quite delighted in. The man is so free from fear & puts in masses of colouring in such a regal imperial way. No fear then of being crude. No hankering after unhealthy yellows & indigestible greens…

Ah-ha, I knew that you would get to feel the same about the nude as I do. The great glorious beautiful lines of the most lovely Creation of God—A woman's body. To think that for centuries they should have been almost regarded as sinful to look upon by this nasty prurient world of ours. Au revoir, *bientôt*—Adrian

HUNSTANTON PRIMROSE DAY, SUNDAY, 19TH APRIL

My own Darling Adrian, Your talk about the pictures interests me so although I am not going to say *amen* darling to *all* your remarks. … Miss Holden (Wally Gurney's fiancée) is so uninteresting, a character made up of negatives & decidedly dull…she does not care for reading at all she told me—nor does Wally—for *any* books so they never read when they are together. *Do you think they kiss all the time?*!! …

On coming home late (from Seymours at Barwick) we found that we had an hour to wait at Heacham so instead we walked home three miles along the beach in the moonlight, a crescent moon & millions of bright stars lighting up a lovely grey sea with tiny waves splashing up on the sand. When you are here in the summer we will wander out in the evenings for it is so delicious by the sea—like being *in* one of Whistler's Harmonies in grey and silver, or Nocturnes I suppose he would call them. ... It would be good practice to draw from some plaster of Paris life figures as you suggest but what I want to get are some casts, life size, of hands & feet, to draw from to learn the forms better. Your *petite Laure—qui t'aime un peu*

BACHELORS' CLUB, 8 HAMILTON PLACE SUNDAY, 19TH APRIL [JO'S ROOM]

My darling Laura, ... today I lunched at the Wildes' & found Charlie [Orde] there. Besides us there were two very dull people there, a brother who has acted at the Lyceum & a sister at Girton. Both hideous. They called themselves Stickert [Sickert][44] or some such name. Charlie & I agreed that we had rarely met such dull people as these—but it was very entertaining. Charlie gushed so in a way that made *me* feel quite surpassed. I can write no more for Jo has come in. *Ma petite Laure, Adieu*, Adrian

HUNSTANTON 20TH APRIL

My Darling Adie, Last night talking over the fire with Amy, I approached the subject of the painting lessons. To my surprise and pleasure she was quite *enthusiastic* about it and said she thought it would be selfish & *unpatriotic* of them to stop my going, and she would do all she could to help me to arrange it, though she would hate my being away for so long. She saw how far easier it would be to *really* work at painting quite away in Paris where I know no one, to London, where I could not help seeing friends & would sure to feel bored after a time as I am so used to amusing myself there. I *was* delighted Amy should take this view of it. With Amy on my side, I know I could work Uncle Sommy & Aunt Bache—for as they are our guardians they like to be consulted about our plans. ... I feel convinced that I *do* care sufficiently about painting, and I feel such a strong wish to learn more of art that I know these would carry me through the discomforts of the Ourliac ménage that you told me of. Sep., October & November would be best for me. It would be a long time for *us* to say Goodbye—but it has been my wish for *so long* to learn to be more than a feeble amateur and so my ambition would help me. … You did really mean your suggestion about Paris—didn't you? Ever your own *Laure*

York Club, 8 St James' Square   23rd April

My own sweet Darling, … I am very anxious to see the copies you have made from the nude studies. Do you think you could get hold of any little boys or girls & study the nude from them. 1/- [shilling] down would surely produce a child ready to strip to the skin in the sacred cause of Art. Or what say you to asking Clem's little angel of a boy[45] & making studies of him as a Cupid? … Things do look very bad out in the East[46] but somehow I do not think that we shall have war this time. [Laura had written: 'I suppose there will be war now— or we shall have all Europe sneering at us.'] The great increase in the Navy will be of use to Ernest I fancy & we shall see him coming back as no end of a Swell of the Ocean some day. … *Ma Laure adieu*, Adrian

Hunstanton   25th April

My Darling, It is too funny about your political friends McIver and Hume wanting to help them in Torquay. Do you mean to say that Hume is the *Conservative* candidate or merely another Liberal? If the former he must have very hazy ideas about your politics—or perhaps with him you talked of some of those real old Tory ideas I used to hear you let out sometimes—for you know you *have* some darling, under the outside *froth* of Radicalism that you love to declare. … Farewell Darling, I think of you so often, yours ever, *Laure*

York Club, 8 St James' Square   25th April

My loving Sweetheart, … As I was walking home on Thursday I ran into the arms of Oscar Wilde who insisted on my dining with them, which I accordingly did & sat up talking with him in his vermilion garret until 2. of the clock. We discussed some strange subjects. Among others the effect of matrimony on Man. Our conclusions were on the whole favourable to that remarkable institution though Oscar had distinct leanings to a system of Contract for 7 years only, to be renewed or not as either party saw fit. It arose from Constance having said during dinner that she thought it should be free to either party to go off at the expiration of the first year. What think you darling of these matters? … Have you read Mrs Praed's novel *Affinities*? There is a rather coarse caricature of Oscar Wilde in it.' *Bon jour, ma Laure, j'embrasse tes épaules*, Adrian

Warwick House, Albert Road, Battersea Sunday, 26th April

My dearest Love, I must begin by telling you that I find myself forced to stop in town till Saturday [so is unable to meet Laura on the Friday for their weekend with the Cresswells at Lynn]. It is a great bore, but I have several engagements on that day besides which Lady G. has written to beg me to come to her first Evening party on her return from Cannes. As she has been very ill & is very useful to me it would be ungrateful of me to refuse. Besides I have really got business which ought to be done. ... Do not think it is because I love you less my Sweet that I think of humouring any other person than you. ...

I went to lunch with Mother Higgins and her daughter, her son Capt. Higgins & his wife Lady Hilda H. (and others). They were all rabid Tories & attacked me violently on following such a crew as the present Govt. Lady H.H. told me that the Royal tour[47] had been nothing like the triumphal tour reported by the papers. But all the unpleasant part of it has been kept quiet. ... I saw Prince George of Wales in Piccadilly walking with Prince Edward of Saxe Weimar. No one knew him & I was actually chaffed by a friend for having taken off my hat 'to that little Counter Jumper'.[48]

Mrs Amherst is full of the Bazaar she is to have in June for her hospital at Hackney. She will have a book on sale full of short stories by celebrated people with Poems & Illustrations [see page 122]. I at once suggested that possibly if she were very pressing you might do an illustration for her. I am going to try & squeeze out a poem from Oscar Wilde for the book & a little story from Mallock [author of *The New Republic* (1877), a satire on English society and ideas]. ...

The news is again more warlike. In fact now I can see no hope of peace. If we have to fight both France & Russia we shall find ourselves in a hole deeper than we have been in for four hundred years when we fought the whole of Europe pretty well. ... My Father for a wonder is at home & is sitting working out horrible sums about his Gun & its wonderful powers. This seems to suit him much better than trying to make money by it for my Mother & us all. He is the most perfect specimen of a selfish man I ever saw. ... Now my Parent has pounced on the hapless Charles who was quietly reading a book in a corner & now the poor boy is working out sums in cube root to check his Father's calculations. ... *Toujours ma petite Laure, ton Adrian qui t'adore,*—Adrian

Laura's reaction to the Wildes' attitude to matrimony [see Adrian's letter of 25th April] took up ten pages, of which an extract follows:

HUNSTANTON   SUNDAY, 26TH APRIL

My Dearest, ... That a discussion on Matrimony between a newly married man, and an engaged man, should have ended 'favourably for that venerable institution' is not very surprising—is it? The vague theories you speak of are rather amusing for idle discussion—to build up & then bowl over again—but...if one attempts in one's mind to make a *personal* application of them, they appear simply *revolting*. ... I dislike Constance Wilde for her remark even more than her opinion on dancing [?]—unless by the by it was a *desperate* attempt at originality. No wonder she has a sulky, dull face if those are the thoughts she has to talk with when she is alone—If I found any such in my heart I should *kill* them. Darling I find I am getting quite angry—it is absurd, but do not laugh at me for raging about this. I confess it *did* get a rise out of me. ... I know, my own dear Adrian, that your thoughts are with mine on this—and not with theirs—with their one, or seven, years *lease of a heart*! ... darling, goodbye L.

YORK CLUB, 8 ST JAMES' SQUARE   28TH APRIL

My own sweet Love, ... On Friday I had breakfast with Austin Lee at the F.O. & then went into the City on some business. Coming back I had a long talk with Marston who has been trying yet another process for the 'Little Mermaid' drawings. He frankly advised me to urge you not to run the risk of bringing out the book at present. For he said that this War cloud was affecting the Book trade as well as every other. Then I went & saw Bodley who was not able to give me any encouragement as to the probable death of any Auditors. On I came here and found Jo and we went to see an Amateur Photography Exhibition which I thought a bore. Then on to the Bachelors' for Cocoa, where we were joined by a cousin of Jo's, Fitzclarence Paget, a little lame man who paints his face as much as Alec Yorke [groom-in-waiting to Queen Victoria] but not so well for it shows more. You will wonder how I was away all day but the fact is that Roberts has had little or nothing for me to do of late at his Workhouses. Only three whole days till we meet again dear Love, Your Adrian

---

40 *17th Apr* Mlle Ourliac (later Mme Boucher Ourliac) had studied under Carolus Duran (1837-1917). She became a friend of Adrian's sister Laura and their aunt Annie Cunninghame Graham when they were living in Paris and had painted an oil portrait of Adrian when he stayed with them there in 1883/84. This was accepted for the Paris Salon in April, 1886.
41 *18th Apr* Edwin Long RA (1829-91), historical genre and portrait painter.

42 *18th Apr* Richard Cosway RA (1742-1821), an able miniaturist. He was a friend of the Prince of Wales (later George IV).

43 *18th Apr* Hans Makart (1840-84), Austrian historical and figure painter.

44 *20th Apr* Wilde was friends with the Sickert family. Walter (1860-1942) was then aged twenty-five and a pupil of Whistler but he had been briefly on the stage before spending a year or so at the Slade and Whistler rather foisted his protégé on the Wildes. The younger sister, Helena Maria (1864-1939), had become a favoured protégée of Wilde in the late 1870s when they kept up a friendly correspondence. She took a degree in Moral Science at Girton in 1882, became a writer, lecturer and keen promoter of women's rights under her married surname as H M Swanwick. When Wilde was editing *The Woman's World* she contributed only one article, on 'The Evolution of Economics Today' (February 1989). Wilde had hoped for further contributions.

45 *23rd Apr* 'Dodsie' (Ernest) Wright, then aged six and a particular favourite of Laura's was the son of Willy Wright, the Gurney steward at Runcton, and Clemence née Vleminck. Clem had arrived from Belgium in 1866 to be governess to the young Troubridges before their mother died. She was then nineteen years old and Laura aged eight. The sisters all adored her and little Dodsie. Laura's journals record constant meetings with them in Lynn after Clem's marriage in 1877. Dodsie was to become secretary at the Royal Academy in London and he remained friendly with Laura's daughter, Jaqueline, throughout all his life.

46 *23rd Apr* On 30th March, the Russians, thinking the British were more than occupied in Egypt, perpetrated an aggressive 'incident' in Afghanistan to test Britain's reaction to this possible threat to her position in India.

47 *26th Apr* The Prince and Princess of Wales and their elder son, Prince Eddy, spent much of April touring Ireland where they were constantly booed by the nationalists.

48 *26th Apr* Prince Edward of Saxe Coburg ('that little Counter Jumper') was in fact British-born, a Field-Marshal in the British Army and married to a daughter of the 5th Duke of Richmond. Prince Edward was not acknowledged as royalty in British Society although in his own country of origin this courtesy was extended to his wife.

MAY 1885

Hunstanton   6th May

My Darling, … Ernest says the heat in Hong Kong is frightful & their Captain is *very* strict about frock coats & collars which are martyrdom to the poor Rough Seaman. He was delighted with Kandy & with great difficulty refrained from spending all his patrimony on cat's-eyes & sapphires. He found several people who knew you…especially one *White*—a bird stuffer—whom he found stuffing some peacocks, who spoke affectionately of you! Goodbye, your own *Laure*

York Club, 8 St James' Square   7th May

My own Darling Laura, … I have been busy all the morning seeing people about Courtenay Boyle's Inspectorship, now vacant as he is now made Asst. Secretary of the L.G.B. I have written to Dilke a letter about it which Lady G. will herself give him. However I am not a bit sanguine but I feel it is better to try all round. … Here is a letter from my sister in Paris about Mlle Ourliac. The price for a month's board & lodging & fees is about frs 230 (or £9.3 [shillings]). Now I shall go to see Miss Miller & ask her whether she thinks the advantages of Paris are so superior as to be worth the journey etc. *Au revoir bientôt*, Adrian your faithful lover

Adrian's sister Laura's note on art classes in Paris

'It would be dull to work all the time with Mlle O. A nice plan would be to work with her at drawing & go to some studio as well for painting & models. Miss Miller worked for 3 years with Duran & Henner—they teach conjointly in the studio at Quai Voltaire & of course believe they are the best masters in Paris. Miss Miller's address is: The Boltons Studios, Redcliffe Road, South Kensington "after 5 o'clock". '

Mlle Ourliac	board and lodging	180 fr/month
	teaching, drawing, use of studio	50 fr/month
Colarossi Studio, Avenue d'Eglan	drawing well taught, painting indifferent	40 fr/month

Colarossi Studio, Rue de la grande Chaumière, Rue de Notre Dame du Champs	drawing as above	20 fr/ month
Carolus Duran, 17 Quai Voltaire	for painting only then	100 fr/1st month 85 fr/ month

HUNSTANTON   8TH MAY

Darling Adrian, … What I feel is that I am not yet *up* to lessons from such swells as Carolus Duran etc. Supposing I could this year have *thorough* good *grounding* lessons in figure painting in London with 'the handsome Miss Miller' (or in Paris), it would be more real use to me to have the better lessons from the French masters later on. … I long to hear that Dilke's heart has been softened & to hear which way things turn out. Goodbye my *own* love, ever your *Laure*

YORK CLUB, 8 ST JAMES' SQUARE   8TH MAY

My Sweet Heart, [After leaving the Goldsmid's Friday night party] … It is now 1/4 to one & all the gay world is on its way to dance at Lady Abergavenny's even Lady G. who having got rid of her people goes on to make herself more unwell. She is obliged to do so poor thing as Royalty is to be there & they have allowed it to be understood that she has been avoiding houses to which they go of late. This is true for she hates the Prince of Wales. I have been asked to do some literary work for the *Morning Post*—nothing very grand but work of that kind has always had a strong fascination for me. … My father is quite pleased as he sees a prospect of a new law suit before him. This is always unbounded joy to him. Meanwhile I hear nothing about his Gun. *Je t'adore à la folie*, Your true lover, Adrian

WARWICK HOUSE, ALBERT ROAD, BATTERSEA   9TH MAY

My Darling Laura, The answer from Dilke is not favourable but Lady G. told me he was not offended with my letter but that he does not intend to make another Inspector but to economize the post. Also that he thinks me too young [at twenty-seven] which is rather absurd. …

I went to see Oscar Wilde about the little poem for Mrs T. Amherst's Bazaar. He very graciously consented on condition that you would give him a drawing on the subject and he stands out for a sheet all to himself. The size of the book is quarto i.e. 6 inches by 4 inches, the poem to be printed on one side of a sheet. Will you do something pretty either a vignette and Initial letter or border of small children. … You have *carte* blanche. … Goodbye, Adrian

[CONTINUED]   11TH MAY
(FROM YORK CLUB, 8 ST JAMES' SQUARE)

My Sweet Heart, I will explain about Oscar's poem as I fear my letters were rather wanting in courtesy. Mrs Amherst's book[49] is to be sold for the benefit of the Children's Hospital at Hackney in which she takes an interest. Oscar gave me the poem which I sent to you. But he made several conditions as to its publication. One was that unless you undertook to illustrate it, it was *not* to be used. Mrs A. to whom I at once referred the matter was very happy to accept the condition. So darling you must not fancy that I have been promising things in your name should you feel inclined to illustrate this poem will you send me as quick as possible your sketch. If you find it distasteful or if you think one sheet is too small, write to me today. … Oscar favoured me with his views about you last night. He said you were like a young Greek Goddess & had a certain fierce Chastity about you which was fascinating. Oddly enough he too [?] called you '*une femme de glace*' [Ice-maiden] but he said that he shrewdly suspected the existence of a Volcano beneath the exterior crust of ice. I turned the conversation onto his own Constance & we had a very curious conversation which I will tell you about some time. She seemed happier & less taciturn. … Goodnight *ma petite Laure*, Your Adrian

The last of the five verses of Oscar's poem, 'Le Jardin des Tuileries'[50], is quoted here:

> Ah! cruel tree! If I were you,
> And children climbed me, for their sake
> Though it be winter I would break
> Into Spring blossoms white and blue!

HUNSTANTON   12TH MAY

My own Darling Adrian, Of course I will do the drawing—rather try to. It is rather tiny for the poem & design to be on the *same* page, isn't it? … I don't *want* to say anything disagreeable about O.W. *especially after his comparing me to a goddess*!!!! but I *think* I could have written as good a poem myself! and what on earth is the species of tree in the Tuileries Gardens that bears *blue* blossoms!! How horrid & *philistine* of me to make these impertinent remarks—almost worthy of Grigsby [?] ... After all it suggests something to draw and is not too *nebulous* as I feared it might be or at all Swinburnian!!! so I will not say anything more—but take out my pencils & paper and try to do justice to this latest cobweb from the poet's brain spinning. ... I should love to rest your head & to talk your worries away together till we both laughed—oh darling, this is *not* quite the *femme de glace* is it!! I know Oscar Wilde so slightly that I am rather amused he should have any opinion to give about me—and oh so glad you turned the conversation when it became dangerous. I should like to hear the talk about Constance ... those 2 rather interest me.

I wonder what you will tell me about the Journalist work—no leaders for the *War Cry* or *Band of Hope*, is it?—I should love to read anything you wrote for any paper—unless it were ultra Radicalism—you will forgive me this I know. ... Roland Le Strange (now aged 16) was at home yesterday & at luncheon he made conversation with me & talked like a man about town of 40 at least! discussing theatres, both before & behind the scenes in the most casual way. ... He has become *so* grown up I found I felt rather indignant & *almost* blushed when he put his arm round my waist & said something very complimentary. Is *he* growing up—or am *I* growing *Prudish*! ... Ever your loving *Laure*

Warwick House, Albert Road, Battersea   12th May

My own sweet Love, ... I quite agree with your criticism of Oscar's poem, it is twaddle. ... I went to lunch with the St Aubyns—the family was nearly all there, Sir John & Lady Elizabeth, 6 girls & Bean & Mike. Lill [Laura's 'greatest friend'] is just adorable. I think her eyes lovely & her figure delicious. ... The Herbert Jones's [Laura's uncle and aunt] asked me to come to their hotel in Dover Street to meet Amy who was full of lamentations because you were not with her at Abbey Lodge. She said that Marie de Bunsen made her do what she did not want to do & would not let her get away to see the people whom she wanted to see. For without you, Amy said, to keep her up to her engagements they all fell through. Also that London without you was robbed of more than half its charm. The dear good Jones's were too killing about Oscar Wilde whom they met at Lady Dorothy Nevill's & with whom they are fascinated. He too told me that he thought them charming. Your uncle went to the Levee yesterday &, we were told, looked angelic in his gown & shoes & stockings. ... *Ma petite Laure, à bientôt,* Your Adrian

My Dearest, ... Sometimes when I am here for long I know I have my *Hunstanton* face every day—and a Hunstanton mind too now—that does not seem to care very much about anything in particular except perhaps drawing, and *you* are so *far* down in my heart. Quite out of sight all day—or *very* nearly. Only in this way can I live here cheerily—& as before. Then in the evening late, Darling, just before I sleep, I draw aside the veil and think of you—and have my waking dreams—of *you*, and weave the beautiful castles in the air that we dwell in together & I am always happy thinking about the future. For me—I think I would rather have a 2 years engagement or even longer, meeting as we do—than that you should leave me for a whole long year—like Julian Orde and his Alice. Not that I do not really love you *truly* & *faithfully*—but you would find me frozen over! Grown estranged from your *presence*. Although I might love you in *the abstract* just as well ... I could *not* possibly, like Alice, begin joyfully to make preparations for a wedding—no Darling, you would have to woo me all over again—a second courtship from the *very* beginning! ...

If Madame de Bunsen had wired for me to join Amy in London this week there would have been no visit as planned for me later, in June, when there may be summer weather at Hurlingham, & the night lights & piano organs etc., Strauss Band & Illuminations at 'the Inventories'[51]—& other mild dissipations of our *season*. ... Darling, I shall insist on your wearing some sort of *blinkers* when you take your walks abroad—if you *will* amuse yourself by looking into shop windows such as Himuss' [of which Adrian had written: 'they had some most ravishing garments hung up for public admiration']. Darling what *possible* interest can such chiffons have for you? *Qu' allait il faire dans cette galère?* You see you are *only engaged*. Of course if you were *married*, it would be *quite* different—and you might see something that you thought I should like—and we go & buy it together—that is if you were not too *shy* or *I* was not. This last is more likely perhaps—for you are *not* much troubled with shyness I know, and I should rather like to *pinch* you. ————

An interval of time—now it is after dinner. We have dined I hope *wisely*—but not too *well*! Menu: Fried Soles, Chicken, Jam & cream in red tea cups—rather fattening!! I have begun to illustrate Oscar Wilde's verses—I think one page will be enough for us both. I am drawing it larger & it will have to be reduced in the printing but this I believe is very simple. Vi & Helen are crooning over the fire with books, a maid is warbling a hymn, I think one of Moody & Sankeys'—outside in the passage. I must go and *implore* her to stop—it is a *dreadful* sound. ... Goodnight Sweet Heart, from your *Laure*

SUNDAY, 17TH MAY

My dearest, I am sending you the pen and ink sketch for the lines Oscar Wilde wrote when I think his *Muse* was out of town—will he say the same of my sketch I wonder! Well, I hope you & the Amherst Committee will approve of it. The space given me is so tiny that I could not attempt anything at all ambitious. ... I think we will go to Gloucester St. for a month in the summer and *winter in the workhouse*!! The idea is to let The Castle for August to the Gemmells, or longer, & visit about. I *long* for a little distraction & life. I have an idea you do not much want me to come to London—and I cannot quite think why. ...

I have had a *dreadful* wedding present from an old Quaker cousin—quite beyond! Imagine two *gigantic* shawl pins—moored together by a massive silver chain, the pins formed of enormous topaz set in sort of filigree silver. *Hideous* beyond all description—and *shawl pins* for *me* of all people. I must immediately take to shawls, I think tartan fastened with the pins would look very chic. I *suppose* they are real stones but they are so large that they look like glass, about an inch deep. We thought perhaps we might use them for salt cellars ...

If we come to London I should so like to have some fencing lessons. After a severe course of lessons & a violent rage for practice between times, you would be surprised to be greeted by a tall *bony* woman with hard knuckles, hollow cheeks & only *one* chin, & plenty of angles instead of the Laura you had crumpled & kissed before—would you be pleased Darling? ... Ever your own *Laure*

YORK CLUB, 8 ST JAMES' SQUARE   18TH MAY

My Darling, I think your drawing for the poem is very pretty & will carry it off to Mrs A. I am not yet pleased at the idea of your coming up to London, even though Lady G. longs to see you at her Ball on the 10th June, and to know who will chaperon you etc. Also Mrs McIver tells me that 47 Hill Street shall have a room reserved for us in case we like to make it a sort of meeting place.

[CONTINUED] (FROM WARWICK HOUSE, ALBERT ROAD, BATTERSEA)

I have my heart so full of you...my guiding Star. To you I shall owe it if ever I do anything worth doing in the cruel struggle of this bitter world. ... Today I spent four hours at the British Museum reading up the subject on which I am to write an article for approval. I have been asked to try & enliven the *Morning*

Post by Stewart, who is a sub-editor there. Of course I cannot write any political Leaders as my feelings are directly contrary to what they publish as news. The subjects I am to write on are to be social. I am trying to make up one on Italian Opera as we have not got an Opera this year. ...

I went to see Lady G. in her glory, for she had been to the [Court] Drawing Room today. She had a train of pale blue silk rather ribbed & lined with pale pink satin. Corsage of blue. Dress of 'point d'Alencon' over which was draped crêpe de Chine covered with tiny pink & blue flowers. The effect was spoilt I thought by the contrast between the crêpe de Chine, which looked for all the world like flowered muslin, and the train. I told her so which by no means pleased her. She was covered with Diamonds & looked very tired & cross.

Bea Gurney had been to see Mr & Mrs McIver today & seems to have said such delightful things about our Engagement that I forgive her all her oddities. It *would* be curious if she were to end by marrying Montefiore [Claude, Mrs McIver's brother]. Would they be happy? He has £50,000 a year at least & will have more some day. I like him much for he is a *good man indeed*.

[CONTINUED]   19TH MAY

Last night I spent a couple of hours trying to write my Opera article made up of a sort of Hodge Podge of what I read at the British Museum. There is I fancy too much war news for them to put it in just now. ... I wish I were there instead of Tanner tomorrow morning. Then I would kiss your Arms when you put them out for this letter from—Adrian

22ND MAY

Darling, your letter gave me a stab for it seemed so hard that you should expect me for Whitsun and that you should wait in vain. ... Oh how I do long for something certain, some fixed point in the shifting sand. I have work to do on Saturday [23rd] at St Pancras Workhouse and Monday I have to keep an appointment. ... I think Whit Sunday will be a very sad day for me here in London. ... Goodbye dearest, Your Adrian

HUNSTANTON   SUNDAY, 24TH MAY

My own Darling, I was not *angry* with you—not for one little minute. I know you would not refuse to spend three days together here unless there were good reasons. By the end of the week I think the weather must change and be fine & sunshiny again, when *perhaps* you are coming—from Friday to Tuesday.

... Mary Amherst wrote that she thought my little drawing would be the prize picture in the book—but I am afraid Oscar will not think it very *subtle*. ...

Lothar de Bunsen is here—alone with 4 young ladies to talk to—he seems to like it very much. He and I sat by chance together in Church—away from the others, watched with intense interest by the Congregation who have quite settled by this time that here at last is my fiancé! Isn't it too bad? You would have laughed if you had seen me carefully securing 2 hymn books so that we might *each* have one & keeping an empty chair with umbrellas & books between us to *discourage* the idea!

Vi & Helen enjoyed their ball very much—the Norfolk Artillery Militia one for the Prince. It was a very smart occasion—lots of H.R.H.'s London friends turned up but poor Limpet fell into the clutches of old Papa Duff who devoted himself to her, boring her to death—but of course she was too shy to get rid of him & is quite pathetic on the subject. After some negotiations over the exchange of houses with the Miss Gemmells the date of our arrival in Gloucester St. is settled—23rd June. I know it will be good for me—a sort of pick me up to come up to town again & see something of my friends and I cannot disguise from you that I think we shall have some very happy occasions together...I am very busy with attacks on the 2 huge signboards I am painting for Mr Le Strange & Uncle Hay [Gurney] as I have to finish them before we leave as we shall probably not come back here till October. ... Ever you own *Petite Laure*

26TH MAY

My Darling Adrian, Lothar's visit was a success—he is easily amused & he played so well to us, *not* always the same tune over & over again! He did not bore me at all. Clemency Hubbard had as usual been airing her opinions on our engagement to Lothar—you will perhaps darling be rather surprised to hear that I am 'not at all the sort of girl who will suit you in any way'!! I do *wish* to be philosophic about her remarks on you & me but I cannot quite succeed. ... Goodbye for the present, your Laura

YORK CLUB, 8 ST JAMES' SQUARE   26TH MAY

My darling Laura, ... I dined last night at Abbey Lodge. Oh! Darling, the badness of the dinner!!! I sat between Mrs Monteith [sister of Poppy Herbert, Amy's great friend] and Marie de B. Marie gave a long explanation of how difficult it was to get your visit to them squeezed in...After dinner Old de B. gave us a lecture on Oranges which he declared were a passion with him & he described when he bought them in the Edgware Road feeling them all himself. I took such a fancy to Monteith & stayed to have a cigarette with him after the others retired. We had a long talk on all sorts of queer subjects. He is an Ardent Catholic & really got quite warm trying to convert me. He told me something about Moritz [de Bunsen] which I was sorry to hear. He seems to be a male flirt of a bad description. I found that I had sat up just long enough to miss the last Underground train to S. Kensington. So, the night being fine & I in the mood, I walked all the way home to Battersea, taking an hour and a half only to do the distance in. … Goodbye for the time, from Adrian

28TH MAY

Darling of my Soul, Yesterday I went after dinner to 'the Inventories' which was nice but the party was dull. … All the lighting is now done by electricity & the effect is I think superior to the Lanterns of former years. The countless small lights look like jewels hanging on the outlines of the buildings. My thoughts wandered off to the happy evening last year when you & I were together. Now for a bit of sad news, at least it is to me. I cannot come down for this next Sunday as I particularly want to meet some men on Sunday. Besides my poor Mother is in bed once more and I do not like to go away & leave her all alone. … *Toujours à toi ma Laure*, Adrian

HUNSTANTON   29TH MAY

Dearest Adrian, This morning I dreamt I had your letter to say you could not come alas—but a long letter & very sorry—but when I woke there was only a little note describing the lamps at 'the Inventories' which I have read about in every newspaper—and at the end just a little word to say you want to meet— not me—but 'some men' on Sunday. … That your Mother is ill I am sorry for—but she has been more or less ill in bed since Xmas—& it has never stopped you coming before. Ah—now I find how Love can punish—if once you let it take possession of your heart—for see how you can give me a sharper disappointment than anyone in the world, because I love you so — — — — — — — and make me feel dull & sad even on a day of sunshine. It is no use looking forward to anything. … Goodbye, from your *Laure*

YORK CLUB, 8 ST JAMES' SQUARE   29TH MAY

Ma Chérie Your telegram has made me feel so very wretched. Darling I am quite miserable but I cannot get away. Last night my Mother was so ill & fainted away for so long as to frighten us all. This is one reason but not the one which keeps me here. You see I am so very anxious to get something fixed & to get out of this uncertainty which weighs upon me like a black cloud. So I feel that I ought not to throw away any chance of getting on. ... Don't be too angry with me for I am quite wretched enough as it is just now...Goodbye, your Adrian

HUNSTANTON   30TH MAY

Darling, I feel *rather* better since I have had your answer to my telegram—but I always feel that Hunstanton is such a dull stupid little place to ask you to come to, and London is full of nice things and nice people – – – – – – –. I cannot ask you to come here again—you must write yourself & tell me you are coming when you really wish to. But not another disappointment please. I cannot stand them from you—they take all the life out of me. Always yr L.

YORK CLUB, 8 ST JAMES' SQUARE   30TH MAY

My darling Laura, Your letter has given me such pain. I feel I should have been frank with you & told you at once last week that I could not come down but I hoped so to be able to manage my little glimpse of Heaven somehow. ... You cannot imagine that any desire for amusement or wish to meet anyone except for business, could keep me away from you. I could not afford to come for several reasons. First I am very hard up just now. Second I cannot run the risk of having it said that I am always away in Norfolk. Also I have had to see people on business. ... But I have never found that I could do what I liked always however much I may have wished to do so.

What can I say more to you my dearest love? ... So many things are pressing hard upon me just now so that you must try to forgive me if you can. ... It is an agony of pain to me, thinking of you & that it is I who have hurt you so. Your lover, Adrian

HUNSTANTON   SUNDAY, 31ST MAY

My *own darling* Adrian, It is *you* who must forgive, not *me*. I do not know what shadow has been over me the last two days. ... It did not need your sad and gentle letter this morning to open my eyes to this. Yesterday afternoon, about 5. I heard some *very very* sad news about some friends of ours. I was dreadfully shocked, and I went out alone to think quietly of this real great sorrow that has come to our friends—and I felt suddenly as if I had awoken—out of a bad dream. I saw that I had conjured up imaginary grief & given way weakly to disappointment. Ah darling, I—your *Laure*—have made anything but the happiness of your life the last few days—and I feel *so* remorseful. ... I imagined from your note on Thursday, you did not really want to come—and I fretted so over this—& the necessity of being just as usual with the others, made me *think* even more. ... There is so little really to distract one's attention that any naughty evil thought will grow apace, if once you give way to it. ... Faith and Hope—I have, and what I pray for is the 'Charity that thinketh no evil'. Goodbye darling, some day your wife, *Laure*

---

49 *11th May* In a Good Cause—a Collection of Stories, Poems and Illustrations—For the benefit of the North Eastern Hospital for Children, Hackney Road. Dedicated to Her Royal Highness The Princess of Wales by the Editor—Margaret S Tyssen-Amherst (Wells Gardner Darton & Co, 1885).

50 *11th May* Oscar Wilde's poem '*Le Jardin des Tuileries*' ('The Tuileries Gardens') of five four-line verses was illustrated by Laura's vignette of children playing on a tree trunk. Wilde had made notes for these verses while on honeymoon in Paris a year earlier.

51 *15th May* The enormously elaborate International Inventions and Music Exhibition at South Kensington, known as 'the Inventories', had opened on 4th May. It was to repeat the success of the previous year's 'Healtheries', with the addition of a promenade as a fashionable venue in the evenings.

JUNE 1885

HUNSTANTON   2ND JUNE

My own dear Adrian, I am sitting writing outside the drawing-room on this lovely summer's day. The little garden is quite gay with flowers, laburnum & purple iris—the grass is covered with daisies & butterflies & insects are dancing about in the sunshine which is quite dazzling. The sea is so still, like a bright sheet of glass. If one shuts one's eyes to the lodging houses it all looks quite pretty. I hardly remember a more perfect day here—for it is not *too* hot, but a little wandering breeze makes it deliciously fresh. Logie has just marched out of the house—he evidently agrees with me that it is far too nice to stay indoors—so he is spending his time rolling backwards & forwards among the daisies. I have not tried that yet! I have too much consideration for the feelings of our opposite neighbours the Finches.

We have seen a good deal of the Finches since they arrived—indeed rather *too* much perhaps of *Mr* Finch for he frequently surprises The Castle by appearing at an upper window opposite, whilst we are at breakfast. We suppose him to be in an absent fit—or a brown study—but otherwise in a state of nature!! He is stiff & shy & rather formal and would probably have a fit if he knew this. Mrs Finch is a dear gentle woman, *perfectly* devoted to her pretty little girls. They come here every day & play about in the garden, & we have been drawing them. One dear little thing of six spent the morning alone with me yesterday, and we discussed fairies and birthday treats together whilst I sketched her. ...

I wonder if you would really be better pleased if I did not take things to heart. I used often to wish I did not feel so much, one way or the other, that I could have a sort of calm neutral view of life like my Aunt Kitty for instance, but that was before I knew you darling—now I would not for anything miss the joy & the gladness that I feel sometimes—and even a cloud like this—*when it has passed away only seems to draw us nearer to one another.* ... Ever your own *Laure*

WARWICK HOUSE, ALBERT ROAD, BATTERSEA   3RD JUNE

My Dearest Laura, Your long letter has been delightful to me. It was a delicious piece of word painting & I could see so plainly the lawn with Logie rolling on it & you writing to your absent lover. ... It will be a terrible feeling for me if you come back to London to find me no further on my way to certainty. Altogether my life at present consists of running after people of all sorts which is galling to a certain pride that you wot of. ... Here is a little scrap from a Latin poet called Terence which has been running in my head all day. What think you of it? *Amantium irae amoris integratio est* [Lovers' quarrels are the renewal of love].

1 *Five young Troubridges outside Knocklofty House in Ireland (1884);*
(left to right): *co-host Edward 'Bean' St Aubyn, Amy, Helen, Adrian Hope and Laura, Vi, Tom.*

2 North Runcton Hall, near King's Lynn, Norfolk, home of Daniel Gurney.
Painted by Katharine, eldest daughter of his eldest sister Elizabeth Fry, in 1878.

3 Above and 4 Right: On grandfather Daniel's death in 1880 the young Troubridges moved to this ordinary seaside house in Hunstanton but enlivened it inside with parasols and peacock feathers.

5 Below: The Hunstanton Band of first cousins (1887). Left to right, standing: *Laura Troubridge, Kat and Winny Gurney (of Runcton Rectory) and Violet Troubridge.* Seated: *Chen (another 'Runcton Rec' sister) and Amy Troubridge.*

6 Dandies of the opposite kind:
Charles Orde (left), and 8
Adrian Hope (far right).

7 Below: 'E' (Evelyn),
handsome eldest Orde daughter
and great friend of Laura's.

9 Below: The Ordes at Hopton
near Yarmouth in mid 1880s.
(Left to right): *Charlie on the*
banjo, his sisters Betty and 'E',
Laura next to Aunt Maggie,
Sybil, and Daisy with parasol.

ROYAL · NAVAL · LUNCH

GOODWOOD, 1884.

❊ MENU. ❊

ROAST BEEF. / **CORNED BEEF.**

Salmon.   Mayonnaise of Chicken
Roast Boned Capon.
Braised York Ham.   Roast Chicken.
Pigeon Pies.   Braised Ox Tongues.
Aspics of Fore Gras.   Aspics of Prawns.
Vanilla Cream, Cherry and Currant Tarts.
Greengage Tart.   Gooseberry Tart.
Raspberry and Currant Tarts.
Cherry and Currant Tarts.
Lemon Jelly.   Maraschino Jelly.
Macédoines of Fruits.
Savoy Biscuits and Philberts and Cakes.

Ices.

Pine Apple Cream.   Strawberry Cream.
Lemon Water.

Dessert.

Grapes.   Pine Apples.   Gooseberries.
Cherries.   Greengages.   Raspberries.
Plums.

10   *Goodwood, 1884, the 'very swagger' picnic lunch which restored Adrian and Laura*
after their late night dancing of the night before — until 3.30 a.m.

11 Right: Roland Le Strange of Hunstanton Hall in 1887 when he flirted outrageously with Laura, ten years his senior.

12 Below, right: Eva (née Gurney of Runcton Rectory) married widower George Cresswell in 1882 and often invited Laura and Adrian to stay in King's Lynn or at their Hunstanton holiday house.

13 Below left: Rosy Gurney (of North Runcton Hall) in 1882, a year before her marriage to Johnny Birkbeck. She was to arrange many meetings between Laura and Adrian in London.

LIEUTENANT HOPE SAVING THE POWDER MAGAZINE

14 & 15 Adrian's father, William Hope VC (inset), in the Crimean War (1855) with his volunteers, in the midst of 'eattle, covering exposed powder boxes in 'The Windmill' with wet tarpaulins.

We have a happy letter from my brother Charlie saying that the Dons at Oxford have given him his Scholarship of £60. As he is to have a school ditto of £50 this will I hope enable him to go to Oxford. Dear boy, I am so glad for his sake at this news. Also a long letter from poor John in Bechuanaland, very woeful at there being no fighting. He deplores quite gravely the extreme cowardice of the Boers which deprives him of his chance of getting on. ...

There is a quaint Arab motto which some magazine has rediscovered this month but I have loved for years. 'This too will pass'—whenever I am all but driven wild I try to think of it. Darling I do not see how I can get down to you at all—I must see Lord Acton on Saturday (a man of much influence with the Liberals or rather with Gladstone & Granville), & Arthur Guest on Monday.[52] Will you think it is really perhaps a greater trial to me than to you. For no one can tell how much I enjoy getting down to you at Hunstanton, away from London & its detestable inhabitants. *Ma petite Laure*, believe always in the love of your—Adrian

SUNDAY, 7TH JUNE

Ma Laure chérie, I must tell you that Dilke & Chamberlain gave Gladstone to understand on Friday that they would resign if the Crimes Act be renewed for more than one year.[53] This is horrible news for me & has kept me on the rack ever since I heard it. Goldsmid has induced me to apply for the post of Secretary to the Children's Hospital in Gt Ormond St. They want a gentleman & it would not prevent my getting the Auditorship or anything else that chance might send my way. I cannot go on any longer giving my services gratis & my Father does not give me a penny as you know. I have been trying the sharpest economy for I do not want to have debts hanging round my neck. But still one has to live & that costs money. How horrid of me it is to fill my letter with these sordid details. ... I am really looking forward to your coming up to town when I hope to have, with you, a few jolly days. My Father has dined with us & has not opened his lips *once* since he came in. He eat his food having pen, ink, & paper beside him to make calculations with. I more than suspect him of having inked his beef & mustarded his paper. ... Adieu, *mon amour, je t'aime, je t'aime*—Your lover Adrian

YORK CLUB, 8 ST JAMES' SQUARE   8TH JUNE

My own dear Laura, ... I went to the Great Ormond St Hospital & my cousin Mary Hope showed me all over & introduced me to Miss Wood, the head Lady. Everything was clean & airy. ... Did you know that the Wildes have a boy? I rather pity the infant don't you? … Dearest goodbye, Your lover Adrian

Hunstanton   9th June

My own dearest, … Of the infant Wilde—I agree that it is much to be pitied—will it be swathed in artistic baby clothes—sage green bibs & tuckers I suppose, & peacock blue robes? … Ever your Laura

York Club, 8 St James' Square   10th June

My darling Love, … Yesterday I had an interview with Ld Aberdare (the Chairman of Gt Ormond St Hospital Committee). Of the Sec'ship of the Hosp. I am certain if I choose to take it. At least I think so. Arthur Guest is very anxious to make me go into the office of the Railway Co., the London & South Western of which he is Boss. So that I don't feel so very dependent on Dilke as I feared. *Petite Laure bien aimée*, Your Adrian

11th June

My Darling, Your two letters were a very delightful 'pick-me-up'. Dilke's resignation destroys his list of Candidates, so that on the appointment of the Conservative Ministry I shall have to worry a new man to get my name replaced which will need some considerable amount of running to & fro. … At the moment I stand reviewing the respective merits of Hospital & Railway Co. The first means more money now, the second may lead to better things by & by. I have been secretly wishing that—we were married. Then I should have the benefit of your cool head & judgement to help me.

The Goldsmid Ball was last night. Everything went off most brilliantly & the Cotillon leader, a Spaniard, achieved a success. I danced it with Miss Dennistoun as she is ugly, deaf and middle aged. A sort of mortification of the spirit Dearest. … By the way, Lothar de Bunsen tells me that he is determined to marry as he finds Wisbech dull for one. I fancy he is open to any eligible offer. From what he told me of his talks with Amy, she is not in a very happy frame of mind, dreading your marriage & Vi's & Helen's, wondering what will happen to her. Poor Amy, I am so very sorry for her. … I see Charlie's name down in the newspapers as having got the Henniker Scholarship at Trinity College Oxford. I feel very proud of him. Now I must say goodbye my dearest love, *ma petite Laure*, Your Adrian

HUNSTANTON   12TH JUNE

Dearest Adrian, ... I should so like to talk over the two appointments with you because even though we are not yet married, darling, I do not see why we could not discuss together what concerns us both so much. So I have used one of the only 'Woman's rights' that I care about—i.e. I have *changed my mind* and asked you by telegram to come here, although my *mémoire féroce* tells me that I said I would *not* do so again! I daresay you will not be able to get away...if it is not to be, you need not fear another disconsolate note from your *petite Laure*. We go up to London on the 23rd and arrive about 4. at Gloucester St. The first thing always is on our arrival to make hay *frantically* all about the house and stir up all the 'Gemmidge' household Gods! There are various Parian marble *bathers* under cruel glass shades & various other abominations that have to be carefully hidden, besides the large portrait of the mother 'Gemmidge' in her youth and side curls which has to be artistically draped with curtains & fans before it is possible to remain in peace in the room. If I do not help I shall be in disgrace and if you dearest are anywhere near it would be impossible to leave each other wouldn't it? After dinner the whirlwind will I hope have subsided. If you have any nice invitation that night you must accept it ... but if you are doing nothing, there I shall be, sitting on *the* balcony, resting, and thinking, and—if you come to spend the evening—well, it would be rather a nice beginning of our visit. ... Your loving *Laure*

YORK CLUB, 8 ST JAMES' SQUARE   MONDAY, 15TH JUNE

My Darling, I look back on the day we spent together yesterday with such intense pleasure. I got up to Liverpool St, left my bag there & went to see the Hospital Committee Man who assured me that he would vote for me. Then back I went for my bag & took it by Sewer to Charing X when again I left it & rushed off to the House of Lords to see Lord Napier whom I missed, on I went to St James' Place & missed him again. Then home to write a letter. Then off to Hill St to catch McIver where I found his wife there. She has arranged a party for the first Sunday in July to go to Hurlingham & spend all afternoon there & if possible dine. Will that do my sweetest love? Then I came here & wrote 5 letters with Jo sitting in front of me glowering. Now he has gone & I am free to write to you. Oh, *ma Laure* I did so love to be with you *all* again. Of course you come first but I loved being with the others too & only longed for Ernest to be there as well. My testimonials have all gone to Lord Aberdare & I do hope that Arthur Lucas (who is the Chairman of the

Hospital Management Committee) whom I saw this afternoon will get me elected on Wednesday. Now I shall have a chop & then go to 'Bitter-sea'. ...

I shut my eyes just now & kept murmuring Darling, Darling, till I saw the man opposite look nervous. My chop awaits me so ... *au revoir à bientôt*, your Adrian

HUNSTANTON   16TH JUNE

Darling Adrian, I am so glad that you made the effort to come. It was a delightful long summer day that we spent together—and the others too—I loved what you said of the visit & of them. Amy goes up to stay at Abbey Lodge on Saturday till we come to Gloucester Street. They send me messages to say they are very sorry they have no room to ask me too. However I think I am really wanted here to help to move on the Tuesday with our goods and chattels. Vi and Helen tell me they would be in despair if I left them to manage it—so this is consolation. Rosy and Johnny Birkbeck are at Runcton, the former so weak she can do nothing. Johnny has just been made a guardian of the parish of Kennington—I think it has to do with his work there. ... Goodbye my own Sweetheart, Ever yours, *Laure*

YORK CLUB, 8 ST JAMES' SQUARE   17TH JUNE

My sweet Laura, All day I have been on tenterhooks waiting to hear the results of my Sec'ship application. I went to Lucas's rooms and waited for him until 7.30 when he came in & told me that the Committee had chosen 3 names out of the lot. Myself, a man called Whitmore, & a Mr Hawkins. We are to go before the Committee on Thursday week when the final choice will be made. It really lies between me & Whitmore. Lucas said that between us there was not a pin to choose. Sir Julian with whom I have dined, is quite excited & is going to canvas personally for me. I shall ask Ld N. & E. [Napier & Ettrick], who has already recommended me to two influential Committee members, to go to Ld Aberdare himself as he has offered to do so. Then I shall go round all the Members of the Committee & try to impress them with my fitness for the post. ...

I went to see the Wynne Finch [his widow admirer]—you know I like her & she has been a true friend to me. Old Lady Galway, the sister of Lord Houghton, was there & others. We heard a lot of Tory gossip. Gladstone *fils* was offered an Earldom & W.E.G. refused his consent, so said the old ladies. Lady Galway pulled my ears for an impertinent Radical pup & then told me that if I failed to come to her party she would never speak to me again. ...

How bitter it must be for Northcote[54] to be thrust on one side by Randy Churchill. I saw Northcote in the street today. He looked so old & broken hearted that I felt sorry for him & took off my hat to the 'Conquered'. ... *Ma petite Laure, je t'aime plus que la vie, Ton* Adrian

HUNSTANTON   17TH JUNE

Dearest Adrian, I have been painting all day. I believe the old monster 'King of Prussia' (my signboard for Uncle Hay) looks rather well. I have given him a lurid blue sky background, suggestion of battle fields, and he is surrounded with *Laurel*s. Today I had a letter containing some criticisms on some drawings of mine by Kate Greenaway. I think some of it would amuse you—we have all been laughing over it—she is very gushing & complimentary about some. ... Have you had your hair cut??!! Ever your own *Laure*

19TH JUNE

My darling Adrian, Only 3 whole days now before we meet again. I think of this to keep up my spirits which have rather clouded over from several small causes. Do not laugh darling when I confide to you the greatest reason which is that I have been trying on a new frock—and *do not like it*!!!! also it's going to rain and we are going to a picnic. I have been working all the week at my signboard & now I find it impossible to finish the old wretch before I leave. I have come to the conclusion that I do not like the trade and shall not do any more. It is such coarse painting—and all the time I am longing to sketch or to paint little fairy pictures. The most flattering criticism from Kate Greenaway was on the little moonlight scene I called 'Fairy Ships'—do you remember it—she says she will never cease to regret that she did not do it herself—& that there is no a single line wrong! I suppose she did not observe the little boys' *knees*! but I remember what *you* said darling—& I know you were right. Some of the letter is really *too funny*. I should think she was first cousin to the 'British Matron'. She cannot be the original as she is an old maid, Miss K.G. I mean. ... Yours ever, Laura

BACHELORS' CLUB, 8 HAMILTON PLACE [JO'S ROOM]   20TH JUNE

My dearest Laura, Yesterday I spent in a round of visits to the Members of the Committee. The result was satisfactory as I found that neither of the other 2 Candidates had thought of doing this. I called upon a dear old bachelor, Dr Sturges, who kept me nearly an hour. I had no introduction & found him rather gruff at first, but when he shook hands with me at parting, I felt that I had made a friend of him. Nothing could have been nicer than his manner. He said that the only thing which seemed to him against my coming in an easy winner was that I was *too good for them*. Dear old thing, I was very pleased as this personal canvassing goes horribly against the grain with me. Then I saw in the afternoon a Mr Dickinson, a lawyer to whom I took a fancy, Telling him about the Dr he said 'Oh, that is my uncle'. Dickinson too was very nice & will I fancy vote for me. Altogether I saw 7 people & left cards on 2 more. Of course I had to turn up at 105 Piccadilly where I found Sir Julian quite excited about my chances. He regards me in the light of his horse running for some Stake. ...

Today the rumour is that the Liberals must come in again as Lord Salisbury cannot form a Cabinet & will not take office without a pledge that the Liberals form no factions opposition. Fancy Dilke & Chamberlain consenting to the muzzle.

(from Warwick House, Albert Road, Battersea)   [*Later*]

... Only *two whole days* now before we meet again. I am so grieved that the frock should have turned out wrong & quite sympathize with you my Laura under this annoyance for it is so vexing to feel that one's ideas have not been rightly carried into effect. ... About Thursday, I am not to go before the Committee till 4.30 but we might spend the day together if you will? I would come quite early & fetch you to look at pictures or something. Then we could lunch somewhere & after that you might, if you liked, wait at the York Club where I would join you. ... What makes you compare Kate Greenaway to the B.M. [British Matron]? Is she shocked at your nudities? Why they are too charming & tender. Though I still hold to the knee of the boy being out of drawing. How nice of K.G. to say such pretty things to you. ... Your lover, Adrian

Hunstanton   Sunday, 21st June

Darling Adie, I can imagine this canvassing must bore you. I mean it is just the sort of thing you would dislike. How lucky that the others have not thought of it—it would be so embarrassing if you all met on the doorsteps of the various Committee members! ... I *may* have to write & ask you to help us in something about our arrival. Do not laugh when I tell you we are so afraid of those horrid rough men from the streets who run after the omnibuses on the chance of helping with the luggage. We fell into their clutches one year & they were so rude & dreadful & the maids could not manage them a bit. They

would not leave till *I* had to march down & order them out of the house—&
threaten to send for a policeman instantly if they did not go—but I know they
are really thieves & I am secretly as frightened of them as anyone. Last year
we engaged a respectable man to meet us—& had no difficulties. This year
we have written for the same man—a strong sort of porter—but we have not
heard yet if he can be there to meet us. If *not* I was going to ask if you knew of
anyone you could send to defend us—but we may hear tomorrow ... Ever
your *Laure*

The episode of the 'porters' was described in Laura's published
Journals (*Life Amongst the Troubridges*)[55] for June 1883:

> 'Arrived safely at Gloucester Street with 32 packages in all and
> there had rather a *mauvais quart d'heure* [bad quarter of an
> hour]—two horrible gaunt men, clothed in rags got into the
> house and insisted on taking our luggage upstairs, then of
> course they refused to go and demanded loads of money ...'.

---

52 *3rd June* Lord Acton's widowed mother had married the 2nd Lord Granville in 1840. Arthur
Guest was then head of the London and South Western Railway.

53 *7th June* In the event, Gladstone had resigned on Friday, 5th June, at the government's
defeat over the budget amendment.

54 *17th June* Sir Stafford Northcote, leader of the opposition until the recent collapse of the
Liberal government.

55 *21st June Life Amongst the Troubridges—Journals of a Young Victorian 1873-1884* by
Laura Troubridge, edited by Jaqueline Hope-Nicholson (John Murray, 1966; reprinted, Tite
Street Press, 1999).

TOGETHER IN LONDON

23RD JUNE

TO

4TH AUGUST 1885

The London visit lasted six weeks, during which period Laura's journal entries were very scrappy owing to her hectic social life. Much of her time with Adrian was spent in walking from picture gallery to picture gallery, with many calls on friends and relations fitted in between, but the chief attraction was to go to 'the Inventories' in a party, for the afternoon or after dinner, and then to 'roam about' there on their own. Laura also managed visits to the dressmaker and frequent shopping forays to Gorringes and other shops with one or more of her sisters. Meal-times were vague and the sisters often made do with chocolate, or strawberries and cream at lunch-time if everyone they called on happened to be out. All the friends and relations would have luncheon or tea on offer to callers, provided they arrived at suitable hours. Luncheon was never served before two o'clock, which allowed for much activity to take place in the mornings, while afternoon events often lasted well into the evening and ended up with a late supper at ten o'clock.

The great day was 25th June when Adrian had his decisive interview at the Great Ormond Street Hospital for Sick Children, to give it its full name. By the following day he knew he had been elected Secretary by fifteen votes to two and that they wanted him to start work as soon as possible. Although the salary was not good—£300 a year to begin with—at least it meant he would be earning something, and there was always a chance of the promised auditorship bringing in a few more hundreds, so both Adrian and Laura felt they were one step nearer to marriage. For Adrian the great excitement was his decision to leave Warwick House, his unloved family home, for two unfurnished rooms with service in Great Ormond Street so as to be near to his new place of employment and to avoid the long journey from Battersea and back every day. Chaperons appeared to be required only for social events as they did very well without one on the occasions when Laura helped him to arrange his new rooms and they would picnic there together or, for instance, when they made an expedition by train to Richmond Park for tea and did not get home till ten-thirty 'rather tired'.

The following journal extracts give a flavour of Laura's activities during this much longed-for visit to London:

At 45 Gloucester Street,
Warwick Square

Saturday, 27th June The others off to find a Chaperon for the park. I waited for Adrian. After he came & we had talked a little we walked to Battersea to see Mrs Hope & Jessie, then to the Albert Exhibition Palace there, where we lunched together & afterwards saw the pictures. The V.C. Gallery was interesting.[56] Then home again & I changed my frock & we set off together for the Club & on to 105 Piccadilly to tea with Lady Goldsmid—I liked her very much, that is to say much more than I expected. It was nice there. I came home by myself.

11th July Went off to meet Adrian at the Goldsmids. Stayed some time looking at Sir Julian's lovely collection of snuff boxes, miniatures and watches. ... Later, to the Horse Guards where Colonel Hope met us & we saw his regiment, the London Artillery Volunteers, inspected. Vi & I spent a quiet evening together. The others were at Lords all day & Amy & Helen dined at Hampton Court with old Charley Clifford and Lady Elizabeth Townshend.[57]

16th July Colonel Hope & Adrian came to fetch us at 11.30. Went off to the Wellington Barracks to see the Camel Corps march in—from the Soudan. Found a great many friends there & the sight was very interesting.

25th July Off at 10.30 for my first lesson in oil painting which I enjoyed very much, from Miss Miller at the Boltons Studios, painted from a live model. Then to lunch with the Goldsmids, afternoon at Ranelagh [at Barnes] with Amy and friends, boated on the lake & enjoyed ourselves, dined there & drove home with the Deichmanns—on their coach.[58]

27th July Another lesson, & struggled through my first painting alone. ... Afternoon to Great Ormond St & helped with the rooms. Adrian's youngest sister Madge (now aged 12) and the old nurse there. I brought Madge here to dine with me. I liked her— she is quite a little girl. ...

At Somerhill, Tonbridge,
[with Sir Julian & Lady Goldsmid]

Monday, Bank Holiday, 3rd August A year today—or rather last night—since we two were engaged. Drove over to Penshurst, the de L'Isles were away but saw over the house & wandered about the place with Adrian. Like a curious dream to be there with him and engaged. [As already described, they met there briefly in 1883.]

And so the long summer visit to London was over, and on 4th August Laura started a round of family visits in Norfolk. The engagement correspondence then continued into its second year. What neither Laura nor Adrian envisaged was that their engagement would last for another three years before they would be able to marry.

---

56 *27th June* The Albert Exhibition Palace, then in Battersea, contained a VC Gallery with portraits by the Chevalier Desanges of all the VC-holders from the time of the Crimean War to the Indian Mutiny. These were probably commissioned by Lord Wantage who in 1900 presented the collection to the town of Wantage in Berkshire. The portraits are now dispersed to various museums or to the families concerned. The one of Adrian's father, Lt Col William Hope VC is now at the Fusiliers Museum, Tower of London.

57 *11th July* Sir Charles Clifford 4th Bt, son of Adml Sir Augustus Clifford (illegitimate son of 5th Duke of Devonshire) and Lady Elizabeth Townshend, an aunt of Laura's godmother Lady St Aubyn ('Lady Booba'), née Townshend.

58 *25th July* Hilda de Bunsen's second husband, Adolph (later Baron) von Deichmann, had a famous four-in-hand coach drawn by brown horses with black manes and tails, in which he was a familiar sight driving all over London. Hilda was the elder sister of Amy and Laura's great friend Marie de Bunsen of Abbey Lodge.

YEAR TWO 1885–86

LETTERS OF ENGAGEMENT

ADRIAN – LAURA

5TH AUGUST

TO

22ND OCTOBER 1885

YORK CLUB, 8 ST JAMES' SQUARE AFTER DINNER, 5TH AUGUST

Darling, I went to 105 (Lady Goldsmid's) & was received with open arms & sat & listened to a long rave about you which naturally I loved to hear. Then I went to see Jo who was very low as a man called Walpole has been appointed Sec.y of the Naval & Military Club. ... Did you see the reference in the *World* to my Father? I wonder what it means. ... Your Adrian.

The paragraph in the *World* of 5th August 1885, in connection with the Colonel's gun read most plausibly:

> 'That clever enthusiast, Colonel Hope, V.C., has at last induced the Government to look with some favour on his invention, "the gun of the future." By an ingenious contrivance in the chamber of the gun he is able to distribute the strain caused by the exploded gunpowder to such an extent that charges may be used in guns of various sizes of six times the strength of those now in use, thus increasing the velocity, penetration, and range to an enormous extent. Colonel Hope's gun weighs 7½ tons, but it is to fire the same weight of powder as our 38-ton guns.'

SCULTHORPE RECTORY, NR FAKENHAM 6TH AUGUST
[WITH UNCLE HERB & AUNT BACHE JONES]

My darling, Julian Orde and Alice [newly-married] came yesterday. They are *so happy* and do not seem at all to mind the vagueness of the £.s.d. prospects. ... I *do* miss you sadly darling & feel that work is the best thing for me. Indeed for *us both* and the only thing that will help to pass the time till you come to see me again. Now letters from you are going up again in value—and I long to hear from you every single day, my darling. Ever your *Laure*

GREAT ORMOND STREET HOSPITAL, BLOOMSBURY 7TH AUGUST

My darling Laura, Your letter made me feel so bitterly jealous of Julian Orde & his bride. I just ramped about the room with envy of them. Darling I do so want you at every turn of the day & the thought of other people not *having* to wait makes me rage as do the Heathen. ... *Je t'aime toujours et passionnément,* *Ton* Adrian

Sculthorpe Rectory, nr Fakenham 7th August
[with Uncle Herb & Aunt Bache Jones]

My darling, ... I long for the Millers' presence to help me out of my painting difficulties. However I daresay it is a good thing to puzzle them out by oneself & buy one's own experience. The 15th of August is a Saturday—and also—do you remember what? [her twenty-seventh birthday]. It would be awfully nice if you could manage that Sunday at Eva's at Hunstanton where she and George [Cresswell][59] will be on holiday. Poor old Jo, I am sorry that he has failed with this appointment. There will be even less rose colour now—in the eye glass through which he takes his view of things in general. ... The past is so greedy—it swallows up all the happy times we spend together so soon—that even a few hours after we have said goodbye they all begin to fade away into a sort of dreamy unreality. Don't you find it to be so too? ... From your Laura who loves you best

Great Ormond Street Hospital, Bloomsbury 8th August

My own dear Laura, Last night I went down to 'Bitter-sea' where Charlie who has grown taller looks very overworked with dark rings under his eyes. Poor boy, he had to go through a trying leave-taking of his School where he had been 7 years & of which he has been the head boy for some time past. He had to tell the Head Master that two boys were thieves. One was proved to have taken a marked 2/6 [two shillings & sixpence] of Charlie's & the other had tremendously strong circumstantial evidence against him about some more money of Charlie's. The money was taken out of trouser pockets in the dressing tent for cricket & curiously always Charlie's money. One boy was flogged & publicly expelled & as he was a nephew of Miss Vizard who is at the Hospital in Rhyl with my Aunt Cha you may guess how all this has upset my brother to whom this boy of 16 had been recommended when he came to the school. The other boy was allowed to leave.

Tell me what you thought of Alice Orde as a bride. Is there much change about her, visible to the outward eye. Or is she the same as before? The French have a theory that you can always tell by a woman's eyes whether she is married or not. I must say that I have never been able to do so—can you? ... I do not agree with you about the Past. I think it is the 'hard cruel Present' which swallows up one's recollections. But then the future with Golden Rays gilds the outlook. *Je t'envoye un bien doux baiser, au revoir,* Adrian

YORK CLUB, 8 ST JAMES' SQUARE   SUNDAY, 9TH AUGUST

My dearest Love, I went to the Chapel Service at the Hospital yesterday afternoon. It was touching to see those children who were well enough to attend, the boys in their sailor suits, the girls in little Red jackets, white pinafores & a kind of fishwife's cap. … No more can I write for I see you too plainly before my eyes & I long to kiss those eyes of yours, my own. Au revoir, *Ma Laure*, from Adrian

SCULTHORPE RECTORY, NR FAKENHAM   SUNDAY, 9TH AUGUST
[WITH UNCLE HERB & AUNT BACHE JONES]

My darling, … As to Alice Archdale—she always was a very stolid downright unemotional little person—I did not see the slightest change in her. She always had red cheeks & a smiling face—she was always rather dull & *very* practical to talk to & not over burdened with ideas & so she remains. … I don't like the French theory you tell me of somehow—neither do I believe in it—if I did & you took me to Paris—I should always defeat them by wearing a pince-nez— or blue goggles! for it would annoy me to think of it. … Ever your own *Laure*

GREAT ORMOND STREET HOSPITAL, BLOOMSBURY   10TH AUGUST

My darling, … Blue goggles, my love, would suit you so well—you have just the kind of nose on which they would rest quietly & firmly. But why does it annoy you so that people should be able to guess that you are no longer a happy Spin.? … Goodbye, Your Adrian

12TH AUGUST

My Darling Love, … I walked down to see Stewart at the *Morning Post* & found him at work translating telegrams & preparing bits of news from the French papers for the *M.P.* It rejoices my heart to hear him say that he should not want me to stand in for him before November. Then he asked me to come to his Box for *Excelsior* after dinner. So I went & there was a very droll little Ballet before *Excelsior* began…one of the two girls dresses up in various disguises. She appears at first in a conventional peasant's dress only cut down to the waist behind & before (nearly, really) & with the tiniest apology for a skirt. As she changed her costume in the wings just in front of me I was able to 'faire des études précieuses' [make some valuable studies] on the equipment of a second Prima Ballerina. I think of reserving the details until we meet. She had such a pretty back with 3 or 4 dimples in it which really were pretty even on

148

the Stage. ... Today I have had £10 drawn from me by a Creditor whom I never meant to pay for ages & I feel very cross & angry with myself for having debts. Your Adrian

SCULTHORPE RECTORY, NR FAKENHAM   12TH AUGUST
[WITH UNCLE HERB & AUNT BACHE JONES]

Darling, Do you know you have more than 200 miles to travel for the pleasure of spending less than 24 hours with me! Oh I hope that unfortunate Cresswell Baby won't go & have another tooth or something on purpose to annoy us! Ever yours, *Laure*

    P.S. I have sent the sketch (done largely from photographs) to Lady G. but it does not do her justice I know, & told her so.

BACHELORS' CLUB, 8 HAMILTON PLACE [JO'S ROOM]   17TH AUGUST

My dearest Love, ... I fancy you are in bed & asleep tonight, having had no tiresome lover to keep you sitting up till past 2 in the morning as was the case last night & the night before. ... This morning I rushed to the Hospital where I found such a lot of letters to be opened & answered that I never stopped till my poor Clerk told me with a sigh that it was past 7 o'clock. He wants me to go away on Saturday 29th August for one month & he will then be able to have his week in October when I come back. ... Always your Adrian

NORTH RUNCTON HALL, KING'S LYNN   18TH AUGUST
[WITH UNCLE SOMMY'S ELDEST UNMARRIED DAUGHTER LILL GURNEY
AS HOSTESS]

My darling, I have been all the morning beginning my portrait of Audrey. I think it will be a success—& Uncle Sommy will probably buy it—she is very nice to draw. If you think of me, imagine a *very* industrious *Laure* in the midst of her paint & brushes—quite happy—(that is *very* nearly so) & hard at work till the poor model Audrey can *sit* no longer. ... I was glad I had not settled to stay on with Eva and George. He must be too dreadfully oppressive in his affections unrestrained even by *our* presence—which we know he sometimes seems unaware of!!! I should have felt *so* lonely but here it is not the fashion to have a lover! & so we amuse ourselves all together. My frock is waiting for me to get into it for a tennis party at Congham so I must finish. Get up lazy one! draw down the blinds & lock the door & have your bath! Goodbye, ever your *Laure*

GREAT ORMOND STREET HOSPITAL, BLOOMSBURY   18TH AUGUST

My own dear Love, ... After dinner I came back here to get my work ready for my Committee tomorrow. It is now 10.10 & I have just finished. The good ladies were awfully frightened just now when they saw a light in the office & thought the burglars had come at last to steal the contents of my Cash Box. I daresay they are marvelling at my untoward zeal for doing work at the wrong hours. ... I was very down this morning as I did not get to bed last night till 2.30. Do you think my Dear that matrimony will make us as fond of early hours as George & Eva? So sleepy Sweet & I have not got you beside me to rouse me & make me oblivious of my tiredness & of all else but the fact that your sweet mouth is there to be kissed & you to be cuddled. Goodbye, Your Adrian

NORTH RUNCTON HALL, KING'S LYNN   19TH AUGUST
[WITH LILL GURNEY AS HOSTESS]

My darling Adrian, ... I liked the tennis at Congham yesterday & played well for *me*. There were lots of friends to talk to—the only thing that rather bored me was being asked so constantly first by one—then the other—*when* we are going to be married. It really *is* rather tiresome, and everyone seems to think it is *such* a hardship to have a long engagement and I don't believe any of them are *half* so happy as *we* are darling, in spite of our cruel fate!! I really think I shall put a paragraph in the *Morning Post* to say that it is no use asking that frivolous question as we do not intend to marry just yet awhile. I have been painting *all* day and have not done good work. It is the study of Audrey & all the cousins tell me it is so like or so good but it is really *very* bad—and I long for some helpful criticism, that the Miller would give me, instead of vague admiration. ...

By the by I was told by someone (Ethel Chapman I think) yesterday that a friend of hers was going to try for the Sec'ship of the Bachelors' & that it was worth £500 a year! besides rooms & living! I remarked that it was not worth so much and also that it was not vacant. She then informed me that it soon would be—as Mr J. was *so much disliked* they were going to get rid of him— which she declared several members had told her. I should not like poor old Jo to hear these *on dits* [rumours]but it is just what you said you thought would happen. ... Goodbye my own Adie, ever your Laura

20TH AUGUST

My darling Adrian, ... human nature could stand it no longer—the bad pen *and* the thought of the cake & cocoa that were waiting for me prevailed, & I have come to finish my letter in my bedroom (for peace sake), feeling very much refreshed but I am sure that cocoa is *not* a thinning beverage, & we will not have any in our house—because it would be such a temptation to *me* & even *you* might get fat upon it!

This morning I was so disheartened about my work—Audrey looked so pretty & my painting so very much the reverse that I felt really X. If there had been a fire I would have thrown it into the flames. However, a palette knife did as well—& I rubbed it all out & began another. I have only tomorrow morning to finish it as I leave after lunch for Rosy's. *Adieu mon bien-aimé, Toujours ta Laure*

HIGH HOUSE, THORPE, NORWICH   21ST AUGUST
[WITH JOHNNY & ROSY BIRKBECK AT HIS PARENTS' HOUSE]

My dearest, Am safely arrived chez Rosy & Johnny. To be dining with those two without you to help me to talk was not very amusing. Now it is just 10 o'clock—and they have *already* disappeared—really these married cousins—and the hours they keep it is *rather* ridiculous, don't you think so? ... This house is so nice—I had quite forgotten there were so many pretty things here. The old Birkbecks are at Cromer now. Rosy is very cheery—for her—but leads quite an invalid life. ... Oh my darling—how I wish you were here. I think when I stay about alone I must always go where there are vague parties of people *unattached* for even the few hours I have been here with these two who are *in their way* devoted to each other, I have missed you more than all the week at Runcton. Ever your *Laure*

SUNDAY, 23RD AUGUST

My darling, ... Johnny is playing the piano—and something pretty for once. He is going up to London tomorrow. I am rather glad of it *entre nous* for he bores me—he is always going off into long absent fits and droning out ghastly Georgian chants like a bumble bee with a bad pain somewhere. He is a most *curious* being. I would not be his wife for anything in the world. However Rosy does not seem to mind his vagaries. She is looking much better—and I think she rather likes lying still—and being lifted about and waited upon.[60] ... Ever your love, *Laure*

SOMERHILL, TONBRIDGE
[WITH SIR JULIAN & LADY GOLDSMID]

SUNDAY, 23RD AUGUST

My dearest Laura, When I came down here yesterday and got out at Sevenoaks for the Tonbridge train, the only person who paced up & down too was a rather red-faced young man who looked as if he drank a good deal too much. When we got into the Carriage I found that he & I were the only two going in the Wagonette & we had to talk. The young man is called Alfred Thornhill & is a brother of the Conservative Whip who has just been made a Bart. I found Julian playing tennis with all his daughters, Milady in the Library with a headache & a stockbroker called Derenbourg who plays the violin divinely. … Dinner was amusing & I found myself taking a fancy to my drunken looking neighbour Thornhill. Afterwards we had music and when Milady went to bed I had some games at Billiards with Thornhill while Julian & the musical stockbroker had a quiet gamble together.

This morning my hostess took me for a drive in her pony carriage. We started at ½ past ten & drove a round of six miles to get to the other end of the town of Tonbridge without having to pass through the town which is only a mile off. We had to do this as G. is so dreadfully afraid of hurting prejudices by doing anything on a Sunday that political Adversaries might get hold of. The object of our drive was to call on a man called Hardinge[61] who plays the piano very well indeed. He was not at home but we left word that he was to come & dine. The ponies were sent home & we prepared to walk across the fields. An old woman muttered to me of drowned Girls & bodies being found but I took no heed & off we started through the pleasant fields down which flows the Medway when we saw a crowd coming along with the dead body of a poor little nurse maid who had fallen in yesterday trying to get a child's toy out of the river. It seemed so sad this sight under the summer sky & with such a lovely view all round. Milady was of course impressed & has talked of little else ever since. …

[CONTINUED]
(FROM GREAT ORMOND STREET HOSPITAL)

24TH AUGUST

… A certain Belgian by name Jamtel appeared, scented like a civet Cat & dull!! & with a look of intense weariness. Hardinge came. He is a queer compound of the Musician, Man of letters (he writeth novels) & Masher. We had some heavenly music, then I enticed my poor little hostess down to the Billiard Room & got her to play me a game & beat me. This sent her to bed happy. I have been permitted this morning to see your sketch which I think very pretty, very sympathetic, very artistic but not very like. The mouth is all wrong. Lady G. has a very ugly mouth & you have given her an amended edition. Jamtel came up with me & made his beastly French servant come first class in the same Compartment with us. I was furious & cross as 10 bears.

By the way, just before we left G. got a telegram to say that his mother who has been ill for a long time was dead. Lady G. had discussed with me the day before the question of mourning & had exulted in the idea that black suited her well. ... So you like Johnny's home. The exertion of talking for three must be peculiarly trying *to you* my darling. ... The Bachelors' shuts for its Autumn cleaning & I proposed to Jo that he should have my rooms instead of going to the York Club. He jumped at the idea. ... You talk of growing fat & indolent after your visit. Does Johnny carry you about too as well as Rosy. Oh my faithless Laura. However I am consoled by one thing. He will Break His Back. Only 5 more days now till we meet. Goodbye my own, Your Adrian

High House, Thorpe, Norwich   24th August
[with Rosy Birkbeck]

My darling, Yesterday I drove with Nita Birkbeck, Johnny's sister, to lunch at Keswick with Uncle Hay & Aunt Minnie. I did *so* enjoy my day there—we played racquets and lawn tennis all day with interludes of picking gardenias and eating apricots & grapes. Only 4 girls and 2 brothers at home—and 2 men who had come over to play. Vi (who was staying there) and I were so glad to meet, they have made her quite energetic about tennis & boating. ... Today I have been painting all day, a small study of Rosy which she is going to give Johnny on their wedding day—it is far more like than anything I have done yet—& has quite cheered me up about my portraits. It is rather nice, with her pink cheeks and pink peignoir to match, & some dark red cushions behind her. As to your dreadful idea about Johnny, I could not help laughing out loud when I read it—why he cannot even carry his *own* wife—far less me great gawk! He always has a fit of giggles and nearly lets her drop which frightens her so that now *he* looks on and grins while I pick her up from the sofa and put her in her wheel chair, helped by old Quicky who is installed here as nurse—or lady's maid, & so we procession into dinner. ...

Is that a little sarcasm, Darling, about my having to talk for 3 & finding it a peculiar exertion—if so *beware* when we meet when we are *very* near together! ... Ever your *Laure*

Great Ormond Street Hospital, Bloomsbury 25th August

My dearest, Jo is sitting here in my office cleaning his nails & scowling ever & again as I write. He guesses that this is no longer Business letters that are keeping me. I have had Lady Dorothy Nevill & her daughter here & showed them all over the Hospital. The old lady gave me a Sov. & I blushed & felt like a boy who was being tipped. ... Oh I was sad today for no letter came from my Laura. Goodbye, Your Adrian

Hopton House, Great Yarmouth 26th August
[with Aunt Maggie Orde]

Darling Adrian, I have been here about 2 hours—and I have already laughed more than all the time I was at Thorpe. Rosy asked me to come to Thurloe Square when I am in London in November & stay there for some more painting lessons if I like to. The Lindseys want us to fix a date for our visit to Uffington, and I must write to Mrs Finch to arrange our visit to Burley on the Hill, and to the Lawrence Joneses first when we leave here. You see I am really being *very* practical, not a bit Troubridgey & vague about our round of visits. The Runctoners want us to go there if we can manage it.

Tardy [Charlie Orde] is going to march from Yarmouth this aft. at the head of his Company of the Volunteers. They are to have a sort of sham fight, 50 of them & the band & I believe Hopton is to be taken by assault. Then a supper & speeches for the men here, so we have been decorating a huge barn with flags for them. Tomorrow there is a 2 days tennis tournament. ... Alas we have not let 'The Castle' by the Wash after the end of this month, so I am writing to the agent to tell him to lower the drawbridge, let down the Portcullis & thoroughly put the Castle in a state of defence & then it must take care of itself. *Toujours à toi, Laure*

Great Ormond Street Hospital, Bloomsbury 27th August

My dearest, Today is cold & I am miserable. I don't know why but I should like to feel your strong white arms round me & to cry myself to sleep on your breast. Darling, I do so love you so & the waiting seems too awful. Like a cloud between us. Tomorrow night think of me at the Pavilion, Folkestone, with my – – Aunt Cha. It sounds too absurd. I am putting her on the boat for her visit to Paris and so I can only catch the train from London which arrives at Yarmouth at 10.47 when I will drive out at once & hope your Aunt won't mind my coming at that hour & clamouring for food. ... To my own, goodbye, Your Adrian.

Nothing was recorded of the first two weeks of Adrian's month-long holiday, spent at Hopton and Runcton, but Laura picked up her journal again when they moved on to her new friends from Hunstanton, the Finches, at their 'delightful 18th century house'.

---

59 *7th Aug* One of Laura's Keswick Gurney first cousins, Constance, had married another cousin—George Cresswell—in 1878 and sadly died within six weeks. In 1882, George married yet another first cousin, Eva of the Runcton Rectory Gurneys. They lived in Lynn and Eva was very kind in constantly inviting Laura, and Adrian when he could manage it, to spend weekends with her and George there or at *their* house in Hunstanton.

60 *23rd Aug* After producing still-born twins in March 1885, Rosy Birkbeck was pregnant again and leading the life of an invalid. The following March she was to give birth to a son.

61 *23rd Aug* Hardinge is probably Charles Hardinge, grandson of Rev Sir Charles Hardinge 2nd Bt, and gt nephew of Frances Hardinge, wife of Rev Stephen Woodgate, vicar of Pembury, Kent. It was his ancestor, John Woodgate of Stonewall, who had originally bought the house Somerhill, nr Tonbridge—now the home of Sir Julian and Lady Goldsmid.

SEPTEMBER 1885

At Burley on the Hill, nr Oakham, Leicestershire [with Mrs Finch]

Sunday, 20th September After church tried to go for a walk *à deux* but Alan Finch (the stepson) would come too & lionize everything with us. It is an enormous house & the most lovely woods all round. I have a comfy very ghostly tapestried room. …

22nd September In the morning little Jasmine Finch sat to me for her portrait. She looked lovely in a little low frock & pale blue silk sash, but keeping still was simply impossible to her & so the drawing was difficult. …

23rd September A Lady Knightley arrived to stay, to speak to a meeting of the G.F.S. [Girls' Friendly Society]. Adrian & I went to tea with the children in the schoolroom & played games with them. Afterwards in the smoking-room—banjo playing, a dull dinner-party of parsons. …

24th September Adrian rifle shooting with Alan. I had 3 shots & hit the mark twice…evening very jolly playing nap & Lady Knightley came out as 'a great gambler'. …

25th September Worked at the piccy of Jasmine, and also finished the sketch from their Hoppner.

At Cranmer Hall, Fakenham, Norfolk [with Sir Lawrence & Lady Jones]

26th September Goodbye to Burley & dear Mrs Finch and all…had a long journey & arrived at Cranmer about 6. They seemed stiff after the Finches & we had such a dull evening. A Mr Mansfield *such* a duffer—an oppressively good young man—staying in the house and more coming next week.

Sunday, 27th September Lawrence & Evelyn went off early to a Sunday School and a Volunteer Parade. Mr Mansfield officiously waited for Adrian & I, so we had to walk to church *à trois* which was a horrid bore. To church again in the afternoon. Went to tea at Scully with Uncle Herb & Aunt Bache but that wretched

Mansfield would come too! so we had another walk *à trois*—a dull evening—& very long prayers.

28th September Escaped with Adrian after breakfast & walked down to the Keepers to see little Juliet, the dachshund Vi had given him. We loved her...played tennis in the afternoon, billiards afterwards. Uncle Herb & Aunt Bache dined, & two men came for shooting, a Mr Eaton and a Capt. Ward. A dull evening.

29th September The last day of our long delightful holiday together, both very sad at heart. Evelyn sent us together in the Victoria to Houghton.[62] The house is beautiful. I had not seen it for years & Adrian had never been there. Lunched together at 3. when we got home...to tea at the Rec with Uncle Willy & Aunt Amy. ... Our last evening together, alas.

GREAT ORMOND STREET HOSPITAL, BLOOMSBURY 30TH SEPTEMBER

My Sweet Sweet thing, ... Juliet is making havoc with my heart & my Clerk adores her already. Mrs Brooks [his housekeeper] has grown thin under Jo's tyranny & trembled at the sound of his name. He seems to have made a fearful impression on her, at the same time she spoke of him with great pride. ... Make up a civility to the Lady whose name rhymes with groans—to Lawrence, greeting. Your lover, Adrian

---

62 *29th Sept* Houghton Hall, King's Lynn, then seat of 4th Marquess of Cholmondeley. *See also* p363 for extract from Augustus Hare's autobiography mentioning his visit to Houghton with the Herbert Joneses, Adrian and Laura, 19th/22nd Sept 1887, and footnote 106.

OCTOBER 1885

CRANMER HALL, NR FAKENHAM, NORFOLK   1ST OCTOBER
[WITH SIR LAWRENCE & LADY JONES]

My own dearest, Today I have been indoors painting the little girl Hester. Yesterday Lawrence took me in to dinner and little Eaton flew to sit the other side of me. They both talked. In the evening Helen (who has joined the house party) & I made them play Cork grab. It had a *succés fou*—I suppose it was reaction after the dreadful solemn evening we had spent but everyone played and there were shouts of laughter all the time, especially when a great heavy loutish Mr Digby who was dining here broke through 2 chains in his frantic efforts to get the cork. I wish we had started games before—but I don't think we ourselves felt quite cheery enough—did we Sweetheart these last 2 evenings? … I have been reading Rossetti's poems, sonnets called 'The House of Life'. I think you would like them, they are all love songs. Ever your own *petite Laure*

    P.S. I miss you darling *very*, *very* much, *mes yeux te cherches constamment* [my eyes look for you all the time].

GREAT ORMOND STREET HOSPITAL, BLOOMSBURY   1ST OCTOBER

My darling *Laure*, … When I woke this morning I found Juliet sleeping curled up in my arms, and she is quite a comfort to me already. After dinner last night I had a long smoke & talk to Jo who was most amusing about his rattles with Mrs Brooks when he stayed in my lodgings. He used to lecture her on her lazyness in not drilling the maids properly & she used tearfully to promise she would try to amend her ways. The servants are certainly improved since his worritings. … I have spoken to a man about staining my floors & making my bookshelves. … Goodbye my dear Sweet *Laure*

CRANMER HALL, NR FAKENHAM, NORFOLK   2ND OCTOBER
[WITH SIR LAWRENCE & LADY JONES]

My darling, Last night we had a cheery dinner but a dull evening. Little Eaton sat on the sofa with me—and we talked theatricals, which I find he is very keen about—I mean amateur acting, & amused each other but the rest of the party were strangely silent. Whole companies of angels passed overhead during the evening—and legions of monks were born! … I have been walking about the garden with Mr Eaton and eating plums & figs—and laughing about various eccentricities here and elsewhere but I do not think you would have minded darling at all—even if you had been like Zacchaeus up aloft in the fig tree! & had heard his thinly veiled compliments, which I pretended not to see & turned a deaf ear to. ... Most of last evening L. & E. sat together hand in hand talking in whispers about their babies! I thought they might have waited till 10.30 when they retired to their V.C. or Virtuous Couch. ...

I am so glad Jo has thoroughly hustled Mrs Brooks. I hope you get your things brushed now sometimes, darling. Do the rooms look nice? Have you bought a lamp, they are so much cheaper to burn than candles. You seem to have taken dear Juliet quite to your heart. Have you exorcised her *boarders* or f– – – s yet? I hope so darling if she sleeps in your arms. ... Is not it just a year since we left Knocklofty and spent that long night in the train together, side by side? Goodbye my darling lover, ever your *Laure*

GREAT ORMOND STREET HOSPITAL, BLOOMSBURY   2ND OCTOBER

My darling Laura, Juliet has sulked all day because I have not gone out & taken her to see nice ladies who give her Partridge bones instead of nasty Dog biscuit. Eaton I felt sure was eager to take on himself the post of Consoler & Amuser. Does Helen attend Morning Prayers? Oh! if only we had played Cork grab, how I should have pounced upon Lady Jones, her knuckles. ... How does the picture get on of little Grease Spot. How have you managed to make that wretched Hester interesting except as a study of flesh tints, or have you been working at the copy of the Sir Joshua [Reynolds]? My love, *bon soir*, Adrian

3RD OCTOBER

My own dear *Laure*, About my rooms, I find that I must have a Coal box so I shall get an oak chest. It would be more useful to have a box than a scuttle for the latter holds so little that one is perpetually running short of fuel. Will you get me at Runcton ½ a dozen nice plants of ivy? Tomorrow I am going to see my Mother & dine in the bosom of my family which will give me the glooms for a year or more I fancy. ... Goodbye my sweet love, Your Adrian

NORTH RUNCTON HALL, KING'S LYNN   SUNDAY, 4TH OCTOBER
[WITH UNCLE SOMMY & AUNT KITTY GURNEY]

My *darling*, ... I finished the picture of the infant Jones before I left for here. They were delighted with it—and bought it for £3.3 [shillings]. I was glad to sell it because I could not *possibly* have kept it—there is nothing the *least* artistic about the child and my piccy was very like a coloured Christmas Number— with prize red cheeks and round blue eyes, both repeated in its coral necklace and sash. Helen was always down to prayers! & joined in the hymn that *boomed* through the house every morning. She liked Evelyn J. very much and was not offended at being treated like a stupid child. She has now gone to Aylsham to stay with Lady Jones the Dow. and her deaf and dumb daughter. It does not sound lively, does it?

I left Cranmer yesterday afternoon & sent Ann to her home as they do not care for one to bring a maid here. … Last night we sat in the library—round a large fire—it was rather comfy. Uncle Sommy made us laugh so. Having been out working all day he was nearly asleep in an armchair when he suddenly dashed up & began a wild ballet all over the room. We thought he was rather mad, but when he had quite finished he explained that he had had the cramp in his leg & was just dancing it off! All the evening I sat in a corner of the sofa and worked at some rather *old maidish* things for *you* darling ['little lace sacks of lavender'] which I will send tomorrow. They said they had never seen my work—and had no idea I *could* & I was rather chaffed. … I had a long letter from Amy from the Mount. She says that she and Lill [St Aubyn] miss me dreadfully in their talks over the fire—I am rather glad for we have always been such friends *à trois*—it is so nice to be missed, isn't it? … Tomorrow I am going into Lynn to make a sketch of the picture of 'The Fortune Teller'[63] that we did *not* see at Houghton. Ever your loving *Laure*

BACHELORS' CLUB, 8 HAMILTON PLACE SUNDAY, 4TH OCTOBER [JO'S ROOM]

My Darling, I walked across the Park to Jem Hope's stables where your poodle pup was exhibited to me by the Coachman's wife. It is a very handsome dog with a little white shirt frill showing off his black curly coat. … I dined at the Criterion where Juliet had chosen to behave like an owl & lose me & her wits. She rushed trembling from table to table & I had at last to catch her & carry her off & make her sit beside me on a chair while I had my steak. … Today I walked to Battersea at tea-time. My Mother was certainly looking well & Jessie was walking about quite bravely on her crutches. Charlie goes up on the 14th to begin his life as an Undergrad at Trinity College [Oxford]. He has large old fashioned rooms on the ground floor. John has got into Carrington's Horse. I trust that this will be a good thing for him in the long run.

… Jo has been having such a row with his Servants. As the Bachelors opens tomorrow no doubt many things want looking to. But there cannot be any reason for such violence when dealing with Servants. Were you not glad to leave the Goody atmosphere of Cranmer. Oh! Darling how glad I am that you are not so sternly good as that Bundle of all the Virtues. *Ma petite Laure bon soir, ton* Adrian

NORTH RUNCTON HALL, KING'S LYNN 6TH OCTOBER
[WITH UNCLE SOMMY & AUNT KITTY GURNEY]

My darling Adrian, ... How startling to find the Napiers [his cousins, Mrs Napier, Eliza and Francis] had gone to California. I hope poor dear Eliza does not wear the apple green dress in mid ocean. It really would not be fair on the other unfortunate passengers. ... I have painted the little people in the shell for Mary Amherst. We have arranged all about the piccy for Uncle Sommy— it is to be of Audrey, Ruth & Philly, & the old woman fortune teller copied from the original Opie picture. ... Goodbye Darling, Ever your *Laure*

GREAT ORMOND STREET HOSPITAL, BLOOMSBURY 6TH OCTOBER

My dearest Love, I am just off to the Bachelors' Club to lunch with Jo on purpose to meet the [Scott] Gattys whose sister Miss Gatty (dec'd this month, alas!) was for long Editor of *Aunt Judy*. So this is really a business meeting & not a mere frivolous lunch with Jo. ...

[CONTINUED] 5.30 P.M.

Mr Gatty,[64] who writes songs & is Rouge Dragon [a pursuivant at the Royal College of Arms], is a very nice & hideously ugly man with a pretty fat little wife possessing a lovely voice. The lunch was a great success & the Gattys both asked me to go & see them one Sunday & sup. This I accepted with some joy for I want to hear that little woman sing again. The Dragon is in face like a Gargoyle with a bad ache somewhere. Of you we talked a great deal as the Gs have your book *Little Thumb* & love it. I find a telegram from that most shifting of men 'Stewart' asking me to go to him at Sackville St at 6. tonight. I do hope he will do something certain for me at the *Morning Post*. ...

WANDERERS' CLUB, PALL MALL [CONTINUED] 10.30 P.M.

Jo came with me to Sackville St where I signalized myself by pulling out the handle of the door bell & falling back into Jo's arms. After a tender parting with him I went in & found Stewart waiting for me in his room where I remained hard at work till past 8. If they take the *Morning Post* in you will be able to admire my handiwork for all the foreign telegrams are concocted, translated and arranged by me. Also the Leader on French politics is expanded from my notes. I go there again tomorrow & hope that this time I shall get fairly into the saddle so that when Stewart leaves I may be able to do his work & draw the pay. I found that I could translate & write as fast as if I were only writing English but it has tired me very much, indeed I feel quite exhausted. This is only the excitement I fancy & tomorrow will not be so difficult for I shall feel more confident & not so afraid of breaking down.

When I came in here just now (the York Club being shut) I thought I would ask if there were any letters for me. The Club porter grinned & produced 17 to my horror. Some were dated August & were invitations & there was only one bill. … How I wish that I could rest my head on your cool white shoulder, *ma petite Laure*—Your Adrian

8TH OCTOBER

My own sweet *Laure*, After dinner yesterday I really felt too done up to write & hated the look of writing materials. Two columns of French telegrams take a lot of writing & the work has to be rattled off in such a hurry. I wrote with a pencil, first skimming through the Article & marking any passage which I think worth taking entire. Then I write a rough précis translating verbally & putting in the bit which I have marked. It is rather fun but Oh! so very exhausting. I can't think why it should be so, but it is. I begin at 6.30 and it goes on till 8.30 about. … Do you know Juliet was sick on my bed & made two messes last night in my room so today she is rather in disgrace. Tomorrow I hope to have my Divan in place & the shelf up round the alcove. What kind of matrasse would you advise? The top of the divan is to be of sacking & I thought of having a sort of matrasse made, & covered with Turkey red, to fit the whole top. Then if you will do me a Dragon or two on some more Red stuff we will cover two or three large Cushions with it. These will do for the back or to sit on whichever you please. … I am so grieved that you should have had no letter today, my Darling. Try to forgive me. Your Adrian

NORTH RUNCTON HALL, KING'S LYNN   8TH OCTOBER
[WITH UNCLE SOMMY & AUNT KITTY GURNEY]

My darling, I read every word that you had edited in the *Morning Post*—I felt so proud of you and I thought you was very very *clev* darling to be able to do it. How do you manage the German & Italian news? … You have come in for a very busy time as there is so much on the *tapis* [going on] just now in France. … My canvas came and all day till 4 o'clock I have been busy sketching in my picture. Every evening here I work making dolls' frocks—I feel like a good little girl again, but I am dressing some old wax babies to send to the Hospital for Christmas. Ever your own *Laure*

P.S. How I wish we had a telephone.

9TH OCTOBER

My own dearest Adrian, I am so glad to hear you are going to Somerhill for Sunday. I suppose Sir C. & Lady Dilke will not be there!! Did you hear what Lady Goldsmid thought of that marriage?[65] ... Today I have been painting Ruth—she sits perfectly still & looks pretty in her costume and disordered coiffure, with the most beautiful white throat & neck. ... I suppose the *mattress*—vide Nuttalls *Dictionary!* must be made at an upholsterers & stuffed with wool. I know Maple is not at all dear. If the cushions are covered with plain red Turkey twill & you tell me the size I will work something which can be put *over* them. I should love to do some vague dragons—rather vaguely embroidered on red twill which I can get here as I imagine it is the same all the world over. ...

It really would be rather nice if Stewart was to have a fit (not a *very* bad one) and you were to step into his place on the *M.P.* staff. ... I send my best love to dear kind Lady Goldsmid and those nice little girls [her eight daughters]. Ever your *Laure qui t'aime—un peu—beaucoup* ...

BACHELORS' CLUB, 8 HAMILTON PLACE   MIDNIGHT, 9TH OCTOBER (JO'S ROOM)

My dearest, Today I have seen Tom [Troubridge] in Piccadilly. He was on his way to Hythe where he has to spend a month instead of going with Amy to Scotland. Tom was very blooming but rather furious at having to go to such a dog's hole. Also he had tried to get old Egerton[66] to help him and Tom's account of their interview was very funny. He wound up a great speech by saying that he should be forced to go to India (meaning this as a sort of way at hinting at suicide at least) when old Egerton warmly shook hands with him & said 'how very nice for you'. Fancy Tom's face of *disgust* at the way of taking his last words. ... Goodbye my dearest Love, Your Adrian

GREAT ORMOND STREET HOSPITAL, BLOOMSBURY   10TH OCTOBER

My own dear Love, ... Lady G. is great on the Dilke match which enrages her though she says that she means to call on the happy pair directly she returns. I wonder if Lady D. has extracted any guarantee of faithfulness from her too amorous spouse. Or is she too much of a blue stocking to care? ... From all that Tom told me he and Amy had a very jolly time at The Mount but he seems to have got into great disgrace for desperate flirtings with Evelyn St. A [St. Aubyn]. He was too funny about her & raved of her hair, legs, & figure & then wound up in the most practical way by saying, 'And you know this is no use for of course we could only amuse ourselves, nothing serious at all'.

... Give my love to Uncle Sommy. Does he sit for the old woman—the 'Fortune Teller'? Juliet is learning to jump & can now get into or out of a Hansom quite nicely. ... Au revoir *ma Laure*, Your Adrian

SOMERHILL, TONBRIDGE   SUNDAY, 11TH OCTOBER
[WITH SIR JULIAN & LADY GOLDSMID]

My dearest Love, ... There is no one here but myself. V.G. sang & played to me & then they both went off to bed & left me to sit up & smoke by myself. Julian has been taken ill & is obliged to take care of himself. I read an illustrated edition of Keats' *Endymion* which was very nice. Poynter was the Artist & some of the pictures were fine though I could not admire his Diana. The figure was not my idea of nude feminine loveliness. Here are some cuttings from the *Pall Mall Gazette* of last night as to nude models. Would you like to have the series? ...

Julian & I had a political talk this morning. He told me that he expected a Liberal majority of 72 over Conservatives & Home Rulers combined. I have almost decided to return here tomorrow night for a Liberal meeting at Southborough as Fred Verney[67] is to come down & speak at it to meet some more of his Electors. Julian speaks too. Verney was here last week & spoke of me to them both in very friendly terms. It might be of use to meet him here & make him realize that I am *'un des amis de la maison'* [like one of the family]. If the Liberals do come in with such a majority I do think they might do something for me which would enable me to marry soon. I do long for a date to be fixed for us two to think of, dear one. ... My love to them all, Your Adrian

NORTH RUNCTON HALL, KING'S LYNN   12TH OCTOBER
[WITH UNCLE SOMMY & AUNT KITTY GURNEY]

My darling, ... The Library I have taken for my studio & it makes a capital one with a north light & no other. I have my easel in the bow, the fireside end of the room. Today I worked from 10. to 5. with half an hour for lunch. I had to get on with the picture as tomorrow I am going to spend the whole day painting at it from the original 'Fortune Teller' at this Art Loan in Lynn. I don't like it because of the people—but it is the greatest help for the piccy & no one is there I hear till 2. ... Last night the cousins sang to the violin, and then the organ accompaniment. It was very pretty—so soothing & peaceful, and the music wafted all troubling thoughts from one's mind & left it in a sort of dream, when there seemed to be only you and me. ... Ever your loving fiancée, *Laure*

GREAT ORMOND STREET HOSPITAL, BLOOMSBURY   13TH OCTOBER

My own Darling, ... Our Meeting last night was very successful. Fred Verney made a capital speech which was well taken. Sir Julian & old Morley[68] made some good hits & a lot of country chaps talked nonsense. V.G. was tremendously excited & kept poking me with eager delight. The French Cook whom we had brought, at his special request, was in a wild state of enthusiasm. ... My rooms looked rather lovely when I got back. The Divan is pronounced a stunner. I do so long for you to see it, my dearest. ... Your Adrian

NORTH RUNCTON HALL, KING'S LYNN   14TH OCTOBER
[WITH UNCLE SOMMY & AUNT KITTY GURNEY]

My darling...Uncle Sommy is very excited about the Picture. Yesterday I worked at the Exhibition. It was rather shy work when people came & looked over my shoulder—I thought of the very last time I had copied a picture in that way with only strangers coming through the room! It was at *Penshurst*. I wished that history would repeat itself. At 3. Uncle Sommy came & took me to have some luncheon at the Exhibition—a cup of coffee and some jam sandwiches!! Presently Bea Gurney appeared and I shut up my painting—and we went together to see a *very* amusing show of *Live Waxworks* done by Lynnets. They made me laugh so it was quite refreshing.

A plan has been made—it is *almost* settled that I shall be in *London* having lessons from the Miller for the whole month of November—at Rosy's empty house in Thurloe Square—with the two youngest Gurney girls Audrey & Muriel & their old German Fräulein Elfrich for governess and chaperon. First there are the lessons that I am simply dying for—and when I feel so glad about it I know that *through it all* is the thought that we shall be so near each other and every Sunday darling we shall meet—at all events. Aunt Kitty has entirely made the plan—& has written to Rosy who is delighted to lend her house and servants. Aunt K. has long wanted her little girls to go for different lessons—& my lessons were an additional reason. She has been so awfully kind about it. Uncle Sommy has been against it because of the expense but she is so keen about it that I think & feel pretty certain we shall go. ... Goodbye Sweetheart, Your *Laure*

GREAT ORMOND STREET HOSPITAL, BLOOMSBURY   15TH OCTOBER

My dearest Laura, This idea of Aunt Kitty's is really splendid of her & shows that she has more originality than one would have supposed possible. Why not reap up Daisy Orde as well, that would lessen the individual expenses of housekeeping. Oh! Darling, it seems too good news to be true. … I never told you that when my Aunt came to stay in my rooms I could not get a bed for myself in the house so Juliet & I had to turn out & sleep at a Temperance Hotel in Queen Square. I *was* so uncomfy the servants had only sent over the lower half of my sleeping things. There were neither shutters nor curtains, though everything was beautifully clean, I must say. And only a thin, very thin partition divided me from the next Bed. As I put my boots outside the door, my neighbour did the same & having her own & her husband's boots could not retire so hurriedly but that I could see what a lovely girl she was. Darling, they were a newly married couple & I never slept a wink till past 3. Juliet was so shocked that she barked & growled at every sound we heard & we heard so many——sounds!!! …

Juliet is a terrible Old Maid by nature. Her love for me is tiresome for she will jump suddenly on my knee when I am writing, which makes me curse a few. Give my particular love to Aunt Kitty. I feel inclined to give 3 cheers for her when I think of the happiness we shall owe to her. Tell Uncle Sommy not to be so fearsome. Goodbye *ma petite Laure*, Adrian

16TH OCTOBER

Petite Laure, … Let me recommend you to insist on bringing the Picture to show to Miss Miller, for of course the dear Aunt will get her way or there is no more any virtue in a Hamond lip!!! Hunstanton will seem a little flat after your four months away, but you must draw steadily from Jem Hope's casts. Do make me a set of Copies from Jem's ugly naked women, putting in pretty faces.

By the way, Stewart & I are furious with the *Morning Post* Editor for *not* putting in my Article on Burmah. I hope you did not think the rubbishy one that did appear on the 15th was written by me. Borthwick (the Proprietor) is also very angry and the Editor must have passed a bad quarter of an hour about this. Stewart may go to Paris today in which case I am to be left in charge. When he does go away for his 2 months holiday it has been, I think, finally settled that I am to do his work getting his pay. So far I have done all this *pour ses beaux yeux* [—for free]. … I have had a note from little Mrs Finch who tells me that Count Mattei's medicine is really curing her deafness which much rejoices the poor little woman. ... Darling I must stop now, with a passionate longing to see you again in my heart, Your Adrian

North Runcton Hall, King's Lynn   16th October
[with Uncle Sommy & Aunt Kitty Gurney]

My darling, ... The objection to taking Daisy Orde to London is that there are so few servants left in the house and that Aunt Kitty will have to send one—if not two—with us as it is. If Wally [Gurney] & his young lady marry in the Spring we shall be almost the only fiancés left—except Dear Lill St. A. [St. Aubyn]. I had a long letter from her yesterday. Nothing has turned up for Dot Cuffe! Lill says she has heard of a couple who waited 12 years for each other & then married & lived happily ever afterwards—& this has cheered her up so much that she feels quite jovial—as they have only waited 6!!! I don't like the idea, do you? ... Ever your own *Petite Laure*

Great Ormond Street Hospital, Bloomsbury   17th October

My dearest Love, ... All these marriages make me quite wild & I long to go & rob a church or do something to get money. ... Juliet sends her love. She is sitting behind me on my office chair with her head & paws up my back as there is positively no room for her otherwise. Goodbye my precious *Laure*, Your Adrian

North Runcton Hall, King's Lynn   Sunday, 18th October
[with Uncle Sommy & Aunt Kitty Gurney]

Darling, ... Did you get the 6d spasmodic telegram that Uncle Sommy sent to you for me? The 'Fortune Teller' Picture is all but finished. They are *very* pleased with it, which is repaying after the way I have fagged the last 10 days. I have come to the conclusion that besides what one can possibly evolve of the 'sacred fire' the next thing absolutely necessary for portrait painting is an *infinite* amount of *patience*. ... I *think* on Saturday next I will be in London, so I shall have the Sunday with you—& my first day at the *drawing* class—from life— 10. till 4. on Monday. ... Ever your *Laure*

Great Ormond Street Hospital, Bloomsbury   19th October

Ma Laure chérie, ... The 'Tanagram' has never yet reached me so I rather think Uncle Sommy must have forgotten all about it. Yesterday I dined in Battersea with my Father & Mother. He is in great spirits as I believe a Gun will really be ready to blow up the family when tried, in December. I talked to him about Houghton & he said quite gravely, 'That would do for me when my Gun has succeeded.' He also adjured me to keep 'my eye on it'. Still, if I were you, Love, I would not indulge in dreams of being the future mistress of Houghton. ... ... Saturday rings in my ears. The thought of it fills my heart, dear love of mine. Your Adrian

HUNSTANTON   19TH OCTOBER

My own darling Adrian, ... The plan is *settled*—Uncle Sommy has given his consent and is going to pay for my lessons—£5. 5 [shillings] in payment of the 'Fortune Teller'. The little girls and the old Fräulein are *delighted*. Of course we are going to live very quietly—you darling are to be our only guest! and you are to come to tea with us—and spend the evening *whenever we* wish— Aunt Kitty said no particularly. ... Darling won't it be fun, and so charming to see each other again. ... Your *Laure*

21ST OCTOBER

My darling, Last night I dreamt that poor Jo was trying to give a lecture on *White Bats* (not Rats!) and he had hundreds to show the audience—and you were so naughty & tiresome and *would* interrupt—& everybody shouted 'turn him out!' and I was *so* ashamed that I got up & whispered in your ear 'Darling, *do* be quiet', then you were and Jo had nothing more to say & everyone laughed. When I woke, it was so vivid, it made me laugh—remembering Jo's angry face!

Really your Father is too *impayable* [priceless] with his ideas for the future— well, Houghton would not be bad for *one* of our Castles—How surprised he would be if he realized how very little we think about *the* Gun with regard to our prospects. ... I see Miss Hope-Vere is engaged to the painter Millais' son. He, the son, used to be in Norfolk learning farming or something, but he was rather a failure—or very much so—I know 2 girls at whose shrine he used to worship—but I never heard any good of him. ... At Thurloe Square we have settled to have 5 o'clock tea—& then that inferior meal called high tea at 7.— as it is easiest to manage so with Audrey and Muriel. Aunt Kitty talked over all these sort of arrangements with me before I left. ... Letters will soon rather decline in Value—won't they? Ever your Laura

GREAT ORMOND STREET HOSPITAL, BLOOMSBURY   22ND OCTOBER

My Sweet Love, I have been obliged to spend all the middle of the day at Highgate [Cromwell House Convalescent Home for Sick Children, a branch of Great Ormond Street Hospital] looking at drains & talking to a builder which has so scattered my ideas that I can hardly collect them to write to you. Tonight I go to a Liberal Meeting, to hear Labby [Henry Labouchère][69] speak for Goldsmid...I have had a desperate fight with my Committee & beaten them over two points which are dear to me. *Ma Laure, je t'attends avec une impatience fiévreuse*, Your Adrian

---

63   *4th Oct* 'The Fortune Teller' group by John Opie (1761-1807) who at one time had a studio in Norwich. This painting is said to be of the Gurneys of Earlham and was on view at the Art Loan Exhibition in Lynn in 1885.

64   *6th Oct* Alfred 'Jack' Scott Gatty (1847-1919), Rouge Dragon pursuivant at the English College of Arms, and composer of operettas. His mother, Margaret Gatty née Scott (1809-73), was a successful children's writer who had originated the popular *Aunt Judy's Magazine* in 1865. Her daughter, Juliana Horatia (1841-85), married Major Alexander Ewing and as Mrs Ewing wrote many successful children's books and took over *Aunt Judy's Magazine* on her mother's death, for which she commissioned writers of the calibre of Lewis Carroll, Mrs Molesworth and F Anstey.

65   *9th Oct* Sir Charles Dilke had been married less than a week earlier to Emilia Frances née Strong whose first husband, Rev Mark Pattison, Rector of Lincoln College, Oxford, had died in 1884. She was an art historian and also interested herself in the conditions of working women. Dilke and she had been friends from before her first marriage.

66   *9th Oct* Capt Francis Philip Egerton RN, son of Gen Sir Charles Bulkeley Egerton and Charlotte Troubridge, Tom Troubridge's great aunt. Egerton, who was a trustee for the young Troubridges, seemed to resent their Gurney-orientated upbringing and there was certainly no love lost between them.

67   *11th Oct* Sir Harry 'Fred' Verney 2nd Bt, MP for North Bucks, had first married a daughter of Adrian's four-times gt uncle, Adml Sir George Hope.

68   *13th Oct* John Morley, Liberal politician, historian and biographer, late editor of *Pall Mall Gazette*.

69   *22nd Oct* 'Labby'—Henry du Pré Labouchère, MP, Liberal political leader and journalist.

TOGETHER IN LONDON

26TH OCTOBER

TO

14TH DECEMBER 1885

At last Laura achieved her desire of several weeks' training at Miss Miller's Studio, from ten till four, most weekdays, and Saturday mornings. She and Adrian resigned themselves to not meeting every evening in the week as he was so busy with his *Morning Post* work after leaving the hospital, but they corresponded frequently.

At 30 Thurloe Square, South Kensington
[Rosy Birkbeck's house]

26th October Adrian arrived at 9. bringing the 2 easels & the paints. Audrey & I set off for Miss Miller's Studio but the model who had been engaged never came. The other pupils left in despair but we did other work.

27th October My first day painting, sketched the model Emma, did not much care for her as she is so ugly.

28th October Drew from a life model for the first time in my life, an ugly little woman who sat as still as a wax figure. Then Adrian took us all to the Inventions Exhibition for tea in the Chinese pavilion. Home at 9. dined & sat & talked with Adrian afterwards.

29th October Adrian's cold so bad he stayed home & we lunched together there off a grouse Jo had sent & spent the afternoon hanging up pictures.

31st October Finished my head of Emma, it is hopelessly ugly. Met Adrian for lunch at the Goldsmids, afterwards went down to Battersea to see Mrs Hope & Jessie, Adrian to dinner—no work for him tonight—Saturday—for once.

At 30 Thurloe Square, South Kensington
[Rosy Birkbeck's house]

2nd November All day at work. Did a study from the nude model[70] rather a pretty one, & felt pleased but the room was so hot I had a headache & a cold. …

10th November In the evening Adrian called for me & we went together to the Albert Palace to meet Midget [Lady Wallscourt] & George Macdonald[71]—who never appeared. We saw an Indian nautch & jugglers—& had an excellent little dinner *à deux* & enjoyed ourselves.

13th November A long day at the Studio. Thought of Vi & Helen at home preparing & prinking for the ball tonight at Sandringham. Spent a quiet Cinderella like evening tête-à-tête with old Fräulein but I like her. She is such a nice old thing.

18th November To tea with Midget. George Macdonald there, & Lincoln & Dudley Stanhope (her brothers). They all eat oysters & drank beer—instead of 5 o'clock tea. They are very cheery. Wally was out—such a mercy.

19th November Went to the Albert Palace—met Mr Jolliffe there—saw the Indian entertainment & came back to tea. Adrian had already arrived, & stayed to dinner. Both rather down as there does not seem a chance of my staying on next week.

20th November Our last day at the Studio. Afternoon went with Audrey to Abbey Lodge on the chance of the de Bunsens asking me to stay on & found they were in Germany. Adrian to dinner—our last evening in Thurloe Square.

21st November The Twinks & Fräulein all very sorry to finish the good time we have spent here. Adrian & I were sitting over the fire, rather miserable at saying Goodbye when at 3. Midget suddenly arrived with an invitation for me to stay at her old aunt Mrs Hughes' house nearby & to live with them in the day at Earls Court Road from Monday.

At 34 Abingdon Villas, Kensington
[with Mrs Hughes]

23rd November Arrived about 5, unpacked, talked to Mrs Hughes, dressed & dined at 99 Earls Court Road with Midget. Mrs Hughes thought I was too late back (midnight) & was rather X, I don't like her.

24th November To lunch at Midget's & stayed till 11. helping with her Bazaar things. Amy arrived at 8, very weary after a journey from Carstairs—the Monteiths. *So* jolly meeting again. When I got in had a row with Mrs Hughes who was awfully rude to me. I shall go.

York Club, 8 St James' Square   23rd November

My Darling, After a rather stiff day's work I had to go to the Rag [Army & Navy Club] & sit for nearly 2 hours while my Father discoursed on his past life. He announced to me his intention of making a will & appointing me his Executor. This is very proper but oh! the weariness of his oration. And he had an appointment so left with a promise to continue tomorrow. What I want to know is when he is likely to finish for as yet we have only come down as far as the year of grace 1864. So I have 21 years more of life history before me. Besides it is his intention to put me through a cross examination to ascertain my knowledge of the Lecture on the Hope Gun. Said Lecture having been put into my hands & I adjured solemnly to master its contents by tomorrow. My Father anticipates that he will die in about 3 weeks or a month. Really if it were that I am crying for I should laugh at the Grim Joke. As it is it has satisfactorily achieved the result he wanted I suppose, for I feel most miserable. How all this is to end I do not see. It is too horrible.

Poor man, I am so sorry for him all the time & yet I sit watching with fear his next word for I fear all this is only the prelude to another great fight over the Marriage Settlements of my poor Mother [a few years earlier he had already tried to borrow on these]. However as he has never made a will it is as well to humour him so far. His Affairs seem perfectly desperate by his own description of them. In appearance he seems well as usual, but evidently there is something very wrong about the prospects of the Gun. Only it is so impossible to get out of him how it really stands. I trust that tomorrow will finish it for it is quite heart-breaking & does no good. ... If I were to read this again I should probably burn it so you might do it for me. Goodnight my own, Your Adrian

24TH NOVEMBER

Darling, … I have found out one reason for my Father's gloomy state of mind. He was one of the Pall bearers at Lord Ranelagh's funeral[72] on Saturday which evidently had turned his thoughts in the direction of the Grave. I have had another fearful long harangue, at the end of which I was forced to tell him that being a very busy man I could really not afford the time which seems to be required to properly appreciate my Father's life & to really understand the principles of the Hope Gun. He took this fairly well though he resented deeply my suggestion of getting advice from a good Doctor. … But the state of his Affairs, as he explained them, is simply appalling. He has so far as I can make out run through everything he has in the world. Dearest I am filled with sadness … I must go to bed as I never slept last night. Your Adrian

99 EARL'S COURT ROAD, KENSINGTON 24TH NOVEMBER
[WITH LADY WALLSCOURT]

My darling, … I long to fly & see you & try to cheer you up a bit. I hope muchly you and your Father have got through the remaining twenty years. … I am awfully sorry he is down about the Gun for I thought it was the only trump card he had left to play. … I do hope you have been able to steer clear of another row. … Midget wants you to come here whenever you can. Tomorrow, if you can get away early, the Bazaar opens at 2 o'clock at the Kensington Town Hall, then you must stay to supper which we are all going to have together rather late. … I do want to see you badly my Sweet. Ever your own *Laure*

At 99 Earls Court Road, Kensington
[with Lady Wallscourt]

> *25th November* Midget arranged that I should stop with her & leave that old hag Mrs Hughes, thank heaven. A long day at the Bazaar—from 11. to till 9, a thick yellow fog & pouring rain so hardly anyone came, such a disappointment. Adrian did not come either.

GREAT ORMOND STREET HOSPITAL, 2.30 A.M. 26TH NOVEMBER
BLOOMSBURY

My Darling, I quite forgot the Bazaar in the excitement of the Election. Sir Julian Goldsmid has just been elected by a majority of 222. All 4 Liberal

Candidates in for St Pancras. Hurrah! I have been at work all day taking Voters to the Poll. One old man I dressed & took from his bed to vote. It has been a great fight. The scene at the declaration of the Poll was wonderful. An enormous crowd wild with joy as Liberal after Liberal was announced as Member. I was of course inside & knew the result as soon as Julian. C. Baillie looks such a duffer. Poor chap I am sorry he did not get in. But oh! I am so thankful that Julian is safe. Hurrah! Tomorrow I will try to turn up if I can. Forgive me for my silence all today. I had to be present as my personal influence has become of some value in the district which I was canvassing. I took 35 men down to poll for us. Oh! so tired *but* triumphant. The Mob was wild with joy. Good morning from Adrian.

At 99 Earls Court Road, Kensington [with Lady Wallscourt]

> *27th November* Adrian came & we sat over the fire & talked. The Liberals are creeping up—& have a majority of 20.

> *30th November* Say goodbye to Midget, and off by myself to stay with the Bill Birkbecks (Johnny's parents) at 65 Cromwell Road.
> …

65 CROMWELL ROAD, SOUTH KENSINGTON   1ST DECEMBER [MR & MRS WILLIAM BIRKBECK'S HOUSE]

Darling Adrian, The number in Mrs Birkbeck's letter that she wrote me is blotted & looks exactly like 15. I had such a hunt for the house. I was *ages* finding it in the dark & the rain. It was horrid, ringing & asking at lots of houses until I got a red book & chanced to remember the name of the man the house belonged to—meanwhile Frank who I had sent to No 15 with my luggage had simply taken it for an airing up & down Cromwell Road till he gave up in despair & went back to Earls Court Road. Wasn't it vague, but now I am safely garnered with all my goods & chattels! It is *just* 10 o'clock. Nita Birkbeck [Johnny's sister] and old Miss Fanny Hamond who are here have gone to their downys—and I am left alone. It is rather dull. …

I wonder what you are doing now. I wish I had one of those crystals to look into, that I might see you. I hope the Committee behaved nicely, Goodnight my *darling*. Ever your *Laure*

GREAT ORMOND STREET HOSPITAL, BLOOMSBURY   1ST DECEMBER

My own Darling, I did get away in time for the Wallscourt dinner & found Lincoln S[Stanhope] & his wife waiting in the Holborn Restaurant. We went in & began. Wally did not come for forty minutes & then took Lady W. into the Grill room below so we dined in two divisions. Afterwards we went on to the Lyceum where we had a box for *Olivia*[73] & Irving sent us in tea. I had found a telegram from Alfred Hodgkin asking me to go to his Box at Drury Lane. So after *Olivia* was over I rushed round to D. Lane & was in time for the last Act of *Human Nature* [a drama by Pettitt and Harris]. Being very hungry I took off Hodgkin to the Holborn & had a modest grilled bone & some of the Ardfrey Oysters & so to bed. ... Your Adrian

2ND DECEMBER

My dear Love, ... I wish that you were near me to drive away the dark thoughts. Ah! me what a sad world it is. I have been much shocked by some wretched cases of poverty which I have been enquiring into as a Member of the Charity Organization Society. Fancy a man, his wife, a daughter of 17 & four other children all living & sleeping in one room with only one bed. And this within two minutes walk of this room. One wonders that London has not been consumed like Sodom with fire from above. These poor people are paying 6/- [shillings] a week for their one room. ... A year and four months now darling since that night in Gloucester Street. Goodnight my Love, goodnight, Your Adrian

P.S. McIver got in for Torquay but Verney was beaten for Tonbridge. I do not know whether my cousin Robert [Cunninghame Graham] got in for Lanarkshire as the result has not yet been published [he was defeated].[74]

At 65 Cromwell Road, South Kensington
[Mr & Mrs William Birkbeck's house]

4th December Off to the Studio at 10. Painted till 4. & finished the study of Rosy. Afterwards to tea with Adrian—we had not met since Monday—to church together to hear Spohr's 'Last Judgement' at St Anne's, Soho. A lovely service till 10 o'clock. ...

10th December ... After dinner I went with Miss Miller to the Royal Academy when Sir F. Leighton[75] made a speech & presented Medals to the students. ...

12th December My last morning at the Studio ... after lunch meet Adrian at the York Club, to the National Gallery together ... a quiet evening, finished off dressing the dolls for the Hospital & afterwards had a delicious hot bath & stayed in for ages reading *The Arabian Nights.* ...

14th December Packed my hard worked painting things, then off with Nita Birkbeck to the British Museum where we lunched & looked at statues & mummies. Then goodbye to everyone ... and arrived at Hunstanton by the 5. train. Found them all there, & Tom & the doggies to welcome me.

HUNSTANTON   15TH DECEMBER

My own darling, ... I had rather too much of the British Museum yesterday. I suppose it was the mummies but I did feel so depressed. There is a great discussion going on about Amy's attire at the fancy ball she is going to and which I have to design – the White Cat in the fairy story who was really a Princess in disguise and had to remain a lonely pussy until her lover cut off her head. Amy is not to wear a mask but a frock of white satin and white fur and a fur cap with pussy's ears ... Cressie has been here making us all laugh. He was in an amusing mind without being too eccentric.

Rather dull this morning when Tanner woke me, and gently and almost apologetically remarked - 'I have no letter for you this morning Miss Laura.' Ever your own *Laure*

---

70 *2nd Nov* In Laura's later memoirs she wrote: 'One day I asked the pretty model what she did on her holiday and she answered: "Well, my little brother and I save up our money and buy as many English song birds as we can, then we go in a bus out into the country and walk till we come to green fields and woods, and then we open the horrid little cages and set the birds free." '

71 *2nd Nov* 'Midget' – Lady Wallscourt, née Jane H C Stanhope (fourth daughter of 7th Earl Harrington), was not getting on with her husband 'Lord Wally' who was becoming increasingly eccentric. George Macdonald had become her constant companion and was accepted as such by family and friends.

72 *24th Nov* The Irish peer, Thomas Heron Jones, 7th Viscount Ranelagh (1812-85) was buried with military honours. Like Col Hope, after service in the regular army he became a Lt Col in the Volunteers, where he commanded the 2nd South Middlesex Volunteers.

73   *1st Dec Olivia*, W G Wills's adaptation of Oliver Goldsmith's novel *The Vicar of Wakefield* (1766) with Henry Irving as 'Dr Primrose', at the Lyceum. The Gaiety then put on a 'bright travestie' of *Olivia* as *The Vicar of Wide-a-*Wakefield.

74   *2nd Dec* Adrian's first cousin, Robert Cunninghame Graham (1852-1936), known as 'Don Roberto' and 'the Uncrowned King of Scotland', had ridden with the gauchos in Argentina, travelled in Morocco disguised as an Arab sheik, and prospected—tongue-in-cheek—for gold in Spain after reading about it in a book of Pliny's. He first entered parliament as a Liberal for NW Lanarkshire (1886-92), became founder and president of the first Labour party, president of the Scottish National Party and was considered to be the first 'Socialist' in parliament long before the Socialists became a party. He was a great promoter of the eight-hour working day as well as a supporter of Home Rule for Scotland and Ireland. From 1896 until his death forty years later he was an inspired writer of short stories, essays and biographies, and as a close friend of Conrad provided background material for his *Nostromo* (1904), as well as the character for 'Saranoff' in Shaw's *Arms and the Man* (1894) and the inspiration for the latter's *Captain Brassbound's Conversion* (1901) which was based on Robert's own adventures in Morocco and his book, *Mogreb-el-Acksa* (1898).

75   *10th Dec* Sir Frederick (later Lord) Leighton RA (1830-96), President of the Royal Academy since 1878.

1885–1886

LETTERS OF ENGAGEMENT

ADRIAN—LAURA

17TH DECEMBER 1885

TO

10TH JUNE 1886

HUNSTANTON   17TH DECEMBER

My darling Adrian, I *am* glad it is settled about Christmas. I will come and meet your train on the 24th and then we will drive out to Runcton together. … I have been reading *How to be Happy Though Married.*[76] Some of it is good—& a good deal is twaddle I think. Amy hates the book & is always crabbing it much to our amusement. It is a serious book. … The black dog has rather got Brer Tom in his clutches. I suppose it is the effect of the tender passion. … Goodbye my Sweet. Keep up your heart. *Au revoir bientôt, ta Laure*

                                              18TH DECEMBER

My darling Adrian, I have had several orders for pictures already—so after Christmas I think I shall be very busy. The Castle seems full to bursting with 5 Troubridges and 4 doggies. Tom is just off to see Uncle Sommy at the Bank. I think the plot is thickening in that direction. I wish they [Tom & Sybil Legh] were 'comfortably engaged' as Cuckoo Wicksted [Aunt Kitty Gurney's youngest sister, née Hamond] expresses it. … Ever your own *Laure*

YORK CLUB, 8 ST JAMES' SQUARE   18TH DECEMBER

My dearest Laura, … Yesterday Aubrey Stanhope made me come to lunch with him & then call on his Mother in Jermyn Street. They asked me to dine & meet Olave Fitzgerald [née Stanhope] & her husband who are also stopping in the same house. We had a most merry dinner. Olave is not a bit spoilt by her marriage & we had a lot of old stories to talk of which Fitzgerald bore with great good humour. Then we all went & spent the evening in Powell's Rooms where we had music & talk. … I am so longing for Thursday to come, Your Adrian *qui t'adore*

HUNSTANTON   SUNDAY, 20TH DECEMBER

My darling, … We want to have some live waxworks at Runcton on Saturday. Will you take a part Darling? You have been cast for the character of King Solomon. Amy wishes to be the Queen of Sheba & wear a black mask to hide her laughing! & bring you gifts—peacocks & apes I suppose. It won't bore you will it dearest? I shall not allow any *wives* to appear in the scene! We have thought of a lot of eccentric characters. Have you got any of your Blue Beard costume? Would it do for Solomon's attire? … I am rather amused with what you said about Olave Fitzgerald, that 'marriage has not spoilt her'—I think it is rather crushing, as if she had had smallpox or something dreadful. Did *you* write *How to be Happy Though Married!* Amy calls it making the best of a bad bargain & she & Cressie say they are going to write another book, *How to be Happier Though Unmarried!* … Goodbye my own dearest, Ever your L.

Great Ormond Street Hospital, Bloomsbury 21st December

My darling Laura, … I went to the Simeons at Eaton Place where we had a jolly little dance & Cotillon lasting only till midnight. About 20 couples, all nice pretty Girls. Stevie Simeon & his Bride, whom I knew as Miss Childers, were there. They have married on £400 a year & seem proud of the fact. Both very happy & advising me to go & do likewise at once. How would that suit you, my Sweet? Yesterday I went to lunch with Jo and afterwards he walked down as far as the Albert Bridge with me. On the way I ran against a man who was standing in the middle of the road, a little man. He twirled round, sat on the bare cold stone & his hat flew off. The little wretch ran after me shouting Police so I faced about rather savagely, when he fled behind a smaller boy & his wife and yelled at me from across the road. Jo held me back & urged me to walk on. Hardly had we gone two paces when a small boy rushing headlong out of a shop came plumb against Jo, falling heavily on his back & staring at us. A regular Mob now pursued us & we had to take refuge in flight. Rather funny to see I think it must have been.

Well I found Battersea the same as usual, only that the Gun seems really in hand at Sheffield. Till ½ past 12 I stopped, talking to my dear Mother. … Much love to all, Your Adrian

22nd December

Darling, I went last night to see *Faust* with Charlie Orde. It was a splendid success and I quite give in about Irving. His Mephistopheles is a wonderful horrible conception of evil. Ellen Terry looks so lovely & her dresses are quite beautiful. Charlie & I both longed for you to be there my Sweet for there was food for many sketches in the tableaux & Effects produced during the Play. One man beside me wept such a lot that I almost fancy he must have had some Margaret on his conscience. Coming back from the theatre, I found my brother & Coleridge eating up their supper. Lord!! What a lot boys do eat. A whole big fowl. A tongue. Welsh Rare Bit & Mugs of Beer. Coleridge, who is 17 and weighs over 12 stone, has succeeded Charlie as Captain of the school at Bloxham. … Only one day now separates you from my arms, my only Love—Your Adrian

At North Runcton Hall, King's Lynn
[with Uncle Sommy & Aunt Kitty Gurney]

24th December Adrian arrived soon after 3. The Wicksteds—cousins of Aunt Kitty's, all the Runctoners but Tony (who is a sailor at Greenwich) & 5 of us Troubridges & Adrian—a party of 19—in the house. A dance that evening—very cheery indeed.

Christmas Day A delightful Christmas morning with lots of presents and cards & letters—everyone's plate full of them. Then to church—down the garden—after lunch singing songs & dancing. ... A Christmas dinner party & a masked revel & games, & songs from Tom till 12.

26th December ... An absurd evening's amusement. Everyone but the elders dressed up & acting waxworks. Katty (a Runcton Rec Gurney) as Showwoman.

28th December... Amy goes to the Cochranes [their gt uncle & aunt] at Quarr for 2 balls, Tom shooting with the Masons at Swaffham, Vi & Helen off to Ketteringham to the Boileaus. Our last evening here together for a long time.

31st December ... Very busy all day helping Lill with the Christmas tree & at 4. about 50 children came. It is the first they have had since they lived here. ... A quiet evening & all too sleepy to sit up—I longed for the others as it was rather dull & lonely. ...

NORTH RUNCTON HALL, KING'S LYNN   NEW YEAR'S EVE
[WITH UNCLE SOMMY & AUNT KITTY GURNEY]

Darling Adrian, ... I shall think of you *often* tonight & I know you will be thinking of me. *Always* & for ever, your own *Laure*

GREAT ORMOND STREET HOSPITAL, BLOOMSBURY   31ST DECEMBER

A Happy New Year to you my dearest Love. May 1886 bring you as much happiness as you have given me in 1885. I am off to the Charity Organization for an hour, then I shall dine somewhere & come back here as I have a lot of work to finish up. ... At 12 o'clock I shall specially think of you & kiss your face. A.

76 *17th Dec How to be Happy Though Married* (John Murray, 1885). Although published anonymously, it was widely known that the author was Rev E J Hardy (1849-1920). He had been an assistant master at the Portora Royal School in Co Fermanagh when Oscar Wilde was a pupil there and he later married a niece of Sir William Wilde. When reviewing this book for the *Pall Mall Gazette* (18th November, 1885) Wilde called it 'a complete earthly Paradise' and its author 'the Murray of matrimony and the Baedeker of bliss'. As this phrase was frequently quoted by the publisher in his advertisements, Wilde used to remark that he should have received a royalty for it. Murrays was known at the time as the major publisher of English guidebooks while the German publisher, Baedeker, originated the famous series of travel guidebooks of that name. (Cf *The Annotated Oscar Wilde*, edited, with introductions & annotations by H Montgomery Hyde, 1982.)

JANUARY 1886

GREAT ORMOND STREET HOSPITAL, BLOOMSBURY 1ST JANUARY

My darling Laura, Last night I was here till after 10. trying to get abreast of the work which had poured in on me. Elsie Hope is ill again & kept on her back all day. It is the same kind of case as Rosy's [a difficult pregnancy]. Just as I was beginning to write to you in came Mr Lucas (my Hospital Management Committee Chairman) to tell me that he was off to Vienna & did not know when he should be back again, so I had to rush into a lot of details & get sanction for an extra Clerk and all kinds of things which have fairly driven out of my head all that I would write to you. My eyes are so tired that I cannot go on by gas light, so goodnight, Your Adrian.

KING STREET, LYNN NEW YEAR'S DAY
[WITH GEORGE & EVA CRESSWELL]

My darling, ... Presently we are going off to a little Cinderella dance for children as well as grown-ups chez Partridge. I have promised Aunt Kitty to see that Philly (aged 9) does not eat more than 6 ices or devote himself too seriously to the champagne. Last night I went off in solitary state to the East Room (my bedroom) where I sat by the fire all alone—and thought and consoled myself with chocolate—and—photographs and wished for the others, and wished for————you ... *Toujours à toi, ta Petite Laure*

HUNSTANTON 3RD JANUARY

My darling Adrian, ... My visit to Eva's was not particularly amusing. The little dance was ghastly as I expected—an assembly of the *crème de la crème* of Lynnets all abominably dressed & talking boring & extremely local small talk. I thought with a shudder how you had often wished *we* lived in Lynn—and if we could ever become so deteriorated as to *enjoy* such festivities. ... By the way, Vi tells me that Bea Gurney appeared at the ball at Ketteringham decked in spoils—or rather offerings sent her by a certain admirer of hers and he also sent a lovely screen for her bedroom at Keswick! I wish you would tell me in your next letter if it is true that Claude Montefiore is going to become a Rabbi himself—and can therefore never marry which is the yarn that the Keswicks have got hold of & believe in. Therefore the gifts are supposed to be offered entirely in a platonic spirit and the letters he writes also! ... Ever your own *Laure*

Great Ormond Street Hospital, Bloomsbury   5th January

My dearest, ... On my return to my Rooms after dining with Jem & Elsie in her bedroom, I found the most magnificent lamp, a big Brass Egg on a stand with a mitrailleuse burner. All this from Jo. The Lamp sheds a most brilliant light over everything & is as good as two Gas lamps. ... Today I have spent in the City delivering my Petitions to the Clerks of the City Companies & coming back here to find as many as 43 letters to be written. ... Your Adrian

At Necton Hall, Swaffham
[with Harvey & Jenny Mason]

5th Janaury The garden is so pretty with woods full of evergreens and quaint temples, statues and summer houses rather moss grown and ruinous. The children's party began at 4 o'clock— about 70 people in all—rather too many seedy looking Swaffham curates and their young lady friends simply bounders. The children evidently loved it & danced hard till 8 o'clock. ...

6th Janaury Made sketches of the little boy Humphrey, aged 2— like a Frohlich child [the Danish artist Lorenz Frohlich, 1820-1908]—with yellow curls all over his head and a frock & fat legs in white socks, a very pretty face. ... After tea played romping games with all the children, but the fact is games are *far* more amusing played by grown-up people—what L.B. would call the *Elder* children. ...

7th Janaury The old Orangery is delightful. They have some statues and antiquities there amongst the trees, and Harvey with doubtful modesty has adorned Bacchus & Mercury with *muslin sashes*—the effect is utterly ridiculous. He has not been so considerate to the Venus etc. who peep out from amongst the orange trees in an unabashed sort of way that would be death to the 'British Matron'. ...

Necton Hall, Swaffham   6th January
[with Harvey & Jenny Mason]

My darling Adrian, Jenny Mason is our cousin[77] in the same way as the Leghs, her mother was a sister of Mrs Legh's. She has been talking about the Legh girls much to our amusement—but has never evidently heard the slightest rumour about Tom [Troubridge] & Syb Legh. ... The dance yesterday was rather fun in a romping sort of way. About 70 people—I was asked to dance by several *plucky* little boys but the country dances & Lancers went the best. There was one very ugly little man who *Bostoned* quite happily & wore yellow dog skin gloves—sewn with black. I watched him with quiet amusement when a halo of interest suddenly shone over him, for we were told he was a sailor just come back from China. So Vi & I made acquaintance with him and find he knew the dear Rough Seaman well and had lived for a time on the *Agamemnon*. Of course he raved about Ernest—but said he looked about 30! with long black mutton chop whiskers—and *very* grey hair (he is only 23). They will have to be quickly reaped off when he comes home again. ... Goodbye my dearest one, *toujours ta Laure*

HUNSTANTON   7TH JANUARY

My dearest, ... We travelled to Lynn with old Tony Hamond—on his way to London. He offered to take me up with him & urged me to come. He said he would take great care of me & that he had lots of money—Darling how would you have liked that! I think he is rather a *naughty old boy* don't you? He looked very fat and jolly in a huge fur coat. ... I found Kingsley's *Water Babies* had arrived here when I got back but I don't care for the piccys much [by Linley Sambourne]—they are not nearly so pretty as Noel Paton's[78] in the old Ed. [1869] so I am going to change it for other books. Ever your very loving Laura

P.S. I was so taken up with sealing my letter to you yesterday that I never put *any* address! It was fortunately found so in the bag & brought in solemnly by the Butler on a tray in the middle of the party and I had to claim it, so everyone who knew me laughed, & I knew they guessed it was for you. Wasn't it horrid, but I think you would have laughed at me too –

GREAT ORMOND STREET HOSPITAL, BLOOMSBURY   11TH JANUARY

My darling, Your Label for the Maude Cot has come & looks very pretty indeed. I have had a worry all day. Tomorrow we have our Xmas Tree & at the last moment the Doctors wrote to say they forbade it on account of Chicken pox & that Visitors might carry away infection. Miss Wood (the Matron) came to me in a rabid state of rage as it is her special treat & she invites everybody to come. I had to summon a Committee—finally we agreed upon having the Tree & shutting visitors out of all the Wards but two. ... Goodnight my dearest, Your Adrian

My dearest Love, Today I have had a meeting of the Medical Committee who are furious that the Treat was held yesterday against their wishes. I rather agree with them. Anyway there seems every chance of a mighty row. ... Goodnight dear Love, Your Adrian

HUNSTANTON   14TH JANUARY

My darling Adrian, I shall have Willy Wright's present of one of his old oak chests cleaned & rubbed up & it will do for the Studio here I daresay, & perhaps some day you will carve some panels for it, & I will design them. In fact we will do them together if we ever learn to carve anything harder than a chicken!

What a crowd of Committees you seem to be having. How lucky that the frivolous Stewart remains in England—so you have not all that newspaper work on your mind besides. What do you think of *the* Miss Goldsmid engagement to Mr Charlie Bethune? Fancy being tied to such a dull woman for life!!! I hear she has left the Synagogue. Did you like Mr Bethune? ... I am quite in love with Arnold's poems ['Indian Idylls' tr. by Sir Edwin Arnold]. ... I think of you *so often*, ever your own *Laure*

15TH JANUARY

My darling, I have sent you the 'Indian Idylls' and have marked in the index those which pleased me most—but I think if old Jo were to see a little X against 'The Saint's Temptation' he would be awfully shocked—but there are such *lovely* descriptions in it. Two things rather surprised me about these poems. One that the women should have played such important parts in the stories— and shown so much character. I thought they were always nonentities in India—as well as other oriental nations. The other thing that struck me was that of all the virtues *Truth* is what is praised the most in all these poems. Whenever a good & great man is described this point is particularly dwelt upon—it is certainly not one of their national characteristics & I should not have thought they would care a pin about it. ... Goodbye my darling one, ever your *Laure*

GRAND HOTEL, BRIGHTON   15–16TH JANUARY
[WITH JEM & ELSIE HOPE]

My dear sweet thing, Jem & I went for a little walk before dinner & already the air revived us to the point of making us quite ready for a ¼ to 7 table d'hôte. … Darling, when I am with Jem & Elsie I feel our separation worst of all. The sight of these 2 & then their constant advice to marry, even if we have to live in lodgings, is irritating. … Brighton seems full of pretty girls & of course the inevitably newly married Couple dined next to us—such a pretty girl! But the Bridegroom was bald & no lovely. Oh! the next morning he did look such a wreck that at once I swore to myself a little vow as to breakfast in the solitude of one's Chamber being the correct thing. … Goodbye my dearest love, Your Adrian

HUNSTANTON   SUNDAY, 17TH JANUARY

My darling Adrian, … Last night I read some old love letters, they were 30 years old—from my mother to my father during the few weeks they were engaged. It was odd, but one or two might have been written by me. … Also a letter of introduction turned up from Lord Napier for your father to give to mine, praising him (Col. H.) tremendously. It is curious that we should have it now. … Ever your *Laure*

YORK CLUB, 8 ST JAMES' SQUARE   SUNDAY NIGHT, 17TH JANUARY

My own dear Laura, I had to go to see Madame Cellini who had given a Concert for the Hospital & realized £700 for us. She had permission to name 2 Cots & now wants to have them christened by Royalty. As she lives in the wilds of Notting Hill I was furious at having to go but found a nice old lady who was very pleasant indeed. I went on to see Lady Wally & found George Macdonald, of course. He soon bolted & I had a long talk with her. Wally seems to be worse than ever. She looked better but was very hard in her expressions about him. … Did I never tell you of Charlie Bethune's Engagement? I meant to do so & of his going about Brighton in a Bath Chair with his Fiancée *walking* beside him, because, as he said, it was more exhausting to make love than to be made love to. I wonder how a certain Arrangement of Charlie's has been brought to an end? As for Miss G[Goldsmid], she gets what she deserves. I have a hearty contempt for her & cannot help thinking that even Charlie Bethune might have done better. I did know him, he is the brother-in-law of John Hope-Wallace. …

I love 'The Saint's Temptation' for its beauty of description—women have always held a very high position in India whenever they have been at all above the average of the Hareem Slave. Though kept apart by custom they have never been in the position of the Turkish women, merely Slaves to the sensual appetites of their Masters. As for the Oriental love for truth, that is one of the reasons of our hold on them. For they admire Truth as an abstract idea. We practise it as far as we can. This they have not the strength to do. ... *Ma petite Laure, je t'aime tellement*, Your Adrian

28 Great Ormond Street   After dinner, 19th January

My dearest, Yesterday I was in my office till 8. when I came back here to dine & after I had about 50 cheques to prepare & sign. Today I have just had a very heavy Com. with Ld Aberdare in the chair. They did a lot of work & sat till 7. which was very virtuous of them. I made them a long speech on the heaviness of my work & wound up by asking for a Sub Committee to go into & report on the work of the office, which was very well received & my request granted at once. The Doctors & Miss Wood are not on speaking terms & I fancy she will resign which would not appal me much. ...

Your account of Tom is very cheering. I really think old Legh might chance the effect on Egerton's mind and authorize the Engagement to Sybil.[79] My own darling Laura Goodnight, Your Adrian

York Club, 8 St James' Square   Sunday, 24th January

My darling, ... Yesterday I had that pilgrimage to Bitter-sea which it required all Van Beers' oddity (again at the Salon Parisien) to help me shake off. Really Van Beers is too mad. There are Masks of Japanese Devils on the Wall & you stoop & having put your eye to the eyehole of a mask you see a Man who, having cut off his own head is flourishing it about—or the face of a girl before & after death. His other pictures are not as good as last year. I miss with regret all those pretty legs & stockings. There is one very large nude picture of a girl lying full length on a great white-rug-covered-sofa with her clothes in a heap in the foreground, which is just a naked girl with naughty eyes who has evidently torn off all her clothes & is now saying 'paint me this pretty body quick, before I get cold' & then 'come & kiss me'. ... Goodnight, Your Adrian

28 Great Ormond Street   Late at night, 27th January

My Darling, ... The whole Hospital is upside down and even I have got into a furious quarrel with my Committee. So serious was this row that on Monday night I all but resigned. They think that I apply for help in order to hide my own laziness & we have had warm words upon the matter. But it has now cooled over & I think will heal up.[80] ... Eva has written me such a dear little note welcoming me down to King St. on Saturday week, but I much fear that I shall have to come to town on Sunday night.

The excitement about the new Ministry is great. I hear that Hartington[81] has abandoned Gladstone. Goldsmid is back from holidaying abroad in the nick of time. ... Goodnight my dear Love, Your Adrian

HUNSTANTON   28TH JANUARY

Darling Adrian, ... It makes me perfectly furious to think of *you* being accused of laziness...I cannot tell you all the same how glad I am that you did not resign—'*in your haste*' although I quite understand your being tempted to shake the dust off your feet and cut the whole thing! but a lot of people I am sure, would have taken a wrong impression of it all. ... With a Liberal Government I know *our* prospects brighten tremendously. ... I hope you have seen the Goldsmids by this time. I cannot help feeling when 'something better' turns up it will be from that quarter. I *am* getting *so* worldly! Goodbye dearest, ever your *Laure*

29TH JANUARY

Darling Adrian, ... Mrs Birkbeck writes & offers me £5 for the study of Rosy—in the hat and green feathers, which I shall certainly accept. I see Dilke is mentioned for the new Cabinet. Rather unfortunate that little affair of Dilke's coming on just now! I thought it was to be hushed up altogether. Goodbye *darling*—are you taking care of yourself? Do rest on Sunday & amuse yourself. Ever your *Laure*

28 GREAT ORMOND STREET, BLOOMSBURY   SUNDAY, 31ST JANUARY

My dearest Love, ... For the last fortnight I have found writing to you very difficult for my mind has been so disturbed by what I cannot help thinking the very cruel & uncalled for remarks of my Committee. It galls my pride so terribly & makes me tingle all over with shame. Only for goodness sake don't mention it for I could not bear being pitied. Even by you dearest. Let me try to forget it altogether when I am once more with you. More & More my whole world begins & ends with you, my Laura. If only we were together I should care for nothing. It is the coming back to these horrid empty rooms that takes the heart out of me. ... *Ma Laure, bonne nuit,* Your Adrian

77 *6th Jan* Jenny Mason, née Wodehouse (whose mother was a sister of 'Cousin Milly' Legh of Lyme Park) and Laura shared a gt grandfather, the 17th Earl of Errol. His daughter Lady Dulcibella Jane Hay (by his 1st wife) married Jenny's maternal grandfather, the Ven. Charles Wodehouse, archdeacon of Norfolk, and his next daughter Lady Harriet Jemima Hay (by his 2nd wife) married Laura's maternal grandfather, Daniel Gurney of Runcton, Norfolk.

78 *7th Jan* Edward Linley Sambourne (1844-1910), chief cartoonist for *Punch* magazine 1880/ 1910. Sir Joseph Noel Paton (1821-1901), painter, mainly of historical, religious, allegorical and fairy subjects.

79 *19th Jan* Tom Troubridge and Sybil Legh enjoyed a long-running flirtation that was now becoming more serious and might not meet with the approval of the Troubridges' unpopular trustee, Capt Egerton RN *See also* p167, footnote 66.

80 *27th Jan* The relevant minutes of the Hospital Management Committee noted that the books were in arrears and accounts not ready for audit, partly as a result of Adrian being new to the job but also because of additional work caused by a new method of collecting subscriptions. An assistant clerk was to be hired at fifteen shillings a week to help with detail work.

81 *27th Jan* The Prime Minister and Foreign Secretary, Lord Salisbury, had just resigned and Gladstone was to form a Liberal government. In June, 1886 Lord Hartington and certain other Liberals would vote with the opposition, resulting in the fall of Gladstone's government.

FEBRUARY 1886

HUNSTANTON   1ST FEBRUARY

My darling Adrian, ... Tonight I shall think of you dining with the Goldsmids.
I suppose it is too soon for anything to be suggested for you. This morning
when I saw in the *Morning Post* it was rumoured that Sir C.D. [Dilke] was to
have Ld Hartington's post at the War Office—in a flash of thought I had
presented you with the *very* best & most lucrative Clerkship in the Department!!
I think it came into my head the more readily—because my father managed to
get one of those appointments for my Uncle James Orde *to enable him to
marry*—and as Sir Redvers Buller has the same post at the Horse Guards as
my father had, & his interest I am sure one could count on—& if you had the
head of the War Office to back you up besides—you see there are materials
for a very nice little Castle in the air—all made up of *Ifs* & *Ands*! Do not laugh
at me darling, for these wandering thoughts help to while away dull times
here...

   Of course I have not mentioned about that odious Committee—nothing
would induce me to—only I should have liked to rage a little. ... Goodbye
darling, from your Sweetheart Laura

GREAT ORMOND STREET HOSPITAL,   8 P.M. 4TH FEBRUARY
BLOOMSBURY

My darling, I have been working away every night till past 8. ... my Committee
really deserve a little hanging. We have got the Archbishop of Canterbury to
take the Chair at our Annual Dinner which is a good thing & will I hope bring
money. ... Goodnight, my own dear love, Your Adrian

HUNSTANTON   5TH FEBRUARY

Darling Adrian, I have been *longing* to hear from you all this week. ... I have
been *longing* to write to you every day this week. I have had heaps of time and
lots of little things to say to you but as you write to me so seldom now—and
never mention my letters—or allude to anything I write, the thought has taken
possession of me that you do not care to hear from me as you used to ... my
heart has been *crying* to write to you—it cannot bear these long silences between
us. ... Au revoir, ever your love Laura

At King Street, Lynn
[with George & Eva Cresswell]

6th February ... At last Adrian came. He looks tired, thin, & overworked—but we were *very* happy. I don't think we *did* anything these 2 days—it was *so perfect* to be together.

Sunday afternoon, 7th February Adrian had some work to do, a Hospital Appeal to invent so we sat over the boudoir fire & did it together. Had to say goodbye tonight for A. had to leave at 7. tomorrow morning, alas. ...

Great Ormond Street Hospital, Bloomsbury   9th February

My Darling, ... Yesterday, after running about all morning & finding myself near Green Street I went in & corrected a proof of a circular at the Jem Hopes instead of coming here & so had lunch & got asked to dine. Off I went to the Printers & then came back to my office where I stayed till ¼ past 7. which fortunately kept me well out of the row in the streets. When I walked to Jem's house there was nothing to be seen except a few broken shop windows. But it might have been very serious if the Mob had been able to get weapons. As it was, their supply of stones was soon exhausted & London streets are so much paved with wood that there was nothing to throw which the mob could get at. It is very disgraceful of the Police & very unfortunate for the men out of work that this should have happened. ... I found Elsie getting better. All thoughts of the baby have been upset for good & all & she is recovering rapidly & will go to Algiers as soon as she can travel. ... Goodbye, Your Adrian

11th February

My darling, ... The Scotch Minister (my fellow tenant) tells me that gold watches were being sold in the streets about Drury Lane for nothing almost. The damage done by the Mob is estimated at £80,000. ... I must part from Juliet very shortly—she has been a foolish Virgin & now the sad consequences are getting very apparent. The Don Juan in question is that beastly yellow Hospital Dog. ... Goodbye my dear Love, Your Adrian

Hunstanton   12th February

My darling Adrian, ... I have been reading a Vol. of Ld Beaconsfield's letters, several are written from Deepdene staying with the Hopes—who he raves about. This was in 1840 or thereabouts. ... How I trust & pray we may spend our lives together darling before very long. I shall love to make your life happier if I may. God bless you darling, Your *Laure*

GREAT ORMOND STREET HOSPITAL, BLOOMSBURY   12TH FEBRUARY

My Darling, I dined with Elsie last night all alone (Jem had had to go out) & we talked of all sorts of queer things. The death of her baby & this last disappointment, of the character of Jem's first wife & her death. Altogether rather funereal. Elsie was very low & impressed with the notion that she had come between Jem & his future career, that now he would never do anything but live a lazy life, that she was not fitted for him etc. I did my best to cheer her up. ... Goodbye dearest, Your Adrian

13TH FEBRUARY

My darling, ... the papers today are full of the Dilke [divorce] case which is beastly enough though he has escaped as I thought he would. Give my love to everybody, Your Adrian

HUNSTANTON   ST VALENTINE'S DAY, SUNDAY, 14TH FEBRUARY

My darling Adrian, ... As to Mr Jem's '*Career*'—I think if he was at all ambitious in that way he would not have waited till he was *over 40* to begin it! [Jem is a qualified doctor but sees himself as an artist.] Besides—if he was not naturally indolent I should think he could begin *now*, if he wished to take up Politics or anything of that sort, & so far from Elsie being in the way–she supplies *all* the sinews of war–in the shape of £.s.d. ... Ever your own loving *Laure*

GREAT ORMOND STREET HOSPITAL,   SUNDAY, 14TH FEBRUARY BLOOMSBURY

My darling, I spent yesterday and today with the Jem Hopes at Oatlands Park Hotel in Weybridge, to see how their house boat is progressing. She is enormous & will be too nice for words when finished. Just like a ship & you go down a hatchway into a big Saloon with two double Sleeping Cabins off it, besides three other Cabins and a large Wine Cellar. I have undertaken to look after the Boat for Jem as he starts for Algiers with Elsie on Friday. ... Thank Tom for letting me enrol him as a Steward for the Hospital Dinner. Though it is only a week today it seems years since I fled from Lynn & you my dearest Love, From Adrian

HUNSTANTON   16TH FEBRUARY

My dearest One, ... the 3 sisters have departed for their ball—& another dance and I am left alone—a sort of 'pelican in the wilderness'! It is rather dull. Have you been able to do anything about getting your name on Chamberlain's list yet? I see such crowds of Appts in the papers every day now—but I suppose they are not really much good, only small secretaryships, etc. ... Always your *Laure*

19TH FEBRUARY

My darling Adrian, ... I am so sorry your work is no lighter—& the quarrels at the Hospital must be *odious*. I shall be glad when you can leave there altogether. ... Today & yesterday I have been drawing—another design for my 'Jaw Crackers' book, for '*Ton thé t'a t'il oté ta toux?*' [Has your tea cured your cough?] It is a little fairy picture, a green lizard with *such* a bad cough—propped up under the shade of a scarlet toadstool sipping tea out of an acorn cup, and honeysuckles growing round him & tall grass. ... Bea Gurney has just arrived to stay. Vi gave us quite a scare as she went down to meet the 1.0 train thinking Bea would arrive on it, and she never appeared again until 5 o'clock. She had been for a little walk on the beach—which had taken 4 hours! She was not in the least tired, had forgotten lunch and thought it *might* be half past two! ... Ever your own *Laure*

YORK CLUB, 8 ST JAMES SQUARE   SUNDAY, 21ST FEBRUARY

My own dearest Laura, Last night's dinner [at Lady Birkbeck's, Jo Jolliffe's sixth sister] was a regular Jolliffe gathering. The dinner was atrocious. I was so hungry when I left that I had to make Jo give me some supper afterwards. I sat beside Miss Stracey, a pretty girl with good arms but an unfurnished front to her dress. ... Today I have done nothing except go to the Goldsmids where I dined after staying all the afternoon. Hubert Jerningham & Sir Julian Pauncefote [both diplomats] came in & we discussed the Dilke business which is severely exercising London Society. Is he to be *received* or not? That is the question. He & his came into the Cyril Flowers' the other day & everyone who was there bolted. I don't think people care so much about the immorality as the cowardly spirit he has shown all through. That poor woman!! I feel so very sorry for her & I really do hope that he will not escape a punishment socially which he has escaped legally. But it is a foul subject anyway. ... The Govt is already on the split I hear, which is a bad thing for me. Goodnight dearest, Your Adrian

GREAT ORMOND STREET HOSPITAL, BLOOMSBURY   22ND FEBRUARY

My dearest, … David, Jem's black servant, turned up this morning & brushed my clothes & varnished my boots & shoes. I do trust that he will keep sober. … While I was at the Goldsmids I secured the Siamese Minister as a Steward. Really I am getting quite keen in hunting down Stewards for the Dinner. Goodbye my Sweetheart, Your Adrian

HOPTON ST MARGARET, GREAT YARMOUTH   24TH FEBRUARY [WITH AUNT MAGGIE ORDE]

My darling, … We were asked to a wedding today but it was too far off, a *pink* wedding it was to be—with a breakfast at 12 and a Meet of the hounds at 12.30 & most people *including* the bride & bridegroom were going out hunting. An odd idea, don't you think so? She is not the least a good rider & generally comes off. … Ever your *Laure*

At Hopton St Margaret – as renamed, Great Yarmouth [with Aunt Maggie Orde]

24th February … I don't see how the Goldsmids could invite Dilke to their house yet—even if they still wish to be friends with him, for surely it would offend a great many people to be asked to meet him? … The programme at the Aquarium was very long, beginning with the farce *To Oblige Benson* acted by some Yarmouth Bloaters, then 3 *tableaux vivants*, then a Statue Gallery of people whitewashed & very much draped in white calico—the whole effect *not* very classical, and winding up with a long 2-act play *Our Wife* in which poor Tardy [Charlie Orde] appeared. He had a very gorgeous costume but too many embarrassing ruffles (his sister—Evelyn—says *frilled drawers*), and he wore a wig, hundreds of little bobbing corkscrew curls to the waist, and a fierce moustache—and somehow it was all wrong. He knew his part perfectly but the heroine was too dreadful, a fat bounding frump who couldn't act in the least (fat *not* fair, and forty at least!). He had to call her *Angel* & embrace her twice!

25th February We had a vague evening of dancing & playing games—only we girls as Charlie had to go through the same performance at Yarmouth again. E. wore her new masher suit which suits her exactly—black velvet breeches & regular (swallow tail)

evening coat fitting very well, blue silk stockings & buckled pumps, white piqué waistcoat with brass buttons—& a most smashing collar & white tie, her hair powdered and done in a queue.

26th February After tea we all dressed up in the most fantastic costumes and danced in the hall.

28 GREAT ORMOND STREET [MY OWN ROOMS] 3 P.M. 26TH FEBRUARY

My darling, I have had to beat a retreat & come home for my cold is so oppressive that I cannot work. Last night about finished me—the dinner at Willis's Rooms for the new Members for St Pancras Borough of whom Sir Julian Goldsmid was one. Lord Rosebery was in the Chair and the large Hall was crammed full of people—about 400. I sat down & began to eat my dinner quietly when I vaguely glanced at the programme & saw—— I send you what I saw. [The speakers listed included the Chairman, several M.P.s, six others—and 'Adrian Hope on The Ladies'.] Imagine my horror, nearly dumb from a bad cold, surrounded with greasy electors & their fat wives. What was I to say or do. Hastily I sent for a Snuff Box & took many heavy pinches which a little cleared my voice though I gave out a chorus of such sneezes as would have driven Amy wild with rage at me. At last the awful moment came for my——? They were good enough to cheer me & I felt what I have always been secretly sure of, that I should make a good Speaker. I talked a good deal of nonsense about backing the 'Liberal Ladies' against the 'Tory Dames'. Also referring to female suffrage I supposed that, as young lawyers eat their way to the Bar, so these good Ladies would eat their way to a vote, etc. Sad trash but as I waited for them to cheer me at the proper moments, I got a good deal applauded. ... Now goodbye dearest, Your Adrian

P.S. I see they have quite adopted *my* advice as to the change of name to 'Hopton St Margaret' [from Hopton House].

HOPTON ST MARGARET, GREAT YARMOUTH 27TH FEBRUARY [WITH AUNT MAGGIE ORDE]

My very dearest Adrian, How I *should* have liked to hear your speech. I am sure it was *awfully good*—though perhaps *I* should not have liked any slighting allusions to 'Tory Dames' because, you know, I *did* refuse to join the *League* yet I am a Tory Damosel myself! ... Adieu dearest, ever your own *Laure*

P.S. By the by is not the great Gun to be fired off on the 1st. Have you heard anything about it lately from *le Colonel*?

MARCH 1886

KESWICK HALL, NORWICH   4TH MARCH
[WITH UNCLE HAY & AUNT MINNIE GURNEY]

My dearest, … We are just back from a long expedition to Thickthorn, the house all these Keswickers remove to this spring—it is rather a pretty place, with an ugly house—at present overrun with bricklayers, gardeners & all sorts of workmen. … It is really very odd that all these people should agree to treat their middle-aged father like a spoilt child. By the by I have another letter from the Colonel about his letter in the *Whitehall Review*. … Ever yours, *Laure*

The Colonel's lengthy letter in the 25th February edition of the *Whitehall Review*, headed 'An Impudent Lie', detailed most convincingly the iniquities of the Ordnance Department in importing *German* swords and bayonets to replace 'the old pattern'—necessary because of the sub-standard steel of the original ones. … 'Would any contractors have dared to supply bad steel to the Duke of Wellington's troops? And if not, why not? Because he would have hanged them if they had, and they knew it.' He revealed that because the replacements were needed in a hurry, 'the Department' was using this as an excuse to place foreign orders as they maintained British manufacturing could not fulfil the total required. One English firm wanted to use German blades because of the difficulty of getting their English blades to stand the test, yet another British firm had no such trouble for their government contract and was supplied entirely from Firths of Sheffield. What, the Colonel asked, was the *origin* of that firm's monopoly? Names were mentioned and he laid himself open to libel. Interestingly enough, he never did get sued by his victims.

GREAT ORMOND STREET HOSPITAL, BLOOMSBURY   8TH MARCH

My own Darling, … I have just taken a large dose of quinine in the hope of stopping my neuralgia…I am low as a Cat. Yesterday I dined with the Goldsmids, and the girls, to whom I was talking about your 'Jaw Crackers' book, were much delighted & they gave me a phrase for you: '*Didon dina dit on d'un dodu Dindon*' [Didon dined, they say, off a plump turkey]. Milady talked much of you to me. We discussed Matrimony under various heads & she gave me details of her own experience which were really too intimate. Really she is an odd woman or I must have some secret affinity to women for

I do get strange confidences from her & Elsie. ... I do so long to see you again after these years of absence from you. How I hate Dilke for having this spill. But for that he would have been in the Cabinet & I should have got something by this time perhaps. Ai! Ai! ... Goodbye my darling, Your Adrian

At Keswick Hall, Norwich
[with Uncle Hay & Aunt Minnie Gurney]

8th March Adrian's birthday. ... Heard of Alice Lee-Warner's engagement to Mr Woodward—the Vicar of Walsingham—just what they will all like, & it is nice to hear of it. They *say* they will wait a year before they marry—but as there is no reason for delay I would not mind betting that they do not keep to this idea. Life is too short to deliberately put off one's possible happiness for a year & they will soon find it out—that is if they really care for each other.

HUNSTANTON   10TH MARCH

My darling Adrian, I know you will be sorry for me about my poor studio—I am sending you Amy's letter that I had yesterday at Keswick to see. A *bonfire* for your birthday it seems to have been, to do honour for the day—but *rather* unkind to choose my studio for the place, and my poor piccys for the fuel. The studio looks dreadful and I have been mourning over a few shrivelled scraps of canvas that remain of the 2 burnt piccys. The flames seem to have run along the ceiling as all the beams are scorched and a piccy of Amy's right at the other end has been *consumed*. Vi ran in when the fireplace end of the room was all blazing and tore down all the piccys she could get at and threw them out of the window, and the things I liked best, till the room got so hot she had to bolt. Isn't it too vague having no fire engine—or any water supply for a hose in a place of this kind? Amy said Beeton the Carpenter who always works for me, nearly cried afterwards & kept saying: 'What will Miss Laura say—Oh dear, oh dear!' The *beautiful* bust of Psyche is decent at last! poor dear. She crowned the ancestral fireplace—and her pale face must have looked out like a martyr from among the flames as they rose around her till she fell with a crash on the floor as *jet black* as any negress—but still smiling, and strange to say not broken. I have written to ask Uncle Sommy about the Insurance—but I am afraid it is no good as it is only the Dwelling house that is mentioned in the Policy—not the premises. ... Ever my darling, your *Laure*

GREAT ORMOND STREET HOSPITAL, BLOOMSBURY   11TH MARCH

My darling Laura, What a terrible catastrophe … I grieve over the loss of your pictures which must be a horrid blow to you. … How lucky it was that the whole place was not burnt down & some of you as well. Yesterday I was too busy to write to you & tell you how I enjoyed Verbeck. Here is a work of art [a rough sketch in pencil of a padlock, with Verbeck's flourish of a signature] with which I was presented. You see it is a Padlock. Well he locked the Padlock & asked me to put it on a Stick & hold it well up in the air so—[Adrian's sketch shows the stick, horizontal, with the padlock hanging from it.]. Verbeck drew his little sketch & applied the Key to the Sketch. At this moment the Padlock fell off my stick, unlocked. There is magic for you. Goodbye my own sweet thing, Your Adrian

17TH MARCH

Ma petite Laure, … When I got down to my Mother's I found my Father was in his Bedroom with Bronchitis. The model of his gun was there & he nearly drove me mad by sitting working it up & down for hours. He had an awful take-in about the Chief Bobby's ship for on Friday night the telegrams in the Clubs stated that he had been appointed & all the members of the Rag were shaking hands with him & he was getting telegrams of congratulation, only to find in the morning that it was a 'Canard'. You may guess what a heavenly temper he had been in ever since & how he abuses Warren [Gen. Sir Charles Warren, Commissioner, Metropolitan Police 1886-88]. … Juliet's puppies are hideous—she was moderately glad to see me & evidently hates her children like anything. Goodbye *ma Laure bien aimée*, Your Adrian

18TH MARCH

My dearest Love, Here is Amy's letter which I return to you. It is most amusing, such a vivid description of the fire. Has she ever tried to write? She really ought to do so for her powers of description are so good. I wish Chamberlain's resignation was not a 'Canard' but there it is, alas! too much truth in it. … My love to all, from Adrian

19TH MARCH

My darling, … Lucas has just been here in the best of tempers which is pleasanter for me than having to fight with him. Would you like to do 3 Cot Labels at 10/- [shillings] a piece? Only you would have to do them *right away*.

I know this is rather a base insult to your Art & I only throw it out in case you thought it worth doing. A new Member of Committee lately elected, Mr John Murray, son of the Publisher, has just come in to see me. He tells me that he knows Tom & chuckled when he saw Tom's name down as a Steward. ... *Ma petite Laure, Adieu, ton* Adrian

HUNSTANTON   20TH MARCH

My *darling* Adrian, ... It is very vague about Amy going up to town as the de Bunsens' plans are as usual most weather cocky—the fascinating Blei Herbert [brother of Amy's friend Poppy] goes back to India next month for *3 years*— I do not think Amy now cares at all, which is lucky—*very*. Darling I have such a wish to see you again already—but it must be crushed. Nearly 3 months of the wretched '86 have passed—and we have only been together 2 days—Heigh ho! I told Amy what you said about her letter—she has never written anything or tried to—but was pleased and thinks of making the attempt with some short story if a good motif could be found. She wants us two to try together! ... Adieu, always your *Laure*

SUNDAY, 21ST MARCH

My darling, ... Yesterday we had more letters from the American cousins, the Wilkes, with details of family history—and now Vi & I are plunging into a *genealogical correspondence* with an old man in New York—a great authority—& quite unknown to us, which is rather fun! He is a descendant of a certain Derrick Dey who was a Dutch ancestor of ours—so that I believe he is what he would call a *kinsman*. He writes of us as 'The cousins across the ocean.' Vi has become quite energetic and has painted ever so many shields of wood with the coats of arms of all our people—some day they are to adorn the *new* fireplace in the studio. I am anxious to finish my book so I do not think I will undertake the 3 Cut Labels but Amy and Helen would like to do them. I wonder if you have been to see the Park Street house?[82] ... Always your *Laure*

YORK CLUB, 8 ST JAMES' SQUARE   SUNDAY, 21ST MARCH

My darling, Yesterday I walked to Jones Thaddeus's studio as he is back from Rome & had brought the picture of the Pope with him. It is a fine study of an old man's face & is quite the best piece of work that he has done. He had some other pictures as well, a sketch of an Eve whom I thought a rather fascinating nudity. Percy French & Mrs Maxse & Barrymore the actor with his wife, were there. We had rather fun & told stories all round to illustrate the effect of danger as bringing out cowardice or courage. ... Jo and I went to work at 66 Park Street. It is a corner house painted red. The house is too tiny for words and if you were but two it might do. You & I would be very comfy there together my darling I think [detailed sketches follow]. The Housekeeper is ready to be Cook. She does not look at all respectable. But still she may therefore be a good Cook, only I fear she will corrupt Tanner & lead her astray. ... I met Wally & Dudley Stanhope in Piccadilly, they told me that Lady Wally was gone to Ascot, so if G. Mac[donald] is still at Windsor they must be inseparable. Wally looked as if he had not had a wash for a year.[83] ... I am waiting anxiously to hear whether you think you are compressible enough to fit into 66. I long to kiss your shoulder my darling, Your Adrian

HUNSTANTON   22ND MARCH

My dearest Adrian, Thank you *so much* darling for taking such trouble to find out all we wanted to know about the house. We would only bring up 2 other maids, besides Tanner, who could be potted out next door—perhaps the 'Naughty French dressmaker' you spoke of would have a room. ... We should have to be *very* stern about frocks & not bring up more than enough for decency for there is evidently no *boxroom* and so the family arks [trunks] would have to remain in a huge cairn outside. ... If this falls through & we do not let but only *lend* the Castle I see *very* little chance of our coming up to town *en famille* this summer. ... I read the paragraph in the *World* about Thaddeus & his picture of His Holiness—praising it up to the sky. I am glad he is getting on. Aunt Bache wrote an article some months ago on Ld Nelson, bringing in his friendship for old Troubridge (our gt. grandfather)—and all that series of unpublished letters that we have. Yesterday she wrote to tell us it had been accepted by the Editor of the *Century*, that illustrated magazine.[84] She is very pleased about it. Adieu, ever your *Laure*

GREAT ORMOND STREET HOSPITAL, BLOOMSBURY   22ND MARCH

My Sweet *Laure*, ... I very much fear that 66 Park Street is an impossible dream. ... At the Goldsmid dinner, Julian was too sulky for words, with a bad throat, & never spoke all evening. She had on a wonderful bottle green peignoir trimmed with & opening over a lace petticoat. Very nice but too hot for last night which was stifling. ... On my way home I looked in at the Lyric Club &

heard some beautiful music. The new tenor Celli with the voice of an Angel, an excellent Violinist & two recitations by Clifford Harrison who is most exciting & he accompanies himself wonderfully all the while. ... My love to you all, goodbye, Your Adrian

HUNSTANTON   23RD MARCH

Darling, ... Ach! your description of Wally as one of the great unwashed—I am not much surprised she has left town although it seems a pity to go to Ascot if G.Mac[donald] is about as it will not make people more silent on the subject. ... I think Clifford Harrison recites awfully well. Charlie Orde had him once at Hopton for a visit & an entertainment when we were there. He is very *stagey* to talk to (you know he began life as an actor) but certainly clever— he also draws very well indeed. I don't know about the Lyric Club but it sounds very nice. Could we ever go together—or is it a real Club—only for the 'Lords of Creation'? Do you know I *hate* that expression. I cannot think why I wrote it unless to mortify the spirit as it is Lent. ... I shall think of you at the Childers party tonight [to which Sir Julian refused to go]. I rather envy Lady G. although I am not in the smallest degree j— — — — — but to have perhaps a lovely frock and to be taken by *you* to a party tonight would make *someone* very happy. Always your *Laure*

GREAT ORMOND STREET HOSPITAL, BLOOMSBURY   26TH MARCH

My own dear Love, ... I had to show Countess Erbach, sister of Henry of Battenberg over the Hospital which wasted my time fearfully and now I have been visited by such swarms of old women with bags coming to pay their Subs. So ugly they all are & they will talk so tremendously. ... I got pitched out of a Cab last night—& smashed my hat besides getting a shaking which was rather a bore. The horse fell & out I went. My love to you all, Your Adrian

At Hunstanton

> *26th March*... In the evening cut out a little cotton blouse, a garment for the unemployed! as I have joined the working guild for making clothes for the poor—not a very great effort as you are only supposed to make 2 a year. Began to read *Daniel Deronda*—thought it clever & not so *ponderous* as some of George Eliot's writings. It is deeply interesting—such a relief after the trash I have been reading lately.

GREAT ORMOND STREET HOSPITAL, BLOOMSBURY   27TH MARCH

My darling, I am spending my Saturday half holiday as I usually do now—I have sent off about 4000 Circulars in connection with this dinner. Fancy what my Clerks must have endured, putting on the stamps? ... Goodnight dear heart, Your Adrian

29TH MARCH

My darling Laura, Yesterday I went down to look after the boat at Weybridge & returned wet & cold in the blues about 7. A happy thought struck me to go & see [Lord] Crofton whom I found sitting over his fire. He was delighted & we sat & talked & then he played till 8.30. we then decided that we had not the courage to go out & eat so we had Bacon & Eggs & B & S! in C's rooms. After this very frugal repast we went to the Lyric together & heard some man sing Shelley's 'Goodnight'. It made me think so of you & when you last murmured those lines in my ear with your warm white arms round me. I did so long to metamorphose poor old Crofton's bald head & grey whiskers into you, love. Oscar Wilde was there, fat & greasy as ever & looking peculiarly revolting in huge white kid gloves. ... This cannot be a real answer to your dear letter for somehow it is not easy to answer here with my Clerk coming in & looking at me. Goodbye, Your Adrian

HUNSTANTON   30TH MARCH

My darling Adrian, ... Did I tell you what Uncle Sommy wrote to me about his Birkbeck *grandson*? He and Aunt Kitty went over to Thorpe to see this small person: 'At present he is *not* a beau but he may become so. He is now rather like *Johnny* [Birkbeck, his son-in-law], when he is playing a *very* difficult passage on the piano!' Cannot you imagine it, with the face all crumpled up! ... Goodbye my faithful one, always yours, *Laure*

82 *21st Mar* Laura's cousin, Tom Cochrane, had asked her brother Tom (Troubridge) to help him let his house in Park Street for the season but that if no one made an offer he promised to let the young Troubridges have it for nothing for their summer visit to London. This Tom Cochrane, son of Sir Thomas Cochrane by his second wife, Rosetta Wheeler-Cuffe, was a nephew of Laura's grandmother Anna Maria née Cochrane, wife of Adml Sir E T Troubridge 2nd Bt. *See also* p274 and footnote 93.

83 *21st Mar* Lord Wallscourt became increasingly eccentric. He would walk round his draughty castle in Ireland in the nude, with a cowbell tied round his neck as a warning to approaching housemaids to hide in the nearest cupboard.

84 *22nd Mar See* 'Unpublished Letters of Lord Nelson to Sir Thomas Troubridge', *Century* magazine, Vol XXXVII-4, p19-28 (1886).

APRIL 1886

HUNSTANTON   1ST APRIL

My dearest Adrian, Today I have been really industrious about my 'Jaw Crackers' book. Ten designs are finished and mounted on smoke grey cards which improves them very much. I want to have 12 or 14 in the set & there are still the initial letters for each—and the cover to design. ... I am very busy learning my part for the theatricals. I have 22 pages! it is rather a grind—but fortunately I can learn rather easily by heart. Charlie and E. [Orde] are coming for Sunday to rehearse *The Happy Pair* (which we are to present at Hunstanton on April 30th). Goodbye dearest one, Ever to the end your *Laure*

2ND APRIL

Darling Adrian, ... What a bore it is for Jo to be so C.D. again—is it that he wants looking after—Guardian *Angeling* as you did once or twice before for him? or is it something new. I always think his life is really rather lonely although he has so many people about him. You see he has no home—or anyone who cares *very* much about him[85]—which would make life rather joyless I think—even without the additional disenchantment of bad—uncertain health. He cannot find any enjoyment in life *by himself* and that is unfortunate as he lives alone. ... from your own loving *Laure*

GREAT ORMOND STREET HOSPITAL, BLOOMSBURY   7TH APRIL

My darling Laura, I had promised the Gs to dine with them yesterday at 7. before we all went, the Gs, myself, & Hardinge, to a Wesleyan School Room Concert (Milady would call it Westphalian!!). Of course this was all with a view of a possible Election soon. The music was not so very bad. V.G. sang twice & loved the applause. J.G. made a very wooden funny speech when the jokes all missed fire. I sat through this very tedious Concert which lasted 2 hours & ½. Not one pretty girl to look at even! ... I have a letter from Paris in which my sister tells me two things. First that she has just got an appointment teaching French & German at Cambridge at which she is delighted. She & my Aunt Annie (Cunninghame Graham) will come over & settle down there in September & Laura says some very nice things about our being able to use their house as a halfway meeting house & that she hopes now to make your acquaintance. The other thing is that Mlle Ourliac's portrait of me has just been accepted at the Salon. ... Your Adrian *qui t'adore ma bien aimée*

York Club, 8 St James' Square 15th April

Ma Laure, At 5. today I had to go down to the Charity Organization Society as I am the Chairman of Committee just now & have to sign all the cheques for Relief. Last night I dined at the Rag & found my Uncle Douglas [Cunninghame Graham] there just back from Paris. He gave a very cheery account of Aunt Annie & Laura whom he declares to be very pretty & most delightful company. I had a talk with him about a post at the Chelsea Hospital & he is going to see if he can do anything to help me in the matter. I have just heard such a nice trait of my Brother John [still a trooper in Bechuanaland]. He has sent Charlie £10.10 [shillings], all his savings I should think, to help him at Oxford. Poor dear boy, it is very good of him. On Saturday (17th) I go to the Longdens.[86] Ever your Adrian

Hunstanton 15th April

My *darling*, ... We all enjoyed our day out yesterday to the West Norfolk Hunt Steeplechases (at East Winch)—there were hundreds of people including everyone that was ever seen or *thought* of in Norfolk. The Princess [of Wales] came over—with her 3 daughters. They drove up to the Course in a huge wagonette with 4 horses driven by the most eccentric Hungarian Coachman— in a costume spangled very freely with silver buttons (about 200 down each leg!) and wearing apparently one of our favourite Spanish hats! He flourished a huge whip and uttered strange cries as they came up full gallop—I think he rather cut out the Royalties in the way of attracting attention or shared the honours with them at all events. Several people we knew were riding—and no one came to grief. Wally was there—from Runcton—he looked so handsome. La belle Lucie—his fiancée—was *not* there. ... The only people I did *not* see to talk to were Uncle Sommy & Aunt Kitty as they were riding about all day—so we did not arrange our Easter visit. It was the anniversary of their 29th wedding day & she was in tremendous spirits *for her*. Uncle Sommy had made her a present of a smart new bridle—because he said she had held the reins so long that they *must* be getting worn out! ... Adieu, ever your *Laure*

16th April

Darling Adrian, ... We have been down to look at the stage for our acting, it is 30 feet wide—and absolutely bare. It looks rather despairing. I am sending you something to look at. What do you think of this description?

'The forehead shows impulse; the eyebrows gentleness; the eyes constancy; the nose love of admiration; the lips tenderness; the chin sympathy. Venus and the moon.'

It is my character told by a physiognomist from my photograph. I am sorry my face told her nothing of my love for Art. Do 'Venus and the moon' preside over my destiny? Amy & Helen's are rather good but they tell H. her nose denotes 'interest in the opposite sex!' so you can imagine how we have teased her. Will you return this precious document. I think I shall have it printed in the corner of my visiting cards! ... Ever your *Laure*

Sunday, 18th April

Darling, ... Tomorrow is Primrose day. I shall have an aggressive buttonhole of them to wear on my journey across Norfolk. I leave here about 1. and get to Hopton at 6. almost as long as it would take me to come up to London, to kiss you, and come back again. I shall be learning my part for an evening rehearsal. Today I worked so hard and at 7. I finished my task—the design for the cover of my 'Jaw Crackers' book. I had a happy thought and designed my first one again on a thick sheet of common brown packing paper. It makes such a good ground to the fantastic letters and the bright coloured flags—and is quite new besides. The last of the 12 designs is for: 'She stood on the steps of Burgesses Fish Sauce shop welcoming him in.' I have made her a tiny mite of a fisher girl curtseying in the doorway to a very grand sort of masher among mackerel, with a proud look and a high tummy, giving her a condescending bow and wave of the fin. It *is such* a relief to have them really done, like taking off a *very* tight pair of corsets—you know the feeling, don't you? you remember it I daresay when—you know—what was it '18 inches? & the admiration of all Paris – – – '. Darling the only advantage I find in being so far away is I can be as *impertinente* as I like without fear of punishment of one sort or another. ... Ever your *Laure*

LONGHOPE, WATFORD   SUNDAY NIGHT, 18TH APRIL
[WITH SIR JAMES & LADY LONGDEN]

My dearest, I found Sir James waiting for me in the Hall, already fuming because my train was late yesterday afternoon. In the Drawing-Room were Lady L. her two girls Emmy & Ethel, the son Arthur & my red-headed pal Bobs. We all plunged into Ceylon gossip & then hurried to dress for a dinner— fat Country neighbours, And others as the play books have it. After the people had all gone old Jimmy & I sat up talking for hours. He is always so interesting to me when I can get him alone. Today the old Chief would not hear of my going to Church in the morning because he said that we had so much to talk over together. So up & down the garden we marched under an umbrella in the pouring rain while he expounded his views on Ireland. This afternoon we have been for a long wet walk all through Lord Essex's Cassiobury Woods.

The house is a red Brick Villa built by himself just 2 years ago on 4 acres of ground, with the High road in front & the Railway, a very deep cutting, behind … then the house inside is a mixture of the vilest vulgarity with some traces of better things. Every comfort carefully attended to, but—dado's with a stencilled pattern? Black & Gold frames to the mirrors in rooms when all the rest of the woodwork was nice polished pitch pine. A Settee!! in the Drawing-room & footstools to tumble over. A teeny wee Conservatory with stages for pots which reduces the standing room to no more than enough for one at a time. I have been shown over every room & had to admire even the way in which the Coal Cellar is filled from outside.

I saw Pearl for the first time since I carried her on board the Ship when we all returned from Ceylon together. Such a pretty little thing with dark eyes & fair hair. Very coquettish too, she was with me. The eldest daughter Emmy is tall, slim, with rather projecting teeth & wears eye glasses. Not pretty & as I never knew her in Ceylon, she being at school, very shy. About 19 I should say. Ethel is a jolly fat girl of 15 with short frock & lovely legs, but the face leaves much to be desired. Arthur is at Cheltenham, a nice boy of 17 who wants to get into the Army. But I rather doubt his passing. Bobs quite loved me again after the old fashion & came to see me this morning dreadfully early, in his night shirt …

[CONTINUED]   19TH APRIL

Darling, Last night I fell asleep intending to finish my letter early this morning. But I had forgotten Bobs who woke me with a yell in my ear as he informed me that he had come to take my scalp & pulled my hair violently. … I found no bath & Bobs guided me to a bathroom. To my horror we found the door shut & Bobs at once bawled through the keyhole: 'Who's there'? Then when a voice answered, Bobs said: 'Oh! It's you Ethel, well make haste for Mr Hope is here waiting outside for you to finish drying yourself.' I fled to my room & did not emerge again till Ethel had made her escape. She got very red when we met in the Dining-Room. Lady L. is a good natured little fat woman, still pretty & very vain of her hands & feet.

The Character you sent me was very curious. 'Tender and True' I think you all that my Love. But I agree with you that love of Art, & power for painting should have been discovered. Only your Photograph dearest *Laure* is not like the face that haunts me in my dreams. Not one little bit. You kissed me last night on my forehead & I heard your soft low laugh as you murmured, 'only a sister's Kiss'. *Ma Laure* I long for you so. Give my love to your Aunt & all of them, Your A.

At North Runcton Hall, King's Lynn [with Uncle Sommy & Aunt Kitty Gurney]

> *22nd April* Felt awfully glad, *not* to leave Hopton but to think of spending 4 whole days with A. We have not been under the same roof for so long since last September. ... Adrian did not come till 9. ...

> *Easter Sunday, 26th April* Collected all sorts of queer things for the Mummy Show this evening. Made up the bodies of garden matting & old oriental rugs on a foundation of bolsters & top boots—most effective. ... After dinner arranged a dreadful Mummy Exhibition in the Anteroom—Audrey & Giddy [Muriel] looking quite ghastly as 2 little Pharaohs—everyone was thrilled—& much mystified. Adrian & I had arranged them, & the evening finished with the most absurd bear fighting when the Mummy's came to life again & joined the fray. ...

GREAT ORMOND STREET HOSPITAL, BLOOMSBURY   28TH APRIL

Ma Laure, ... I lunched with Jo at White's where I found him with Howard Vyse (his nephew) who was very cross as his wife is just about to present him with No 3 which he says will beggar him. He growled as if really she had all the responsibility of it & he none. Afterwards I took a walk & went to Soho Square where I used to learn fencing from a certain Capt. Griffiths. I found him still there & delighted to see me again. Here are his terms for you as he now has ladies as well. He showed me their Dressing-room & their Costumes hanging all round. Griffiths insists only on two things. First that you take off your stays. Second that you wear some sort of Blouse & Knickerbockers. I thought you might like to go & take Lessons when you are in town. If so you ought to get your costumes made before hand so as not to lose time. I asked him, particularly whether it was really good for women to fence & he told me

that he had never had any case when a pupil of his had been hurt in any way which rather relieved me for after all fencing means stretching open those pretty legs of yours a good bit wider apart than you do usually. But it seems that some Doctors recommend it even. I am going to begin fencing again as I am getting so bent & stooping. Griffiths told me that he had a fencing class of young Actresses as they find it helps to give them a grace of motion & to overcome that stiffness of body from which so many seem to suffer. ... After dinner—I really quite forgot where—I wrote 42 letters before going to bed. How good it was to be together four whole days ... Goodbye, your Adrian
　　P.S. Griffiths is old & ugly so I don't mind.

At Hunstanton

> *28th April* Looked at the Hall where they were rehearsing *Turn Him Out*, an all over the place regular *first* rehearsal—all vague about the cues & exits—no scenery has arrived as yet. ... All the Runctoners were mad enough to come over—to picnic on the beach, so we had to house & warm 7 of them for the rest of the day. After our rehearsal of *The Happy Pair* 14 precious souls squeezed themselves into our tiny dining-room for tea—& songs afterwards till they left. Then Aunt Maggie, Sybil & Betty [Orde] arrived to stay at Osborne House opposite & a cheery dinner party here. A fatiguing day.

> *29th April* No tidings of the scenery so 5 telegrams were despatched. A fatal telegram from Lancer who weakly cannot come. Rather too bad of him to throw us over at the last minute. He is billed to provide Songs with banjo accompaniment in the interval. Rehearsed our play in the morning & then hunted up the furniture wanted for both plays and people to move it, the small ornaments we carried down ourselves. Tried on my frock for the acting & tried a nice way of doing my hair. Settled to have a dress rehearsal in the studio with only our prompter Edwin Orde (a cousin of the Ordes) looking on.

HUNSTANTON　　　　　　　　　　　　　　　　29TH APRIL

My *own* darling Adrian, ... I came home long before the others arrived & found Neville Bevan, one of our theatrical party waiting on the platform, a lanky schoolboy of 17 who stammers frightfully. ... Darling, I don't think I could ever have promised to be your wife if you had told me that you 'l-l-l-l-l-l-l-l-l-l-l-l-l-l-ler-loved' me! Yesterday & today we have been wildly preparing for the show tomorrow. All the seats were snapped up instantly & the agent said he could have filled the Hall 3 times over—it holds 300 or more. ... The only thing against fencing lessons is it would be so hot & tiring for June & July ... but I am longing to fight you! ... I hope you will find time for a rendez-vous with the *dentist* for if you put it off too long it may be too late for repairs and I don't want you to have false teeth *please*. They would rattle I know when I kissed you, besides the uncomfy habit of keeping them in a glass of water at night, and looking *quite different* then which would be *too* horrid especially *then*. ... Goodbye for today, ever your own *Laure*

GREAT ORMOND STREET HOSPITAL, BLOOMSBURY   29TH APRIL

Ma Laure bien aimée, I dined with Jem & Elsie last night. They were both looking so well & happy & they presented me with a gorgeous shot purple silk embroidered with gold from Algiers to make a Smoking Suit of. But it is too pretty, besides I have a conviction that it would look best on your white shoulders my love. I hear that Mrs Scott Gatty, who had a 'much read' copy of *Little Thumb*, is wildly anxious to make your acquaintance & she said that with your talent you ought to have more work than you could do. She offered her husband's help to get work for you. Rather kind of her. I feel now is your chance with [Randolph] Caldecott dead & no new name as yet very prominent. If I were you I would write to Mansell [publishers of *Little Thumb* in 1883] a note asking briefly whether they felt inclined to take another book. Would you like me to go to Marcus Ward & Co. with your Book & a letter from you? ... How I do wish that I could be with you tomorrow night to see you act. ... Your Adrian

At Hunstanton

> *30th April* ... Went off with Vi on a foraging expedition to
> borrow lots of lovely flowers to deck the stage & then to
> Callabys to borrow a wooden fireplace. We made up a very
> pretty little drawing-room which needed a great deal of
> contriving, then we had a rehearsal which lasted till 5.30 so I felt
> perfectly tired out ... tea revived me & excitement did the rest, so
> by the time I was dressed in my pretty pink frock—& ready—I
> felt game for anything. The Hall was crammed—500 people
> squashed into a room meant to hold 400. The acting all went very

well which was a great comfort —after all our trouble—I felt in the mind & all the nervousness fled the moment I was on the stage. They were a good audience & applauded a great deal. The farce too made them all laugh tremendously. We had a supper here afterwards—with songs & dancing till 1. when we said goodnight after good rousing parting songs—'Auld lang syne', 'Rule Britannia'—& 'God Save the Queen'!

The printed programme was pasted into Laura's journal:

HUNSTANTON

AN AMATEUR ENTERTAINMENT

will be given in

THE ESPLANADE HALL

On Friday, April 30th, 1886

In aid of the Funds for a

New Organ for St Edmund's Church

Doors open at 7.30 p.m.   To commence at 8 p.m.

It went on to detail the two plays:

Part I
THE HAPPY PAIR
An original Comedietta, in one act, by S. Theyre Smith
Characters

Mr Honeyton...Mr CHAS. SOMERVILLE ORDE
Mrs Honeyton...Miss LAURA TROUBRIDGE

In the interval there will be Music (Vocal and Instrumental)

Pianoforte Duet ...Miss WINIFRED & Miss KATHLEEN GURNEY
Songs ...Mr. L. ORDE
(with banjo accompaniment)

Part II
TURN HIM OUT
A Farce, in one act, by Thomas J. Williams

The characters in the Farce were played by Edwin and 'Charles S. Orde' (again), Neville Bevan, Helen and Amy Troubridge, the latter in her favoured role of the maid.

Hunstanton   30th April

My darling, ... I am so glad Jem, & Elsie are back—for you. The silk must be lovely—it is so like you dear Adrian to think you will keep it for me *because* it is so pretty. Did you think of it for a peignoir in my trousseau? or is it too smart for that. ... Next week I mean to write to Marcus Ward *not* I think to Mansell—because their colour printing is *not* good. Guy Le Strange told me that if one could write a clear business letter to a publisher, it was better at all events in opening transactions, to write straight oneself—& *not* to send the letter by a friend—so I think darling I will take his advice—as he has published books—and knew what he was talking about, but if it comes to anything & we have a correspondence about the £.s.d. part of course I shall ask your advice—& consult *you* before I agree to any proposals about my new book. ... The house is *surging* with people ... Sweetheart Goodbye, ever your *own* *Laure*

---

85 *2nd Apr* Hon 'Jo' Spencer Hylton Jolliffe (1853-1902), d unm), seventh son of 1st Baron Hylton and far the youngest of thirteen children. His mother died when he was nine, his father remarried and died when Jo was twenty-three, and his stepmother died a few years later.

86 *15th Apr* Sir James Longden, ex-governor of Ceylon (Sri Lanka), to whom Adrian was private secretary for three years in the early 1880s.

MAY 1886

GREAT ORMOND STREET HOSPITAL, BLOOMSBURY   MAY DAY

My dearest, … Did you get many Calls before the Curtain? Do tell me all about it dear *Laure*, how Charlie acted & how you felt. … My father's Gun has really been cast & is now being *bored out*, the last words *do so* describe my own feelings on the subject. Darling when shall I see your face again? Your Adrian

HUNSTANTON   SUNDAY, 2ND MAY

My darling Adrian, … Everything went off with the greatest possible éclat, as the local paper will probably say. … Amy said I had never acted better in my life, and I think I felt it too. I know I had the audience in *hand* as it were—& made all my points. … I was a little afraid how Charlie would get through, for he *could not* remember some of his speeches. However he was only prompted twice—& he looked very nice too. … All my impertinences to 'Mr Honeyton' were received with *shouts* of laughter & a great clapping of hands followed both my exits. At the end when I have those angry broken hearted speeches—& then break down & throw myself on the sofa covering my face with my hands & sobbing, *several* people were in tears & *Amy* felt so miserable after weeping (fancy making *Amy* cry!), she said she did not feel as if she *could* act the farce! … Charlie told me afterwards that he never realized till Friday what a rude brute he was in the play—and that several times it was all he could do not to dash & kiss me & make it up *long* before the end of the play—imagine my rage if he had!! … Everyone laughed very much at *Turn Him Out*—& it really was funny. Helen looked wonderful in her golden wig & fly away bonnet—no one hardly recognised her. Amy was very good as the coy parlour maid & did her flirtatious scenes awfully well—she did not laugh either herself—Charlie was made up as the most dreadful masher & snob … with a tiny tasselled umbrella—he quite brought down the house. …

Yesterday I was so done up but today I feel as fresh as possible—and Amy & I have been talking London hard. It is quite settled that Vi & Helen take it in turns to be up in London, Tom does not expect any leave till September & the Rough Seaman does not expect to be home until the Autumn, so it would only be we three in the Park Street house. Helen would come up with us & Vi follow & take her place for the end of the time. This is their own idea—I proposed having a turn in the country too but this was squashed—Vi said that of course I must be in London all the time for your sake dearest so that we might meet often, & Amy said nothing would induce her to be in London with those 2 without me, so I gave a sigh of relief & felt I had done my duty.

Tomorrow I go & see the agent about letting The Castle. ... In a fortnight I shall have collected some of the new clothing demanded by civilization. ... The Salvation Army—bother them—are promenading Hunstanton *bawling* accompanied by a tambourine—singing well known Christy Minstrels to hymn words. ... By the by, we collected about £21 on Friday night, it wasn't *bad* but several of the Hunstanton swells gave gold so there must have been showers of coppers from the back seats—it was about half what we should have got if we had had a license. Now with the experience we have gathered we shall manage the licence & make it a more paying business next time. ... Ever your own loving *Laure*

Great Ormond Street Hospital, Bloomsbury   4th May

My darling, ... How would you like to go to Algiers & manage an Orange & Grape Farm there? Jem & Elsie are full of this rather vague project. ... Your Adrian

York Club, 8 St James' Square   5th May

My dearest *Laure*, ... I am so sorry to have let a day pass without telling you how I love you ... but I feel very low & everything is a burden to me. ... The dinner with the Goldsmids was pleasant but he seems to be going to vote against the [Irish Home Rule] Bill which rather puts it out of the question to ask for anything for me just now. I have had a miserable headache for several days which has worried me a good deal. Now I am too tired to write more than that I love you Oh! my darling, Your Adrian

At Hunstanton

> *5th May* ... Very busy winding up all the business of the theatricals, paying all the expenses, & making out what was left— £14, which I sent to the Chairman of the Church Committee. The expenses were over £7 although we fagged so much ourselves, & all our servants too—however they say £14 is more than anyone has ever made here by an entertainment! ... One man told me they had not had such a treat in the place for 20 years!

20 Duke Street (from Crofton's rooms)   7th May

My own dear Love, Today I accepted an invitation from Crofton to come to 'the Colonies' Exhibition [recently opened by Queen Victoria] & dine & listen to the Band which was infinitely resting. … The Exhibition seemed, from the little I saw of it, to be better than last year's 'Inventories' for there is no machinery thank goodness. I went through the Ceylon Court & was amused to see some people take off their hats to me—they were Members of the Civil Service whom I had known in Ceylon. Milady came to see me earlier today but I was away in the City so she entertained my Clerk with a long account of how I fainted there after our dinner on Tuesday night. He seemed much amused. Really she is an extraordinary woman, so indiscreet. … *Ton* Adrian

SCULTHORPE RECTORY, NR FAKENHAM   7TH MAY
[WITH UNCLE HERB & AUNT BACHE JONES]

My Adrian—darling, … Do you know I can not help thinking, of this vague idea of Algiers, for *many* reasons how delightful it would be. Algiers is the only place out of Europe I could be induced to live in. I think because it is *only four days* journey from home and unless you could have some nice *easy* appointment in *London* I would *rather* live out there, than be buried in some remote country village in England because there would be the compensation of the beautiful climate, which I know would suit you dearest. Also I suppose there would be some society—at all events in winter. … I suppose from the little that you have told me—*we* should have nothing to do with it as a *venture* but merely manage the Orange Farm for Jim & Elsie, being paid large sums to do so—*not* depending on the orange harvest. Is that so? If they make it worth our while—& enough to come to see everyone at home say once a year—I *do* think it good enough to think about *seriously*. It would be better to *begin* life together, even in Algiers than to wait on for *years* indefinitely. … I am rather in the dark as to whether it is a life & work *you would like*—which after all is the most important part. Everyone I have met who knows Algiers always raves about it. … Would there be a chance of making a little pile & returning to live in England? … for if you don't *spec* you cannot well make even a small fortune I fear. *Do* get well—or I simply must fly up to see you, ever your *Laure*

GREAT ORMOND STREET HOSPITAL, BLOOMSBURY   8TH MAY

My own dear *Laure*, About Algiers … Jem & Elsie are wild to buy a Farm & build a house there to which they may come every winter. I suggested half laughingly that they had better buy a bigger piece of land & build a house for two & then I would go & manage the property & live there with you. They both jumped at the idea. As yet it depends on Elsie's father [Sir Peter Coats]. I should have a house to live in with a small salary & a share of the profits. …

Jem says there is plenty of money to be made but I have not looked at figures yet. ... Your Adrian

P.S. I should love the life among the orange groves if you were there to make that life worth living. Especially if I saw my way really to making a little money. Here, beyond my salary I can make nothing, can't even get the *M. Post* to pay me what they owe me for my last year's work.

12TH MAY

My Darling, ... My Father is in great spirits for Jessop promises to have the Gun ready in June for trial. Also, when he was at Portsmouth he examined the Guns on board the *Collingwood* & when he got back, wrote to Lord Ripon [First Lord of the Admiralty] to tell him that those guns were not safe. As Lord Ripon was reading my Father's letter there came the telegram to announce that one of the big guns had burst as my Father prophesied they would do when tried. You may imagine his joy. He at once wrote to *The Times* & they put his letter among the telegrams on the first page & wrote a Leader upon it which delighted him. ... Goodbye my own, your Adrian

28 GREAT ORMOND STREET (FROM 'MY ROOMS') — SUNDAY NIGHT, 18TH MAY

My darling, ... Today I went to Greenwich & lunched with Henry Chamberlain & his wife. They have 3 children & are living there on 500£ per annum. How they do it I don't know. ... The Orange Farm has faded away into thin air. But if a Hartington—Chamberlain Ministry comes in I may perhaps have a chance of getting something. ... Goodnight, your Adrian

HUNSTANTON — 17TH MAY

Darling Adrian, ... I feel quite *Hunstonized* again and our engagement almost seems unreal—but I suppose we *are* really *promessi sposi* and I shall remember it when we meet. This has been rather a trying year for us—as yet—we have only been together *7 days* all this year. ... I think there is only one way to live on 500 a year—with a wife & especially 3 children, and that is to have *lots* of big bills!—unless they eat very little—wear no nice frocks—and *never* leave home—or entertain at all, & occasionally make a pilgrimage by bus, or 3rd Class by the Underground as a birthday treat now & then. ...

My 'Jaw Crackers' book is now neatly packed in a box ready to send to Marcus Ward. I did a dedication page—with an orchestra of green frogs tuning up, & a scroll in the centre of the page on which Jo's suggested title appears—*Odd Alliterations—Artfully Illustrated*—'Dedicated to my brother T.H.C.T.' so Tom ought to feel flattered. Adieu from your *Laure*

Great Ormond Street Hospital, Bloomsbury   22nd May

My own dear *Laure*, … I had a pleasant dinner last night at the Goldsmids. When I arrived I found Milady preparing to faint while he was looking stolidly on. So I made her take a little Brandy which put her all right. I sat between Lady Wynford & Lady Cecilia Rose. Lady Cecilia talked of her black Poodle but Lady W. & I talked of you. She knew your people & got very confidential, told me she was as fond of Lord W. as when they were married 28 years ago. We discussed Honeymoons & she said that both she and her husband had been bored by theirs but that they had a real honeymoon about 3 years after they were married. … My Father should be in good spirits for 3 Members of Parliament badgered Govt about him last night & Goldsmid would keep on introducing me to people as son of the celebrated Col. Hope. Which I disliked excessively. Dear Heart goodbye, your A.

York Club, 8 St James' Square   Sunday night, 23nd May

My darling, … After lunching with the Batemans (I knew them long years ago—before Lee had begun to trouble) I went to call on my cousin Eliza Alexander who begged me to bring you to lunch. If you can stand her blunt rudeness you may find out her sterling good qualities. But she is very terrifying at times. At least I find her so. … Last night Jo & I had such a row. Fancy the old ass was angry because I said that I *would, would, would* dine with you at Abbey Lodge on Friday instead of going to a Gatty concert & having supper with them & him at the Club. I think he must be mad not to see that I am just dying to meet you again oh! My Love. Really he has annoyed me this time beyond my patience. Fat Fool. Goodbye *ma Laure*, your A.

Hunstanton *Vive la Reine*!   24th May
[Queen Victoria's birthday]

My darling Adrian, It is really *too silly* of Jo to expect you to be ready to give up our very first meeting to please him. He can *never* have cared for anyone to think it for a moment or so long ago he had forgotten what it was like. But it always pleases Jo—for some reason or other—to ignore the fact of our engagement, it is quite *absurd*. … There is nothing to tell you except the arrival of a second Cresswell son at King St. on Sunday. I am rather sorry it is not a little god-daughter. Eve is a wonderful person, all Saturday aft. she was out boating with George! Marie [de Bunsen] writes today that her people dine out on Friday & she is going to a ball—so she wants us to devise some amusement because she thinks we would be bored spending the evening with her aunt 'old Ellen' Gurney—and *I* think so too. I don't want to do a play our first night because we *must* talk. Amy suggests 'the Colonies' Exhib.—she has asked Cressie to dine—an early dinner—at Abbey Lodge, then we 4 could go in a brace of hansoms & amuse ourselves. What think you? Amy suggests a play for Saturday. If you can come then we must collect a chaperon. ...

I have been painting all the morning—Charlotte Noel—she is a child I don't much care for, *so hard*—like a little old person to talk to & with the most baby face—a child who *hates* fairy stories & fairies, and crabs most things & most people. She is curiously like her mother Freda—who sent me this from last week's *Army and Navy Gazette* about the Colonel's new gun—had you seen it? How I *hope* it may be prophetic—especially the 'substantial fruits of success'. Eh, darling? ... Goodbye for today, ever your *Laure*

The *Army and Navy Gazette* editorial hedged somewhat, as follows:

> '... we trust that he will have every facility which can be given by the War Office authorities to test his system fairly and fully. Should Colonel Hope produce a gun which justifies his specifications, he will not only be entitled to an ample *amende* from those who, like ourselves, did not admit his pretensions to be an "artillerist" and to sit in judgement on the professional experts ... but from the authorities themselves; and he, moreover, will receive what no doubt he values much more,— the thanks of the country, in addition to the substantial rewards which will be the natural fruits of success.'

GREAT ORMOND STREET HOSPITAL, BLOOMSBURY 25TH MAY

My darling Laura, ... Today I was able to get away in decent time to go to Apsley House to the Duchess of Wellington who very kindly asked me to an Afternoon with music. I have rarely enjoyed anything so much in my life. The Waterloo Chamber was thrown open. A room twice as big as Milady's, hung with red satin & covered with magnificent pictures. Lots of smart pretty people whom I knew. But I had a nervous time of it walking up the whole length of the room to introduce myself to the dearest little Fairy on Ebony Crutches who was charming to me. The music was delightful & it was a dream of pretty women. Crofton introduced me to the Duke who is very fat & looks like a prosperous butcher, however he showed me the pictures very goodnaturedly & seemed jolly. ...

I shall be delighted to go with you to 'the Colonies' on Friday after dinner. Hopetoun has bidden me to Grosvenor Square that night to an At Home & I think I ought to go there about 11.30 as he has been kind about the Hospital & also when he asks me for the first time it would be rude not to go. Oh! Darling if it had only been you & I together today I should have been so proud of you my wife. ... Only two days and a half now before I see the dearest face to me in this whole world. *Carissima mia arivederla*, your lover Adrian

27TH MAY

My dearest, I had such a worry yesterday. All my Speakers for tomorrow's Dinner have failed me at the last minute. Lord Aberdare lost his daughter Mrs Whately, while Sir Charles Tupper, the Canadian High Commissioner, has lost his voice & all my M.P.s are kept in the House for the Irish Debate. So at 6 o'clock I started on the war path to get substitutes. Jo came with me, first to Sir Samuel Wilson then to Teignmouth Shore [3rd Baron] & then to Oscar Wilde who refused though much tempted by the idea of speaking along with an Archbishop—the Archbishop of Canterbury is to be in the Chair. Jo sat amazed at Mrs Oscar & at Oscar who seemed to confound poor Jo's wits altogether. I got back here at 9. & had to set to work for an hour or so. Then, having had no dinner I dressed & went to see Jo & made him give me some Sandwiches & Claret. I felt so lively then that I went to my first Ball this season. It was rather a good one. Lots of people one knew. The women seemed to be very naked, at least so I thought. I was introduced to Mrs Millais (Miss Hope-Vere that was). We made great friends though I don't like her much. Jo left in a temper about something. ...

If *possible* I will be at the Station tomorrow at 3.30. how good it is to write that word tomorrow. I feel very bad at the idea of your going with Charlie to the play on Saturday but still feel that I ought to get my work cleared up & not have it hanging like a cloud over next week's happiness. My Darling, I do love you so & hunger so for a kiss from you, Your Adrian

At Abbey Lodge, Regent's Park
[with Chevalier Ernest & Mme de Bunsen]

> *28th May* Amy & I & Tanner arrived at St Pancras—Adrian met
> us, then off in a luggage laden growler to Abbey Lodge. ... After

tea Amy & I feeling energetic set off walking for Park Street to
see Number 66 where we hope to pitch our tents. A teeny corner
house painted red—a very dirty outside, a nice little pill box
inside—with pretty little double drawing & dining-rooms. A
civil housekeeper left in charge showed us over—& begged us to
come. Walked partly home talking it over & also a delightful
invitation from Lady Wallscourt to join her pay party & stay with
her down at Ascot for the week. However felt we really couldn't
afford it. Tom is going & lots of jolly people—& she offers to
take us 2 for £15—half price. ... After dinner off with Adrian to
'the Colonies', a very happy evening. The Exhib. is quite lovely
though we didn't see much of it.

29th May Adrian has got us tickets for the Trooping of the
Colour for the Queen's birthday this morning & Jo to escort us.
... Such a crowd at the Horse Guards & we were too late to see
much—afterwards to St James' Palace to hear the band. Then we
shopped a little at Gorringes & walked to the Leghs for a very
nice luncheon party—everyone so glad that we have reappeared
on the scenes again—Gilly Legh, Bean St Aubyn & Mary Millais.
Gilly bought my picture of 'Fairy Ships'. Then to the Grosvenor
Gallery where I met A. & we looked at some piccys together,
then to have tea *à deux* in Green Street at Jem & Elsie's house,
they being away. It was very nice, we pretended it was *ours*. ...

JUNE 1886

At Abbey Lodge, Regent's Park
[with Chevalier Ernest & Mme de Bunsen]

1st June … Off feeling very happy with Amy to dine at the
Bachelors'—to meet Adrian at Jack Hay's party, but alas all
pleasure was spoilt, for me at least, as I found A. quite lame &
suffering secret agonies with a bad sprained ankle. He had run
downstairs just before we arrived to see if some lovely flowers
had come that he had ordered for me—he slipped the last 3 steps
& this happened. He made nothing of it & *would* come with us
afterwards to the Goldsmids party. I couldn't enjoy it for a
minute. … Good news when we got home at 1. Found a letter
from Tom saying we may have the Park Street House from the
11th. Joy, Joy!

ABBEY LODGE, REGENT'S PARK   2ND JUNE

My darling, … The 'Jo & Flo' Monteith luncheon at Bailey's Hotel was very
smart, like a *young* wedding breakfast, with all sorts of *gobbits*, but it was
rather a fiasco I thought for Flo is such a vague hostess that she did not
arrange or sort her guests at all, & all the men were together & all the
girls. … I waited there until it was time to go to the Millais. There I had a
very successful visit. The old boy was so nice & jolly to me, showed me his
studio—& all the pictures he had about—& was *very* nice about my drawings
which he criticized sternly, perspective & anatomy etc. but he said many nice
things too—and urged me to work. He said he *never* paid compliments so if
all he said about my things was true, I ought to do some good in time.[87] He
gave me no advice about publishing. I think Mr Gatty will be more useful in
that way. …

   Then on to the Leghs—where I found Amy & Mob Legh gossiping over
their tea, & Cousin Milly & Syb—all most sympathetic about you darling.
Cousin M. was delighted to hear about my visit to Sir J. Millais & I have
arranged to go with her & spend every Tuesday drawing at Mr Fitz's studio
in Fitzroy Sq. when I come up again. A long day, 10. to 4. with a live model,
a *head*. …

   I tried to find Jem & Elsie to tell them about you but they had rushed off
again to the House Boat, then I was driving disconsolately Abbeywards when
I suddenly thought I would go to Hereford Gardens & found Lill St Aubyn so
I dined & we saw off the 'Royal Family' to the Queen's ball—all looking

more or less bored. ... *I wish* I was Mrs Adrian to take care of you, my own dearest. I *think* we go down to Hunstanton at 5 o'clock tomorrow, ever your *Laure*

3RD JUNE

My darling, old Ernest de B. has toddled off & means to *enquire*—I hope he won't bore you but I could not help his going—& he is a nice old boy too. Madame de B. has been making *the* most impossible & frantic suggestions— that you should be brought *here* to be nursed by her & 'Aunt Gurney', my *not* staying on etc. etc. I wonder which of you would die first, you of ennui, she of fussing! We stopped at the Bachelors' on the way out & Jo came & talked at the door of our hansom. I told him about you & he said he should come & see you this afternoon. In the park I found you some more visitors, Tardy & Lancer. Charlie was most sympathetic & said he would call this evening. I thought darling it would amuse you & make the day less long to have some visitors. I also wrote a note to Uncle Sommy & also to Jem & Elsie—but *no one* else, not even the Colonel. ... Get well darling for our return *tomorrow week*, your loving & for ever your *Laure*

28 GREAT ORMOND STREET, BLOOMSBURY   3RD JUNE

My dearest Love, Crofton was my first visitor about 2. today. I must tell you that he dressed me & carried me into my sitting room where I am now lying on my bed chair which is most comfy. I have got on my smoking suit & really feel better though my foot still tweaks a bit. After he had gone in came Jo who stopped till after 5. And then came old Ernest de B. who was most charming. We sat & discussed all manner of early forms of religion till ¼ past 7. He was really very interesting. How good of you to tell all your nice Relations to come & see me. Old Ernest & I made great friends & he is coming to read me some of his new book on Sunday. I hope it will not be very dry. The idea of being taken to Abbey Lodge nearly gave me a fit. Here comes the Doctor to put me to bed, so Goodnight my own dear *Laure*, from Adrian

4TH JUNE

My own Dear Love, This morning Elsie burst into my bedroom wild to carry me off there & then to the Boat at Sonning. She only left me on my promise to ask the Doctors if I might go tomorrow. I have done so & go down tomorrow till Monday. ... After lunch in came Uncle Sommy. He *was* so nice. After he had gone a funny thing happened. Milady & Stewart (of the *M. Post*) came &

had just sat down & taken cigarettes when in came Mrs Orde & E. Milady chucked her cigarette but Mrs Orde was so very shy & stiff & though I introduced them all to each other they would not amalgamate one bit. I felt almost glad when the dear Ordes left me though I should have loved to talk quietly with your Aunt. The others stayed on & began again to smoke when in came Uncle Douglas [Cunninghame Graham] who made himself most nice & we had a pleasant half hour's chat. Uncle D. stopped on for a bit & after he went Charlie Orde came in & we had a long talk about you. Then he went away & Jo came in & brought me books but he seemed so glad you were out of town that I was quite angry with him. Jo says that London sans Troubridges is so dull that he must go out of town tomorrow also. I wish we had been going down together to the Boat for the first time, Your Adrian

THE HOUSE BOAT *CROCODILE*, AT SONNING-ON-THAMES 8TH JUNE

My own dear *Laure*, Life on board is simply perfect if you were only here. Jem carried me into the Saloon where he put me on a sofa on which I have spent most of my time since. Anything more delightful, you can hardly imagine & the boat is full of comfort. On Saturday night after dinner Jem put me into a boat where I lay with my head in Elsie's lap & we rowed about in the River for an hour. Sunday afternoon we went for a long row, E. as before being my pillow. Yesterday a Steam Tug took the House Boat up the River so as to get by the Weir where Jem left me with my foot in the water for an hour. The cold water hurt me a good deal but will do me good I hope. I am still quite helpless & can only hop a very short way for it hurts me so to let my foot hang. As to letting it touch the ground, that is out of the question yet. It is such a dreadful bore about Whitsuntide. They had made up their minds that you should come here & join me. Now a pair of *cussed* Coats have asked themselves down on the strength of an old invitation. Elsie had arranged for you to sleep with her & for Jem to sleep with me in the Saloon on the other sofa. They are unfortunately unable to put up more than one extra lady. It is such a blow for I don't know what we can do with our little holiday. ... [unfinished]

HUNSTANTON 10TH JUNE

My darling Adrian, ... I am *so disappointed* ... I think it is *very* unkind of Jem & Elsie *to invite you & not me*. I do *really*. Of course the Coats cousin is only a feeble excuse. I don't see why Elsie should have two husbands—& I should not even have one. It is quite evident they do not want me, they only care to have you alone—for we have been engaged for so long & this is the first time they have even *thought* about asking me to meet you—and now they have asked someone else instead. ... Of course *you*, darling, must stay for your holiday & try to get well. Your poor foot, it is 10 days since it happened and I daresay it would have been nearly well if you had not been so mad—& insisted on going to Lady Goldsmid's party, and then it was not a bit *nice*. You would not even speak to me—which gave me a heartache. However much you could laugh & talk with others you could not hide from *me* how much you were suffering. Standing so long *must* have done mischief to your ankle. ... Now the summer is spoilt for me—I have not felt happy for a single minute since I saw you standing in the hall at the Bachelors' with your face full of pain. Darling what shall I do without you in London? I have purposely made no engagements these 3 days of Whitsuntide—but I suppose something will turn up—and if I see anyone I care to speak to I shall *flirt de—li—be—ra—te—ly*. I believe grass widows always do.

Darling I feel so naughty & discontented—I wish you were here to scold me—or to—well comfort me as you do best. ... Darling if I was an old frump I would come & stay at the 'White Hart' which sounds like an Inn, & see you sometimes—but no, I must just try & forget that such a dear dear person as you exists. How I wish I could—but *Love* is too hard a master for *that*. ... I don't send my love to anyone only to you Sweetheart. I don't think you can put *this* letter near your heart. I am sure it would feel like a mustard plaster & leave a red mark! ... Goodbye—Oh Goodbye, your *Laure*

CROCODILE HOUSE BOAT,   10TH JUNE
THE WHITE HART, SONNING-ON-THAMES

Darling, I have decided to come up to London on Friday & will do my best to dine with you at Park Street. ... How I wish you were here for I feel so much better today & not so low-spirited as I did. My leg is a fat black leg up to the knee. It looks as if I had on a black silk stocking rather showing the flesh through it. ... Here one day passes like another in a heavenly calm except that Jem & Elsie are too indecently loving. It is really an awful trial to my feelings & I dream of you every night & Darling you are never kind to me but as at Abbey Lodge you always beat me & ask me why you married me. Last night you said you would go off with Jem & leave me with Elsie. Was not that very cruel. I fear that Salmon & Champagne Cup are not a wholesome mixture when one can take no exercise but this of writing to you. Goodnight my own dear love, from cripple Adrian

87 *2nd June* In Laura's later memoirs she added to the account of her visit to Sir John Millais' studio.

> ' ... Of the drawing of the Little Mermaid dancing at the court of the Prince he said: "Now that arm is wrong—she could not have got it into that position—surely your model did not?" When I confessed rather shyly that I never had a model for these illustrations he said: "My dear young lady, you write poetry before you have learnt grammar!" He drew the arm as it should be on the back of the drawing. He also said I ought never to draw anything unless I had a model—by that time I was no longer in awe of him, so said: "What about mermaids?" He laughed, but said I might have a bowl of goldfish to study their scales, adding: "I see the work of about thirty young artists every year. I advise twenty-nine of them to give it up—but to you I say—go on!" '

TOGETHER IN LONDON

11TH JUNE

TO

31ST JULY 1886

At 66 Park Street, Grosvenor Square
[Tom Cochrane's House]

11th June Oh the delight with which Amy & I greeted the day of our departure for London, beloved London. … Adrian has come back from the boat & is laid up at Jem Hope's house in Green Street, it is quite near here which is my only comfort. A note asking me to dine there.

Whit Monday, 14th June Adrian alas is not so well after the exertion of dining here last night & hopping down Park Street on crutches. … I went in to Green Street on my way to a Garden party at Abbey Lodge, a very nice party, crowds of cousins—a sort of family gathering and a performing pony doing tricks in the garden. Dined with Adrian tête-à-tête. His foot is *not* so well.

15th June First day at Mr Fitz's Studio. Cousin Milly Legh called for Helen & myself & we went together about 10 o'clock. Enjoyed it very much, worked from life, in charcoal, till 3 o'clock, a large head study—of a girl in peasant's cap. Then the full length, a small sketch to be done in an hour. Fitz is rather an alarming little man, rather jerky & rude—but a capital master I am sure. Knocked off for an hour at 12 o'clock & lunched with Cousin M. at Shoolbred's shop, we had great fun. … Dined in Green Street, A. is better—home about 12. & found a drum [party], Amy & Cressie.

On the Crocodile, *at Henley*
[with Jem & Elsie Hope]

26th June Wore my new frock, pink & white stripes. Adrian came for me at Park Street at 10. & we went off together to Henley. Jem & Elsie met us, rowed down to the House Boat, the *Crocodile*. Very pretty & comfortable …

Sunday, 27th June Got up at 7. put on my new *costume* & went off to swim with Jem, enjoyed it very much. After lunch painted on a panel in the Saloon with Jem, both painting at once, it was great fun.

28th June Had to leave this delicious place. Very sorry our holiday was over. After lunch found Adrian still at Green Street & stayed with him till it was time for him to leave for Great Ormond Street.

A note of Laura's personal expenses during June was pasted into her journal. She came up to London with '£10.7 [shillings] in the L. fund' and spent £11.7.3½ [shillings & pence].

	£.	s.	d.		£.	s.	d.
White osprey		1	6	flowers		1	6
black suede gloves		2	9	lace & hankies		2	0
gloves & stockings	1	1	9	grass mat		3	0
ribbons, pink & white,				field flowers			
hat & veils		11	3½	& ribbon		9	10
drawing pencils etc.		2	6	flowers		3	11
lace for sleeves & lisse		8	9	church		1	0
Prints for Audrey & Adrian		10	6	black dress	1	17	6
muslin & screens		4	9	gloves		1	6
flowers		4	0	Japanese temptations		5	6
net & ribbon & belting,				book – Nelson's life		1	2
pink & white stripe dress		12	6	hat & stockings,			
white peignoir		15	6	suspenders		1	9
Japanese things		5	0	velvet for hat		2	10
ribbons		10	6	flowers		10	6
German reeds		3	0	ribbons		4	0
gloves		4	6	lowers		1	6

66 PARK STREET, GROSVENOR SQUARE 1ST JULY
[TOM COCHRANE'S HOUSE]

My darling, ... I have telegraphed to your mother proposing to go down there this afternoon. Amy & Vi go to the Oscar Wildes' party for which it appeared we had a card sent us long ago though I did not know it. I have just been reading the manuscript he brought me, the fairy story called 'The Selfish Giant'. It is very prettily written, quite Hans Andersen's style & would be delightful to illustrate.[88] ... Ever your *Laure*

Laura found the time—or inclination—to write up only a few days in her journal for July. One reference was to Rachel (then aged nineteen), younger daughter of Laura's 'unacceptable' Aunt Alice Gurney: 'We had not met since Rachel was seven, we thought her so pretty & nice.'[89] Her sister Queenie had noticeably failed to grace the Troubridges' tea-party a few days earlier.

At the end of the month, three balls in a row were noted. On 21st July the Ordes found the Marlborough House Ball 'disappointing, & they had not enjoyed it'. The next day there was no question of resting before the Amherst Ball—first Laura went shopping, before walking with the Ordes in the park, then on to lunch with the Lamingtons and to go driving with them afterwards, then she 'vagued' about, shops & *flanéed* [Laura's version of *flaner*—to stroll about] with Vi before landing up at Charbonnel Et Walker for iced coffee & 'delicious cakes'. On their return they found Adrian having tea with Amy; Elsie Hope called and took Adrian and Laura back to meet Jem at Green Street before they returned to dine at Park Street—all this before dressing for the ball, of which Laura wrote: 'Vi enjoyed it immensely but I did not much, it was so tantalizing that poor beloved Adrian could not dance.' The last ball, the St Aubyn's on the 23rd, was the best: 'Dressed for the ball directly after dinner as Adrian was coming at 9.30. Wore my pale pink frock with lots of pale pink roses—it looked very well. Adrian did not come till 10. and Cripps [Cressie Cresswell] arrived directly afterwards—when the others went to dress & I had these two who don't hit it off a bit to talk to till 11.30. it was *such* a bore, however I revived at the ball & enjoyed myself.'

The Park Street interlude came to an end on 31st July and Adrian was able to spend the August Bank Holiday weekend with Laura at Runcton and celebrate—or commiserate on—the *second* anniversary of their engagement on 2nd August, 1884.

88 *1st July* It seems as if Wilde initially wanted Laura to illustrate his story 'The Selfish Giant' but Walter Crane was chosen for the first book edition in which it appeared, *The Happy Prince and Other Tales* (1888).

89 *3rd July* The great gap in the friendship between the young Troubridges and their Gurney first cousins Queenie (Laura), and Rachel, was partly explained on p33. In the aftermath of the Overend, Gurney Bank smash in 1866 the Charles Gurneys sent their young daughters to be cared for temporarily by Alice Gurney's maternal grandmother, Mrs Thoby Prinsep (née Sara Pattle), at Little Holland House in Kensington. There they made great friends with the permanent house guest, the artist G F Watts. In 1879 for the next seven years—from when Queenie was thirteen and Rachel a year younger—they were brought up by their mother's first cousins, the daughters of the beautiful Virginia, Countess of Somers (née Pattle). Queenie was taken by Isabel, who had separated from her husband Lord Henry Somerset, and Rachel by Adeline, wife of the Marquess of Tavistock (later 10th Duke of Bedford). Thereafter they went back to living with their parents between paying long visits to their friends and relations. Despite the animosity between the remaining Gurney uncles and aunts, the young Troubridges were open-minded and Tom started to 'frivol' with Queenie as an alternative to 'flirting' with Sybil Legh. *See also* p271 and footnote 91.

YEAR THREE 1886–87

LETTERS OF ENGAGEMENT

ADRIAN – LAURA

4TH AUGUST 1886

TO

28TH JULY 1887

Colonel Hope continued his long-term vendetta against the War Office, mostly through the letters columns of *The Times* in which he accused high government officials, and especially those of the Ordnance Department, of corrupt practices resulting in the supply of: 'guns which burst, rifles and cartridges which jam, bayonets which bend, and swords which will not cut'. The airing of these criticisms led to a Royal Commission to investigate the charges and the colonel became a willing witness against the War Office.

By the end of the month, the colonel's accusations that the corruption stemmed from certain War Department officials being also shareholders in a firm that supplied ordnance to the Ordnance Department was taken up by the *Fortnightly Review* of 1st September by its then Editor, Frank Harris. He published a somewhat convoluted two-page contribution by the colonel (dated 24th August) under the heading, 'The Ordnance Department and Colonel Hope – A Personal Explanation'. Harris's letter to his own periodical followed on and referred to the Secretary of State for War, Mr W H Smith, as having given on 24th August an unsatisfactory reply to a question on the subject from Gen Sir William Crossman. He went on to state: 'Evidently an English official can serve two masters whose interests are absolutely opposed to each other. He can serve himself as seller and his country as buyer. It is manifest that the sooner the Secretary of State for War applies to Parliament for power to put an end to so scandalous a condition of things, the better it will be for the country. ...' All this was balm to the colonel after his thirty years of proclaiming against the 'iniquities' of the Ordnance Department.

London did not feature much in this third year of Adrian and Laura's engagement as Adrian was now frequently invited to stay with Laura's friends and relations in Norfolk and elsewhere.

Great Ormond Street Hospital, Bloomsbury   4th August

My darling, ... For a penance & feeling that I could not feel more depressed at having left you at Runcton yesterday, I went & saw my Father who gave me authentic news of the Gun which seems really to be nearly finished. He is also in great spirits about his success in attacking the War Office Gang though I do not quite see how this will do him any good. He looks triumphant & told me that the Prince of Wales after first being furious now says that he must be right as the W.O. seem so afraid of meeting him. ... Goodbye my own dear Love, Your Adrian

5TH AUGUST

My own darling Laura, ... Crofton & I tried a Vegetarian Restaurant last night but the food was composed mainly of cabbage steak stuffed with carrots. So, our hearts lusting after meat, we went to a little place in Leicester Square & had a second feed. ... Goodbye Sweetheart till Saturday with the Goldsmids, Your Adrian

BURWAY, LUDLOW, SALOP   10TH AUGUST
[WITH CHARLES & CUCKOO WICKSTED]

My own Darling, I had a comfy journey here from the Goldsmids—it was not hot—& there was no dust only I had to change three times. About two hours I was alone, which I like best—then I travelled with 2 rather nice men—who were very civil—and the last part of the time I was tête-à-tête with such an odd woman—very smart with heaps of things with her—all pretty & all new, a pretty face—but rather got up. She talked hard and rather amused me. She told me amongst other things her husband was mad. She herself had landed only that morning from Port Said. We found some mutual friends to talk of and it beguiled the time. I have quite forgotten her name which she told me, the Baroness M——. She had been wintering at Cairo & knew the Norths, Laura Gurney, the Somers Cocks etc.

I found Helen safely established, the Wicksteds [Cuckoo was Aunt Kitty Gurney's youngest sister] and the 2 Harbord boys, Lionel & Cecil, nice handsome boys with good manners. The house is quaint & old fashioned, with queer little oak panelled rooms—and old carved furniture they have picked up—it is very nearly *very* nice—but rather too homely. The river is delicious. Helen is quite happy fly fishing all day. I spent my morning swimming about with Lionel whose *costume* by the by is a great deal more extensive than Jem's. Cecil rowed about with a boat and we had great fun floating down the rapids—which are *very* swift and quite shallow so one flies along. I have been asked to take a part in the theatricals at Downton Castle on Friday but have refused. I hear the acting is to take place by *daylight* in *the garden* and no one got up at all—I think it would be awfully difficult to feel inspired under those circumstances. I shall look on and criticize instead. ... Farewell my own dear Adrian, ever your Laura

York Club, 8 St James' Square 11th August

My dearest Love, Who do you think woke me up this morning about 8? A very smart pretty young lady who was half kneeling on my bed & shaking me by the shoulders. I kissed her in a dreamy sort of astonishment & tried to gather together my poor wits & guess her name & business. Shall I tell you? I am not quite sure I will after the way you so evidently flirted with the '*two rather nice men*' who '*were very civil*'. ... I hope you are really wild with curiosity to know who was my early bird that caught me. I think I will tell you. My sister Laura came from Paris last night with Aunt Annie [Cunninghame Graham] as my poor Aunt Cha [her sister] has had a stroke of paralysis at Rhyl [where she was Matron at the Royal Alexandra Hospital for Children]. ... Laura was looking so well & pretty that I longed for you to see her. But she looks such a fragile little thing. I had forgotten how tiny she was. They have left Paris for good & have got a house at Cambridge where they will settle down in October. ... Today has been such a busy day with me. I have written 92 letters so my hand & head both ache much. ...Goodnight my *Laure*, Your Adrian

Burway, Ludlow, Salop 12th August
[with Charles & Cuckoo Wicksted]

Darling Adrian, Do you think I did not guess at the *very first* words who your visitor was. I do not think there is more than *one* young lady in the world, darling, who could run in and wake you in that way—impossible even to me!! It must have been startling, darling. I am so amused that you kissed her 'in a dreamy sort of way' I imagine before you really knew who it was! What bad news about your dear little aunt, & it is so sad for your mother to hear this when Jessie is so ill too. ... It is little more than a week now to our meeting here. Goodbye my dear, dear Adrian, ever your Laura

    P.S. Do you think your sister L. seemed so small & fragile—because you are used to seeing another Laura?

York Club, 8 St James' Square 13th August

My Dearest, ... The Col. is in a state of triumph at the result of his letters. All the papers one after the other are taking the matter up. I really begin to fancy that he may do some good to himself & his Gun by all this mud throwing. ... So you guessed at once it was my sister. Well that was more than I did my dear. It was so odd walking about with another Laura who was so *much* smaller

& different all together to my own dear Love. How is Helen recovering from her town dissipation? Goodbye, your Adrian

14TH AUGUST

My Darling, I dined last night with Jo at the 'Cavour'. He was grumpy & cross until after dinner when he cheered up a bit. ... As I was walking home I met Thaddeus & we went & had a poached egg together along with a strange creature, Oscar Wilde's brother, a certain Willie Wilde. ... Just fancy, my Aunt is going to have her Swiss Cook over to Cambridge. Rather nice for us if we ever get a dip into their platter. Your Adrian

BURWAY, LUDLOW, SALOP   MY BIRTHDAY, SUNDAY, 15TH AUGUST [WITH CHARLES & CUCKOO WICKSTED]

My darling Adrian, I was *rather* disappointed when I read your letter and found you had quite forgotten my birthday! but we will keep it next Saturday, won't we, when I trust we will be here together. The idea is to stay here until Tuesday week and then go to Hopton. ... Cuckoo has just gone off to teach a class of Ludlow louts she has every Sunday afternoon and they suddenly began bawling a hymn in the next room at the very tops of their harsh voices. The noise was so awful that I had to bolt until the hymn was over & they settled down to more peaceful religious exercises. ...

The theatricals at Downton Castle were really too funny. They began to act in a lovely little glade in the garden all arranged with flowers & ferns, in a gleam of sunshine with huge black clouds all round—it was perfect madness. In 2 minutes it was raining in *torrents*, a perfect deluge with thunder & lightning. They continued to act although not one single word could be heard for the violence of the rain beating on the umbrellas under which the audience were crouching & huddling together. It was the most *absurd* sight, we were simply convulsed with laughter & could hear & see nothing...at last there was a general stampede to the house & after a bit the actors dried themselves & went through their performances in a large hall. I was so *thankful* I had nothing to do with it. It was a most feeble performance—and so much was heard of the prompter that it was more like a rehearsal than anything. I went fishing yesterday & caught 2 in about half an hour. Goodbye my own dearest, ever your *Laure*

P.S. I cannot take up a paper without seeing something about the Col., he is really getting on swimmingly.

YORK CLUB, 8 ST JAMES' SQUARE 15TH AUGUST

My Darling, I have been quite wild with myself for forgetting when I wrote to you yesterday that today was your Birthday. How can you forgive me. I do so long that your next Birthday may see you my own dear Wife. ... I have been trying to get at the Tory successor to Dilke on the Local Government Board, a Mr Ritchic, & have written two letters which are to be shown to him. Also I am trying to work up a feeling among the Coats family that they should give me something to do. Last night I dined with Jo at the Bachelors', Bean St Aubyn was there & asked me how long I was going to be before marrying you. But he was very nice after & sympathetic. ... Goodnight, your Adrian

20TH AUGUST

My darling, I have been up to the neck in private affairs as well as Hospital work. My silver mines have been a great worry as I have been trying to get Coats to go into them. Tonight I dined with him & we have settled a good deal. ... Goodnight my own own dear Love, Your Adrian

The next day Adrian joined Laura and Helen at the Wicksteds for the start of his month's holiday, which included visits to the Ordes at Hopton, the Herbert Joneses at Scully, ending up with a few days at Hunstanton.

SEPTEMBER 1886

HUNSTANTON   24TH SEPTEMBER

My darling Adrian, After nearly 4 months we four sisters are together again under the Castle roof. ... How I wish Jo could get Spottiswoode to take my drawings. Augusta Webbe came today and was full of ideas of stories she wanted me to illustrate—but in my mind I felt discouraged from fresh ventures, thinking of the 'Mermaid', & then 'Jaw Crackers'. ... I want to get up a rage for studying anatomy in the winter evenings. I have a capital book, *Haydon's Lectures* & have been reading some already. He is an enthusiastic writer—& I like that, making out that the study of bones is essential almost to one's life and happiness! & all skeletons are deeply interesting & beautiful! I don't think I shall ever quite appreciate this—but one cannot help catching something of his fire—when he writes in this way instead of teaching it as a dull & mouldy subject. ... Ever your *Laure*

SUNDAY, 26TH SEPTEMBER

My own dearest, ... The Colonel sent me his long letter in Friday's [24th] *Morning Post*, his justification—or rather challenge—I hardly know what to call it. I thought it a very clever letter. I wonder if he will rouse them to action with it. I was rather amused by Cuckoo Wicksted, she said in a letter a few days ago that they had been very interested reading the Col's letters—and adds—'What a Capital Huntsman he would have made, he does so "stick to his fox" '! ... No more writing today, ever your *Laure*

Colonel Hope sent copies to *The Times* and to the *Morning Post* of his letter to the Secretary of State for War in which he explained at great length why he was turning his original private statement against the Ordnance Department into an official letter to the Secretary of State to be forwarded to the Royal Commission, and went on to say:

> '... I now calmly await the summons of the Secretary of State to adduce the evidence for the Crown before the Royal Commission, or his notification of my arrest on a charge of perjury, whichever he shall consider it to be his, perhaps equally painful, duty to send me.'

The Colonel did not mince matters in his letter to the press:

'The Attorney-General, speaking on behalf of the accused [at the Ordnance Department] made yesterday in the House of Commons (in your absence) a personal attack on me. Cowardice is what he accused me of ... that I "dared not" place my charges before my countrymen; that I hoped they would never be investigated, and that I stab in the back. ... As I have been publicly and falsely attacked in a place where I could not defend myself, and where privilege covers the words used, I trust you will not think I am doing wrong in publicly defending myself by publishing this letter. ...'

Great Ormond Street Hospital, Bloomsbury   27th September

My dearest Laura, ... Jo's nephew Howard Vyse offered him £25 for the 'Mermaid' drawings but he thought you would not care for this as you want them published. ... I got a letter from Elsie begging me to return Jem back before Wednesday. Poor little woman. She is far from well which makes her a bit unreasonable. I was right unfortunately about a coming event & she is trying to be ill as she was before. [Their first baby had died a year earlier and she had miscarried in February.] Although I am deeply sorry for her I think she really ought not to try to turn poor old Jem into a Sick Nurse. ... I did not like the Colonel's letter for I thought it was pompous & showed too much temper. ... Goodbye Darling, *je t'embrasse dans le cou, Ton* Adrian

Hunstanton   28th September

My own dearest, ... Of course Elsie ought to be able to get on without Jem for a few days. It is most fatal—her wish to tie him always to her apron strings, she must end up by boring him. ... I read some more of Froude's studies, the *Times of Erasmus & Luther*, awfully interesting I thought it. The Essay on the Colonies is behind the times now—for they have been made so much of lately, but the writing is *very* clever, he has such a good grasp of his subject & reasons it all out so clearly. ... Adieu, ever your own *Laure*

Great Ormond Street Hospital, Bloomsbury   28th September

Ma Laure, Jem & I had a hurried dinner at the Café Royal during which Jem poured out his soul to me. Elsie gets bursts of wild crying—and she cries just the same whether he is there or not. Her nerves must be very much out of order poor thing. I suppose in her state it is difficult to be quite rational but it is certainly hard on Jem. Dining at the next but one table were 3 old Ceylon friends of mine. Hardinge Cameron (a son of the photographing Mrs Cameron) & two brothers called Saunders, one of whom is Govt. Agent at Colombo. When Jem left I joined them & they made me go with them to the Pavilion & afterwards gave me Supper at the Continental which was full of gilded vice. I was rather annoyed to find some ladies attached to the party when I arrived. However there was no help for it so I sat down & had some oysters. But it has left a taint upon me & I feel unhappy that I went near them. … Goodnight my Sweet, Your Adrian

OCTOBER 1886

YORK CLUB, 8 ST JAMES' SQUARE   1ST OCTOBER

My dearest, I have been busy getting up the Ceylon Dinner which is to take place at Willis's Rooms with Sir James Longden in the Chair. They have made me the acting Steward which is rather a trouble. When I came into the Club last night before dinner I saw Freddy Bateman, to whom I nodded, & his brother Lee sitting beside him. Lee had the impudence to say 'how do you do' but I cut him dead at which he is I believe furious. Much as I dislike having a row I am not prepared to know that man.[90] His wife is in town, but they are going back to Spain soon. I dined with Jo & Wallscourt who told me that his wife was terribly cut up still over the death of their young daughter. He himself did not seem to care much. I was told that he went to the Aquarium on the day of the Funeral which sounds an odd thing to do. … Goodbye, your fond lover Adrian

GREAT ORMOND STREET HOSPITAL, BLOOMSBURY   4TH OCTOBER

My own Darling, … Do you think that the Catton people would give me some thing for my Hospital? We are dreadfully hard up just now. I can see my way to paying the October bills but we shan't have a penny for November. … I wish that I could put my arms round you my darling, Your Adrian

CATTON HALL, NORWICH   5TH OCTOBER
[WITH GURNEY & MINNA BUXTON]

My own darling, … This place looks so pretty, a big garden a mass of roses and a park full of deer. The house is hideous but large & comfortable & they have an excellent Chef. I do not envy my newly married friend much—with her grey haired husband & eight ready made grown up children. Minna is such a nice creature & a very kind hostess, and looks like a Japanese on a screen. The men here are not very interesting. Last night we played Cork pool—on a wretched little make believe table. They are all so short sighted, they say they can not see to play on anything larger. … I am afraid these people would not be good for a subscription, they have the rage that so many rich people have of imagining they are hard up—& I believe they do loads for the local charities. … Last night Minna came to my room—she talked about our engagement & was nice & sympathetic, but I will never say much about our waiting so long—one must keep a brave front before the world—don't you think so darling? … Ever your *Laure*

Great Ormond Street Hospital, Bloomsbury 5th October

My Darling, … Jo looks very much out of spirits & cannot yet realize that he has to go from the Bachelors' on Jan.y 1st. He will talk on about the Club affairs as if he were to be there for the next 100 years instead of as many days. Who is the Muriel Hoare? Is she one of the lot with whom Daisy Orde went a-Hoaring!!! I don't think I should like her for the word she uses—'awfully' is a word I hate & the users thereof likewise. [Laura had written of her as: 'the sort of girl who says things are "awfully beastly" & calls people "awful beasts" about 30 times a day.'] … Goodbye darling, your Adrian

York Club, 8 St James' Square 6th October

Darling, … This evening I met the man who is making my Father's Gun. He told me the gun was really coming up next week to be finished by Maudslay's. They ought to be able to fire the first shot by the middle of November. This man is the most thorough going believer in the gun I ever met & he seems clever & to know what he is talking about. … Goodnight my own dear Love, Your Adrian

Catton Hall, Norwich 8th October
[with Gurney & Minna Buxton]

My darling, … The men here are not at all an interesting lot, as my hostess remarked to me. She thought people who were very keen about shooting hardly ever could talk about anything worth listening to. Ld Westbury goes today—his conversation is mostly racing and double entendres. Sir W. Ffolkes always bores me, though he tries to be civil. Mr Wilson is rather rough but more amusing—he took me in to dinner last night & discussed engagements & matrimony. I am certain that he had not the *slightest* idea I was engaged because he spoke as if I also was free to make up my mind to what sort of man I could care for. I did not tell him—was it naughty darling? I really did not flirt with him, at least I don't think so. … Has Mr Lucas been more civil [at the Hospital]? I hope so. … Your loving *Laure*

York Club, 8 St James Square 9th October

My own *Laure*, What a dull party you must have had. Of Westbury I have never heard any good & he comes of a shocking bad lot. But this Wilson—Oh! darling I think you have been flirting with him. … Lucas is vile. I dread losing my temper with him. Tomorrow I mean to tackle old Longden & ask him to apply at the C.O. & find out whether I could not get an Appointment, though if I can only manage my Father I believe there is plenty of tin to be got out of the Gun. ... Goodbye my dearest, Your Adrian

SUNNY HILL, THORPE, NORWICH   SUNDAY, 10TH OCTOBER
[WITH GEOFFREY & MARY BUXTON]

My darling Adrian, ... I really enjoyed my week at Catton. ... Someone told Mr Wilson of our engagement—and he immediately devoted himself entirely to me! much to my amusement, especially when I was told why. He is it appears a great *partie* in Yorkshire—and being rather weak—is terribly afraid of being married by someone against his will, so he was delighted to hear I was safe! Yesterday all the party left Catton and I arrived here & was quite horrified to see Mary Buxton. She used to be quite beautiful but after eight years of matrimony she has become completely *embedded* in fat! very tall & stooping with a huge unwieldy figure. She is only a year older than I am but looks about forty. They have 5 little children. The one I am going to paint, Ivor, is such a sweet, only 2 years old with a pretty little face. ... Darling all the people I meet when I am far from you only make me feel how much I love you & how far happier I am with you than with anyone else. Ever your *Laure*

YORK CLUB, 8 ST JAMES' SQUARE   11TH OCTOBER

My own dear *Laure*, ... Today I had had the Audit, a Meeting of the Medical Com.tee, & a row with Lucas who is getting quite unbearable. His hostility terrifies me for I feel that he is determined to have me kicked out. ... Your Adrian

SUNNY HILL, THORPE, NORWICH   11TH OCTOBER
[WITH GEOFFREY & MARY BUXTON]

My own dear Adrian, ... There is a Nonconformist gathering of sorts in Norwich this week and the *Shepherds* are billeted about in various houses, 3 come here today—Nonconformist parsons, one is a Yankee the head of Yale College—*Noah* Porter his name is. They have just made their *entrée* and a queerer set I never saw, really awful. However they leave at 9. every morning & return at 9. at night—so we shall survive it somehow. ... Take care of yourself—my own dearest—ever your *Laure*

GREAT ORMOND STREET HOSPITAL, BLOOMSBURY   12TH OCTOBER

My own Laura, ... Do you think your Piccy of the boy Ivor would do for either the Grosvenor Gallery or the Academy? The idea of your having to fraternize with Dissenting Parsons amuses me. Dr Porter is rather a celebrity in his way & ought to have a lot in him [his *Kant's Ethics* had been published earlier in the year]. ... Goodnight my Sweetheart, Your Adrian

SUNNY HILL, THORPE, NORWICH   13TH OCTOBER
[WITH GEOFFREY & MARY BUXTON]

My own dearest, ... Since I have been here Mary has altered her hair—& done it in coils on the top and the change is wonderful—sometimes she looks quite *beautiful*, like an old picture, a Titian or a Rubens—only she is white instead of that dreadful pink. ... Old Dr Porter left today—he was far the best of the fogies—but *very* weak & ancient. Geoffrey quite expected him to die in the house!! He invited us all to see him in America!!! The other two are quite *dreadful* old fossils & *so* dirty. ... I think it would be too ambitious to try & get my Piccy in at any exhibition. I must paint some little fairy picture. ... Goodnight dear heart, ever your *Laure*

GREAT ORMOND STREET HOSPITAL, BLOOMSBURY   14TH OCTOBER

My darling, My Aunt Cha has arrived from Rhyl. I carried her out of the Invalid Carriage into a Bath Chair & wheeled her into the Eastern Hotel when tomorrow she will be seen by a good Dr. Her speech is quite recovered from her stroke, her arm nearly right, only the leg is helpless. She talked so much of you & sent you her love. I will take her down to Cambridge to Aunt Annie on Saturday & have ordered an Invalid Carriage by the 2.35. ... Goodbye my own, Your Adrian

SUNNY HILL, THORPE, NORWICH   14TH OCTOBER
[WITH GEOFFREY & MARY BUXTON]

My darling Adrian, ... All my time here is given up to the portrait. I even dreamed I was painting all last night! Little Ivor's favourite amusement is grovelling under the sofa—where he lies quite happily eating the apples I want to paint! I have him in a little white frock & sash—playing with the apples—& sitting on a fur rug. ... Ever your *Laure*

YORK CLUB, 8 ST JAMES' SQUARE — 15TH OCTOBER

My darling, My Father is in the greatest spirits. The Admiralty (within a month of being cut free from the W.O.) have accepted his offer & will try his Gun. If he is successful that must mean an order. Besides what a slap in the face to the W.O. who have ever contemptuously refused to have anything to do with my Father or his Gun. You may guess his over mastering delight in this. Really it is a point scored to him for he has always said that if the Sailors were free of the W.O. they would give him a trial. I am very pleased & have been urging him to be practical & speedy. He was in quite an amenable state. Ever Darling, Your Adrian

SUNNY HILL, THORPE, NORWICH — SUNDAY, 17TH OCTOBER
[WITH GEOFFREY & MARY BUXTON]

Dearest Adrian, I dreamt of you all last night, most horrid dreams. I thought I found you lying by the side of a river drowned. I know just how you looked, and all the time I was crying and trying to warm your hands in mine & they were as cold as ice. It was a most evil dream, so vivid. … I like these cousins particularly. They *never* fuss & are evidently devoted to each other without spooning. I am so glad they are not so affectionate as some couples that we know—it is so hard on one when one is alone! Don't you agree? The picture is finished and is liked very much. I believe I am to have £10 for it. I am so glad it is a success, it repays one for all the hard work. … Always yours, Laura

Adrian's father wrote to Laura about his gun on 18th October, and on the envelope she noted much later: 'Letter from Colonel Hope written before he was really insane'.

'Dear Laura, Thank you much for your kind note. It is not many that I get! Yes it is great news about the Gun, especially in view of the last letter I had written to the Admiralty, denouncing the Ordnance Dept in the plainest & most categorical terms.

'I fancy Charlie Beresford [Lord Beresford, Junior Lord of the Admiralty] has given me a leg up, at least it was at his suggestion that I sent my offer to the Admiralty on the 2nd September. Today the Peruvian Naval Commissioner is coming to me, & I think I shall get a Contract from him, and I also have a negotiation on with the Greek Govt & another with the Turks, while on the 3rd Sept. I rejected peremptorily a flattering offer from the Russian Govt to whom I said I could *never* sell *any* Guns.

'Things are therefore moving at last, & it looks as if the turning in my long lane, & therefore in yours & Adrian's, is coming in sight. The first £5,000 of net profit is to go to provide for Jessie, & the second is to go to Adrian, & I believe that you will give him instructions as to what use to put it to. Aff.ly yours, W. Hope'

HUNSTANTON   26TH OCTOBER

My own dearest, ... Our invitation for the Sandringham ball has arrived—*figure toi* Laura Gurney's name is on the card with Tom's and ours! We are rather amused—imagine how disgusted the Ordes & Sommys will be. The other 3 wish to go—& so I shall play Cinderella again. It is so dull to be at home—and be positively the only girl in the County not going to this ball. I am told I ought not to care to go as I am engaged—so I suppose it is my natural depravity that makes me still care about dancing & seeing my friends even though I am, and shall always be—only your *Laure*

GREAT ORMOND STREET HOSPITAL, BLOOMSBURY   26TH OCTOBER

Dearest, ... I went to 105 Piccadilly, where I sat & listened to a weary tale of Julian's misdeeds in Switzerland ... and the misery of a hard bed when Milady was haunted by the possibility of fleas! I dined with them. He was really very nice & she was fairly so. Her boil is a terrible distress to her. Just on the end of her chin, there was such a putting on of ointment & a large black satin patch. After dinner they went to a meeting at S. Pancras, leaving me to my Coffee & Cigarette. The old Butler came & had a long talk to me which was very amusing. He was so naively sorry for my poverty & could not help showing it. ...

My Love, I fully realize your feelings about the Ball. Poor Sweet, shall I ever be able to make up to you all you have lost for my sake. Darling I will try to do this one day when it will not be goodbye so often. Is this why Heaven is so peculiarly happy a place, that there are no more partings there? If so, I wish we there together, out of this very dirty cold world—Goodbye my own, Your Adrian

90   *1st Oct* What was it that Lee Latrobe Bateman had done to warrant Adrian's violent disapproval? At one time he had been devoted to Amy, then he switched his affections to Laura who later recounted how she burnt his love letters to her when she became engaged to Adrian in 1884.

NOVEMBER 1886

HUNSTANTON   2ND NOVEMBER

My own darling, … Eva and I went to see the wild beasty show in Lynn with George & their 'fat boy'. It was rather a good show *but* the atmosphere!! They had a lion cub in a cage with a fat white woolly lamb—they seemed great friends & it was rather pretty to see them together. 2 lions fought in a wretched little cage—with most feeble iron bars—& a door opening towards the audience tied up with wire! They had to be separated with a pitchfork, altogether it was thrilling—and I nearly fled from the scene in tears. … Tom has sent 3 letters & a telegram about his coming tomorrow with Queenie [Gurney], rather unlike his usual habits. Dear heart, Goodbye, ever your own *Laure*

4TH NOVEMBER

My darling Adrian, … Well, the fair cousin has arrived—Tom & she muffed the journey somehow in spite of all their letters & telegrams & Tom arrived first, alone, & talked hard till 9. Poor Queenie was very tired when she did appear having started from Freshwater at 9. She will never be so beautiful as *madame sa mère* was but has much the same sort of fascination about her. She is certainly clever & says the *most* amusing remarks in a very gentle quiet little voice—& her manner is the same—most unlike any of the cousins. Tom tells me she is frantic with the Gurneys & has made him promise not to introduce her to a single one at the Sandringham ball. She is most friendly here—& laughs with us & is very sweet—but there is something insincere about her that would prevent one really caring for her. Perhaps it is rather unkind to say this when there has only been time for first impressions as yet & I may change my mind [she did not]. There is evidently *no* affair *de coeur* going on with Queenie & Tom—such a good thing. They only chaff one another. … Ever your *Laure*

GREAT ORMOND STREET HOSPITAL, BLOOMSBURY   5TH NOVEMBER

My own Laura, … At our House Com.ttee they discussed the question of my lunch & asked me to leave the room to which I agreed if Miss Wood did so too. She got up looking like Vinegar. And then I was recalled to hear them say that they did not consider me entitled to my lunch with the Resident Doctors. How I kept my temper I don't know. But I was just dying to curse them all round & to resign. It is so galling to be put on a level with a footman being reproved. … The Gun was finished yesterday & will be in town almost at once, so you may imagine how the Colonel vaunteth to me of his younger &

solely loved child. ... Tom will be a great fool if he lets the other L. fill his head with prejudices against the Gurneys. Your loving Adrian

York Club, 8 St James' Square   Sunday, 7th November

My dearest, I dined with my Father to meet the rich American who wishes to become a Partner in Hope & Co. Gun matters, a 'Mr Norris' to whom I took a great liking. He is a very quiet gentleman of about 60. The Gun is finished & if the trial be a success it ought not to be long before the Colonel makes enough money to enable him to redeem his promise to us. Both Norris & he offered me the part of negotiating with Foreign Governments for the sale of the Hope gun on behalf of Hope & Co. This if they pay well I should feel disposed to accept. ... By the way, did you see that the Great Oscar has another son, [Vyvyan]? Goodnight *ma Laure*, Your Adrian

Great Ormond Street Hospital, Bloomsbury   9th November

Dearest, Jem has got Pleurisy & is very sorry for himself. Elsie is a fearful worrit in a sick room & would certainly fidget me out of this world. We had a vegetable Dinner beginning with my famous Cabbage Soup which was pronounced to be a great success. This was a Rehearsal for a dinner to be given to a Buddhist named Mohini the next day. Today I have thrown over George Macdonald (who had invited me to dine at the Palace Guard) for Goldsmid as I wish to get G. to join in a letter to the papers which my Father is about to send concerning the Ordnance Scandal. ... Of Riots there has been no word though I daresay that Trafalgar Square has not been as peaceful as Hunstanton. Your loving Adrian

P.S. I dare not let myself think of the Gun too much for as it is I have the most fearful dreams.

11th November

My dearest Laura, I long to hear of your safe arrival at my old cousins. Darling I am so afraid that you are being bored to death. Old Louis Hope I like but he requires an operation to make him talk. ... I have been so busy getting up a new Appeal for we are in a fearfully bankrupt condition & unless we get £3000 shall have to begin the New Year by shutting up a couple of Wards. ... I see you have got quite fond of your Cousin Queenie & I am curious to know if she ever mentions her Mother to you.[91] Next Monday's goodbye already casts a shadow on the joy of our meeting this Saturday at The Knowle. Goodbye my dearest Love, Your Adrian

THE KNOWLE, HAZELWOOD, DERBY   16TH NOVEMBER
[WITH HON. LOUIS AND MRS (SUSAN) HOPE]

My own dearest, … Yesterday, about tea-time there was quite an awakening in the family—Aunt Susan cleared the room, old Miss Campbell played (very well by the by) and we all danced wildly—Highland Scottisches, polkas & country dances—in which Aunt Susan joined & nearly died of puffing & panting. … I don't know whether my presence has demoralized them already but we wound up with Shoeing the Grey Mare, & other gymnastics. Isabel & dull little Laura danced a Cachoucka—quite the most ungraceful performance I ever witnessed! it requires much waving & wreathing of arms & pointing of toes—Aunt Susan and I looked on in fits of laughter as they stumped through the mazes of this seductive dance. After dinner we played *Cork grab* & *Old Maid* & did all those writing puzzles & some card tricks. Aunt Susan was so stirred up by these performances that she actually proposed to invite the *louts* of the neighbourhood & give a social hop!!! … Ever darling, your true love, Laura

18TH NOVEMBER

My darling, … In my letter from Eyre & Spottiswoode they are complimentary about the 'Jaw Crackers' drawings but think they are too disconnected to be published as a book & they ask to see illustrations to some poem or story so I have sent them the 'Mermaid' today. How I wish they would do the 'Mermaid', even if I had to colour the drawings. … Some people are coming tonight & a ball takes place beginning at 7.30!! … Goodbye Sweetheart, ever your *Laure*

GREAT ORMOND STREET HOSPITAL, BLOOMSBURY   18TH NOVEMBER

My own *Laure*, … I have a note from my Father to say that he has already got Sir E. Watkin[92] to promise £50 for the fund to unravel the War Office frauds. But no word of the signing of the Partnership. Have you heard how the Sandringham ball went off & if there were any moving incidents? I expect Uncle Sommy was delightful & left Aunt Kitty to fume with Mrs Orde about Queenie's presence. … I send a long loving kiss my darling not over the Batiste [a fine cotton lawn often used to fill in décolletage], Your Adrian

SHANE'S CASTLE, ANTRIM
[WITH LORD & LADY O'NEILL]

SUNDAY, 21ST NOVEMBER

My own darling Adrian, We arrived here about half past 12 yesterday and Oh we were so *dreadfully* tired. We had some soup and went to bed about 3 o'clock in the afternoon, woke up to have some tea, went fast asleep again, woke up & had a little dinner at 8.—and then went fast asleep again without waking once till 8 o'clock this morning. The journey was *not* a complete success. Imagine my dismay when a telegram was brought me at The Knowle just 15 minutes before I had to start for Derby, saying: 'Your plan an utter failure—cannot possibly reach Derby till 11 o'clock'. This wire was from Tom at *Cambridge* where they had no business to be at all. The Inspector at Derby had written to old Louis Hope saying we should be too late for the Stranraer boat if we left Derby at 11.40 but we must go to Trent and catch the mail there at 10.50.

Old Louis immediately encamped amongst a host of Bradshaw, A.B.C. & other railway guides and found out that I might be able to stop the others at Trent, if their train to Derby stopped there. So I set off on my lonely journey in the darkness with only a chance of meeting the others. I had an hour to wait at Derby where I had to see the Inspector & fuss generally. I then changed trains twice & waited a long time at Trent. I was *so* afraid I should have to go all the way by myself & get into such hot water for making them miss the boat. It was past ten before the train came in—& there to my joy I found them, half asleep & very vexed & tired, having been travelling since 2 o'clock. It really was rather their fault as they had not looked out the trains to Peterboro from Lynn and found there was not one till 6. so had to go to Cambridge instead & wait for hours—but at last we subsided into the Pullman Sleeping Car Mr Hope had engaged for us. It was such a shaking noisy long journey, we slept a little but could not really rest. We revived at 7. & went on board & sat together & chatted & laughed as we steamed away.

The first hour it was lovely & calm—but oh when we got really out to the open sea! Before very long that fatal feeling of *fatigue* crept over your poor *Laure* … over the rest of the passage I will draw a veil. We felt such sad wrecks when we arrived & were so glad to hear we only had 2 hours more in the train. The carriage sent to meet us was too late so we finished our long journey by arriving on 2 jaunting cars, reminding one so of Knocklofty.

This is the most beautiful place but the house is modern, a huge house built round 3 sides of a square, with a great pile of buildings at one end with what looks like a great Chapel—but is really a ball room & music room with a splendid organ. The old Castle was burnt down nearly 100 years ago. It is a lovely ruin, with 2 great round towers & a wide terrace mounted with cannons—right over the lake and you can just see the misty blue mountains on the other side. … At present there is only Louisa O'Neill,[93] her brother Tom Cochrane [a cousin of his Park Street namesake] & his wife Lady Gertrude. Wallace Baillie (from Lamington) & some more men for shooting come in the middle of the week & on Thursday there is to be a great ball. They make us very welcome here. … Ever your loving *Laure*

22ND NOVEMBER

My Darling, … Amy & I have a large room together here, with 2 beds side by side—& I have a dressing room. Next door is Tom's room & we are in a tower rather apart from the other spare rooms. There are great corridors with niches, each occupied by a life sized Venus—or other Goddess—that would strike terror & dismay into the heart of the British Matron—I am afraid *you* would rather like them. There is a good billiard room opening in to a long library where we generally sit. The books are shut up in glass cases—which always spoils a library I think. … There are some lovely walks near the lake through woods & rockeries filled with every sort of fern & flower & shrub, the sort of winding sheltered walks with seats & bowers that you & I would love to wander in. …

We have already heard stories of the Banshee—but it fortunately remains wailing round the ruins. Far more alarming is *another* ghost that has a mysterious legend which they are going to tell us this evening—whatever it is *these* people believe in it for the ghost is supposed to tramp around the house at night & Louisa O'Neill made us solemnly promise *not* to look out of the window if we heard it. Every night at 10 o'clock there is a perfectly unaccountable rushing sound & a bang against the drawing-room window—we heard it last night. They say nothing is to be seen, but it *cannot* be explained in any way—except by the legend. I long to hear the story for it may do to write out for the 'Runcton Annual' this Christmas. Tom Cochrane chaffs his wife & says nothing will induce her to sleep alone in this house. Luckily for me I have Amy as I cannot – – – – –! … You must fancy or dream the kiss I cannot give you—ever your *Laure*

23RD NOVEMBER

My dearest Adrian, I was *so* disappointed today, the 3rd day without any word from you. Lord O'Neill came back last night—he is *so* shy & quiet—about 5ft 4 [in.] which although the perfect height for the Venus leaves something to be desired for a man. He is rather nice & kind but too shy for a good host. Louisa is a nice creature but very quiet too. The children do not appear except the eldest girl Etta, a pretty little thing of 7 with long old fashioned corkscrew curls. ... I used your tonging lamp present for the first time last night to do those little curls in the back of my neck—that I think you like. Don't forget to write to your *Laure*

Great Ormond Street Hospital, Bloomsbury   23rd November

My dearest Laura, At Cambridge, I dined at Scroop House (where I am staying with the Clarkes as there is no room for me at Aunt Annie's house) and met a Mr Pollock, Editor of the *Saturday Review*, who would only talk of the Colonel & the War Office. After dinner we all went to see the A.D.C. dress rehearsal of the first part of the divine William's *Henry IV*. A Mr Newton acted Falstaff admirably. The rest acted too vilely for criticism. ... The dresses were magnificent—and we were all amused. On Sunday the Clarkes gave a dinner party. Two girls were stopping there—Miss Cole is a handsome brown clever girl not quite a.1, Miss Welldon was fair, stupid, a sister of the Head Master of Harrow, too tightly laced but with a pretty figure, only drawn together so much in front that the effect in an evening frock was peculiar as the natural depression was squeezed out. No room for Cupid's head to rest. ...

Yesterday I had more work at the Hospital than I could get through but had to leave at 4 to go to the Gattys who had music & had begged me to come & talk about the Hospital with some frumps who want to help me get money. There was such a nice Mrs Molesworth who writes children's books as you may recollect. ... I used to know Lady Gertrude's grandmother, old Lady Abercrombie, & I have danced with her at her Mother's house. She was such a nice girl. Goodbye my best beloved, Your Adrian

Shane's Castle, Antrim   24th November
[with Lord & Lady O'Neill]

My Adrian Darling, A whole lot of people arrived yesterday—but I am afraid they are a very slow set—everyone seems so shy & stiff. ... I have made a conquest of the old General Montgomery Moore & have been much chaffed by Lady Gertrude. I must ask her if she remembers her partner—but she has had six years of matrimony & probably has forgotten those frivolous days. She *is* very nice indeed & we have made great friends. I don't think her husband seems to care much for her. They are more like brother & sister & *never* seem to have any *asides*. He is good-looking & rather a flirt. Two more men arrive this evening & more tomorrow for the dance. ... Our Tom has just come in— he says they had an awful day—all bad shots & all shooting recklessly at each other! not giving the pheasant time to rise ... Amy has come in & silence has departed. So goodbye my own darling Adrian, your *Laura*

26TH NOVEMBER

My darling Adrian, Yesterday, tired of the dull girls here, Amy & I—by special request—joined the shooters, lunched with them. Amy is perfectly happy shooting, & tearing about the garden & shrubberies with a loaded gun, while the 2 Toms beat the bushes for her. I had had to tear myself away from Wallace Baillie's fascinating society—to write to you dearest. ... Last night the dance was fun—Amy & I both enjoyed it—but I don't think everyone did. The ball room is so *very* large, we were not enough people & several of the men didn't dance. Mr O'Neill (Lord O's brother) sprained his ankle trying to show us an Irish jig! ... Old General Moore has come out as a wit- –& is a jolly old boy. We are all rather mad about a new game called 'telegrams'[94]—which we introduced & Mrs Moore let out that she and the General had played it in bed before they got up the other morning. There's an Irish couple here who are *very* uninteresting, almost bordering on middle age, & 3 other girls remain hopeless dull—but we leave them to depress each other. Old Mrs Moore is nice & Gertrude we like *immensely*. She said directly she heard your name she remembered hearing about you at Lady A's & also your Mother, & meeting you too dearest. ...

Our engagement is often talked about—but sometimes sympathy rather unnerves one. Do you know what I mean? ... Adieu, my dear dear Adrian, ever your *Laure*

YORK CLUB, 8 ST JAMES' SQUARE   26TH NOVEMBER

My own dearest, ... I am so glad you liked Lady Gertrude. She *is* plain, but rich my love. The match was made up by the two families. Tom C. was alleged to be the one virtuous Guards man in London. What think you? Tomorrow I am going to see the Gun with my Father. He has been summoned before the Royal Commission on the W.O. Scandals on Tuesday 30th Nov. I shall be very anxious to know how it goes on. The partnership is not yet signed which maddens me. My visit to Cambridge did not make me one bit low. My sister is I can see very nervous about meeting you & yet wants to very much. She has never said so but evidently she feels ashamed of those two unhappy letters she wrote after our engagement. However I have forgotten them now. ... Goodbye *ma petite Laure*, Your Adrian

Great Ormond Street Hospital, Bloomsbury   27th November

My dearest *Laure*, Today [Saturday] I rushed off to go to the Rag by 11. where I met my Father & Norris [his prospective partner]. We all went off to see the Gun at Maudslay's. It is really too lovely. The steel is so pure that it looks like a huge silver pencil case 10½ feet long. I really never thought a gun could be so elegant in its figure & yet so evidently strong. Now I see why the thought of its bursting never occurs to Jessop or to my Father. Maudslay's Manager is really quite enthusiastic about the quality of the Steel and the brilliancy of mechanical invention shown in the breach. I am amazed that the Colonel should have been able without any pattern or workshop to completely work out in his own head so great a revolution in Gunnery. As Norris said to me, 'This is a Revolution not an Improvement.' Here is a very rough sketch of the 'Hope' 2½ inch armour piercing Gun to throw a Steel Bolt 15 inches long with a charge of 19lbs of Powder. Prodigious!!! ...

Amy must be thoroughly enjoying herself but I hope she won't shoot you. I think the old General sounds charming. You ought to make a fancy sketch of the General & Mrs Moore playing 'telegrams' in bed. I am much flattered that Lady G. should recollect me at all. Her dear old Grandmother was really a great friend of mine, one of my old Dowagers to whom I was devoted years ago. ... By the way, would your cousin Laura [Gurney] like to send me one of her stories? I will show it privately to a man who might help her & I would not reveal her name of course. ...

I have got hold of 5 ladies now to beg for us & to send out this appeal to their friends. I send you a copy of it that you may see what I have been doing. 2000 have I sent off, many with private notes as well. Up to now I have only got £70. It is horrible to think of shutting up 40 beds at Xmas but I fear we shall have to do it. Goodbye, Your Adrian

Sunday, 28th November

My own dear love, I had a very pleasant little dinner at the McIvers but really the house is too hideous for words. It is a nice house in Brook St but their combined taste is too disappointing. The Dining-Room is hung with pure ivory white stamped & embossed leather. The effect is that of carved ivory fruit & flowers. Each boss is padded out so as to make it stand out well. The leather is Japanese & the first hung here. I do not like it at all. Then with such a background they have Chippendale chairs, a black carved oak side board & a Cairo screen. Such a jumble & the whole house is the same. They have been to many Sales & have bought all that they took a fancy to. In fact it is like an old curiosity shop in some way. ... Mrs McIver was in grey satin with old black Spanish Lace over it. This looked very pretty. If only the black Lace had also crossed the poor thin little brown breast which looked like a Chocolate Souttlé that had never risen. ... Goodbye my little Laura, Your Adrian

York Club, 8 St James' Square   30th November

My dearest, The Col. has scored a great success before the Royal Com.n. He is sitting beside me & has told me how his evidence was received. Nothing could have been better. [Mr Justice] Stephen, the President of the Royal Commission, has treated him as a friendly witness. This removes a terrible weight from my mind. This is great news for if the Col. establishes his charges they are bound to take the Gun when it proves successful as I am sure it will. Goodnight, Your Adrian

---

91 *11th Nov* According to Laura (Queenie) Gurney's later memoirs when she was Lady Troubridge, *Memories and Reflections* (1925), she was always devoted to her mother and fond of her stepfather. In 1897 Alice Gurney married her long-time friend, Col John Bourchier Stracey-Clitherow CBE (1855-1931) of Hotham Hall, ER Yorks, and her younger son, Thomas Claud Gurney, assumed the name and arms of Clitherow in 1932. *See also* p249 and endnote 89.

92 *18th Nov* Sir Edward Watkin 1st Bt, Chairman of the South Eastern, the Manchester, Sheffield & Lincolnshire & Metropolitan Railways; Labour MP for Gt Yarmouth (1857-58), for Stockport (1864-68, for Hythe (1874-86), and Liberal Unionist (LU) for Hythe (1886-95).

93 *21st Nov* Lady O'Neill, née Louisa Cochrane, was a great niece of Laura's maternal grandmother Anna Maria née Cochrane, wife of Adml Sir E T Troubridge 2nd Bt. Her brother Tom Cochrane (later Baron Cochrane of Cults) was a second cousin once removed to his namesake, who let the Park Street house to the Troubridges in the summer of 1886. Wallace Cochrane-Baillie of Lamington was also a great nephew of Anna Maria Troubridge and so related to both Louisa O'Neill and to the young Troubridges. *See also* p217 and footnote 82.

94 *26th Nov* 'Telegrams' was a popular paper & pencil game in the mid to late 1880s. A *subject* was suggested, then the name of a *place*—say a city or county. The players then had to write a telegram bearing on the *subject*, of which the initial letters of each word had to spell out the chosen *place name*. The telegrams would then be read out anonymously so that guessing the author often caused much amusement. Lady (Constance) Battersea gave the following example in her *Reminiscences* (1922): '... (*subject*) the approaching election, (*place*) Brighton. In the space of a few seconds Mr Gladstone handed in his paper which read: *BE READY IN GREAT HOUSES TO OPERATE NOBLY*'.

DECEMBER 1886

SHANE'S CASTLE, ANTRIM   1ST DECEMBER
[WITH LORD & LADY O'NEILL]

My dearest, … I think the London Dowagers you spoke of were right about Tom Cochrane. He is a particularly nice fellow—so cheery & *modern* & yet very nice & gentle—quite charming with Louisa O'Neill, his sister. We both like him very much indeed. I think he & Gertrude are really great pals but they are quite without romance. At least she is—the most matter of fact sort of character, with a touch of the *Squaw* about her—but he is very unselfish & nice—so doesn't take advantage of it. I like her too, she is so good-natured & kind, but rather untidy, & not troubled with many ideas. After all, her riches have taken to themselves wings—which seems very hard lines for them both. Her father Ld Glasgow has lost any amount of money—& is selling all the property he can, everything that would have come to her. Their 3 little children come tomorrow. Tom [Cochrane] tells me that *little Tom* is a 'ripper' & had already asked me to make a sketch of him. …

I am so sorry to hear you have had neuralgia. Did you try quinine? Is not that the thing to take? … I have learnt to play chess here & rather like it—but it is very brainy. We play billiards here a good deal as there is a capital table—we play from tea-time to dressing-time. … I should like to meet that Mrs Molesworth, her books are very pretty. Goodbye dearest, ever your own *Laure*

GREAT ORMOND STREET HOSPITAL, BLOOMSBURY   4TH DECEMBER

My dearest *Laure*, … I am engaged in negotiations about a new Rifle (a Magazine Rifle) in which I see a fair chance of making money speedily. Also I have been begging money in the City for the Hospital. I got £500 in three days. But then I was cunning. I went to Rothschild & asked for money. He said, 'What is Baring going to give you?' So I rushed off to Barings & told them R. was waiting to see what they would give. Tom Baring behaved like a trump & gave me £100. Back I went to R. & got another £100. Then I went to Glyns & got a 3rd £100 out of them. Was not that capital? … The Colonel is very ill. He has got something the matter with his kidneys & won't go to the Doctor. I am just being worried to fiddle strings. I shall have got over £1000 for the Hospital before Xmas. As we want £3000 it is rather hopeful. No thanks though from anyone. Your A.

28 GREAT ORMOND STREET ['MY ROOMS']   SUNDAY, 5TH DECEMBER

My darling, I have been to see the Colonel today. He is very ill, I fear. This is most disastrous at the present time when nothing is really settled about the Gun. I am really at my wit's end. I got a letter from Lothar de B. [Bunsen] asking me to be his best man on the 6th—7th Jan at Edinburgh. ... Jo will, I hope, get a post in the Royal Insurance Co. which I am glad of. Poor Grev. Wells (one of Jo's nephews) has died in Egypt. This is a great shock to Jo & me for he was a dear good fellow. ... Your letters are the only comfort which I have. My soul is among the lions just now & I have not the luck of Daniel. Every lion takes out a bit just where it hurts most. Goodbye, Your Adrian

17TH DECEMBER

My own dearest Laura, I have been working like a horse both here & at the Burton Gun [Magazine Rifle]. Today we had a long wrangle all together with a lawyer about the Agreement. However I think it is at last settled to everyone's satisfaction. I have just got £700 more for the Hospital. They have given me three days leave to go to Edinburgh. I am not going to get a new coat as best man. Lothar must take me as I am. ... Now goodbye my sweet Laura, Your Adrian

18TH DECEMBER

My darling, ... My dinner with the old General, Sir Edwin Johnson, was pleasant. The other guest was a fellow called Theobald who had been in the Bank of England with me. He has just left as he has been made Sec.y of Guinness & Co. With a £1000 a year. I could not help envying him dreadfully. ... Sweetheart mine I do feel so tired out. Tomorrow Battersea claims me for its prey. Goodbye darling, Your Adrian

HUNSTANTON   SUNDAY, 19TH DECEMBER

My own dearest Adrian, I am sending you a play book—don't think it very cruel of me—but we do so want you to take part in this little play we are going to act at Runcton. I think it might be made very funny with comic make ups— and you know it does not take much to bring the house down at Runcton. We want you to be the old widower if you will—your speeches are *very* short and easy to learn. Amy is to be the sporting girl—and *I* am to be the jeune premier—her lover! In a fair curly wig and blue spectacles and an ulster. You will not know me. *You* must be thoroughly disguised—with grey hair & long whiskers. I was so glad to hear the Rifle affair was solid enough to be actually on paper. ... Goodbye Sweetheart, Ever your *Laure*

GREAT ORMOND STREET HOSPITAL, BLOOMSBURY 20TH DECEMBER

My darling, What a shell to burst on me, unprotected & in bed. I suppose I must do as I am bid. You ought to wear a pair of Tom's knickerbockers under the ulster. I will trust to you for powdering my moustaches. Have you got any make up paints? Do you want a little black moustache darling, or will – – – – –? ... By the way I will not act unless you go to the Doctor & exhibit your little white knee. It is a very serious thing to have anything the matter with one's knee. Goodbye, Your Adrian

HUNSTANTON 21ST DECEMBER

Dearest, ... The old Doctor thought rather badly of my poor knee and says the joint is badly bruised and has forbidden me to dance—such a shame at Christmas time. Fancy my only being allowed to dance *squares* on Christmas night. Uncle Sommy is most glad we have found something to act. I shall not allow you *any* tender passages with the widow! I know how dangerously fascinating they are to you as a rule!! When Amy read the play she insisted on taking the young man's part instead of me & I don't feel a bit like the sporting girl but I shall get through it somehow—burlesque it I think. Amy is simply killing as Horace, a dreadful milksop with a lisp. ... Ever your *Laure*

Adrian had barely a week off at Christmas and Laura's Journal recorded nothing of their time together at Runcton, nor of the Christmas theatricals there.

HOPTON ST MARGARET, GREAT YARMOUTH 30TH DECEMBER
[WITH AUNT MAGGIE ORDE]

My darling Adrian, Tardy [Orde] telegraphed me to come here by the 9. train. I had to get up early—before 7. When I went down to my solitary breakfast at Runcton, I had a little chat with Uncle Sommy who appeared in a red tartan dressing gown—he was about to plunge into his Bubley Ubley bath! ... We have a rehearsal at the school at 3 o'clock and the Hopton play begins at 9. ... Now alas we are parted again, Adieu, ever your own love, *Laure*

My dearest Adrian, A happy new year to you. Darling how I *hope* it may be a happy year for both of us. ... I have been skating a little. I really could not resist it—the ice on the lake looked so delicious. I have now quite recovered the long tiring day I had yesterday—getting up at 7, the journey, the rehearsal & the acting—followed by a supper, games—& a soirée with E.[Orde]—in my room till 2 o'clock, making a good long day of it. *The Happy Pair* went off very well but we had a *wondrous* dull audience, of local parsons and their wives, & they were so *dreadfully* silent, although they *said* they had enjoyed it. ... Goodbye my *own darling*, ever your *Laure*

.

JANUARY 1887

MIDDLETON TOWERS, KING'S LYNN   4TH JANUARY
[WITH SIR LEWIS & LADY JARVIS]

My own darling Adrian, ... The play last night was a great success. There were more than 200 people and they were a capital audience, shouting with laughter at every point. ... I wish you had been there dearest, I know you would have enjoyed my little triumph. There was rather an excruciating village Band, also patriotic & comic songs—ad lib—and conjuring tricks—not bad. *The Happy Pair* came as a sort of *pièce de résistance* in the middle of the programme. One very funny item was a duet by Amy & Louey Jarvis—which utterly broke down—as from some cause—probably the thaw last night— the piano suddenly went *perfectly* dumb & there they were hammering away frantically, Amy *dying* with laughter, & only an occasional vague bass note responding to their efforts. ...

Ah darling, I do miss you *sadly* sometimes, your *never* failing love and sympathy and your tender care for me, and *long* for the time when we may be together. ... What a pity the Happy Pair in Green Street take to pecking at each other. Of course it *is* very trying for her to be left alone but if she is so X she will make him *glad* to get away from her. ... Will you make a speech as best man at Lothar's wedding? Goodbye my own darling, ever your *Laure*

HUNSTANTON   5TH JANUARY

My own darling best man, ... I am so sorry to hear this Royal Insurance Co. affair turns out to be such a small thing for poor old Jo [only £200 a year and Commission]. I think it is horrid of his brother not to help him with an allowance. I found yet more New Year cards here yesterday—& our fireplace is decorated with 125 of these offerings—Amy's, Vi's, Helen's & mine. ... Ever darling Adrian your own *Laure*

GREAT ORMOND STREET HOSPITAL, BLOOMSBURY   8TH JANUARY

My dearest *Laure*, After all I went by 3rd Class to Edinburgh & tipped the Guard to let me travel alone so I was quite comfy & really not too cold. After a bath & breakfast at old Jane Buchanan (my cousin) in walked Lothar [de Bunsen] & we went off to look after Bouquets etc. & went to the old Cathedral Church for a sort of rehearsal of the ceremony. Then we lunched at the Kinlochs & I met 'Mrs Lothar'—May Kinloch. She is a nice girl with a pretty figure, small, rather too much colour in her face, enormous hips of which she is evidently rather proud. A pleasant little person who will drive the good Lothar with a tight rein. ...

After giving Mrs Lothar my little offering I spent the afternoon calling on Great-Aunts, first on three Miss Hope's (sisters of my Grandfather) who live together. Each is an Invalid & stops in her own room. It was like the picture of the wolf dressed up as Red Riding Hood's Grandmama when I was led in & saw an old face with gleaming eyes & such a beard lying swathed in shawls on a bed. Rather horrible to kiss, however I shut my eyes & was awfully scrubbed. But Oh! the state of exhaustion I was in after having had to answer 3 sets of questions about everything from you to the Gun. Then they confused you with your Aunt Chatty Troubridge [aged about 66] & they had never heard of your Father's death for their poor old heads were much addled. By that time I had to bolt home for a 7 o'clock dinner to which two ancient virgins, cousins of mine, had been bidden. They were dull & I was sleepy so I rejoiced when they went. Jane Buchanan & I had a long & dreary form of prayer & then to bed at 10.15.

The next morning when I woke there was a furious Snow Storm in the middle of which Lothar arrived to beg me to rush round with him about the final arrangements. There are always so many little worries. Then we arrayed ourselves in our best raiment & went up to the New Club to lunch with Davy Kinloch, one of May's brothers. The Wedding was at 2. The Bride had on a lovely old brocade but her cheeks were too red & they shone through her plain net veil like apples through a Spider's web. The six Bridesmaids were wonderful plain about the head. They had brown velvet tailor made frocks which looked very warm. Bonnets of the same with mauve & violet feathers which matched the two shades of Chrysanthemums in their bouquets. Where the Altar usually is there was a Pew of seats for the Elders. In front of that a large Oak kitchen Table flanked by two black robed Presbyterian Ministers, one of them being the Dean of the Chapel Royal of Holy Rood & Dean of the Thistle, & wore the Collar & badge. There were no Altar Rails but there were steps. A row of hassocks was put right along, for the Bride & Lothar in the middle, three Bridesmaids on either side & myself on the extreme right next to Lothar's elder sister Marie de B. [not the Abbey Lodge Marie]. I felt as if I were being married to her by some horrid mistake. The Service was very nice, simple & short. None of the plain speaking of the English one. No reference to future little Lothars, nothing which need have made the youngest Bridesmaid blush to hear. There was an Organ & two hymns. We went to the Vestry, signed our names & then processed down the Aisle, first the happy pair, then the six Bridesmaids & I closed the procession with the Hats & Coats.

Then off to the house of Mrs Dundas—a cousin both of Kinlochs & of mine. She gave the Reception as her house was more suited for it. ... The presents were all there, very pretty & useful. Lots of silver things, a silver Sugar Basin from Clemency Hubbard—was it poisoned? Some nice rings & a few diamonds, 10 fans. My gift was a Spider whose body was a Pearl & with Ruby eyes. It was on a Stick like your fly & not so pretty but as there is Bruce blood through the mother there was an implied compliment.

Harry Kinloch, the second brother, and I had a jolly dinner all by our two selves & then joined Lady Tweeddale in her box at the Pantomime. The thing was called *Crusoe* & there were one or two pretty girls acting, one pair of legs we all admired, they were really fine & the face & body passable. ... The next day I had promised to show Lothar's two sisters Edinburgh which was really looking lovely. ... All this we did on our toes ... & after lunch I went to see another Hope Gt-Aunt, Margaret, where I was shown 2 of my pictures—Landscapes with Cattle by Bürger [possibly the Dutchman Nicolaes Berchem] ... Marie de B. is a dear girl. We struck up quite a friendship & talked away tremendously. From my old relations I got no tips but vague promises of marriage gifts. But it did me good to be so warmly greeted by everyone. One feels in Edinburgh that one is not such an absolute cast away as in London. I have got quite a rage for my nation land again & for my countless Cousins who said kind words about our future together. But it *was* trying to see Lothar go off looking so happy. I felt it like a stab thrust. This must really be the last wedding before our own dear love. ... My love to everyone, Your Adrian

HUNSTANTON   SUNDAY, 9TH JANUARY

My own dearest, I was *so* delighted with your long letter this morning—it was all so *well* told and *so* interesting. ... What a lot you managed to cram in to the 3 days—quite a *Troubridgey* whirl. You can no longer chaff us about our energy & love for being on the go. ... I have only just seen *that* Marie de B.—she draws & paints (landscapes) quite *beautifully*. ... I hear from Eyre & Spottiswoode, returning the 'Mermaid' this morning—the reason they give is that the story—Hans Andersen's *The Little Mermaid*!—is too poor to make a good book—I did not feel the least disappointed—or scarcely at all—I am getting more philosophic—& neutral. I thought it just like my luck. None of my drawings seem to prosper somehow. I have heard not a word of the 'Jaw Crackers' drawings that Ld A. Hill took when we were staying with the O'Neills. Ever your *Laure, qui t'aime bien*

28 Great Ormond Street, Bloomsbury ['My Rooms']   9th January

My own dear love, Today I have lunched with Elsie whom I found all alone. Jem's doctor had ordered him to go abroad but forbade Elsie to leave London if she wishes to have a baby so he has gone to the Riviera for a month. Then I called on several people about a concert I want to get up for the Hospital at Grosvenor House in the Spring. Then I came back here, dressed, & went to fetch Elsie with whom I dined at the Café Royal. We had a very good dinner & there were some very pretty women round the room. Elsie attracted a good deal of attention as she had on such lovely diamonds. Some men whom I knew were evidently much mystified as to who she could be. We too were very jolly & drank your health in a bumper my Sweet. Elsie is quite reconciled to Jem's being away. However I expect that I shall be called on to act *cicisbeo* a good deal. You won't be jealous, will you Darling? My love to all, Your Adrian

P.S. Darling I send you one kiss just where the Robe de nuit buttons over— *Ma Laure bien aimée, je t'adore*

Hunstanton   13th January

My own darling Adrian, ... Did you see in the *Morning Post* an account of the inauguration of the Meresia Habitation of the Primrose League at Battersea— with your Father as Chairman! I wish *you* had been one of the glorious band! It is called after that awful Miss Nevill.[95] I daresay you knew. I suppose she is clever, but to me *very* unattractive. I did not know the Col. espoused their cause so warmly—he told me once he was always in opposition—whichever side was in. Wasn't it like him. ... Ever your *Laure*

Great Ormond Street Hospital, Bloomsbury   14th January

My dearest Love, Lothar had begged me to come & see him & Mrs Lothar while they were in London (still on honeymoon) so I went straight from here and found a tea-party of ladies only with Lothar struggling bravely among them. His two sisters and Marie de B. of Abbey Lodge. The bride was uncommon neat & as self possessed as you like. They both looked as if matrimony had agreed with them. His face shone like a Moon, hers like a Sun. By the way, Marie quoted long extracts from my letter to *you* about the wedding, & I thought the Bride looked rather queerly at me. I only mention this because as neither Amy nor this Marie are models of discretion it would be well to avoid anything like a *colportage* [retailing] of little talks which are only between you & I. I sat with them for a bit when the rest left & she pulled out a sock & began to knit away quite in a Matronly way. They did seem so happy. ... There are times when the thought or sight of the happiness of others makes me perfectly furious. ... Good old Aunt Susan's [Hope] slippers are not bad & as I was awfully in want of a pair I shall get them made up if I have time to think of it. ...

Young Stanhope [one of Midget Wallcourt's brothers] made me dine with him & go to the Gaiety where we saw *Monte Cristo* only without Nellie Farren. Her part was taken by a girl who did not fill her tights in front & nearly burst them behind. She also would wear 'his' waistband up under her arms thus accentuating the fact that she was not of the male sex. The Yankee Actress I thought poor but she had on the most lovely grey tights I ever saw. Only they came right up into what Tailors call the fork without any fullness to hide anything. I never saw such a thing before on the English Stage. Her back view was grotesque. I dare not say any more. There was also a French girl to whom I rather lost my heart for she acted & danced with so much enjoyment. Then there was a really lovely Dancer. Quite as good, I thought, as Kate Vaughan. The Prince & his Son were there & he evidently shared my opinion for he never took his glasses off the Dancer & clapped her vigorously every time. She did not look pretty but her dancing was lovely & so were her petticoats, to the knee like Kate V. always had. She did look so much more graceful than the fat little grey Yankee piece of nakedness. I saw some Ceylon friends of mine in a box—she is the lady who lost one side of her figure playing lawn tennis in Ceylon. There was a girl in a box who excited my amazement. Apparently only 18. Pretty face, beautifully dressed but with a line like this to her stays [graphic outline here of the side view of a very prominent and pointed breast]. It was not, I am sure, a case of padding. Otherwise she was thin enough. Can she have been an Advertisement for that preparation you always see in the French Papers '*le lait mamillaire*'. Really everyone in the theatre was looking at this bust hanging over the box.

What a naughty letter this has become dearest. Well *I should* like to present some one with a pair of those dove coloured tights all the same. Goodbye Sweetheart. Your own lover Adrian

P.S. I guess you won't read much of the latter part of *this* letter aloud to the fam.—A.

HUNSTANTON   SUNDAY, 16TH JANUARY

My darling Adrian, ... Darling what a *naughty* mind you were in when you wrote to me on Friday! but I am afraid it only made me laugh. I should like to see *Monte Cristo*. I feel that I require frivolizing after a few weeks at the Wash. I don't think I have ever seen such very *tighty* tights as you describe—it makes one feel quite *knock kneed* even to *think* of wearing them. I was amused with dear old Aunt Susan's tragic appeal to you not to humbug her about the slippers. She will not believe you unless you have them made up. Are those nice old snakeskin shoes dead? It is too bad that I have never made you any slippers— quite one of the 'first duties of a fiancée' and neglected by me. ... I am so sorry you had the annoyance of hearing your letter about the wedding quoted by Marie—it was quite my fault for reading it aloud. I will be more careful darling—for it would be simply unendurable if we could not write freely to each other. It seems curious to me that Lothar & his wife give tea-parties & receive their cousins *already*. What sangfroid! After a few days or a week of marriage I think it would be distinctly a bore to have one's girl friends in shoals to visit one so soon. What is your opinion?

Yesterday we had such an invasion—our privacy was rudely intruded upon by a total stranger without a shred of introduction. A *missionary from Canada*— was shot into the very bosom of the family. We four—at twilight—all talking & laughing round the fire when he suddenly appeared—his reception was *chilling*—for as he timidly advanced carrying some papers—Amy, Vi & Helen all thought it was a summons!! & gave him a stony stare of horror—ending in a gasp of relief when he murmured that he was a missionary from Canada, & immediately seated himself upon the best arm chair without waiting to be asked to sit down. A more perfectly idiotic specimen of the race I never saw. He rambled on about enlisting our sympathy and interest in this great work without attempting to describe what it was. We asked him a few questions and I think he was horribly frightened. The only fact he dwelt upon was that the poor Emigrants had such large families. Then he rambled on about the enormous amount of poor people who came out to Canada every year—& ended by asking dramatically, 'What would England do if all these poor labourers returned upon her hands'. It was just like a riddle. He looked round triumphantly as no one gave the answer. (I am sure this is a great *point* in his lecture.) I entirely spoilt it by instantly asking another riddle—'Yes that is all very well, but *what would Canada do without them*? & scored one as he had just told us labourers were so much wanted and could earn 5/- [shillings] a day. However he remained such ages that we had to promise a subscription to get rid of him. The parting words of the missionary were—'May you be watered'. ... Goodbye, ever your *Laure*

GREAT ORMOND STREET HOSPITAL, BLOOMSBURY   22ND JANUARY

My darling, I have been in such a rage since the Com. Meeting that I have not been able to do anything. There is a regular plot to turn me out formed by Miss Wood & two Members of Com. In my absence they got at my little Clerk, Whitford, & made him write a letter to the Com. saying that he could no longer do so much of my work without increased pay. They asked me to leave the room while this was considered and appointed a Sub-Com. which meets on the 26th to go into this matter. I think that they will ask me to resign. Miss Wood told me to my face the next day that for the past year she had made up her mind that I must go & that she had done all she could to bring this on. I feel so sore & angry at being treated in this way. It has come to this that either I or Miss Wood will have to go & possibly my clerk, Whitford. I fully expect to be beaten. But last night I dined with Jem & Elsie & was comforted by their sympathy & Jem's wrath against Miss W. & Lucas. Tonight I shall go to Battersea & get my Father's opinion on my defence which I am writing. *Ma Laure*, I hate pouring out my woes to you but I can think of nothing else at present. Goodbye, Your Adrian

HUNSTANTON   SUNDAY, 23RD JANUARY

Dearest Adrian, I fully expected some bad news from you when yet another long day passed without a word from you. I am *very* sorry darling that this has happened—what a reward after the way you have slaved for them. If *only* you can clear up their accusations and tide over this row I shall simply *long* for the moment when you send in your resignation but I *hope* it can come from *you*— & not from them. For I am afraid in that case there would be many who would never hear the rights of the story, and it might get about and count against you. Supposing Miss W. fails this time, it is certain that she will make up some other story on the next possible occasion and so I long for you to leave them. It is not worth fighting her for their wretched £300 a year. ... Cannot you write to all your friends and make a *great effort* to get something else—*anything else* merely to get you away from Great O. Street. I cannot help thinking the best course is to pull every single wire you can—*pride* darling returning to the pocket. A concerted attack on your friends might lead to something.

... I was really wounded by your silence—darling do you wish me to be 'your *Laure*' only in fair weather? ... I would far rather know whatever trouble you had—and share it than be left out in the cold—a prey to all my thoughts & fancies. It takes the heart out of me far more than anything. I am afraid it is no good hoping for a political appt. now—but there are others to be asked & tried for. … *Always* your own loving *Laure*

GREAT ORMOND STREET HOSPITAL, BLOOMSBURY   25TH JANUARY

My dearest, Today I feel full of fight & much comforted by Jem's advice & backing. He wrote a letter to Lucas which I fancy spoilt that worthy sneak's digestion for breakfast today. Jem—a doctor himself—is really quite worked up about this affair & means to canvass all the Doctors. He has been to see one of the Special Com.ttee, Mr [John] Murray, & is also going round the other Members of Com.ttee just to tell them that I am neither friendless nor to be kicked out without a fight. Tomorrow will settle the matter one way or another. You must not think dear Heart that I love you less because I did not write & tell you of the affront put upon me—I would tell you but I hate to write about it. … Goodbye my own dearest, Your Adrian

YORK CLUB, 8 ST JAMES' SQUARE   27TH JANUARY

My darling, The Com. sat from 4.30 till past 7. My Clerk produced a Journal in which he had marked down the most astounding lies. All of which he swore to. He said that my usual time for turning up was 12.30 & that I left as early as I came. In fact he made out that I had never done a thing. The Com. sat & drank in all he said with apparent delight. I am in despair because I cannot at this distance of time recollect why on a particular day I was out or away. The whole thing is a very cleverly concocted lie. And how to prove it beats me hollow. I know it is not true but then my word apparently goes for nothing. … My honour is at the mercy of a little scoundrel who apparently sticks at nothing. Your Adrian

GREAT ORMOND STREET HOSPITAL BLOOMSBURY   28TH JANUARY

Darling, Here is a list of days—14 in October, 1 in December—in which he said that I had been out during office hours. That is to say that Whitford declares his diary shows that he saw people for me. [Laura is able to send him many notes as to dates when he worked both early & late at the office.] On Wednesday the Com. were most nasty to me but also to him. They took all his evidence & then asked me what I had to say. I told them that it was absurd to call on me at moment's notice to refute charges I had only just heard. But as they insisted I tried to explain why on one or two of these occasions I had to be out. Then I read a letter I had written & then they adjourned till Monday. Your Adrian

29TH JANUARY

My darling, … I fully expect to be beaten on Monday but then I have an Appeal to the Man.Com. on Feb. 16 when Jem & all the Doctors will stand up for me. All I want now is to retire with grace for I cannot go on as I am situated. This worry has really knocked me up. My Sweet you must forgive these short letters of mine for I am too hurt to be able to write fully even to you. It is so brutal to turn on me like this after one has worked like a dog. Only the other day I worked with the Accountant from 8 o'clock in the evening till 4. in the morning on the Annual Report. … Your Adrian

HUNSTANTON   SUNDAY, 30TH JANUARY

Dearest Adrian, … I am quite alone here—and feeling sad—I have had nothing but those poor little notes for nearly 3 weeks now. … All my letters remain unanswered. I feel *thousands* of miles away from you—and will try not to write you such long letters, or so many, for you *cannot* care for them now. I see your mind is too full of other things. What a pity I am a girl—if I were only a man I could go up to town & see you—dine with you at the Club, hear all you have to tell me, over our brandies & sodas—afterwards—& then stroll down to Great Ormond St with you. Perhaps you would offer me the hospitality of the chair bed in the alcove! All this is so impossible—it really is a pity. … I go to the Cromptons for a ball on Tuesday. … Think of me sometimes, Your *Laure*

GREAT ORMOND STREET HOSPITAL, BLOOMSBURY   31ST JANUARY

My darling, … I have prayed for help to clear off these lies of Whitford's after all his talk, to go & lie about me & to write lies, for I know that they are sheer inventions artfully grafted on to a homeopathic dose of truth. … My Sweet your second letter hurts me very much for I feel that I have been wounding & neglecting you during this row. Oh! do forgive me & think of what a nasty time I have had. The Com. met again today when I read them a letter composed by Hastie (my solicitor friend) saying that I would answer any written charges but that I must decline to go on being harassed. Then I left the room followed by Whitford & I am now sitting waiting while they wrangle about me. We had some talk first when I was treated fairly well by the Committee who were very rude to Whitford, but I am sure they mean to ask me to resign when this is over. In any case they will have to report to the Man.Com. on Feb. 16. I will finish now & write again later.

[Continued] The Com. has called me in to inform me that they have decided over their Report. I found them all standing up. They went at once & never even condescended to answer the request in my letter. Your A.

---

95 *13th Jan* Meresia Nevill, only daughter of Reginald Henry Nevill, third son of second son of 1st Earl of Abergavenny and Lady Dorothy Walpole (daughter of 3rd Earl of Oxford).

FEBRUARY 1887

GREAT ORMOND STREET HOSPITAL, BLOOMSBURY   1ST FEBRUARY

My dearest Love, … I have loved getting your letters even where there have been a few thorns in them. Please never say I cannot care for your letters. Unfortunately for me I have been far from well & this worry has not been my only one. I have had to help Charles to go back to Oxford as we could not extract a 'sou' from the Col. This out of my present income is not easy. Especially at a time of year when one is always bothered for cash. I was very ill at the Club (on Saturday the 15th) after dinner & had to sleep on Jo's bed in the Club Chambers that night. It was an odd sort of fainting attack which frightened Jo horrid. But nothing really serious. … Yesterday Jem & Elsie made me bring my things to Green St where I hope to be for a few days. They ask if you would come up to them from Derbyshire. Oh! *ma Laure* do say yes. …

By the way please understand that all my Clerk says is untrue. I have not been away from here & telling you taradiddles about the work, though I have at times been out a good deal begging for an ungrateful crew. Your Adrian

LILIES, WINDLEY, DERBY   3RD FEBRUARY
[WITH MR & MRS JOHN CROMPTON]

My darling, On the whole I enjoyed the Meynell Hunt ball last night, not rapturously—but I liked it. The men here danced nicely, and there were some *lovely* diamonds & a live Princess—Hohenlohe. There were some sights that would have amused us both. I thought of you very often dearest—especially when I dropped a large hard crumb down my frock at supper—it was hopelessly lost! … I did not get to bed until 4.30 and we got up soon after 8. to drive to an 11 o'clock meet miles off. It was at a pretty place, Osmaston—Sir Andrew Walker's—he is a gin and beer king. The house is gorgeous—money oozing from very pore—& crammed with beautiful things old & new, higgledy piggledy. … At lunch there I found a *very* nice Miss Okeover (Maude—the one in-waiting I have met chez Cochrane). We fraternized a great deal and found lots of mutual friends to talk over. I like the married sister here, Mrs Arkwright. Cecil—Cecilia—Crompton is so dreadfully spoilt & gets cross & sulky, which is such a bore. … It is so comfy having Tanner with me to dress me & take care of me. Now darling goodbye, Ever your own *Laure*

52 GREEN STREET, PARK LANE   SUNDAY, 6TH FEBRUARY
[WITH JEM & ELSIE HOPE]

My dearest, ... At the Hamiltons' party we had thought reading by a Mr Capper
& some tricks with string, rather clever, but such a crew as was collected there
I never saw. All the women dressed very aesthetically without stays or any
apparent reason for wearing such a support—no 'tournures' but flat clinging
frocks with puffed sleeves. Notwithstanding this disguise some of the women
were pretty. The only woman there who was in ordinary black evening dress
was tremendously cut out with a straight piece of white stuff tightly stretched
across at the *lowest possible* point. I got introduced to her, a Miss Froome. She
was very amusing with a very long chin, besides I was quite interested by the
modesty tucker. So very little seemed to be required for a catastrophe. ... I am
full of longing for next Saturday when we two will meet at Lynn, darling. ...
Goodnight dear Heart, Your Adrian

LILIES, WINDLEY, DERBY   7TH FEBRUARY
[WITH MR & MRS JOHN CROMPTON]

My darling Adrian, ... I had a letter from Lord Arthur Hill, enclosing one
from his friend Mr Colnaghi (not the shop of that name). Colnaghi says he
has taken *Whistler's* advice about my 'Jaw Crackers' drawings! & has sent
them to Messrs Field & Tuer—who have them now under consideration. I
wish this would turn up trumps. ... I have just been finishing a sketch for Mrs
Crompton of one of her beloved monkeys, Quadromanus—a sort of tawny
coloured chattering imp with a puckered face looking about a thousand years
old, & lean skinny black hands. She had it on her knee like a baby & *kissed* it
at intervals!! It was amusing to draw but nothing would have induced me to
kiss it. ... My Sweet, my dear Adrian, Goodbye, Ever your *Laure*

    P.S. It will be comforting to be together after the ordeal of your Committee
on the 16th.

THE KNOWLE, HAZELWOOD, DERBY   8TH FEBRUARY
[WITH HON. LOUIS & MRS HOPE]

Darling Adrian, One of my three long days here is nearly past—poor Aunt
Susan is upstairs, she has congestion of the lungs—and cannot talk. I miss her
very much—they seem decidedly a shade more gloomy without her. ... I was
so amused about your party—I thought the race of waistless, hipless, bustless,
aesthetics was extinct—but darling it was like you to get introduced to the

only one who was *not* of that persuasion. It is curious but at odd moments I feel *so* naughty here —I wish I had a funny book to read. ... Goodbye, Ever your *Laure*

Great Ormond Street Hospital, Bloomsbury 10th February

Dearest, ... Tonight I dine with a very dear pal of mine, [Sir Alexander] Swettenham who was in Ceylon. Dear old Swetty, how frightened he will be when I tell him you are coming up next week & that he must come to Green St. He will go to Brighton to avoid this or anywhere as his hatred of women is funny & his shyness a standing joke. ... I did dream of Eva's boudoir at Lynn last night. You had your hair down & I was kissing you through it & round it which perhaps may prove a reality the day after tomorrow. ... Your Adrian

11th February

My Sweet, ... Last night I dined with Swetty & we talked at his Club & then after in my rooms for hours. He was so horrified to hear that I was engaged & leaves for Darlington on Sunday. I believe really to avoid seeing you. He is just as nice as ever only more queer & odd & looks older. He asked a lot of questions about you in a shy reluctant way which much tickled me. My love to George & Eva. May they sleep heavily tomorrow night when we are once more together. Your Adrian

Hunstanton   Valentine's Day, 14th February

My darling Adrian, After you had left I got through yesterday evening alone with George & Eva better than I expected. We went up to the boudoir directly after dinner, talked a little & then all settled down with books. I read the story *A Bit of Human Nature* & Eva was chuckling over your naughty little book all the evening. She wanted to finish off *Le Vieux Garçon* & was not at all scandalized—she said after all there were no *details*, which amused me. I think she was a trifle disappointed!! ... Ever your *Laure*

At 52 Green Street, Park Lane [with Jem & Elsie Hope]

> *16th February* Amy & I bound for beloved London—she to Abbey Lodge, I to the Hopes in Green Street (where the birth of the baby is imminent). Arrived about 6.30. Adrian came presently

from the Committee, it had been favourable to him as far as it went but the pith of the discussion was put off to another General Comm. to be held on the 23rd. The house is nice with a lift in which one soars aloft.

17th February ... *Such* an awful yellow fog, dark & stinking. After lunch Elsie lent me her brougham & pair & I went off to Abbey Lodge to see Amy & we went off shopping. Bought books at Hatchards & cakes at Buzzards. ...

21st February ... Dined with the Bethunes. Adrian took me in, & on the other side was Mr Comyns Carr, Ed. of the *English Illustrated Magazine*. We made great friends & he has asked me to design for him. I think this may be a good business.

23rd February Heard of the earthquakes in France & Italy. ... In the afternoon drove to Macmillans where I had a very satisfactory business interview with Comyns Carr. ... Wait for Adrian—the great Committee meeting today, & after all most successful for him, quite a triumph.[96] We were so *delighted*, also we heard he was elected to White's Club which pleased him much.

Great Ormond Street Hospital, Bloomsbury 26th February

Darling, Your sweet sad face is so present to me as I write this first letter after all these days together. My sweet you must not think over & analyse your feelings & actions sadly. Of course being in Green St was a very trying thing to you especially, as well as to me. How could you help being chafed at the contrast of settled married life. ... Your Adrian

White's, St James' Street 27th February

My own dearest Love, ... When I went to 105 Piccadilly I found V.G. [Milady—Goldsmid] dressing for dinner. However she saw me in her boudoir when she came in dressed in a wadded scarlet silk dressing gown & nothing else much. Her temper was seraphic & she was full of sorrow for her bad temper. ... Last night's Molesworth[97] dinner was a dull affair but I got Mrs Molesworth to write to her Publishers giving your name & address as that of the Artist whom she wished to have to illustrate her next story. It may lead to something perhaps. ... Your Adrian

GREAT ORMOND STREET HOSPITAL, BLOOMSBURY   28TH FEBRUARY

My Darling, … You see the visit to the Arbuthnot Guthries was a good move on our part. My sister writes to me: 'Aunt Annie is much pleased at hearing today from Mrs Guthrie of your having taken your Laura to see her. She says you "are a grand looking pair". I always imagine that your good Laura might make Guthrie restore you the plate as a wedding present.'[98]

… I left your precious sketches with Comyns Carr. Are you going to accept his offer? It would be a good Advertisement. Goodbye my Sweet Love, Your Adrian

---

96   *23rd Feb* Adrian's clerk, Samuel Whitford Junior, was the son of the late Secretary of Great Ormond Street Hospital and he may well have thought that *he* was going to inherit the post. Whitford Senior had been the first and only secretary since 1852, a few months after the hospital had opened (with H A Bathurst then being the Hon Secretary). He was highly thought of and only retired when 'Scrivener's palsy' prevented him from holding a pen. No doubt Adrian's work could not at first compete with that of his predecessor with his thirty-two years of service. Young Whitford started this trouble by writing a letter on 8th January complaining that he was: 'compelled to turn out a large part of the Secretary's duties', and demanding a proper 'Appointment' with more authority. At first the management committee accepted his view, was hostile to Adrian and appointed a sub-committee to consider the work of the secretary.

On 31st January Adrian submitted a letter, composed by his solicitor friend Hastie, refuting the accusations and there the matter rested until 16th February when the committee went so far as to pass a motion that the earlier record of Whitford's letter in the minutes should be cancelled, as it had not been sent, as it should have been, to all the members. Whitford's letter was then reconsidered a week later when it was resolved that: 'Mr Whitford has given no justification for the step he took in writing the letter … [and that] he be censured severely for sending the letter to a few Members only of the Committee and for the unsatisfactory explanations given to the Committee on that point.' There was, however, a veiled criticism of Adrian in their reference to the work of the hospital being: 'such as should generally be transacted by the Secretary and the two Clerks within the specified office hours'. All previous references to this unhappy episode were crossed out in the minutes and initialled by the chairman, Arthur Lucas.

97   *27th Feb* Adrian's friend Alfred Scott Gatty had introduced him to Mrs Molesworth, the children's book author, with a view to her helping to raise money for the Great Ormond Street Hospital. She became a stalwart friend and supporter of Adrian's, and later of Laura's as well.

98   *28th Feb* James Alexander Guthrie, 4th of Craigie (1823-73), one-time Director of the Bank of England, had been at Rugby with Charles 'Rufus' Hope (Col Hope's elder brother who had died while still at school) and became a great friend of the colonel. His brother, Arbuthnot Guthrie, had bought the Hope family silver and other *objets*—which Adrian had expected to inherit—from the colonel to save him from a threatened bankruptcy.

MARCH 1887

GREAT ORMOND STREET HOSPITAL, BLOOMSBURY   1ST MARCH

My dearest, ... Mrs Bethune told me that C. Carr had again dined with them to meet Burne Jones to whom he had talked of your drawings praising them muchly. B. Jones was quite interested & wanted to see them. C. Carr tried to find out whether you were going to accept his offer for the 'Mermaid'. But Mrs Bethune was diplomatic enough to doubt if you would. I have a letter today from Mr Hatchard saying that he would like very much to see your drawings so tomorrow I will worry Cole [Jem Hope's solicitor friend] who has them & take the 'Jaw Crackers' there as a sample. He will I hope ask you to do some illustrations for Mrs Molesworth's stories. ... Your Adrian

HUNSTANTON   1ST MARCH

My darling Adrian, How very dear of you to get Mrs Molesworth to mention me to her publisher who by the by I believe is Macmillan, and just now Mr Comyns Carr is showing them my drawings so it is wheels within wheels & if they like my work it may mean business. About Mr C.C.'s offer for the 'Mermaid', he told me I need not decide immediately—that his offer would hold good for some time, as he would only bring out the drawings in his Christmas number. I would send them also to Lady Harrington before deciding—Midget's mother. I forget if I told you that she was very anxious that Field & Tuer should see them. They have just published a book for her & she asked if I would like her to take my drawings to them as she knows them personally. They were so civil the day we went there together that I think this would be worth trying. ...

Will you send me some more of the Hospital Cards, those for collecting 120 pennies, a dozen I am sure I could get taken. ... Farewell my darling A. Ever your *Laure*

GREAT ORMOND STREET HOSPITAL, BLOOMSBURY   3RD MARCH

My own darling, I saw Cole last night who said that Mr Harding of Clement Smith & Co. had valued your 'Jaw Crackers' drawings at £60 but that they were not prepared to publish them. This morning I took the drawings to Mr Hatchard who was much pleased with them but asked to see some of your black & white drawings. Will you send him a copy of *Little Thumb* – A. Hatchard Esq, 187 Piccadilly. He told me that before getting Mrs Molesworth's letter he had already asked Miss H. Bennet to do her book. However I will go on Saturday to see Mrs M. & find out whether she can use any pressure.

Hatchard said he would offer you another book to do & said he hoped to be able to give you some work besides. ... Your Adrian

HUNSTANTON   SUNDAY, 6TH MARCH

My dearest Adrian, Cole writes that he is in league—or rather in treaty, with some Manchester firm about my drawings. ... I have a very nice note from Mr Hatchard. He says of *Little Thumb* 'the pictures are certainly very clever and charming'!! but he wants to see drawings of mine of men, women & children in *real* life—something less fanciful. I think of sending him 'Friends & Fancies', it is the only thing I have by me with drawings of modern people. I think I *could* illustrate a book with any kind of figures—but I think I should always be more successful with a child's book. ... Dearest, I am very well in body but *not* in mind. Sometimes I have dreadful visions of you working on for *years* at Great Ormond Street, years & years till we are both dull & old—& don't much care whether we marry or not. I do so long to be able to say we have something to look forward to when I see all my relations at Mabel Gurney's wedding next month ...

Everything will appear to me in what I fear is its true colour, i.e. *en noir* [in black]. I long for my rose coloured spectacles again. ... Ever yours, but today rather sad Laura

GREAT ORMOND STREET HOSPITAL, BLOOMSBURY   7TH MARCH

My darling, ... The Colonial Secretaryship of Trinidad is vacant through the sudden death of the man who had held it 30 years. It is £1200 a year. [Sir James] Longden has sent in my name for it. One need not stop 30 years there & we could end our waiting. Would you be terribly grieved at going away so far? ... Your Adrian

HUNSTANTON   7TH MARCH

My own darling Adrian, Was it not prophesied for you according to your horoscope that *30* was the eventful age when you were to be made happy with many wives and camels? & I think you are 29 tomorrow. I suppose I shall have the honour of being the *first* wife! ... Would you care to have that design you always stop at in my book, to the song of Gounod's, '*Mênez moi, dit la belle à la rive fidèle*'—or anything else? I have in thought put my arms round your neck, my face to yours—& wish you a very happy year darling—and God's blessing be with you. ... Ever your *Laure*

YOUR BIRTHDAY, 8TH MARCH

Darling Adrian, ... I suppose as this Secretaryship is so well paid it is rather a plum. ... Of course, as you know, I have always dreaded living far away from everyone but *one*—however many times today I have remembered your gold advice, '*C'est inutile de traverser un pont avant d'y arriver*' [Don't cross your bridges before you come to them]—quite one of the best pieces of advice you ever gave me! so I have not worried at all. I had the curiosity to look up an account of Trinidad—in an old Topographical dictionary here. The account was not very fetching: 'There are two very active *mud* volcanoes on the island, and much *wild cattle*!!!, also a breed of wild *hogs* of an exquisite flavour! ... Ever your own *Laure*

GREAT ORMOND STREET HOSPITAL, BLOOMSBURY   9TH MARCH

Dearest, ... Trinidad is not a bad place at all. Climate healthy but hot, renowned for Chocolate & Sugar. A large Spanish mixture of blood. But the thing that may be offered to me now is Cyprus. Darling I know well that you dislike the idea of leaving England...so I am torn many ways. Last night I was at the House again & got quite a lot of M.P.s to write for me to Sir Henry Holland (the Sec. of State for the Colonies) who has the sole right to appoint whoever he chooses. ... Oh! I am so worried just now by a lot of things all at once. Your Adrian

   P.S. Ma Laure, you won't let me go anywhere away without you, will you darling?

37 BURY STREET, ST JAMES' [CHARLIE ORDE'S ROOM]   12TH MARCH

My darling, ... I was in a very blue fit when I wrote to you the other day. It makes me so sad to think that I am trying for anything which is repugnant to you, such as leaving England so evidently is. Still at Cyprus we should never be more than two years without spending six months in England on leave. ... Restless & uneasy is my Soul within me. I hardly like to wish for success now...I am so sick of being told that we ought to marry by the very people who would hoot at us if we did. ... Your Adrian

HUNSTANTON   SUNDAY, 13TH MARCH

My own darling Adrian, ... Your letter this morning was rather comforting— my imagination foresaw ten years of exile & then about ten days at home, barely enough to visit all the graves of my friends & relations who had died off in my absence. ... I think it would not be *loyal* of me not to help you in this—in the only way I can so I have written to my cousin Mr [Samuel] Hoare (who is the M.P. for Norwich) to ask if he would use his influence to help you in getting an app.t at the C.O. ... He is 2nd rate rather but so nice & kind hearted. ...

The others are *frantic* at the bare idea of your trying to get a Colonial app. I told them it was on the *tapis* [under consideration]—but it created such a storm it has been a forbidden subject since. This is their attitude towards it— Helen mournful, almost funereal. Vi—pessimistical in every way—Amy most wrathful & bitter—*violently* opposed to the whole thing. It is because they care so much for me that they hate the idea. ... Adieu, ever your *Laure*

For some two weeks Adrian's letters were short and largely an account of his canvassing for the Trinidad or Cyprus appointments. Sir Henry Holland's reply to Lord Hopetoun's letter made it clear that Adrian was not in the running. Samuel Hoare promised to use every effort with Holland 'who is under personal obligation to me, private & political' but without success as regards Trinidad although he told Adrian that he would have the offer of a good post from the C.O. before long.

WHITE'S, ST JAMES' STREET   SUNDAY, 20TH MARCH

My dearest Love, I have a dreadful confession to make. 'Jaw Crackers' is lost. I have done all in my power in the way of advertising & offering rewards. I am so ashamed & so wretched darling. The drawings were left by me in a Cab & I have failed to discover the Cabman. This has made me quite mad with rage & helpless anger. *Ma Laure*, do write & tell me that you can forgive me. Myself I cannot forgive. It is too horribly careless of me. I feel it like a crime upon my soul. Never have I lost anything before & now to go & lose your beautiful drawings. ... Will Amy be very angry with me when we meet at Hopton? Goodnight, Your Adrian

HUNSTANTON   21ST MARCH

My dearest Adrian, I am *very* unhappy about my drawings—they represent so many weeks' patient work—and I did so *hope* they would help to make my name. How *could* you lose them! I would rather you had lost *anything* else than my best work. I have not a tracing of a single one—so can never do them again even if I had the courage. ... I want you to write and tell me just how it happened, on *what day*—and *exactly* what steps you have taken to find them again. What daily papers have you advertised in? I want to offer a reward & to advertise—it is the only chance of finding them. ... I imagine that the next fare who took the cab found the parcel & stole it. You see my name is on the designs so if they had fallen into honest hands there would not have been much difficulty in returning them. ... Have you had Handbills printed? £5 we would offer to begin with—& advertise in the *Morning Post* but perhaps you have already done this. *Please* don't be vague about it.

I cannot tell you what I felt when I read your letter, not angry, only so utterly cast down and disappointed...when they are found I will forgive you. Yr. L

P.S. I am too out of heart to write about anything else. That it should be *you* hurts me so. I thought you cared about my drawings & wanted to help me on—but this is not the way.

Great Ormond Street Hospital, Bloomsbury   21st March

My dearest Laura, I felt very bad today without one little line from you...I feel under such a guilty cloud & long to be well punished for my carelessness. It comes between me & my wits. It will be nice to see you again at Hopton for I feel that we are quite out of touch with one another. I do so want to meet you & talk over our chances together. ... Darling, don't let the little cloud thicken between us any more but write me a long letter of hearty abuse which will make me feel better & more at peace with myself. ... Goodbye *ma Laure*, Your Adrian

Hunstanton   22nd March

Dearest Adrian, ... I have not in the least got over this crushing blow. What I *cannot* understand is that you could *sleep* away the whole of Saturday [5th March, when Adrian lost them] and dash about & see your friends all Sunday instead of trying to find my drawings. ... When I know what you have done I mean to write to Mr Jolliffe—and ask him to take up the search which you seem to have entirely abandoned. Jo is full of ideas & expedients. ... If Jem had lost them—or Cole—I should at least have had the small satisfaction of a cheque for the amount they were valued at—but even this is denied me for I could not take money from you, even if it was offered me. ... I do not think I ever *boast* about my drawings & seldom speak to you of the amount of ambition & all the hopes & fears that are bound up in my work but you could hardly have chosen a more cruel way to wound me. I could not have believed of you that you would stroll away & leave my precious work alone in a hansom— *c'est incroyable* [it's unbelievable]. I believe there will always be a cloud between us until these drawings are found—or it is proved they have been destroyed. I feel like a *stone*. I *cannot* find it in my heart to forgive you—yet. ...

This morning I had a M.S. of a fairy tale—*Child Elves*—sent me to illustrate by Griffith & Farran. It would have delighted me before, but now I don't care the least about it & have no heart to begin the work. ... I wish we were going to meet sooner—perhaps you could soften my heart. I never felt like this towards *you* in my life & it makes me so unhappy. Oh *do* find them. L

GREAT ORMOND STREET HOSPITAL, BLOOMSBURY   22ND MARCH

My darling, Here is the Hand bill which I had printed & circulated. I have also advertised in the papers. I will put an Advert in the *Morning Post* but think the *Daily Telegraph* more useful. I had taken the drawings to show Mrs Molesworth who was out. As I did not like to leave them at White's I took them with me to show Sir James Longden at Longhope who I hoped would offer to buy the originals as he is very fond of having Portfolios full of original drawings. I had the parcel beside me in the Cab on my hatbox. As I was very late I jumped out telling the Porter to be careful of the Parcel, & rushed for my ticket. When I got to the R. carriage I at once saw the Parcel was not there. The Porter rushed to find the Hansom which had gone. I told the Station Master & telegraphed to Jo who went to Scotland Yard. Of the Cabman we have no trace. The reason why I put 'supposed to have been left in the Hansom' when I know that it was is because the Cabby is liable to punishment if he had kept it. So he may send his wife to say that she found it. I did not tell you because I hoped that the Drawings would have been recovered before now.

I am so grieved at having lost them. The Station Master informed me that the Porter was getting blind & so we suppose that in the twilight he failed to notice the Parcel. Unluckily it bore no address. It was by the advice of the Scotland Yard people that I offered £2 as they said it would not do to offer too much. I have advertised also in two papers read by Cabmen & the *Daily News*. You can imagine how I feel about it. ... I have distributed these bills to a large number of Cabmen ... Your loving Adrian

23RD MARCH

My dearest, ... All I could I have done. ... You must believe that I feel this very acutely & that I cannot forgive the accident which caused their loss. ...

If only I had the money I would gladly buy the Drawings from you. Your Adrian

P.S. I feel too disheartened to care about coming down to Hopton & really do not see how I can manage it at present for I have a Com.ttee the day before Good Friday & to travel on that day is so unpleasant, & then I have another Com.ttee on Easter Monday.

HUNSTANTON   23RD MARCH

My Poor Adrian, After all it is not much use my feeling so angry & so disappointed in you—it only makes me even *more unhappy*. I have had 200 & more bills printed. They are like yours—only describing the book more fully & giving my name, & I have offered £5 reward. I have today sent off 200, one to *every single Cab Proprietor* in London! Will you distribute the ones I am sending you to every Cabman's *shelter* in London. ... I can't get over your leaving the parcel to the tender mercies of a blind & probably idiotic porter— alas I feel as if I could *never* trust you with anything of mine again. I did not think a man could be so vague. This seems to have taken all the spring out of me. I can not draw a stroke. ...

All the time since we parted last I seem to have been more or less worried or anxious about something. ... I imagine you having *this* on your conscience every day when you write to me. Well I do not envy you my A. poor darling. Goodbye your *Laure*

24TH MARCH

Dearest Adrian, ... Of course I believe that you have tried your utmost to find my drawings—but I thought from your letter you had given it up. You say 'write me a letter of hearty abuse'—I am sure my letters have been unkind enough. I did not feel as if I was writing to you at all. Oh I have such a *longing*, a wild craving to see you again. I feel that if I could only *see* you, at the very sight of your face so dear to me—all these strange hard feelings would melt away—and forgiveness would creep into my heart & we might feel happy again. I own I have had a heartache ever since we last parted—only one thing will cure it—to be with you again & feel your arms round me. I feel sadly out of tune with my life here—everyone always is talking of the wedding at Runcton—it is like so many little swords to me—but I shall forget everything sad or unhappy if we meet—I stretch out my hand & cry for you—will you come? or will you spend Easter away from me—& let the cloud thicken, Your *Laure*

26TH MARCH

My darling Adrian, I feel just as if I was awake after a long bad dream—I still grieve very *very* much for my lost drawings—more perhaps than you can understand but all the bitterness has gone out of my heart—and I want to write and tell you darling that I forgive you—whether you will come to me at Hopton or not. I mean without conditions. I can see things more clearly now— and I know that my first letters were very hard—& cruel—and I too have something to be forgiven by you. ... Did you get my violets? I meant them for a token. Goodbye my own darling Adrian, Ever your loving *Laure*

GREAT ORMOND STREET HOSPITAL, BLOOMSBURY   28TH MARCH

My dearest, I am so glad to hear that you are coming up to Thurloe Square for a week [a sudden invitation to keep the very pregnant Rosy Birkbeck company]. This does seem to be good news indeed. I long to see you & I have managed to get one Com.ttee put off so that we may be quite able to travel down together to Hopton on Good Friday. I have been so very miserable because I did not think you realized either, how painful it was for me to lose your drawings or how I really had done my best to recover them. So many things have made life a worry & a torment of late that writing even to you has been difficult. ... The kiss was so faithfully brought me by your violets & I felt it was a kiss of peace, *ma Laure*, from your own loving heart.

Today I met Robert [Cunninghame] Graham & he introduced me to his wife[99] & we lunched together at the Grosvenor Restaurant. She is such a funny little thing with black hair cut short & ragged as Helen's used to be, only real black Horse hair. Little black eyes which flash suddenly at you. Altogether she reminded me of an Indian. She is very pleasant & as you know I love Robert & am so glad to see him & be with him again listening to his wild talk. We felt like boys again together & it has made me very happy talking to dear old Don Roberto [then aged 34 to Adrian's 29] of you. We three sat & laughed & longed to be in the sunny south once more. *Adieu ma Laure adorée, je meure d'envie de te voir, ton* Adrian

---

99 *28th Mar* In 1878 Robert Cunninghame Graham, Adrian's first cousin, had ostensibly married a Chilean, Gabrielle (or Gabriela) de la Balmondière, whose background was always something of a mystery until the late 1970s when Robert's great niece Lady Polwarth (née Jean Cunninghame Graham) discovered her true origins. She was in fact Caroline ('Carrie') Horsfall, one of the large family of a distinguished doctor in Yorkshire. Carrie, a talented amateur actress, had run away from home at the age of sixteen to go on the stage, after which

her family would have nothing to do with her. She became fluent in French and Spanish in order to join a company of players in Paris and it was there in 1877 that the twenty-five-year old Robert fell in love with the eighteen-year old actress. They came to London the following year and secretly married under the assumed names of 'Roberto Graham and Gabrielle de la Balmondière. Nevertheless, his mother welcomed them, and after they had shared a three-year adventure in San Antonio and on to Mexico City where they encountered Indians and gun-slinging cowboys, Gabrielle was happy to help Robert to keep his Gartmore estate in good order.

Later Gabrielle developed her mystical side and after visits on her own to Spain, she wrote an acclaimed biography of the sixteenth-century St Teresa of Avila, *Santa Teresa: Her Life and Times* (1894). She died from tuberculosis at the age of forty-five in 1906, and Robert published her 'haunting little verses' as *Rhymes from a World Unknown* (Chiswick Press) in 1908. Despite spending interludes in their life apart, on their various travels, they were a devoted couple.

APRIL 1887

At 30 Thurloe Square, South Kensington
[with Rosy Birkbeck]

6th April ... Went to see Hatchard the publisher by appointment. Most satisfactory. I am engaged to illustrate a story for him for £25. Started off after lunch to see Mr Comyns Carr at Macmillans—he was away. Then on to Griffiths & Farran. Saw one of their firm & had a most satisfactory interview there also.

...

At Hopton St Margaret, Great Yarmouth
[with Aunt Maggie Orde]

Easter Eve, 9th April... After dinner we all dressed up but the evening I cannot say was altogether a success. Tardy & Amy were children 50 years ago, Adrian a French chef, I appeared in Carnival costume. We danced & played games, sang, but there was not much *entrain* [go] & it died away rather early & left rather a flat impression.

Easter Monday, 11th April After breakfast a very good piano organ arrived & we all danced in the hall for about an hour. After lunch we played rounders & hockey, & tip & run, but Adrian rather hurt his ankle. After dinner we all went to a little dance at Fritton, unfortunately A. could hardly dance because of his foot but we got what we could out of it.

GREAT ORMOND STREET HOSPITAL, BLOOMSBURY   15TH APRIL

My own darling, I was so glad to visit Sunny Hill [the Geoffrey Buxtons' house]. G.B. seems to be so nice. What a pretty foot Mary Buxton has. I noticed it & thought she had a lovely shoe. Who boots her? ... Don't you worry about Amy. I paid no attention to her manner & have forgotten it in the recollection of our happiness together at Easter. ... Did you see a Leader in Wednesday's *Times* & also in the *Globe* of the same evening upon the Colonel's experiments at Portsmouth with the bayonets of his Volunteers? This will please him greatly. Now goodbye my own dear love, Your Adrian

A Mr Henry C Burdett had written a long letter to *The Times* (13th) headed 'The Arms of our Volunteers' in which he recounted the testing of sword bayonets by the City of London Volunteers commanded by Col Hope during Easter manoeuvres at Portsmouth. No suitable animal carcass being available, a dummy target was improvised from cotton waste wrapped in a truss of straw. As an experiment, the colonel's sword—which had seen him through the Crimea—was tested first and remained straight after each thrust whereas the sword bayonets of his volunteers 'bent up like billhooks' until bent back again by hand. This scandal prompted *Punch* to portray a British Tar asking, 'Ain't nobody to be wopped for this here?' On the following page, a *Times* leader took up the subject and castigated those unknown people responsible for supplying 'pewter' bayonets— '... following as it does upon many similar revelations, it proves the entire rottenness of the War Office...'.

Never one to miss a chance, the colonel followed this up with yet another letter to *The Times* (20th) in which he corroborated Mr Burdett's account of the bent bayonets, and at the same time referred to his charges of corruption against the Ordnance Department in connection with this subject which he gave to the Royal Commission the previous November, but whose terms of appointment precluded them from inquiring into the 'patterns' of warlike stores or the 'processes' by which they were manufactured. The report on the 'Ordnance Inquiry' was not to be published for another month.

Hunstanton   15th April

My darling Adrian, ... Yesterday we all went off to the wedding [Mabel Gurney, Uncle Sommy's third daughter, to Sir William Curtis]. I think our brown frocks & hats were rather pretty. There were crowds & crowds of people at Middleton Church. ... They had quite spoilt Mabel's appearance with her wedding trappings. The Brussels lace veil, which has already adorned seven brides, was arranged on a *perfectly* flat head—with a large white flower pattern over one eye! Her frock had hardly any train & she looked so small & not at *all* smart, the dress was of some sort of plush in stripes—& had none of those shining lights in it like satin has—so the train looked almost grey—& the body was miles too big. The bridesmaids looked pretty in their red frocks & hats, & smart red shoes & stockings. ... We thought the Shropshire [bridegroom's] contingent of guests very frumpy on the whole. A grandmother with a heavy moustache & imperial, & other antique relations. After the service Runcton became a seething mass of people all talking at once & looking at the presents. The girls had told me Uncle Sommy thought your glass [mirror] *lovely*. ... I fully expected to feel rather unhappy but I really did not. I never want to have such a large crowd of vague people at our wedding whenever it is—I should hate it. No one seemed to have anything to say to Mabel, which rather amused me, but all congregated round Uncle Sommy. Aunt Kitty looked very well & quite smiling. I think she liked her 30th wedding day! & could *not* find a grievance. ... While Mabel was changing her frock we went into the garden in a gleam of sunshine—a band was playing there all day—& we were just going to try a country dance when another snow storm damped our ardour & drove everyone back into the house.

Old Herb [Rev. Herbert Jones, Laura's uncle] was *most* amusing, putting on an extra old greatcoat in the house and that dreadful black fur boa! He was quite happy in the middle of the crowd besieging the refreshments in the dining room. He said: 'I have had *three* glasses of champagne already—& am going to drink a *fourth*. Perhaps *then* I may feel better. I have had *nothing* to eat since eight o'clock. I am *completely empty* & can find nothing but small pieces of sponge cake wherewith to fill myself!' meanwhile tucking in to all the *gobbits* he could find. Goodbye my own darling Adrian, Ever your true *Laure*

WHITE'S ST JAMES'   SUNDAY, 17TH APRIL

My dearest, ... Today I began by sleeping until 4. in the afternoon. I had the most heavenly dreams of you. We were together in some wonderful sort of after life where our spirits were floating together, locked in each other's arms. The air was heavy with the scent of orange blossom & we were quite alone drifting down eternity lost in each other's love. Your hair floating round you seemed our only covering & it reached your feet. I woke with a long sigh to find it was 4. ...

[*Later*] In that after life darling, when you & I are together for ever, how strange this endless striving to forget our separation will seem. ... How sweet it will be to begin life side by side. For 10 years of such a life how content I would be to give up the rest if we could go together or if I had only to wait a short time on the other side of the River which divides us from the rest. Goodbye *ma Laure bien aimée*, Your Adrian

In the eighteenth year of her widowhood Laura had noted here: '"They reckon not by days & years where *he* has gone to dwell". L.H.— alone, May 11 1904 – May 11 1922.'

HUNSTANTON   PRIMROSE DAY, 19TH APRIL

My Darling Adrian, The Davys brought a Mr Sidney Streatfield to our tea party yesterday. He said he had met you at those theatricals when you appeared as 'Blue Beard'. I liked him so much, he is *very* handsome but quite lame— from rheumatism ever since he was a boy. He sang to us, banjo songs with a very good tenor voice. Vi & I quite lost our hearts! His moustache had undergone the ordeal by fire—& appeared in two tight little tonged curls at each end. I think it looks rather affected for a man. ... It is such a bore about Hatchard. I had a letter from him about the drawings in my 'Friends & Fancies' album which he wanted for a magazine. He has chosen eight but only offers £5.5 [shillings] for the whole eight drawings *and* copyright. It is far less than I have ever been offered without the copyright. I shall write a civil little note declining this offer. ... It is sad that this last chance about Euston Station lost luggage department [for 'Jaw Crackers'] was tried in vain. ... Ever your *Laure*

GREAT ORMOND STREET HOSPITAL, BLOOMSBURY   20TH APRIL

Darling *Laure*, I dined in Green Street yesterday. Emily Heywood Smith came in & we had a long theological discussion which was interesting. She expounded to us what she really believed & it was very curious to listen to. For a wonder Elsie went to bed without having to be told 20 times of the lateness of the hour. Her Dr suggests that she should try a drive in a good old rattling four wheeler. [Her baby is long overdue.] Today I walked to the F.O. where I saw Ld Salisbury's Private Sec. about an appointment who was very nice to me indeed. Then I went to see Sir Robert Herbert at the C.O. who told me that he did not think I had much of a chance for Trinidad but that he thought I should be offered a vacancy somewhere else. Your Adrian

WHITE'S, ST JAMES'   23RD APRIL

My own *Laure*, I had a driving hard day yesterday & found it impossible to write to you before I went to the Charity Organization Society where I was kept late & (as Chairman) had to investigate a case of a man whose wife & week old baby were starving. After I got back I had to dine at 105 Piccadilly. There was a lovely dark French beauty whom I knew in Paris, a certain Madame Porges & her husband. She had the most lovely ropes of Pearls round her neck with a sort of Sailors Knot in the rope just where there was a valley. People used to say in Paris that that valley had been as often invaded as Italy. ... A very delightful Frenchman, Comte de Dillon, I made great friends with.

He is the Elder branch of the Lords Dillon & he represents the famous Dillon who raised & commanded that 'Regiment Dillon' or Royal Irlandais of which one reads so much in the Louis XIV wars. He loved to be drawn out about the five brothers Dillon who each in turn commanded this gallant corps. ... Lots of people came in the evening. Among them Morny & his Duchesse who is pretty but I think her Corsage would have made you jump. Down to the waist band behind & in front.!!!

Elsie has a little girl. What a comfort that is over at last. Now I am going off to Charing X to meet my sister. I wonder if she will walk in the Park tomorrow with me. It is to be hoped her costume will not be too eccentric. ... *Je t'embrasse sur les deux jumeaux que j'adore*, Your Adrian

SUNDAY, 24TH APRIL

My dear love, ... Today I lunched with the Guthries [where his sister Laura was staying] & had the pleasure! of recognizing many things which once belonged to my father. I also had to dine there. The dinner hardly went round but the Claret was superior. Guthrie tried to be pleasant & kind. In the dining room I saw a picture of ours, a table, some vases & much silver. All of which had been ours. Laura told me that in her bedroom there were lots of things she well knew from old association. It makes one feel so jolly to see a house positively furnished with spoils from one's father. I felt in mad spirits. It is very difficult to be humble & to thank your host kindly for the bone you have been permitted to pick at his table. Darling tonight I am full of prickles & my temper is horrid. ... Laura & Aunt Annie are anxious to ask you to Cambridge for the night. ... Your Adrian

CONGHAM HALL, KING'S LYNN, [WITH MRS WILLIE DAVY]   25TH APRIL

My darling, ... What does Sir Julian G. think of your chances of success with the C.O. now? I do not *worry* about it—but it is often in my mind and the thought is not so distasteful to me as it was at first. All you said that Sunday afternoon when you told me how much your heart was in it—& painted the happy life we might lead together in some lovely foreign place—has told I think—and then it would end this weary waiting ... sometimes it all seems so dark & hopeless. ... Darling, I mean to work hard when I go home—so do not think I shall be fretting. We must keep up a good heart. Ever your loving *Laure*

Hunstanton   27th April

My darling Adrian, I feel rather excited about going to Cambridge on Saturday, especially seeing Laura—she interests me, and I fancy we shall be friends. ... I have been drawing all the morning for *Child Elves*—but I find the pen & ink work rather trying & it goes but slowly. After lunch we met all the Cousins at the photographers and were photographed in groups with the guitars etc. me with my tambourine. The dear little Up [Tom's dog] was in the middle with a trumpet tied round his neck with a pink ribbon. Then we had a wild game of hockey. I have come in as the house agent is coming to see me directly on business. We hear a rumour that a fish shop is to be built close to our house. I want to stop it if possible, it would be a horrid nuisance to have anything so near, *especially* a fish shop smelling horribly all the Summer—not at all 'salubrious, salubrious'. ... Ever your *Laure*

29th April

My darling Adrian, ... I have had such a hard day's work at my book illustrations—from 10.30 till 4. only stopping 15 minutes for lunch. I am so anxious to send off half a dozen specimen drawings (the first of 60 for *Child Elves*) to Griffiths & Farran before I leave for Cambridge tomorrow. Pen & ink goes very slowly—it has to be done with so much care & precision, & I am not used to it yet, but I think they are rather nice. I am going to ask £30 for the book.

I heard such a disgusting engagement yesterday—Maude Okeover, pretty & 27, to Sir Andrew Walker, *at least* 60, *hugely rich*, a grandfather with 6 grown up children. She is quite poor, & one of seven daughters. How she *could* sell herself...Osmaston [Manor] is so lovely I suppose she couldn't resist it—& unlimited dollars as well. Adieu darling, Ever your *Laure*

White's, St James   30th April

Darling *Laure*, ... On Thursday I went down to the House & saw Hoare, Goldsmid & Amherst. They all say that I can only wait now until the C.O. chooses to make up its mind about Trinidad. Very trying it is. ... I was so chaffed at the Goldsmids last night because it seems that there is a picture at the Grosvenor of a man in a Fur Coat which everybody takes for me. They were so positive that at last I wondered if my picture by Mlle Ourliac had been sent there instead of to Cambridge. Goldsmid told me today that the picture [by George Richmond] was absurdly like me but was really of Ld Pembroke.

… By this time you have got to Cambridge & have made acquaintance with the other Laura. I am so dying to hear how you get on. My Aunt's very stiff manner hides a good nature & she does not mean her very sarcastic little speeches. Probably they will both jeer at me. … I feel utterly tired & worn out that I can write no more, Your Adrian

MAY 1887

6 PANTON STREET, CAMBRIDGE   MAYDAY, SUNDAY 1ST MAY
[WITH AUNT ANNIE CUNNINGHAME GRAHAM]

My darling Adrian, I am so happy here darling. I like them both so much. ...
When I arrived Miss Graham brought me straight into their very pretty little
salon to see your portrait.[100] I love it—but you look so sad I long to comfort
you. There are faults but the whole effect is *wonderfully* like you. I think Aunt
Annie has quite taken me to her heart—& accepted me as your wife. Her utter
want of faith in men is very curious. She speaks so bitterly—but makes I think
a few exceptions in your favour. ... When Laura came to my room & helped
me to unpack she was so friendly. There is a great charm about her. She is
intensely French and it just suits her—but I cannot like her white stockings—
she asked me if I was horrified at them. I could only say *chacun à son goût*
[everyone to his own taste], though I preferred black myself. I wore my pink
& white teagown—an old friend—for I thought the new one too smart after
what Aunt A. wrote in her note ['Pray do not trouble to bring evening dress as
toilette is quite out of place in this little habitation'].

I am so *fêté-gâté* [fêted and spoilt] here. I think you would be pleased to see
how they pet me—it is for your sake of course. We had a delicious dinner—
bouillon, vol au vent, & asperges & a sweet—all beautifully cooked by the
old Suissesse. She made a sauce Maître d'Hôtel *quite* as well as any French
Chef. ... The evening was rather short—we went up about 11. Laura provided
me with the *Vie Parisienne* & *Françillon* which I read before I went to sleep. ...
Aunt Annie looked in this morning to wake me. You would not have thought
her stiff if you had seen her perched on my bed talking & laughing. ... But I
see what you mean about her. It is curious how she pursues a subject even if
she sees you do not much like it. ... Ever your *Laure*

On the same day Aunt Annie wrote to her 'Dearest nephew':

'Just one line to tell you that Laura Troubridge came &
conquered at once. I think her a most beautiful woman, and
an enchanting Creature altogether. Such an honest single-
hearted girl is only to be met with rarely...I do not wonder
you cling to such a rare possession. I only think the world does
not possess a man creature good enough for this charming girl
...'.

My darling Adrian, ... I cannot tell you how glad I am to find that I can really love your sister—and Aunt A. too who was kindness itself to me. ... We had several walks & talks together—and I felt all the time how happy you would have been living a university life. No wonder you have felt this very bitterly at times. It quite saddened me to think what you had missed. ...

After lunch on Sunday an open fly appeared and Laura & I drove off to Girton together—which amused me very much. She wore her dark blue frock & jacket & high Paris hat, looking as you said just like a Mars [the Belgian artist Maurice Bonvoisin, 1849-1912] drawing. We talked & laughed all the way. ... She told me of her life in Paris, & talked, Aunt A. too, a good deal— of the past—of the Col., of Battersea etc., Aunt A. most bitterly, Laura more sadly—& she confided in me what she hoped to do to help Madge & Jessie. It is quite a new experience to me to meet a girl like her—she is clever in so *many* different ways & is so bright & full of interest to talk to. ... It is so curious to meet a girl like her, pretty & attractive & gentle & yet full of aim & purpose—so utterly unlike all the cousins, who just live out the lives that are arranged for them—& take no thought of the morrow. I suppose it is partly circumstances that have made her like this, but she is very interesting to me— & she has so much heart. She wept darling speaking of the letters she had written to Knocklofty [so bitter about their engagement]—& I forgave her freely. Her *motive* was good. It shall be forgotten now. We have many thoughts in common, our love of *liberty* & *freedom* particularly—& she has a ready laugh, which is *so* nice.

Well, all this time we were driving along a sunny road to Girton. Her friend there, a Miss Ramsay,[101] was at home so we went in. There was a curious atmosphere of *emancipation* about the whole place—in the way the 'sweet girl graduates' *slouched* about with unkempt hair & uncouth bustless figures! In the way they perched about the window ledges of their studies—chattering & eyeing Laura & I through their goggles & pince-nez as we drove up looking rather fashionable & frivolous. One felt somehow that here all coquetterie was thrown to the winds—that mankind was unknown in this strange place— & the girls the sole object & centre of the huge building, the tennis courts, racket courts, gymnasium & everything. It was an odd feeling. If it was a home of the *arts* I should have enjoyed such a life—anyhow for a time.

We are shown through long corridors—with doors opening on to them all along, with cards & the girls' names outside—no Miss—only their initials & surnames. We waited in a tiny little den rather prettily arranged for Miss

Ramsay—who never appeared at all—so after having sat & chatted in her study till we quite forgot what we had come for—we moved on to see another girl, a Miss Sheldon—Mathematical Lecturer to the College!!! She had a large bare room with solid masculine furniture. She was at home—a rather pleasant, tired headachey looking young man [*sic*]—with dishevelled hair, dressed in a skimpy grey dress. She received us in a sort of absent minded grave way. Her frock would have been rather pretty if it had not been *raked* on—she had absolutely no figure at all—perfectly flat—as everyone appeared to be at Girton. Busts are simply unknown. Isn't it curious darling—*comment l'expliquer?* No *aimables rondeurs* of *any* sort or kind. She gave us tea—putting on the kettle—& making it—& getting it ready—exactly like a man would have done it—in an awkward fashion—& we sat & talked for some time. I made them both laugh, & asked many questions. Then she showed us over the College, the big hall where they all dine together—& the Library, a very good room full of books in good editions—& comfortable nooks. They have a Fire Brigade of their own—which amused me—but they do *not* learn to fence—which seems dull of them—& they only dance once a week for an hour—so it isn't *quite* Liberty Hall. Laura made me laugh so just as we drove up when I asked if men were allowed there at all—she said *yes* but they must stand all the time. No man is allowed to sit down at Girton!! It seemed to me *such* a funny idea. I suppose it is to ensure their not staying long. ...

Laura took me to the station yesterday & we had a tender farewell. They are coming here some time in June when she has her mid term holiday [from her teaching school]. I am sure the others will get on well with Laura—they are much inclined to like her. She recited 2 poems to me on Sunday evening—most beautifully. ... I was so disappointed when I heard the postman's knock—and there was not a letter for me. You had *not* written, naughty one. I felt a little sore about your *very* busy Saturday afternoon, lunching chez Goldsmid & paying calls! Today is only the 3rd of May. Well I must wait patiently till the 27th, the Friday after your Hospital Dinner. Then I have a plan to unfold of which more another day.

Your portrait with the sad face haunts me. Goodbye dearest Adrian, Your *Laure*

GREAT ORMOND STREET HOSPITAL, BLOOMSBURY   4TH MAY

My own Darling *Laure*, What a splendid long letter—full of just what I longed to know. I am so glad that Laura did refer to those letters to Knocklofty & that you were able to forgive her fully. What an odd place Girton must be with its

16 & 17 Oscar Wilde had married Adrian's cousin Constance Lloyd in 1884. His poem, with sketch by Laura(see below), was included in Mrs Amherst's anthology In a Good Cause *(1885).*

Le Jardin des Tuileries.

THIS winter air is keen and cold,
  And keen and cold this winter sun,
  But round my chair the children run
Like little things of dancing gold.

Sometimes about the painted kiosk
  The mimic soldiers strut and stride,
  Sometimes the blue-eyed brigands hide
In the bleak tangles of the bosk.

And sometimes, while the old nurse cons
  Her book, they steal across the square,
  And launch their paper navies where
Huge Triton writhes in greenish bronze.

And now in mimic flight they flee,
  And now they rush, a boisterous band—
  And, tiny hand on tiny hand,
Climb up the black and leafless tree.

Ah! cruel tree! if I were you,
  And children climbed me, for their sake
  Though it be winter I would break
Into Spring blossoms white and blue!

oscar wilde

18 Left: Adrian helped Robert Cunninghame Graham ('Don Roberto', his first cousin) after his arrest during the Battle of Trafalgar Square on 'Bloody Sunday' 13th November, 1887.

19 & 20 Below: Adrian and Laura agreed to differ on the subject of 'Don Roberto', Laura taking a thoroughly disapproving view of his Trafalgar Square involvement.

21 Contemporary engraving showing 'FIGHT AT THE BOTTOM OF PARLIAMENT STREET BETWEEN THE POLICE AND CONTINGENT FROM SOUTH LONDON AND BATTERSEA', a view of confused fighting between police and the unemployed and their sympathisers during the 'Bloody Sunday' riot.

22 Left: Sir Thomas Troubridge Bt, Laura's elder brother, who married in 1893 his first cousin Laura 'Queenie' Gurney, daughter of Uncle Charles Gurney and Alice (née Prinsep).

23 Above left: Portrait of 'Queenie' at the time of her marriage, by her sister-in-law Laura, by then Mrs Adrian Hope.

24 Above right: Ernest, the younger Troubridge brother, was at sea for over four years before he came home on leave, aged nineteen, in 1881.

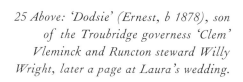

25 Above: 'Dodsie' (Ernest, b 1878), son of the Troubridge governess 'Clem' Vleminck and Runcton steward Willy Wright, later a page at Laura's wedding.

26 Right: Helen, baby of the family, in her early teens dressed as the Sultana Nourmahal.

27 *Selection of Laura's work: Christmas Card, first commissioned by Mansell's in 1879.*

28 *Fifth in the series of six illustrations to the nursery rhyme 'The Queen of Hearts, she made some tarts …', later set to music.*

29 Above: From a set of ten large-page illustrations for Hans Andersen's fairy story, 'The Little Mermaid', not published until 1891.

30 Right: One of Laura's many illustrations to Mrs Molesworth's The Old Pincushion (1889).

*31 & 32 At last, Adrian and Laura on honeymoon on Cousin Jem Hope's luxurious house boat,
the* Crocodile, *at Pangbourne on the Thames. Bellagio, Lake Como was to come later.*

curveless women. Can they ever have lovers & fatten out, think you? Your description is wonderfully vivid & I can see them looking at you & Laura with astonishment. Probably you both got the credit of wearing 'palpitating corsets' among the lean & learned ones. ...

The Colonial Conference ends next week & then Sir Henry Holland [Secretary of State for Colonies], will not be so busy & perhaps he will pay attention to my clamour. But I feel very low about my chances of getting anything. Also I am so doubtful as to how you will endure whatever they may offer me. It seems so treacherous of me to be trying to get anything against which you have a feeling. This is what I think really makes me so depressed. ... The thought that if only I ran about a little more I should get something makes me wild when I am chained here & unable to go after people. How could I get at Ld Claud Hamilton [then A.D.C. to Queen Victoria]? Does Uncle Sommy know him? I have just signed 144 letters which makes my hand stiffish. I am going to work all the evening. I have only scraped £800 together for my Dinner on the 25th & I must get £1500. How to do it I know not but I am writing a series of begging letters.

Did you not think the cooking of 'Jeannie' at Cambridge very superior? It is so different from English nastiness. I am so glad that you & Laura have met so happily for it makes me feel that this is surely a good omen somehow, Your Adrian

HUNSTANTON   4TH MAY

My dearest, ... You say Jem & Elsie are shortly going off to the *Crocodile*— *and* the infant. What an idea. Imagine a crying baby on board & no escape from it. The remedy is so obvious, just to drop it overboard! Dearest, how those 2 at Cambridge do detest Lady G. I had many chapters on that subject, but *we* understand each other so it is all right. I returned laden with French light literature. Some Laura lent me Aunt A. took away again—she said I was too fresh to read them, it would be a pity as they took such a bad view of life. [Laura Troubridge was getting on for twenty-nine while Laura Hope was only lately twenty-seven years old.] I felt rather offended as I had read them, but of course I gave them up. ... Ever your own dear *Laure*

WHITE'S, ST JAMES   SUNDAY, 8TH MAY

My darling Laura, The dinner at the Sydney Jolliffes (an older brother of Jo's to meet Henry Baillie-Hamilton, P.S. to Sir Henry Holland) was very successful. I took in Mrs B-H & made the running with her all the evening.

We broke the ice of conventionality directly we sat down for she asked me if I could take her leg between mine. She meant the leg of the table but still it made us laugh. Sydney had warned me to talk of the Abercorns so I turned the conversation that way & she soon talked of her uncle the Duke. Then we talked about the Haddingtons (her husband is the 4th son of the Earl) & I mentioned that old Maria Lady H. had been my Gt-Aunt. We got on very swimmingly & she asked me to call on her today. Of course I said nothing about my chances either to her or to her husband who was very nice & civil. …

Jem has been in Paris for three days with Cole & he has come back more full of the famous Cartridge deal. … I saw Austin Lee at the F.O. who warned me not to overdo it at the C.O. The feeling at the C.O. is against bringing in a new man. … I am so sorry to hear that your *Child Elves* work is not of much interest to you. I hoped that when you began it you would get a bit carried away. … Poor darling, it must be trying for you—the sleepy monotony of Hunstanton. Yet this life in London alone is very solitary too. This life roaring all round & no place for you & me in it all. It gets on one's nerves horribly. Goodbye my wife, Your Adrian

HUNSTANTON 10TH MAY

My own dearest Adrian, … I cannot be much carried away by this book I am illustrating—because it is *quite* the most stupid story I have ever read, and very badly written—fairy stories can be so charming & poetical that I cannot understand Griffiths & Farran taking this M.S. … However I do my best & have turned out some pretty little fairy scenes but it is so different working out someone else's ideas—especially when you think them stupid—to one's own inspirations. …

It must be very wearing for you running after all sorts of men about this app.t. I should have thought you were a *new* man when without any effort on your part you were offered the Ceylon Sec.ship but now, after 3 years of that you surely must have *some* claim on them. … I think of you *so* often, Ever your *Laure*

GREAT ORMOND STREET HOSPITAL, BLOOMSBURY 11TH MAY

My own Precious Love, … I should much prefer Runcton to any other visit for Whitsun for I don't feel well enough to be civil or to make myself nice to strangers. … The Colonel came to see me last night. He feels very proud that the Gov.t should now ask him for a Report on the Gun that burst last year when at first they even declined his offer to give evidence. This rather puts him in the pulpit as one authorized to preach on Guns. Of his own poor Gunlet I can extract no word, which evidently means another delay. How mad people must think him to be. … Hoare is vexed I think to find that he can extract no promise out of Holland for me. What I hear from the C.O. is really worth nothing for no official ever tells the truth. Indeed they would find life impossible were they to do so. … Your Adrian

KING STREET, KING'S LYNN   14TH MAY
[WITH GEORGE & EVA CRESSWELL]

My darling Adrian, … I forget if I told you I had received the 'Mermaid' from Mr Carr with a nice little note to say his offer for it still holds good. Thereupon I wrote to Field & Tuer (who had asked to see something of mine in black & white) about the 'Mermaid' set and by return I had a snubby little note saying they would not trouble me to send the drawings as all their Christmas arrangements were complete. Then yesterday I had another letter from F. & T. most civil, apologizing for the first, saying the member of their Firm who wished to see my drawings was ill at home when my letter was received & answered, & begging me to send the drawings with a view to their publication. This may possibly lead to something. No word have I had yet from Griffiths & F., only a note to say they had sent my sample drawings for *Child Elves* on to the author—who lives abroad. … Ever your *Laure*

28 GREAT ORMOND   12 P.M. SATURDAY/SUNDAY, 14/15TH MAY
STREET ['MY ROOMS']

My own dear *Laure*, Oh! What a dinner with the O'Neills. First of all Ponsonby had asked me to meet him in the City to see the Queen go by [a Jubilee Procession]. There were some women there & when Ponsonby said he had to go he hoped I would see these people to the nearest Underground. This made me very late. When I got to Eaton Square I found the most awful lot of fossils waiting for Sir Patrick Grant who never came. Lady Grant came at last, saying Sir P. was tired out with the function, & as she brought her daughter we were a man short. Imagine poor Lady O'Neill devoured by shyness & having to alter her list at the last moment. I took down a Mrs Ryder whose back & front bulged equally. She was a jolly old thing all the same. On the other side of me was Lady Colchester who reminded me absurdly of my Aunt Bontine [Cunninghame Graham]. She had exactly the same voice so in the middle of dinner I asked her if Aunt B. was any relation of hers. It turned out that she was a niece. Lady C. said that I reminded her so strongly of Charlie Graham—my cousin—which amused us rather. Bar this I never was so bored. When the ladies left us I was left utterly alone. O'Neill talked to Ld C., the other 4 men paired off & I did not open my mouth the whole time & could not even smoke. He (Ld O'N.) is a miserable little creature, quite awful to look at I think & so shy. When we went upstairs the women were tightly packed together & I stood in a corner like a naughty child for almost the whole time. Lady Gertrude [Tom Cochrane's wife] was there but fenced in by dowagers. Just as everyone was going I had a few words with Lady O'Neill & thanked her for getting her husband to write about me to the C.O. Oh! darling, what a house. I do hope that I may be spared another dinner there. …

Today I called on people & found them out so I left a few cards & then went to see Mrs Baillie-Hamilton. What a woman to talk. She never ceased from ½ past 5. until ¼ past 7. In vain I said goodbye & three times she always began again, holding on to my hand in the most embarrassing way. I really thought that the only way out of it would be to kiss her & then fly. However I was spared the ordeal & got away at last. … Forgive me if I have said anything rude about the O'Neills. Really they tried to be kind but I shall not forget in a hurry the *coup d'oeil* [first glance] of their menagerie. Fancy half a dozen of Aunt Amy [of Runcton Rectory], all in low frocks. One's appetite was quite taken away with such a liberal display of flesh. Ld O'Neill hopped about like a lame Robin looking for crumbs. She looked frightened & stupid. Just as I left I was introduced to Tom Cochrane [later of Cults] for whom I at once conceived the most intense loathing. I am so sorry Dearest but I really cannot bear the little man. He seems to me an abominable little wretch. Perhaps it was only because I was so terribly bored. … Darling goodnight, Your Adrian

HUNSTANTON   16TH MAY

My darling Adrian, I am sorry you had such a dull dinner party at the O'Neills, but you ought to have *enjoyed* meeting so many old ladies. I thought you had such a weakness for them—perhaps they were not quite old enough! … You need not have been so very bitter about the dinner party, & poor Tom Cochrane too. I suppose you forget I like him *particularly*—or you would hardly have called him an 'abominable little wretch'—for after all darling you simply do not know him and it was rather rude & not very kind of you to abuse him to me. … I can imagine poor Louisa feeling the dullness & weight of her fossil dinner party—& totally unable to do anything to improve matters. She is such a painfully shy hostess. Cannot you imagine how she used to depend on Amy & I to get up amusements & make things go off at Shane's … & Edward cannot be a very exhilarating husband. … He really is pleasant but so painfully shy too—and his appearance & walk is *so* odd. At Shane's he always wore boots with gashes cut in them for his poor toes—& waddled about like a duck—it had the oddest effect. …

I would have given anything to see the sight of the Jubilee Procession. I have seen nothing of the sort since I was quite a tiny person & was taken to the Horseguards to see Garibaldi pass. I should have liked to have seen that great multitude of excited people—& have hourrahed with them! … Darling, how you must have been flirting with Mrs Baillie-Hamilton for you to be on such terms already—a 2 hours visit for the very first start off! I imagine *he* was not at home. … Amy is staying at Runcton for rook shooting. There is a great ball at Yarmouth for H.R.H. on Thursday—Vi is going to represent the family. I go on quietly with my drawings & try to forget there is such a thing as life. Do not think I write to pose as a martyr—I only feel low & sad sometimes because I miss you so—and nothing nice seems to happen. … Ever your own loving *Laure*

Great Ormond Street Hospital, Bloomsbury   16th May

My Darling, My long scrawl of last night was I fear written rather in a bad mind. I was cross certainly & pray you forgive me, Love. … I went to the C.O. today but could learn nothing except that they intend to cut down the pay of Trinidad to £900 from £1200 for the next man. … I have been to see Lucas who asked me about my chances. He is very friendly just at present as he hopes to get quit of me. … As I passed the Grosvenor I could not resist looking in to see the picture of Lord Pembroke which I have been so chaffed about. It is absurdly like me though the likeness of a better looking man. Burne Jones has a very hideous picture of Pan there. Thaddeus' one of the Pope is well hung & looks a fine portrait. I chuckled when I found that some women were pointing me out to each other as Lord Pembroke. By the way, tell me if you think my own picture [the Ourliac portrait] is really well painted or only a daub. I recollect that I always thought the shoulders were out of drawing, & that the head looked too small. Goodbye, Your Adrian

Great Ormond Street Hospital, Bloomsbury   17th May

Ma Laure, Mea culpa. It was a cross letter that offending night, so please forgive me. … Last night I dined with Swettenham at the Isthmian … then we went on to White's for a bit & then Swettie fidgeted about until I agreed to go down to the House with him. In the Lobby I met Don Roberto who got us into the Distinguished Strangers Gallery. We came in for an interesting row & I was amazed to discover that the dear old fellow had never been in the House before & had been secretly dying to come all the evening. He is so queer. … He is too mad with his hatred of women. It is a disease with him. You will I think be so much amused with his queerness & oddity. At the same time I do hope you will like him for I am so much attached to him, bear as he is. However, I think Cyprus is improving him for he told me two naughty Storiettes quite nicely & even laughed grimly. For him this was wonderful & a great stride. We two did talk & laugh so over old Ceylon days & he told me of his experiences in Cyprus which must be a charming place. His descriptions are fascinating. Such a lovely hill country & the people so nice. Morality seems quite unknown but they have such nice ways & pleasant manners. …

The Procession was not very imposing or very striking and the Queen is too much of a Norfolk Dumpling to look imposing. … Goodbye my own dear Love, Your Adrian

HUNSTANTON   17TH MAY

My darling Adrian, … I had a civil note from Field & Tuer—but declining the 'Mermaid' which they say is not in their way—but praising it—gilding the pill for me. So now I hope she will find a happy home with Mr Carr [at the *English Illustrated Magazine*]. I also had a nice letter from Mr Okeden of the firm of Griffiths & Farran. They are very pleased with my drawings & want rather more than 60—for which he says I must increase my demands. He is just married, but I forget who to. He asks if I will come and see him and his wife in Chester Square when I am next in town. It is really a nice letter & I will certainly go—as publishers are most useful friends for me. About Hatchard I have heard nothing further & I am thankful for it. I should feel swamped if I had both M.S. at once in my mind. You see it is all work from the imagination & one can not depend upon ideas to order—as one can on hand work. …

About your portrait at Cambridge. It is certainly not a daub, it is very carefully painted—but if anything rather too smooth, not quite *powerful* enough. I mean the paint is too evenly laid on all over—which gives it a sort of uniform texture for both the flesh, coat & background—which I think is a mistake—but the likeness is so undeniably good that these criticisms occur more as you get to know the picture. … I should like to curl your hair one day with my nice little lamp & tongs! just to see if I should like it. Laura said it suited you so well in Paris—& all the Frenchmen did it. Goodbye my dearest one, Always your *Laure*

Laura accepted Comyns Carr's offer for her 'Mermaid' drawings and noted on the July Accounts page of her journal that she was paid £20 by the editor of the *English Illustrated Magazine* 'for the use & copyright of the 'Little Mermaid' series, the originals to be returned.

18TH MAY

My darling Adrian, I have been very busy about our theatricals at Runcton at Whitsun. I am going to appear in my old character—Jenny—in *Sweethearts*. I ought to know the role well by this time so do not mean to sacrifice our holiday to rehearsals. Charlie [Orde] has been longing to appear as my sweetheart for ages—so he takes the part—very safe I think—but it is ambitious of him. Perhaps *you* could give him some hints after nearly 3 years study of the part! We need not begin to rehearse till Whit Tuesday—the day I suppose you will have to return after your tiny holiday. Adieu, Your *Laure*

GREAT ORMOND STREET HOSPITAL, BLOOMSBURY   25TH MAY

My dearest, Everything went wrong at the last but I shall have £1700 to give out tonight which is better than I had hoped. I have had to fill up my Dinner from White's. Quite a large division is coming to sit round me. Last night I dined with Swettie & we read through an Act of Parliament to divert us after dinner. It is all about Colonial Pensions & we want to get it altered. Then we studied the Blue Book with the Report of the Royal Com.n. The poor Col. has had such a slating in some of the papers. I am sorry for him & feel a bit sore. Every paper had a Leader on him yesterday. *The Times* was fair, *Daily News* very bitter. He seems to have been most careless & injudicious. …

The Times Leader of the 24th on the Report of the Ordnance Inquiry Commission, with its revelations of gross mismanagement & inefficiency, censured the commissioners for undue lenience towards certain aspects of a system which it felt 'lacks the very rudiments of intelligent organization'. Not so pleasing to the colonel was its reference to the eminently satisfactory 'dissipation once for all of the charges of corruption … against the officials of the War Office … for which the several witnesses … have manifestly failed to establish even a *prima facie* case.'

The 'copious extracts' from the 100-page report itself covered almost a whole page of *The Times* and Col Hope was mentioned frequently— and usually unfavourably—for his persistent, unsubstantiated charges of corruption, and for introducing irrelevant personal grievances. The colonel withdrew most of his charges, saying 'that he had been mistaken … and when he said that the Ordnance Department was a seething mass of corruption he had made use of a foolish expression'. … The Report continued: 'It should be said, however, that Colonel Hope seems to have had some ground of complaint in regard to his treatment by the War Office … concerning the bursting of the Collingwood gun.' The commissioners offered themselves as a go-between whereby the colonel would be supplied with the relevant information and allowed to inspect the gun. His report would be given direct to them and they would pass it on to the Secretary of State for War 'who did not feel disposed to have any direct communication with Colonel Hope' for observations, and the whole would then be published as a supplementary report.

The Whitsun holiday at Runcton was uneventful, the weather was mostly foul and even the performance of *Sweethearts* had to be postponed for lack of acting support.

---

100 *1st May* Adrian had told Laura that he was particularly unhappy at the time Mlle Ourliac was painting this portrait of him in Paris in the early 1880s.

101 *3rd May* Agnata Ramsay became the second wife of H M Butler, the Master of Trinity College, Cambridge, the following year (1888).

JUNE 1887

HUNSTANTON   2ND JUNE

My Adrian darling, I should love to see the Jubilee procession from Lady G's [Goldsmid] balcony. I see the Queen will pass down Piccadilly twice so No 105 would be as good a place as one could possibly have to see the show. ... One can hardly believe it is already the 2nd of June—how soon it will be 3 years since *that day*—it seems to me half a life time ago. Not because of waiting, or any sad reason, but one seems to live more when one loves—don't you think so darling? I suppose because one shares so much in each other's life—besides one's own.

I see it rumoured in the papers that the very thing you have been saying about Cyprus is to be done, that the Sultan is going to cede the island altogether to England. If we ever go there I shall be glad for it would be nice to have to do with a prosperous place instead of one that is always out at elbow & beggared. ... Today I received what I have been rather dreading—a letter from Hatchard—with the M.S. of *Daddy's Boy* & asking me to let him have some of the illustrations as soon as possible that they may be engraved in the magazine in which the story is first coming out. I should have liked to finish my *Child Elves* book set but it would be too great a pity to throw over Hatchard so I have accepted. He has changed his idea & now wants nothing but full page. I have agreed to do 12 drawings for the £25. ... Ever your own *Laure*

SUNDAY, 5TH JUNE

My darling Adrian, ... About British Honduras [for which Adrian hears he is not being considered] I cannot possibly feel any regret—why even *you* dreaded the possibility & *I* saw it like a huge black cloud on the far horizon—it would have been a *terrible* exile. ... Hatchard has changed his mind & now only wants 7 full page pictures & an initial letter to each chapter (20)—for which I am very glad. The initials are nothing compared to the thought & work required for the full page. He has sent me an example for the full page—which are to be wood engravings. It is so pretty, not pen & ink but washes of soft grey black, done with a brush. Quite new to me—but if I can get into the way of this style they will take far less time to do than line pen & ink work. I believe the designs for all those soft engravings in *Harper's*[102] are done in this way. ... Ever your *Laure*

6TH JUNE

My darling Adrian, ... It is very mortifying about the Colonel but it ought not to affect you—as you fear—for you have never been mixed up with this crusade of his. ... Did you read Lord Randolph's [Churchill] speech at Wolverhampton? I think it would have pleased your father—Lord R. at all events does not mean to let the matter drop. He does not mention the Col. but he repeats all his charges of maladministration—& more besides against the Naval & Military departments. ... Ever your *Laure*

GREAT ORMOND STREET HOSPITAL, BLOOMSBURY   7TH JUNE

My own Sweet Love, ... I arrived very late for dinner at the de Bunsens, they had begun & there was no party so I was forgiven. Mrs Lothar de B. looked so bored on the other side of the table all alone for Lothar was upstairs as he nearly cut off his big toe when he dropped his razor through his foot. Madame de B. talked of nothing but the Jubilee & I tried to tempt her [to have Laura to stay] with an offer of seats at White's. They are going to have no one with them because they hope to get foreign H.R.H.'s quartered on them. After a very filthy dinner I went & sat with Lothar who was very cheery as he has got a month's leave—away from the fens. ... Your Adrian

HUNSTANTON   8TH JUNE

My dearest one, ... I felt sure you would be starved at Abbey Lodge. What was it—mutton & French plums? or something even worser. ... How like Bette [Mme de Bunsen] to have set her heart on doing landlady to Royalty. They really haven't the establishment for it but I suppose they may possibly catch some Grand Dukelet. She is *such* a snob. ... I had a long letter from Ernest, he is on board the flagship *Alexandra* for a cruise. They are bringing the Duke [of Clarence] & Prince George for the Jubilee. ... Ever your *Laure*

9TH JUNE

My darling Adrian, After all we *are* coming to Abbey Lodge—Amy & I for the 21st in the Jubilee week. I see a list published today saying where all the royalties great & small, white & black, were to be potted out for that week—there was *no* mention of Abbey Lodge!! I long to see the illuminations on the 21st, could not we two drive about together to see the show? I wish Jem & Elsie would ask us to the *Crocodile* for the Sunday after as at present we leave Abbey Lodge on Saturday 25th. ... Adieu, ever your *Laure*

WHITE'S, ST JAMES'   SUNDAY, 12TH JUNE

Darling Laura, Yesterday afternoon I went down to the Longdens with Palgrave.[103] He is the same as ever & we sat up talking till 4.30 with Sir James. They were delightful together & I did most thoroughly enjoy my part of listener as the interest never flagged for one instant. We had such a dull dinner party though, the people stared so at Palgrave who always refuses to wear evening dress & who had a Fez & a comforter on. He rather shocked their propriety too by dilating upon the advantages of polygamy (no doubt he practised it). But then when we were alone, how he did talk. It is a liberal education to listen to him. And in argument he employs such quaint apt illustrations. By Allah but he is a wonder that man. Jew to the backbone really I always suspect. … By the by I went to 105 Piccadilly on Friday. There was such a crush & all the native Princes in their gorgeous clothes & with such jewelry. How I wish you could come here for the Goldsmid Ball on the 15th. … Your Adrian

HUNSTANTON   13TH JUNE

My darling Adrian, … Mr Palgrave must be interesting—but I don't think I should care for him—should I? I feel almost certain he is rather dirty! Fancy a *comforter* in this weather. Have you found yet the best way to see the illuminations. I was told waggon loads of people would drive about in huge *vans*, is this true? It would be rather fun. One could hardly walk in the crowd, could one? … Darling I could not write to you yesterday. I was thinking so much about my lost book—it was your going to the Longdens at Longhope that reminded me of it. I can *never* forget it, though I thought at Runcton it had quite passed from my mind—when you could not remember whether or not you had done as I asked about circulating the printshops. I am often unhappy about it & I have not worked with *any* enthusiasm since I heard you had lost my best work. Goodbye dearest, your *Laure*

GREAT ORMOND STREET HOSPITAL, BLOOMSBURY   14TH JUNE

Dearest Love, I saw Austin Lee who was fearfully against my applying for any Consulship. He said the one at Brussels was purely commercial, i.e. filled by some Merchant. Lord Claud [Hamilton] was very kind but not encouraging. He seems to think that my Father has gravely affected my chances. At the C.O. they told me that their list of Applicants was so long that they could see no hope whatever of my being offered anything at all. This is not cheerful is it. All day I have been worried & now I am too fidgety to sit down & write so goodbye my own dearest, Your Adrian

HUNSTANTON   15TH JUNE

My darling Adrian, I am coming up to London on *Friday* [17th] & stay till Monday at Thurloe Square for the christening of the latest arrival there—my goddaughter—on Saturday. I am in a sort of fever lest you should have accepted any *unputoffable* Sunday visit. … Darling I am *very* sorry for your disappointment about the C.O. I am afraid your not being a Conservative weighs against you now. Most of all I grudge the time & trouble that have been given up to this for the last 4 months. … Have you found out anything about the staff they intend to have to work this Imperial Institute. … About Mr Austin Lee—it seems to me he throws cold water over everything you suggest. The man who held that post at Brussels was a solicitor—he is not likely to have been a merchant as well. I noticed this particularly because I wondered if it was necessary to be a solicitor to hold the viceconsulship. … If you had something at the Institute it might be in connection with those Colonies that you love so fondly—& yet be in London—which I love so fondly. … Ever your *Laure qui t'aime*

GREAT ORMOND STREET HOSPITAL, BLOOMSBURY   15TH JUNE

Dearest, My Committee is just over & I have again beaten Miss Wood by getting my Candidate elected for Highgate against hers. Miss Kol is such a nice pretty Dutch woman who has been a Sister here for 4½ years. Miss Wood drove her away & then did her best to stop Miss Kol from being elected & the result was a triumph for I got the whole Com.ttee to take my view. … I have got seats for 2 ladies at White's & a seat for 1 lady & myself at 105 Piccadilly [Goldsmids]. I hardly know which to advise. The Goldsmids have asked 70 people & may ask more so that I cannot ask for Amy but she could go to White's with Madame de B. who is wild to see the show. Jo would attend on them & I can offer a lunch there which is more than we shall get at 105. Your Adrian

At Thurloe Square
[with Johnny & Rosy Birkbeck]

> *18th June* We went off after lunch to St Barnabas for the Xtening—I held Betty—as she is to be called. … Dined early & went off to *Buffalo Bill* the Wild West show. Enjoyed it immensely—a lovely evening. I had a toboggan slide.

20th June Went shopping with Audrey [Rosy's young sister] & then to the Royal Academy—looked at hundreds of pictures, had an ice, walked halfway home for the crowd & block of carriages was impossible. Piccadilly very gay with decorations. Adrian had 2 tickets for the Abbey tomorrow but they were so very high up that I thought it would make one giddy. Went to Abbey Lodge to meet Amy, very jolly—went together on the prance. Saw some people, ices at Gunters. Adrian came in the evening.

At Abbey Lodge, Regent's Park
[with the de Bunsens]

21st June – 'Longest Day' and the Great Jubilee day. Perfect weather. Up very early, breakfast in haste & set off with Amy for Piccadilly—crowds & crowds of people everywhere. Arrived at Lady Goldsmids & Amy went on escorted by Adrian to White's, then he came back to me & we went on the balcony & saw the procession most beautifully. Lunched & out again to see the Queen & her guests returning from the Abbey. … After dinner went off again to see the illuminations.

GREAT ORMOND STREET HOSPITAL, BLOOMSBURY   28TH JUNE

Darling, What a lovely morning it was yesterday. I longed to come & give you one more kiss but instead I had sorrowfully to go off by train leaving my Love behind [on the *Crocodile* house boat]. … Today I have just had an absurd interview with Lucas, who sent for Miss Wood & read us both a lecture on Charity & give & take. I gleefully agreed & said that the only thing I objected to was being bullied by him for sins not of my committing. Miss Wood's face was a lovely study when I forgave her her misrepresentation. Finally Lucas departed having done nothing but moan over the friction between us two. … How I wish Jem's idea could turn to something. But in Coats I put not my trust. Your Adrian

Regatta Week, on the Crocodile at Henley
[with Jem & Elsie Hope]

28th June The infant Violet has been very peaceful & not disturbed me at all. She was lifting her voice when I woke this morning, I was so sleepy I had forgotten all about the little person—& asked Shirley [the Nanny] what it was! which must have surprised her. ... Wanted to bathe & Jem rowed Elsie & I up to the bathing place only to find it forbidden for ladies in the Regatta week—so unkind & selfish of the men. After lunch shopped with Jem in Henley, he bought a melon at famine price—& all the way back to the *Crocodile* was advising Adrian & I to throw everything to the winds & marry immediately with such energy that he squeezed the melon to death—which made me laugh—it was entirely spoilt.

29th June The races began almost directly after breakfast. The river was such a pretty sight. A delicious lunch mostly strawberries & cream, & round about among the crowds of every kind of craft—& every kind of band. Saw a few friends. After dinner rowed about with Jem & Elsie to see the illuminations. ...

---

102 *5th June Harper's New Monthly Magazine* was originally founded in the US (1850) to reprint contributions to English magazines from such writers as Dickens. It later became truly American.

103 *12th June* W G Palgrave (1826-88), the diplomat, travel author, and one-time Jesuit missionary, who had many posts in the Orient. His elder brother, Francis Turner Palgrave, was a poet and critic and editor of *The Golden Treasury* (1861, 1897), and his younger brother, Sir Robert Harris Inglis Palgrave, edited *The Economist* (1877/83). Their father, Sir Francis Palgrave, the English historian and deputy keeper of public records had changed his name from Cohen before the birth of his three sons.

JULY 1887

HUNSTANTON   2ND JULY

[AFTER STAYING WITH ADRIAN'S AUNTS ANNIE & CHA CUNNINGHAME
GRAHAM, AND HIS SISTER LAURA, IN CAMBRIDGE]

My darling Adrian, Charlie [Hope, Adrian's younger brother] came to meet
me at Cambridge & we drove off to Number 6 [Panton Street]. They were
all so kind & nice. Aunt Cha seemed to me to be perfectly well—only a little
stiff in walking [after her stroke] but so bright & full of talk. We sat in the
little garden—there we had delicious strawberries & cream, little cakes, &
long tumblers of fresh milk—not quite cold—a most arcadian feast. ...
Laura was as nice as ever—she told me your brother John was made a
Corporal in South Africa and Charles has taken a third in his exams. ... I
want you to tell me if you have decided to try for the Carlton Secretaryship
or not because Cousin Milly Legh said she would mention your name to
someone she knew on the Committee. Amy told me she had lunched with
the Sam Hoares & he said he feared it was perfectly hopeless, that there was a
long *queue* of people waiting for each vacancy at the C.O., many of whom
had been applying for ages. ... Darling, do not lose heart, so many people are
keen to help now. ...

Such good news for Amy & Vi—dear old Uncle Herb offers them a room
& sitting-room for a week at his expense at Storeys Hotel, & room & board
for Tanner to take care of them. They are wildly delighted, simply standing
on their heads. ... Ever your *Laure*

                                                              4TH JULY

My dearest Adrian, ... I feel happier about the future than I have for some
time. I feel sure you *can* get something worth £400-500 in London. ... I
am sure if we both try we can be splendid managers and stretch out our
income until it does wonders. Why should we not live happily on a modest
£700 if others have done the same? ... Do not forget dearest about enlisting
Mr Hastie to find out for you what could be done about your family
pictures. It would simplify everything very much if they could be turned
into £.s.d.

The Le Stranges are so frightfully anxious about their brother Charles,
Capt. Le S. I daresay you saw in the papers that he had disappeared, having
started one night to visit the environs of Marseilles. Nothing has been heard
of him for 4 days—& his ship had to sail without him. Hamon Le S. is going
abroad directly in search of him. ... Your own *Laure*

5TH JULY

My darling Adrian, ... Yesterday a squall came on while we were out sailing on George's boat, the *Wild Duck*. We rather enjoyed it sitting on deck wrapped in blankets & tarpaulins & the yacht simply flying along before the wind. It was lovely when we started—so we had only our summer frocks & sketch books & guitars: instead of that we had to hold on tight in a gale of wind. ... The Le Stranges' have heard nothing of their brother since Thursday night when he was seen in Paris looking very ill, with all his luggage ready addressed to the *Surprise*. It is most mysterious. Of course they fear he has been murdered. ... Adieu Sweetheart, Keep up your courage, Ever your *Laure*

8TH JULY

My Adrian Darling, ... It is so odd to think I shall not know where you are tonight—if you really turn out of your rooms today. Yesterday I had a long day's work—from early morn to dewy end—& finished off the second full page design for Hatchard as he was in a hurry for it. ... The Col. sent me a message that the Cartridge was finished & he hoped to hear the sweet voice of his Gun for certain by the end of this month. Wolf—Wolf! it reminds one of—& I cannot get up any excitement about it. George [Cresswell] told me there were all sorts of stories going about London about poor Captain Le Strange having disappeared but I am certain they are canards—they say he has bolted with some woman—but one cannot believe he would have chosen this moment for it—which would be the ruin of his whole career ... but whether he is a good man or a bad man it would be absolute madness to desert for such a cause—as not many men have such a chance in the navy as he has. ... They have now tracked him to the Gare de Lyons in Paris & there lost all trace. His brothers have searched every Hospital in Paris—& any amount of detectives are at work. ... Always your *Laure*

GREAT ORMOND STREET HOSPITAL, BLOOMSBURY 11TH JULY

Dearest, I have been busy & besides have had no good news of any kind to tell you. ... Sometimes writing is such pain. I am living at 35 Jermyn Street now, at least if I could sleep anywhere my bed is there. My head spins round so that I cannot write. Goodbye, Your A.

HUNSTANTON 12TH JULY

My own darling Adrian, ... When a day or two passes in silence ... I can not sleep for thinking why it is you have not written to your *Laure*—I lie there thinking & thinking for hours—& when there is no letter I feel I have no courage to begin the day. Though really the day calms one—& brings reason to refute all the wild thoughts & fancies of the night—so one gets through the time somehow. ... Darling, do not lose heart now. We must be getting *very* near the time when we may spend our lives together now we have settled to marry when you can find a settled £400 a year in London. I feel certain you will succeed. ... Ever your *Laure*

13TH JULY

My darling Adrian, ... I do not wonder that you *can not see* whence our deliverance is to come—for this small appt. you are looking out for needs to be hunted—like everything else worth having. Unless you have not mentioned it in your letters, dearest, you have not yet seen a *single* one of the friends we thought might help—& how you are to find anything without asking & giving out to everyone what you are in search of I cannot imagine. I know you are very busy & the weather is very hot ... but nothing can come by sitting at Great O. Street, and in another fortnight everyone will have flown away & it will be too late. ... At the Jubilee day you told me you meant to ask Mr Amherst's advice & you have done *nothing*. Francis Buxton too, & Sam Hoare have not yet been seen. Would it not be possible to turn your French into account—& be French corresponding clerk to some big business house— French or English? ... Forgive my writing all this but I can not help telling you what is in my heart. The fact is the effort must be made *first* to find the idea of something to do—to get away from that hateful Hospital.

How I wish you were coming on the Sunday to Hopton but I suppose it would be utterly impossible. You want the day for seeing people. ... Always your *Laure*

HOPTON ST MARGARET, GREAT YARMOUTH 20TH JULY
[WITH AUNT MAGGIE ORDE]

My darling Adrian, ... I had a nice amusing letter from Laura from Cambridge—I send it you to read. ... Ever your *Laure*

> 'Dearest Laura, I was sorry not to be able to carry out my long intended visit—Charlie [the youngest brother] kindly

struggled to console me by taking me out every evening on the Cam, but as he don't condescend to row in anything but an outrigger, it was a remarkably trembly pleasure for me, also the undergraduates incited thereto by the exceeding warm weather, will bathe in that beautiful stream & then walk about 'in nature' on the banks till they are dry, now all these things add in no wise to the pleasure of boating; one night rowing past a group of bathers I put up a large umbrella & consequently steered straight on to a drift of gravel where we stuck fast, & the bathers obligingly swam out & pushed us off – I shall eschew boating on the Cam for a while. ... When you have any news of Adrian it would be sweet of you to share them—he is too low at present, poor old dear, to write.

Aunt Cha went on Wednesday to Rhyl. She is wonderfully better & received a most touching welcome from her old patients & fellow workers. On the 30th my holidays begin—hurrah & how nice it will be to be free for seven whole weeks. Goodbye dear, when does your story appear in the pious pages of the *Sunday Magazine*—I long to see your pretty illustrations. Ever with tenderest love your sister Laura'

GREAT ORMOND STREET HOSPITAL, BLOOMSBURY   20TH JULY

My dearest, ... Jo is going to try very hard for the Garrick Club Secretaryship which might leave his post open at the Bachelors'. It is only £200 a year but I might combine other things as the work is light & would admit of my doing other work. ... I wrote 6 or 7 letters yesterday begging the people we talked of to help me to find some small post which would make our future possible. ... Goodbye darling, Your Adrian

22ND JULY

My dearest *Laure*, Here are three of the letters in reply—Ld Claud Hamilton is nice & so is F. Buxton. [Henry] Birkbeck writes about the Carlton & you see he takes the same view that I did—that it would be a waste of time to apply. I also send you the music for your 'Queen of Hearts' set[104] & Gatty's letter about it. Tell me if it sounds pretty. You will want to send it soon if it is to come out by Christmas as it ought.

Yes, sleep once more visits me but I have been very headachey every day of late. I think it is the weather as I go early to bed & eat both breakfast & also lunch. A shocking waste of money. ... Goodbye darling, Your Adrian

HUNSTANTON   SUNDAY, 24TH JULY

My darling Adrian, Mr Gatty's song is *so* pretty, repeating the last line or last three words of the nursery rhyme like an echo—'The Queen of Hearts, she made some tarts ...'. How very kind of him to make me a present of the copyright—it is really *very* nice of him for I know him so slightly. I shall illustrate a title page or perhaps the score with some little playing card musicians etc. It is too late already for Xmas as the Xmas books are out by the beginning of September at the very latest. I am not so sorry for this as I must finish off my 2 books I have half done before anything else. I should like to get the 'Heart' series out by next Easter if I can as that is a publishing season. ...

Next Sunday [31st] my *bien aimé* I hope we may be together again at Sunny Hill [the Geoffrey Buxtons] and we will only talk of nice things. The theatricals for Norwich cricket week when I am to be the ingenue 'Molly' in *The Parvenu* are on the 3rd & 5th of August & rehearsals begin on 28th. Charlie Orde is going to act in these plays—I had a wail from him because he is *not* going to be my lover in the play! Adieu, your *Laure*

WHITE'S, ST JAMES'   25TH JULY

My own dear *Laure*, Jem wants me to go & live in Green Street from the 1st August while they are in Scotland. It will save me money for a bit. Tonight I dined with Thaddeus who afterwards took me to the Alhambra when we saw such a pretty Ballet. You would have loved the Costumes, they were so lovely only perhaps a little too indecent. The women seemed to have nothing on at all in one Eastern Scene, & perhaps there was too lavish a display of the female form above the knee for real art. But the whole effect was good. Thaddeus told me to tell you that his wedding present to us would be any one of his sketches that might happen to please your fancy. Rather nice of him was it not? Goodnight my own, Your Adrian

P.S. My Father has been catching it hot in the House of Lords tonight.

This *PS* referred to the Earl of Morley's lengthy peroration in the House of Lords, the gist of which was that as a result of their being totally discredited by the Royal Commission on the Ordnance Inquiry, neither Col Hope nor a Capt Armit—who had also laid charges of corruption against the Ordnance Department—was a fit person to hold high commissions in a Volunteer regiment. In Lord Morley's opinion, the then Secretary for War, Mr E Stanhope, had given an unsatisfactory reply to a question on this subject by Sir William Crossman (reported in *The Times* on 1st July). Here Mr Stanhope had replied that it was recommended Capt Armit (late of the navy before becoming a major in the Volunteers) be removed from the service. As to Col Hope, he felt debarred from taking such action as although the commissioners had considered his charges as 'palpably reckless' they were not 'intentionally false' and that he had 'more or less atoned for his conduct...by the frankness with which he had admitted his mistakes when they were pointed out ...'. *The Times* of 26th July took over two full-length columns to repeat Lord Morley's extensive quote from the published report of the recent Royal Commission, by which time the colonel's character lay in shreds.

To his rescue came Lord Napier and Ettrick who 'as an old friend and a relative of the gallant officer whose conduct has been so severely impugned' proceeded to give a moving résumé of the colonel's past life—his distinguished family, his bravery in the Crimea where he was awarded the VC, his success in the Diplomatic Service (under Lord Napier), and lastly his career as an inventor 'in the pursuits of engineering and mechanical contrivances, for which he had a natural genius' during which period be came into contact with the Ordnance Department. ... Lord Napier admitted all the colonel's failings in his subsequent charges of corruption but appealed to their lordships to refrain from taking any hasty decisions concerning the colonel's connection with the Volunteers. The colonel might yet be prosecuted by the officers against whom he had laid his charges of corruption and in that case should not 'go into the court prejudged'.

The under-secretary for War, Lord Harris, replied to the effect that sympathy should be extended to the officers accused of corruption by Colonel Hope. Lord Harris understood that the Secretary of State for War could not go against the commission's stated view that the colonel had atoned for his wrongful charges, in which case he should be allowed to retain his rank in the Volunteers—but Lord Harris repeated that it was open to any 'aggrieved person' to take proceedings against Colonel Hope. This adverse publicity did not affect Laura, who continued to write about the happenings of her day.

HUNSTANTON   26TH JULY

My darling Adrian, ... I am glad you have decided not to come to Sunny Hill till late on the Saturday for I find we are to have *2* rehearsals on that day, one 11.30 & the other at 2.30 & Sir Kenneth Kemp (the Manager of *The Parvenu* production) gives a luncheon party for the 'corps dramatic' at the Club in between. It is all so business like I don't suppose you would be allowed to look on—& even that would be very poor fun for us two. On Monday there is only one rehearsal—in the morning—I mean to cut it if it is possible. I shall plead a previous engagement (of 3 years standing!). On Tuesday the 2nd there is only one, in the morning, that I should have to go to as the performance is on the Wednesday. It would be *so* delightful to be together on the 2nd—our third anniversary. Last year we were at Runcton—& we have not missed that day yet. ...

How very nice of Thaddeus to say that. I should rather like to have his *impression* of 'The Inventories'—do you remember it—as we saw that scene so often together, but I daresay he has done others since. ... After our talk the other day at Hopton we cannot look forward to anything this year. I try not to think of the future at all now, but just enjoy my life here with the sisters and my profession as much as I can, & learn Patience all the time. ... *Toute à toi,* *Laure*

SUNNY HILL, THORPE, NORWICH   28TH JULY
[WITH GEOFFREY & MARY BUXTON]

My dearest, ... We shall meet so soon—I should be quite happy if it were not for the theatricals, they bore me, but we have Sunday & Monday free. We might go boating one day, just we two if we can, the river is quite near. There will be other people staying here—but mostly cricketers. Do bring some knickerbockers or flannels for the boating on Bank 'Oliday, which we shall enjoy as much as all the 'Arrys & 'Arriets in the country!! ... I am very busy painting a profile of Mary's little sister Maud Harbord. ... Adieu, ever your *Laure*

104 *22nd July* 'The Queen of Hearts', Laura's set of six watercolour illustrations in a square format (8.5 by 8 inches) of this nursery rhyme had the brightly coloured figures, based on playing card characters, in charmingly illustrated backgrounds with the words of 'The Queen of Hearts, she made some tarts ...' handwritten below each picture. Adrian's friend, Scott Gatty, then set these pages to music but they were never published.

YEAR FOUR 1887–88

LETTERS OF ENGAGEMENT

ADRIAN – LAURA

4TH AUGUST 1887

TO

31ST JULY 1888

WHITE'S, ST JAMES'   4TH AUGUST

Darling, I am so longing for an account of how the play went off. I sit & fancy all manner of things. That the tree you have to climb has broken down, that your frock split. That Bourke [her stage lover] kissed you. Never tell me if he did for it would be horrible to know of. ... I must stop for J.M.S. [John Manners Sutton, 4th son of 3rd Viscount Canterbury] is in such a hole that I must do what I can to help him. They are awaiting to arrest him in the Hall. Don't breathe a word of this ... Goodbye, Your Adrian

SUNNY HILL, THORPE, NORWICH   4TH AUGUST
[WITH GEOFFREY & MARY BUXTON]

My own dearest, ... I felt rather frightened about the acting—I think a good deal because I didn't care for the part. Charlie [Orde] came here about 6. and we had dinner together in the Gun room & went off in good time. I took a maid to dress me. The scene at the theatre looked so pretty. I think it went off very well. The local paper has a flourish about it this morning—in which Miss Troubridge is spoken of as 'an actress of great ability, etc.'. Mr Bourke, whether from carelessness or nervousness I don't know, cut out a good many speeches here & there which was rather a pity, especially as it made our reconciliation rather abrupt. The stage embrace was quite a success—not a bit a real one darling. I said I heard footsteps & started back directly! Miss Williams had some rather nice dresses but looked *so* like a professional painted up. Rosy [Birkbeck] was here this morning and said Charlie making long speeches to Miss W. was *exactly* like Uncle Willy preaching a sermon!! This I shall *not* tell him. The tree scene went very well—all our remarks were received with shouts of laughter, so that was satisfactory. ...

I did wish you were with me dearest, but I *am* glad we had the holiday together here. Goodbye my best beloved, ever your *Laure*

WHITE'S, ST JAMES'   5TH AUGUST

My Darling, Yesterday my letter was cut short by poor J.M.S. He is a close prisoner here with men waiting outside to take him to Holloway Jail for six weeks on a debt of £80. He had to sleep here & now we are going to try & smuggle him out late at night & get him off. I have been trying to arrange matters for him with his Solicitors. Of course he has not a sou but has just managed to scrape together £20 which I am endeavouring to get them to accept as a bit on a/c but they are very stony hearted as yet. Perceval [Manager of

White's] has behaved like a trump & given J.M.S. a bed. They tried to arrest Perceval which much delighted him. All the waiters have been splendid & they swear that J.M.S. is out of town. Today I had a stormy scene with the Creditor who at last consented to wait till the 10th before doing anything further but the men are still trying to catch poor J.M.S. There is a comic element in all this which makes one laugh. ... Will you ask [Geoffrey] Buxton for the address of the good School where a boy can learn things to fit him for emigrating? [This was in respect of his brother Charlie.] Goodbye, dearest, Your Adrian

Sunny Hill, Thorpe, Norwich   5th August
[with Geoffrey & Mary Buxton]

My darling Adrian, ... Such an excitement here last night—while we were away watching the other Company act in *Delicate Ground* and *Woodcock's Little Fan* my room was on fire. The housemaid lit the gas & shoved it into the curtains somehow. There was a tremendous flare up—huge blue satin curtains burnt to a tinder & the wall burnt too—such a pity, the curtains were lovely. The butler put it out with 2 of Hardens Sten Grenade things which he hurled at the blazing curtains. Oh the smell in my room when I got home! It had all been put tidy—but the chemicals & the burnt curtains were too horrid. I had to sleep there as there was not another corner empty—we are 12 in the house without the Buxtons. Mary had dashed in through the smoke & rescued *both* my pictures—Maud & Ivor's—which were quite near the flames. I am rather glad all my clothes were not burnt. Goodbye my own dearest, Your *Laure*

 P.S. I have given up trying to love you less for the present.

Sunday, 7th August

Darling, the acting went so well on Friday—I had a lovely bouquet thrown to me when we came before the curtain at the end. I *was* so tired—and I was portrait painting all yesterday, & all this hot afternoon I have done four little sketches for the *Sporting & Dramatic* all because you thought it such a pity to refuse, darling. Now Phil Harbord (Mary's brother) is here & wants to take me on the river but Geoffrey has a Buxtonian prejudice against Sunday boating so we wandered in the woods after tea. Phil was in a discontented mind & very cross because we could not go boating. He really looked quite beautiful— it rather suits him to be angry.

 How too absurd about J.M.S. He is *not* a good subject for disguise. If you had a fashionable wig & dress he would possibly pass as a 'dowager'. I wonder how you managed. Amy says Mrs Brooke's son (Edward) has joined her at

Hunstanton and is very nice & amusing. How unusual to have anyone nice at Hunstanton. Ever your *Laure*

Great Ormond Street Hospital, Bloomsbury 10th August

My dearest *Laure*, I had such a nice little letter from Charlie [Orde] today giving me an account of the acting. He says you were 'very coy' with your lover & gave him no chance of embracing you, that you looked very sweet up that tree. ... J.M.S. is in an awful mess over this debt of his. Poor fellow he has been very stupid & the law is wonderful hard on the poor when they are in debt. Last night I dined at White's by myself on cold fish & a dish of French beans to the horror of the waiters who thought me mad. Then I went & smoked a cigar with J.M.S. in his mother's house. He plays [the piano] so well & has such a soft touch, & his brother paints. By the way my friend Richmond told me that I was as like Ld Pembroke[105] as one pea to another. Very odd. Your loving Adrian

Hunstanton 10th August

My dearest, ... When I got home last night I found a frantic appeal for more drawings from Mr Okeden of Griffiths & Farran, merely this—'Dear Miss Troubridge—please!!! Yours very sincerely Herbert Okeden'. Of course I don't want to get into their bad books & have no more orders, so instead of the few days' rest I rather longed for I had had to fly at these drawings again. I have still 22 drawings to do for the *Child Elves*, including 2 full pages & I am determined to do them in a fortnight. ... Mary Buxton was delighted with my portrait of little Maud & has given me a commission to paint a duplicate for her mother. I am glad as I think I can improve on it. ...

Tom & Amy are going to the Leghs at Lyme. I wonder what will come of it [Tom's possible engagement to Sybil Legh]. ... Mr Brooke has been here today. I think he seems nice & clever, a very neat little ex Guardsman & *so* nice with his poor invalid mother. By the by, my illustration is in this week's *Sporting & Dramatic* & I think is rather nice. Adieu, Your *Laure*

11th August

Darling Adrian, Last night after tea I sat on the pier with Mrs Brooke till past 7. She is so nice & agreeable. I am sure you will like her. She is the kind of woman who knows everyone—she looks so miserably ill though poor thing, one wonders how she can have the courage to talk & laugh. ... I suppose there is hardly ever any smoke without some fire to account for it—& after all, much to the Le Stranges' sorrow it *is* a case of *cherchez la femme* [look for the woman] about Charles Le S. They have found he has been secretly married for ages to some impossible woman. The Duke [Prince Alfred, Duke of Edinburgh, to whom he is Equerry] got wind of this & taxed him with it—he entirely denied the whole thing, & then in the Duke's absence found out who had told the Duke—& that the truth was known beyond a doubt and then with his mind unhinged by illness—a touch of fever & sunstroke—he dare not face the Duke, knowing he was in disgrace with him, & went to Brussels instead, ill and alone. The Admiralty have suspended him & he is now put on half pay. This is sad for he had always been such a success. Of course he had a right to marry any one he chose, good, bad or indifferent but it is a pity he had come to such grief over it. Of course the Le Stranges have not mentioned it to us but Eva told us the story.

Mr Le Strange came to tell us he had seen Ernest—looking so well & that he was very popular on board the *Alexandra*. As to the Leghs, we do not know at all how the land lies there. We believe *Sybil* is abroad with her mother & only Mabel & Gil & her father are giving this grouse shooting party. Still, asking Tom at all looks as if they are trying to revive the affair. I wish you had not the bother of J.M.S. & his debts. Rather stupid of him to flounder so— because we know he has a very tidy little berth there in that Pall Mall office & ought to manage better. I wish he would hand it over to you out of gratitude. … Adieu, Ever your *Laure*

Great Ormond Street Hospital, Bloomsbury   11th August

Ma Laure chérie, I think I have finally managed to get J.M.S. free from his very importunate Creditor who has consented to an arrangement which I proposed yesterday. We then went to the Hammams [Turkish Baths] where we stewed away our cares & dined on fish & curried eggs. To bed I went very early & slept like a top. … If the Leghs do not mean anything they are behaving very cruelly & very badly to all concerned. How strange it will be if Tom does marry her. What a relief to you all as that would prevent his going to India [in the Army] and he would then get no doubt the Court post you have talked about. … So you like the little Brooke. Well, I am glad that he seems better than the usual run of Amy's Admirers. At any rate he must be over 21.

I am counting the days as they go by until we meet again—just a clear 14 days today. I ache to see you again. We seem to have been years apart & I am consumed with a jealous rage of everyone who talks to you while I can not. … Dearest, I kiss your feet & long for you. Your Adrian

WHITE'S, ST JAMES'   12TH AUGUST

My own *Laure*, We had a very nice dinner at Mrs Cooper's last night [mother-in-law of his friend Hugh Trevanion]. Then we drove to the Crystal Palace & saw some lovely fireworks & then the open air Ballet. They were all Mme Lenner's pupils & ranged from 5 to 20. The little mites were such dears & some of them had really fine legs. All in white tights & with their skins whitened. It was called *The Sculptor's Dream* & they were all the Gods & Goddesses of Olympos. The dancing too was first rate but there was wonderful little drapery & if they had been the ordinary fat Choristers I think some of the outlines would have verged on the grotesque. As it was I was quite charmed with it. We drove back for supper at Portman Square & I longed for you to be sitting opposite to me instead of the black moustache of Mrs Cooper. ... Goodbye my own, Your Adrian

HUNSTANTON   12TH AUGUST

My Adrian darling, ... Now Amy does not go to Lyme until Monday. The 'nice little man' [Brooke] seems very *épris* [taken] with her. I cannot help hoping it may be serious—he is very well off—& his old mother seems to have taken a great fancy to Amy & is always trying to throw them together, unlike most mothers of eligible sons—he is over 30 I believe but looks much younger. Amy is in an odd mind—& makes *no* moves—for which *entre nous* [between ourselves] I am most thankful. Consequently the little man is constantly contriving meetings & Eva is here or his mother for chaperonage. I daresay really there is nothing in it—but one can not help hoping. I know she would be so far happier married. He has begged her to put off Lyme till Tuesday when he might escort her to London & part of the way as he goes north that day. She has actually refused—she said if he wished to see her again he could easily get his mother to ask her to their place in Suffolk—but she was not going to change her plans to suit his pleasure! I quite agreed. ... Darling I too am looking forward so much to our long holiday. Ever your *Laure*

WHITE'S ST JAMES'   14TH AUGUST

My own dear Love, ... Yesterday I spent on the river with Mrs Cooper, a Mrs Paget & a Col. Wallace. We went to Cookham by train & sculled down to Monkey Island where we had tea. Then we came back to Skindles at Maidenhead for a very jolly dinner. Oh! the stories which were told. They were most amusing but I fear so improper. I hope that I shall be able to recollect one or two of them for you. Today Mrs Cooper gave us a dinner at the Ship at Greenwich & we went down by penny Steamer. Only one Sunday more before we meet again. Your Adrian

GREAT ORMOND STREET HOSPITAL, BLOOMSBURY 17TH AUGUST

Darling, ... How I hope the Clouds may have broken before Friday next for I have set my heart on our being married this Jubilee year & for this I would pay any price. Would you mind a winter wedding, my own love? I may have to go out of town this Saturday. Now I am going to see my Mother for I feel restless & uneasy. Coming events sometimes cast long shadows before which tinge the soul with gloom until the Sun rise & the Clouds pass away. ... I would rather not tell you where I have to go on the 20th or what it is about until I have something which is definite to lay before you. ... I feel well but very anxious & fearfully unsettled. Forgive me for not writing more. Goodbye dear love, Your Adrian

HUNSTANTON 22ND AUGUST

My dearest Adrian, ... I want you to buy yourself a nice Tam o'shanter cap for the holidays, like that nice old one you used to have at Knocklofty—but you probably won't be able to get a Graham [tartan]—so you may have a blue one, dark blue. I expect Scott Adie has hundreds. George has got such a horrid collection of dirt coloured ancient deerstalkers & I know you would always wear them!! ... I am pining to know this mystery. Ever your own *Laure*

P.S. You will need your *youngest* fur coat if we go on the pier after dinner. The evenings are quite cold now.

25TH AUGUST

Dearest Adrian, I am rather *starving* for news of you, good, bad or indifferent. An idea has taken possession of my mind, that after all it is the trial of the Gun that you are so anxious about, & not the new Eldorado I hoped you had found. It is rather a disappointing idea to me—because I always fancy it will be so long before the Gun brings a fortune, even if the trial is a great success. ... I have a Bee waiting to be drawn—it is buzzing like fury under a glass & I feel sure I can not persuade it to keep still while I sketch it. ... I have now finished the very last of my set of 60 illustrations for *The Child Elves* & feel so delighted & quite free again. Adieu, ever your *Laure*

GREAT ORMOND STREET HOSPITAL, BLOOMSBURY   23RD AUGUST

Dearest Love, Jem camc to Green Street today very full of beans. The scheme has reference to exile I am grieved to say & has naught to do with the Gun which by the way will be fired tonight. I go down by a 6 o'clock train to witness the affair which I trust will prove a triumph. How happy the poor Col. will be if it is. I hope to catch an early train on Saturday, darling. Tomorrow is a Com.ttee day & I am so busy preparing for what I had hoped might be the Com.ttee at which I could announce my resignation. However matters have not come to this pass yet. Goodbye dearest *Laure*, Your Adrian

24TH AUGUST

My Sweet, Yesterday I rushed off at 5. to Green Street where I had wired Jo and Jem to meet me. From there we went down by train to Southall where we found a trap & drove to the Butts. The Gun was being placed in position & looked splendid. The Col. was engaged filling the Cartridges with their enormous charges of powder. Presently everything being ready for firing we were all told to get under cover & there we lay watching the Colonel's tall figure standing out against the evening sky. He pulled the lanyard & we waited for the explosion. But something had gone wrong so I jumped up & ran up to see. The cap was bad & had refused to explode. With singular bad luck every cap in the Cartridges there was also bad. Night had now fallen to cover our dismay. So the poor Col. had to put off till today the virgin shot. It was really wonderful to see how quiet he was over this vexatious little annoyance caused by the petty blunder of a workman. As it was by this time 9.30 we left the Col. & his friends to drive to the Inn where he was to give a dinner. We meanwhile walked off to the Railway Station, caught a train & got back to Green St where Mrs Crawley soon gave us comfort for our hungry bodies & Jem produced wine to gladden our hearts.

Today, while my beastly Com.ttee are droning along the shot will be fired. I wish I could get away. At the last attempt last night Jem, I & the Col. stood all three beside the Great Gun, we felt that we could not leave him to be blown up all alone so we refused to take shelter. I think he was rather pleased. His old Crimean servant, Callow, was there having come over from America just in time. Poor old Callow, he followed his old master about like a faithful dog & was delighted to see me whom he knew as a baby at Washington for he married my nurse. Today Jem & Jo are unable to go so I shall not hear what happens. Everyone was pleased with the look of the Gun & the Breach action was splendid. It worked quite beautifully extracting the Cartridge & doing everything it ought. … Dear Heart, I so long to find myself beside you on the sofa in that quaint back Smoking-Room at Eva's, with my arm round your waist holding you to my heart which is all yours darling. Goodbye, Your Adrian

WHITE'S, ST JAMES' 26TH AUGUST

My poor Darling, I am grieved to have to disappoint you but I fear that it is very doubtful whether I can get away at all tomorrow. The Gun burst into a thousand pieces. It is a wonder that the Colonel still lives for he was the centre of a whirlpool of steel. They say the sight was too horrible & when the spectators rushed forward it was in the full belief he was dead. I went down to the Rag yesterday about 5. & found a group of fellows talking in the Hall. I caught the words 'gun burst' & then someone said 'that's his son'. So for the moment of course I believed him to be killed. Palliser (an old friend of the Colonel's) came forward & told me very kindly all about it. Since then I have had a letter from the Col. & have been vainly trying to catch him. I went down to my Mother this morning with a letter from Jem offering her Green St if she cared to go there, for this means absolute final ruin I fear. However she would not accept this but means to go to Rhyl to her sister Cha if the crash comes. All this must keep me here.

The only thing I am sorry for is that I was not there for then the Gun might have done for the family at one sweep. My poor Mother is dreadfully cut up. The Gun went like glass. It hurts me so to think that you will get this miserable letter tomorrow morning & that I shall not be there to comfort you. But I cannot leave them all alone now, at least until something has been settled about my Mother. Perhaps it would have been happier for him had his own Gun killed him. I am sick with sorrow for him. His agony of mind at this time, the end of the Gun which was to do so much. He won't see me & I won't leave London until we have met somehow. Your Adrian

They did meet and Adrian was, after all, able to join Laura at Hunstanton on the Saturday afternoon for the start of his month-long summer holidays. He said the colonel seemed to have taken the failure very coolly, and was already talking of another gun.

At Cliff Esplanade, Hunstanton
[George & Eva Cresswell's holiday house]

> Sunday, 28th August … Mrs Brooke & Adrian met—came, saw, & conquered in both cases—both telling me how charming &

agreeable the other was! Mrs Brooke has invited Amy to Ufford Place, their house in Suffolk, an invitation I do not think she will refuse.

31st August 'The Castle' is once more deserted. The maids as usual quickly seize the opportunity to clean something or somewhere. I believe they would be miserable if they did not do this the moment we leave the house, it seems to be a kind of religious duty with them!

---

105 *10th Aug* George Richmond (1809-96), the portrait painter, was referring to his portrait of a man in a fur coat, exhibited at the Grosvenor Gallery in April 1887, that was thought to be so like Adrian Hope. It was in fact of Lord Pembroke, 13th Earl of Pembroke and Montgomery.

SEPTEMBER 1887

At Hopton St Margaret, Great Yarmouth
[with Aunt Maggie Orde]

3rd–13th September... Sketched the long-suffering Adrian as the invalid uncle hunched up in a cape & old shooting cap for a drawing for Hatchard's *Daddy's Boy*. ... We fetch Adrian's sister from the station. Luckily Laura is not shy & seems amused by it all. Taught her to play golf on the putting links on the lawn while Adrian went out taking wasps' nests. Laura recited to us which was a great success. ... We all drove down to the beach to arrange a haul with a sieve net. Had great fun launching the boat but after 3 hours and a half managed one haul & caught 4 tiny fish. ... Off to the switchback railway at Yarmouth where we made seven flying journeys. ... Most regretfully said goodbye to Hopton, the comfort was going away together. Rather a tedious journey through wet and mist to Congham but we beguiled the way eating buns & playing écarté.

At Congham Hall, Kings' Lynn
[with Mrs Willie Davy]

13th-17th September ... Off to Narboro' where there was a tennis tournament, joined the three others there to our joy— so long since we sisters met that we at once became what Charlie Orde calls a 'Troubridge Pie'. As it was a public affair for a charity one could do what one liked. ... Nearly finished the etching of the Drummer boy in the wood for *Daddy's Boy*. ... Rain came on in torrents, after tea played écarté, Adrian had his first lesson in piquet, and in the evening played poker wildly till 12 o'clock. Enjoyed the fun of it and lost the modest sum of 6d.

At Hunstanton

17th–19th September Waited an hour in Lynn for our train to Hunstanton & had tea in Mrs Willis' celebrated Bathing machine. ... Found a letter from Griffiths & Farran asking me if I would like to illustrate another book for them.

At Sculthorpe Rectory, nr Fakenham
[with Uncle Herb & Aunt Bache Jones]

20th–24th September After lunch we went off to sketch the old
house at East Barsham, Aunt Bache & I in the brougham, Adrian
& Mr Augustus Hare in the pony carriage. The old house is
lovely but the rain fell all the time & spoilt the afternoon,
dribbling over our poor sketches. Mr Hare very clever &
agreeable—told most creepy ghost stories all the evening till I
longed to be safely married!! my room seemed so lonely. ...
Drove over to Houghton. Mr Hare had never seen it & was
delighted. Adrian always loves it. Had a tea-party in the stone
parlour, a sort of picnic. Then goodbye to Mr Hare ... a quiet
evening, Adrian reading out loud.

In Augustus Hare's *The Story of My Life*, on 19th–22nd September,
1887 he recorded first a visit to the Ordes at Hopton:

'A happy united family, with a very beautiful eldest daughter,
Evelyn. Hopton village is the Blunderstone of *David
Copperfield*. Charlie Orde took me to Caister [the Castle ruins]'.
...

He then went on to the Joneses at Sculthorpe to see the ruined
manor house, once the property of his great-grandfather Bishop Hare
through his marriage to a Miss Alston:

'At Cranmer, Lawrence Jones brought out quantities of old
Hare and Alston deeds to show me. ... My kind host, the
Rector, Herbert Jones, the squire's uncle, was the picture of
old-fashioned courtesy. His wife, a Gurney, sister of Mrs
Orde at Hopton, is well known for her archaeological
writings. They took me with their niece Miss Laura
Troubridge and her betrothed, Adrian Hope, to the beautiful
old brick and terra-cotta house of Wolterton. ... Yesterday
we went to Houghton ... the present Lord Cholmondeley has
sold many of its treasures, but ... it is especially interesting
because nothing has been added since the time of Sir Robert
Walpole ...'.[106]

At North Runcton Hall, King's Lynn
[with Uncle Sommy & Aunt Kitty Gurney]

25th-27th September To service at the new church. I regretted the dear old church—with all its old associations swept away for ever [it had burnt down]. ... My feelings on the subject are quite beyond compressing into these few blue lines, although I admit there is a certain prettiness about this odd new building, but oh for the corners & cushions of our youth & the delightful privacy of the Galleries. ... Goodbye to Runcton, the feeling for which was rather merged into the nearer pangs of bidding each other goodbye after our long holiday together.

At Hunstanton

28th September Worked at the strange coarse garment for a poor person in Newfoundland Aunt Kitty had asked me to make. ... Met Capt. Le Strange (now reinstated by the Admiralty) who takes out a relief crew to the *Ag.* [*Agamemnon*] next month when the beloved Ernest will come home.

GREAT ORMOND STREET HOSPITAL, BLOOMSBURY   28TH SEPTEMBER

My Darling Laura, ... At Green Street I found Jem & Elsie. He had been operating on Sir William Wedderburn, a cousin of his who had just returned from nearly 30 years in the Bombay Civil Service and who had a bad shoulder. Wedderburn came to dinner & we had a jolly little party. We talked a great deal of Cooch Behar's offer of a Secy'ship to me in India[107] which Wedderburn quite approved of. ... I also want to talk to Jem about becoming a City Clerk or something for stay here I cannot. ... There is a letter from my Mother saying that she has moved into a smaller house & is much more comfy as it is water tight, but that the Gun is not finished!!!! ... Jem seems more vague than ever about every thing & I fear he won't be much use to me. I had to go to the Guards Club this morning. It is a nice little Club, very quiet & full of swords & Bearskins in the Hall which looks so queer. ... Your Adrian

HUNSTANTON   29TH SEPTEMBER

Darling Adrian, I have been hard at work and sent off another drawing to Hatchard. I have still 2 to do to end the set. This morning I had another letter from them saying that the work was terribly behind hand (not a *little* behind hand!) as by rights it should be out now. As Meade (the author) has not yet sent me the rest of the proof sheets this is my excuse for not having finished the work. ... I do long for a sight of you already dearest, Ever your *Laure*

Great Ormond Street Hospital, Bloomsbury   29th September

My own dear *Laure*, ... We had such a quiet Com.ttee. Lucas turned up & was civil for a wonder. J.M.S. has offered me 3 rooms for a month at 6/- [shillings] a week. They are prettily furnished & just off Queen Anne's Gate. Canterbury (his elder brother) has been living there. I have decided to go there on Monday as unless they are let I may get the chance of stopping on there till Xmas on the same terms which are cheap enough as the 6/- is for attendance so I get the rooms for nothing. When I leave here today I am going to try to find Kneller & ascertain something about Cooch Behar.

Jem told me that Hopie [7th Earl of Hopetoun who was married the previous October] had a son. They did not lose much time. How glad John Hope-Wallace (his great-uncle) will be as he was always in terror of succeeding. ... Your Adrian

Guards Club, Pall Mall   30th September

Darling, ... V.G. has asked me to Somerhill for Sunday & I have refused as I do not feel up to being bored to death there just at present. ... The Col. is I think raving. He is now inventing a Hair Wash!!! It makes me sick. Goodbye dear Heart, Your Adrian

---

106 *19th Sept* Augustus Hare's grandfather, the Rev Robert Hare, was a godson and protégé of Sir Robert Walpole and the latter's younger brother, Horace, was the last Baron Walpole of Wolperton. *See The Story of my Life* by Augustus Hare (Vol 6, 1900).

107 *28th Sept* Nriprendra Narayan Bhup Bahadur had been created the first Maharaja of Cooch Behar in 1884. On this visit to England for the Queen's Jubilee celebrations in 1887, Adrian had met him and been considered for a Secretaryship in India.

OCTOBER 1887

In the October accounts page of her journal, Laura noted that she was paid £36 by Griffith & Farran for sixty pen-and-ink illustrations for the fairy story *The Child Elves* by 'M.L.', and £25 by Hatchard for eight pen-and-ink illustrations for *Daddy's Boy* by L Meade—both published in 1888. On the first book she: 'worked at this set on 42 days', and on the second, '31 days including an attempt in a different style & 3 initial letters they did not use'.

GUARDS CLUB, PALL MALL   1ST OCTOBER

My own darling *Laure*, My dinner last night with Lady de B. [Jo Jolliffe's elder sister, Eleanor Amelie, widow of 4th Lord de Blaquière] was very pleasant indeed. The young American Canadian who will be Ld de Blaquière turned out to be most amusing. He only knew 8 months ago that he was heir to anything & was a Clerk in a Bank at Montreal. There is an income of £6000 a year which is all in Securities & goes with the title. Jo took us both to the theatre to see *The Sultan of Mocha* which is a poor Operetta but which delighted de B. The Ballet Girls he fell in love with & thought beautiful as houris. But he was really shocked at the low dresses worn by the ladies in the Stalls & said that he had never seen such awful indecency. We were much amused at his remarks. ... White's reopens on Monday I am glad to say as I don't enjoy this place. ... Goodbye darling, Your Adrian

HUNSTANTON   SUNDAY, 2ND OCTOBER

My Adrian darling, ... Amy had a most jovial visit to Gerry Cullum at Hardwick. Bret Harte was there, a quiet amusing man & a little Italian Count Primoli who she liked very much. His mother was a Buonaparte & he was going to stay with the Empress E. in Scotland & would meet the Queen, a Good contrast to the frivolities of Hardwick.[108] ... Ever your true love *Laure*

GREAT ORMOND STREET HOSPITAL, BLOOMSBURY   3RD OCTOBER

My darling *Laure*, I am still in Green Street and tonight I have to take Elsie to a play as Jem wants as he says 'to go out with the "other girl"'. ... I have just finished writing 47 letters & it is 5. & I feel boiled so Goodbye dearest. Your A.

WHITE'S, ST JAMES'   6TH OCTOBER

Dearest, … My rooms—at 7 Carteret Street—are very comfy but as Canterbury suddenly left without paying for the attendance I have had to get a man who comes to call me & wait on me. There is a bedroom & sitting-room & another room, all beautifully furnished with lovely old things. Some rather naughty piccys on the walls which made me laugh, darling, when I found them out last night. There is an Omnibus by which I can get to my office in a ¼ of an hour, & it is only 8 minutes to walk from here across St James' Park. J.M.S. is in another most awful scrape again. Poor fellow, life is made bitter to him by his debts. …

Will you wear a silk handkerchief next to your sweet self inside your Corset for a few days & nights as I am going to see a Clairvoyante about the 'Jaw Crackers' drawings. Then when I write for it, send it to me well wrapped up together with a little bit of your own dear hair, & some little wee Sketch knocked off there & then. I am being taken to a good Clairvoyante one day soon. … Goodnight, Your Adrian

HUNSTANTON   7TH OCTOBER

My own darling, … I will do what you ask me about the silk handkerchief—but I have very little faith in the drawings being traced after so long a time has passed. I expect they are quite destroyed but it would be a curious experiment. … I see the Sec.ship of the Senior Army & Navy *Stores* is vacant, is it any use? Did I tell you Hatchard is much pleased with my last drawing, which he liked best of all. It is the frontispiece so it ought to be the best—he wrote such a nice note. Last week he had written & said he could not wait for the 9th illustration (for the proof the author forgot to send me) but he would be content with 8 for the £25. I did not like this as I had undertaken to do 9 drawings, so I enclosed an illustration cut out of my scrap book—one he had marked & had wanted to buy—& I asked him if he would accept it, if it was of any use. He was evidently pleased & said he should certainly use it in his new magazine for girls, *Atalanta*, next year (Helen has it, it is capital). A little sketch of boys shrimping, with a blue sea. … Keep a good heart, Ever your *Laure*

GREAT ORMOND STREET HOSPITAL, BLOOMSBURY   7TH OCTOBER

Darling Love, … Do you see that Oscar Wilde is to be Editor of a new magazine to be called the *Woman's World*.[109] I shall try to go & see him & suggest that you be asked to draw for it if I find there is any moneyed man behind the venture. … Your Adrian

WHITE'S, ST JAMES'   8TH OCTOBER

My own Darling, I got last night a letter from Bignell in which he says that
Kuch Behar [*sic*] has altered his mind & will not take out anybody with him.
Not a word of apology for keeping me all this time waiting without an answer.
So there is an end of this. Today while walking here I met the Col. who was
on his way to see me. He said that he must have £400 by Monday & proposed
that I should run about to find it for him. So feeling very cross I just told him
that I could not be bothered with his worries in addition to my own. Upon this
he said that he could not imagine how I had the least cause for worry on an
ample salary & with light work. I just left him for I felt right down mad. ...
Give them all my love at Runcton, & tell Uncle Sommy I long to redeem my
promise about his 'shilling Dreadful' if he will send me the copies. [He had
written a novel which Adrian hoped to get reviewed.] Your Adrian

NORTH RUNCTON HALL, KING'S LYNN   SUNDAY, 9TH OCTOBER
[WITH UNCLE SOMMY & AUNT KITTY GURNEY]

My darling Adrian, ... I do think Kuch Behar [*sic*] has behaved shabbily or
Bignell ... Though it would have been a way out of our long engagement
there certainly were drawbacks & as some of the staff were against the appt.
they might have made it difficult & disagreeable for you. ... Rosy [Birkbeck]
is playing so sweetly on the harp. She plays *so* prettily—quaint old airs. Ruth
[Gurney, Rosy's sister] last night sang a new song you would have loved by
Maude White called 'A Finland Love Song', quite unlike anything I ever heard
& most delicious—not the least like one of her passionate love songs but with
a strange fantastic accompaniment supposed to be the Finlander riding on his
reindeer over fields of ice to his love. Uncle Sommy has only got the proof
copy of his story *The Haunted Harp*[110] as yet—for final correction. ... Your
Laure qui t'aime

HUNSTANTON   11TH OCTOBER

My dearest Adrian, ... Charles Le Strange wrote & told me Ernest would be
back by about the beginning of December. I hear he (Capt. Le S.) is trying to
get a separation from his wife—& has refused to live with her—or to see her.
I think my new jacket will be very nice, quite a thick warm one for the winter
with otter collar & cuffs, the coat dark blue & braided. I wish we could have
chosen it together. I *hope* you will not call it *matronly*!! ... Darling sometimes
I do so yearn to be with you. Ever your *Laure*

Great Ormond Street Hospital, Bloomsbury   13th October

Dearest, On Tuesday we sat at the Charity Organization Society till 7.30 and yesterday I had to go back during lunch time. There is a distressing lot of poverty about which upsets one when brought face to face with it. ... After dining in Green Street I went on to Jo's new rooms in Pall Mall where I fell asleep waiting for him. He turned up at last with Hubert Wells (his nephew). A friend of Huby's, Mr James the Postmaster General for India, is now bringing out a book on a part of China never before visited by White men and needs an artist for the illustrations.[111] Mr James has some very rare Vases & Arms which he brought home & he wants these drawn for reproduction in black & white. The collection is at his Rooms in Duke St, St James', too valuable to move. He spends the whole day at the B. Museum finishing his book so places the rooms entirely at the disposal of the Artist. I do not know the number of the drawings nor the price but Huby says James is rich, & asked me whether you would undertake this? ... Now I am going to Highgate[112] where they have scarlet fever badly. I shall go straight back to the Turkish Baths where my servant will meet me with other clothes & the ones I have on now will be baked so that I do not carry any infection about with me. ... Howard Marsh, the surgeon, who saw Jessie was very encouraging & has given permission for her to sit down [Adrian's middle sister Jessie's bad hip had been confining her to standing up or lying flat.] Goodbye dear Heart, Your Adrian

Hunstanton   14th October

Darling Adrian, Will you thank Mr Wells for his message. I was so amused at the idea of playing a sort of *Box & Cox* game with the Postmaster General for India. I shall have to refuse the offer as I am really not free to take any more work just now—on account of these negotiations with Griffiths & Farran for another book to be finished in December, & also 2 portraits for Mary Buxton. ... My humble advice to Mr James is to have the things photographed or produced by one of those photogravure processes. I think myself it is far the best way of illustrating antiquities or curios because it is absolutely faithful. I have seen the Fountain collection & others illustrated this way. The great thing is to get a facsimile. ... Ever your *Laure*

White's, St James'   18th October

Darling, ... There has been a very serious riot in Hyde Park between the unemployed & the Police this afternoon. Many of the Police were hurt &

some of the mob. For the last two days Trafalgar Square has swarmed with Police, Mounted & on foot. I was hurried through & told not to loiter every time I turned round to look. We shall have a serious row before long I fancy. Now goodnight, Your Adrian

HUNSTANTON   20TH OCTOBER

My own darling, I have been busy writing a farce on the lines of something we acted years ago but we had lost the book. So I had to invent fresh dialogue full of sparkling jokes—on broadly comic lines to suit the Hunstonian taste. It is to form the *pièce de résistance* of our Variety Entertainment next week. It will probably be dished up again for Runcton at Christmas if it goes well. Amy had an awfully nice week at Norwich for the Festival. The music she raved about. She was also most amused with the 'Baigneuses' as seen by M. Mars [the Belgian artist Maurice Bonvoisin]. I think we 2 must go to Ostende some day to verify his observations! …

Dearest I suppose you have no *Lady* Candidates amongst the 18 House Physicians yesterday. That will be for the next election. [To which Adrian replied: 'No, there was no female in my lot of 18 thank goodness.'] … Ever your own *Laure*

21ST OCTOBER

Darling, … Off to Lynn with Vi to arrange about some scenery for our entertainment. The man who puts up nearly all the old English fairs, Swiss villages, & other shows in England, & who calls himself a scenic artist, has his stronghold in Lynn. I had a letter from Aunt Annie asking us to Cambridge for the 26th of November when there is a Greek play she thought we might like to see with them. I have never seen anything of the kind & it would be fun to see it together. … Adieu, ever your *Laure*

SUNDAY, 23RD OCTOBER

My own dear Adrian, I am so glad that you escaped from the fogs of London to go to Somerhill yesterday. Do tell me all about your visit, & if Violet [the eldest of the eight Goldsmid daughters] is quite grown up or still kept to her little girl frocks. I wonder if Hardinge is in attendance. [He had more or less taken Adrian's place in this respect.] Jimmy St Leger came yesterday—the advance guard of our party for the entertainment next week. In fits & starts he is really very funny, flitting about & fooling, & dashing to the piano & playing which he does rather well. The whole place is full of posters about it

& we hear it is to be crammed. ... I read up the proposed subject for my tableau—Schéhérazade & the Sultan. How *very* odd the story of the thousand & one nights really is. However I suppose it does not matter. ... I wonder what Tom will do? [Adrian had written: 'Major Wyllie hears at the W.O. that Tom won't get his Company for another year.'] ... Adieu, ever your *Laure*

WHITE'S, ST JAMES'   24TH OCTOBER

My own darling, When I got down to Somerhill I found I was let in for a tête-à-tête with V.G. as Sir Julian had gone to Paris. We had a merry little dinner together, after which she sang to me & then she talked for hours about such odd things. Really her confidences made me feel quite embarrassed—what we spoke of I could tell you but cannot write. One thing amused me, she talked of you as loving me but cast much doubt on whether I loved you, my own dear *Laure*, as you should be loved. That I love you as you deserve is not possible but still I do love and worship you with all the heart & soul that is in me. ... She has taken a turn of good works which is healthy & which I encouraged to the utmost. I have persuaded her to start a village library for which I am to choose the books. ...

On Sunday afternoon Sir Julian returned. He was in great spirits & delighted to see me. Lucas [Chairman of Great Ormond Street Hospital Management Committee] had been with him & had said such nice things of me. Verily the world has turned round since last winter. Violet is half out & looks so nice with her hair up & her frock down. We had a wild 2 hours dance with the girls in the Schoolroom which completely pumped me. After dinner Violet & Edith came down & we played Go Bang together while V.G. sang more out of tune than I have ever heard her sing before. J.G. is most anxious you should do something for the Grosvenor & promises to get your picture in. Do paint one. He spoke of our prospects & told me that the first chance he saw of doing me a good turn he would do it. ...

It was lovely at Somerhill though I kept longing for you. She showed me the most lovely 'pantalons' of rose silk trimmed with Valenciennes with great bows of pink ribbon at the knee & I thought how lovely *someone* would have looked in them. There were Chemises to match, shaped to the figure & she ventured the assertion that a woman never looked better than in her chemise & a pair of stockings to match. ... There were night dresses also which were worthy of adoration, even in a drawer!!!! ... Your loving Adrian

HUNSTANTON   25TH OCTOBER

My own dearest Adrian, ... I have been making up my costume for Schéhérazade—long pink striped muslin trousers very full into the ankles, over them a flowing garment of white striped gauze with trimming of gold & peacock's feathers, yellow satin zouave jacket trimmed the same, with tulle sort of sleeves falling from the shoulder almost to the ground leaving my arms bare, & a wide rose silk sash. I have a little green & gold cap, will wear my hair down & lots of jewels. ... I have to make a coif for Mary Queen of Scots, and my Sultan's turban, and decorate a crook for a Shepherdess—so my duties are rather mixed.

Dearest I liked hearing all about your Sunday at Somerhill—really Lady G. is a *very* odd woman. I could not help rather envying what she showed you—perhaps some day when you are rich you will present me with some. I think they are rather wasted now—for I am sure Sir J. does not care a pin about them, & I suppose they are for his benefit only! I think her suggestion is rather insulting *que* toi *tu ne m'aimes pas* [that *you* don't love me] ... does she think I am incapable of inspiring love in your heart—or does she think if *you* could resist *her* you have no power of loving anyone!! which is it? She is a curious woman. ... It is a triumph to have won over Lucas, isn't it? I shall be glad when this week is over, though it is rather fun too. It is impossible not to be laughing & talking nearly all day—we laugh so we can hardly get through dinner—& go to bed quite tired out. ... How could Lady G. say such a thing? Still, I think as Tennyson says in the last few lines of that lovely poem you read me once, 'The Gardener's Daughter': '*and I know I am ever your only love*', *Laure*

GREAT ORMOND STREET HOSPITAL, BLOOMSBURY   26TH OCTOBER

My own dear *Laure*, How full of work you are over these Tableaux. Can you sketch yourself as Schéhérazade. ... So V.G's remarks hurt you. Well they offended me. What was meant I could not discover but I fancy that she intended to insinuate that I did not really care for women in general & was therefore unable to love you with all my heart & as passionately as I do. ... My whole life centres in you & your dear love. I doubt if she ever extracts much sympathy from J.G. over her displays of 'lingerie'. The show was really beautiful and I really admired the things. But oddly, though, we both agreed that I should be quite furious at my wife bringing a man into her dressing room & displaying the ornaments of *la vie intime* in this way. She read me long lectures on the coils of indifferent husbands, with which I so fully agreed. Altogether we moralized too queerly she & I before the open drawer which should have been sealed to the outer world of men. I did so like those bunches of pink ribbon at the knee & the fall of lace which would effectively cover the place which the silk hose sometimes leave uncovered for a kiss. ...

I dined in Green Street last night—Jem is threatened with another lung attack—so I took Elsie to the Alhambra alone—to the box the Goldsmids had given me as they could not go. We were really too late for the first Ballet but there was an audacious little French woman who sang in the interval some clever little songs. Of course the 'Boulanger' song, all with an amount of action & with dancings which fairly electrified the Good Britons who encored wildly. There was such a pretty woman in a Box with a lovely face but the most enormous bust I ever saw, dressed in black cut in such an odd way. A black scalloped edge against the skin, one side folding across the other but open nearly to the waist, something like this [he sketched the bodice], long sleeves & highish back, only this vast expanse of milk white sea. The effect was certainly very attractive to the opera glasses of the audience. One felt that at the least movement she would move out of her corsage altogether.

The Ballet was well danced but all the Choristers at the Alhambra have such fearfully thick legs & Bustles would be thrown away on them. Two girls sang some idiotic songs with nice clear voices but with a fearful cockney twang, accompanied by some good dancing. The way they kicked was a marvel & they had nice lace things & pretty legs but feet & ankles like Lill. Their stockings had steel embroidery round the ankles in the vain hope that this would lighten the navvy like effect. But it did not one bit, only drew attention. They also had steel work in bands just above the knee. This did look rather well. ... Today J.M.S. has been here in another awful state. He is to be made bankrupt tomorrow. I fear that he will lose his post poor chap unless some miracle pulls him out of all his troubles. Here is a long gossip, mostly I fear in the style of *la Vie Parisienne*. Still it may amuse you darling. Your Adrian

27TH OCTOBER

My Sweet Sweet *Laure*, How I wish I had thought of rushing down for tonight just to see you all. I am longing to come & kiss my Sultana in her pink loose tights. ... J.M.S. is still in tribulation & I have not heard yet if he has smashed ... Goodbye, Your Adrian

HUNSTANTON   28TH OCTOBER

My own darling, ... Well the entertainment was I think a great success. Unfortunately it was the *most* awful day—pouring with rain & a gale blowing

& we feared no one would come out in such weather. However about 370 or 400 people came. We had a dreadfully hard day, Vi & I did everything nearly. Neither Pipps [Harold] Hoare or Jimmy [St Leger] were the slightest help, they did nothing at all, but both come out very well in the evening. Pipps played & sang so nicely & Jimmy acting the Madman was simply inimitable & made everyone *roar* with laughter. I never saw Vi so energetic in my life, she was my right hand in everything, as Amy became frivolous & Limpet vague. Vi said quite spontaneously, 'Oh how I wish Adrian was here—I know he would have been splendid in helping us'. I was wishing for you all the time. Our cook had an accident 2 days ago & cut her hand so badly she was not allowed to use it at all so the faithful Tanner as usual stepped into the breach.

The first tableau was 'Broken Vows', a Shepherd & Shepherdess scene with Vi *poudré* as the lover, leaning over a gate making love to Chenny [Richenda Gurney] who looked quite sweet as a Shepherdess with her crook & flower decked pink dress, Helen as the deserted sweetheart peering out from behind an ivy covered tree. Then Amy and Jimmy St Leger appeared as Claude Duval & the Countess of Desmonde dancing a minuet on the Heath. Jimmy is not quite one's idea of a dashing Highwayman but he had a lovely black velvet suit & powdered wig & really looked very well, so did Amy in a pale blue & gold frock with an old fashioned pink silk coif or hood, curtseying to him. The next was the arabian nights scene, Hughie [Gurney] as the Sultan with *your* Schéhérazade telling him a thrilling story, both on a long divan, she sitting cross-legged at one end facing him. There was a red light burning making it very gorgeous. In the next Chenny appeared as the bride in 'The Mistletoe Bough' [from the song *c.* 1840 by T. H. Bayly (1797-1839)] and I appeared first before the curtain & recited the old ballad while Amy softly played the refrain. It was I think effective. It was so still in the Hall when I stopped you could have heard a pin drop, & then they applauded a good deal. Then the curtain went up & Chen appeared. She looked lovely as an old fashioned bride in white satin, with flowing hair, a lovely veil of old lace, a wreath of orange blossoms & a square, short sleeved dress with pearls, just lifting the lid of a carved oak chest.

Then we had some amusing ones to cheer up the audience, 'Two Strings to her Bow' from the picture in last year's Academy, then 'Christmas gone to the Cats'—Jimmy & Helen all in white wearing white cat masks kissing under the mistletoe. Then a *very* pretty one of Vi looking lovely as Mary Queen of Scots with Hughie as Rizzio, in a most beautiful fancy dress of violet & black playing the mandolin sitting at her feet. The last was most weird, 'The Three Witches'—Helen, Katty [Gurney] & Jimmy with long hooked noses & elf locks of black, swathed from head to foot in scarlet & black, bending over a huge cauldron … and a storm conducted by most of the Company behind the scenes.

We had music & singing between each, & then the farce. The whole thing only lasted 2 hours. If you had run down, you would have only come in for the very end & instead of our Sultana to kiss you would have beheld an old frumpy Quaker lady, with side curls, got up just like the portrait of our immortal great aunt—Elizabeth Fry!! … Ever your own *Laure*—who loves you with an undying love—as she will ever as your wife

Sunday, 30th October

My own darling, … Well we have subsided again—& The Castle is once more clothed in its right mind. Jimmy, Amy & I went up to tea with the Le Stranges, & the entertainment was voted a great success. Roland asked me why I did not always go about as Schéhérazade. He said: 'I never saw you look so ripping!!!'. I dreamt of you all last night—this rather annoyed me darling for I wish only to appear in *your* dreams. … Amy has hurt her wrist, a sort of sprain, it is quite stiff & weak. She is thinking of coming up for one night to show it to Wharton Hood & wants me to come with her … so there is a chance of our meeting. … Ever your own true *Laure*

White's, St James'   Sunday, 30th October

My dearest, I went to Marlborough House yesterday to see Knollys [Sir Francis Knollys, P.S. to the Prince of Wales] who promised to do what he can with the Prince for me—to come to the next Hospital Dinner. Today I lunched with Lady Canterbury & found J.M.S. as merry as possible. … Now Goodnight dear love from A.

31st October

My darling *Laure*, … About Amy, I am so very sorry to hear of her bad wrist. But why go to Hood. Jem has taken up Hutton's practice & sees patients in Green St now regularly. Do come up & bring Amy to him. … I can well understand that young scamp Roland dreaming of my Sultana. … The Brunswick Hotel has come to life again [one of Jem Hope's many projects] & I hope to be able to make a little money out of it for myself. Enough to pay off my debts … if Goldsmid will help me I am sure to make a little but will he? That is the question I am going to put to him. Your loving Adrian

108 *2nd Oct* The Cullum house-parties at Hardwick House, Bury St Edmunds, at which Amy was a favourite guest, were considered somewhat raffish—not that this one would appear to have been so. The American writer, Bret Harte (1836-1902), had recently been US Consul in Glasgow, 1880/85, and then stayed on in London as a hack writer until his death. His best work had been done in America before the late 1870s. The Empress Eugénie, widow of Napoleon III, was being befriended at this time by Queen Victoria.

109 *7th Oct* Cassell's, the publishers, had started a magazine in November 1886 called *The Lady's World*, which a year later they invited Wilde to edit in the hope of giving it a new life. He accepted this offer and persuaded Cassell's to change the title to *The Woman's World* as having a broader appeal. His enthusiasm for the life of a full-time editor waned within a year.

110 *9th Oct The Haunted Harp: the narrative of Evelyn Desmond* by Somerville Arthur Gurney (J W Arrowsmith, Bristol, 1887).

111 *13th Oct The Long White Mountain: or, a Journey in Manchuria* by Sir Henry Evan James (1888).

112 *13th Oct* Cromwell House, Highgate, the Great Ormond Street Hospital's Convalescent Home for Sick Children.

NOVEMBER 1887

WHITE'S, ST JAMES'   4TH NOVEMBER

My own Darling, … The French play last night was very good. Such beautiful acting, & Coquelin such a first rate Stage lover. Mrs Cooper & I agreed that his lovemaking was delightful. … I am just back from the Leg show which bored me immensely. Thank goodness the party was just Jim & Elsie & the Whites. Emily W did love the Ballet enormously but the Alhambra is a place I hate to see ladies in. *It* is not a refined atmosphere & I am glad we never went there together. Rather old-maidish of me. Good night, Your Adrian

On the back of the above letter Laura had pencilled an extract from a letter written to her by her cousin Julian Orde who had married a couple of years earlier: '… No one has any idea what a *friend* is until one is married. Cares & sorrows are light when shared so entirely …' This sentiment meant much to Laura.

Amy & Laura came up to London for one night so that Jem could treat Amy's wrist the following day. They stayed at Storeys Hotel, 8 Dover Street.

SUNNY HILL, THORPE, NORWICH   10TH NOVEMBER
[WITH GEOFFREY & MARY BUXTON]

My own darling Adrian, … Storeys presented us with a most modest bill of fourteen shillings, not bad as we had a nice comfy room with a fire, & a sitting room for breakfast & tea, & did not starve ourselves at all. … I am so glad to say Mary is delighted with my 2 portraits of Maud. [In her Journal Accounts page for November, Laura noted she was paid £12.10 [shillings] for these & a little drawing on ivory of Mary's two young daughters.] Carter,[113] the animal artist is still here—& we talked art in the evening. He was delighted with my drawings, the 'Mermaid' set, 'Friends & Fancies' etc. taking them very much *au sérieux* & positively *begged* me to come up to London & study, if only for a short time, just a few of the technicalities of art. He asked if I often exhibited at the Grosvenor—which amused & rather pleased me. … I am going to try & paint a portrait head of Mary, partly from herself, partly from a new Mendelsohn photograph—I own it is only an attempt & will probably fail. … I bought some rather pretty pink vests of woven silk at the Burlington [Arcade], for the winter. They fit rather like a second skin only with little bows on the shoulder & in front which nature has omitted! Amy thought they were too pretty for underneath, *que penses tu?* Goodbye dearest, when shall we live without that little word—Ever your *Laure*

GREAT ORMOND STREET HOSPITAL, BLOOMSBURY   10TH NOVEMBER

My own dear Love, … Last night's French play was most delightful & we all agreed that Coquelin was far better than Irving. … I am finishing off a lot of Xmas work beforehand so that I may be able to ask for leave with a clear conscience. The outside I can get will only be till December 29th, but then I can come down on the Friday [23rd] early. This planning for another Xmas Meeting depresses me fearfully as I did not think we should still be parted. Everything seems to go all wrong & it all seems to be my fault but I don't know what to do or try for now. The future has not one ray of sunshine in it for you & me, my own *Laure*. Nothing but black clouds & this eternal life apart which is such a pain. … Your Adrian

SUNNY HILL, THORPE, NORWICH   SUNDAY, 11TH NOVEMBER
[WITH GEOFFREY & MARY BUXTON]

My Adrian dearest, … I have just been reading about Mrs Jopling's ladies art classes in last week's *World*. There is no chance of your *worrying* me about these. It is one of the wishes of my heart to have more art study—besides I see there a chance of making money which ought not to be neglected. [Adrian had written that: 'a couple of months work could be done there for about £25 if you had a room in a house at S. Kensington'].

Carter left yesterday with his picture. I don't know if they are going to buy it. He wants £300 for it—but to them, as they supplied their dog Ross, baby Olive and cradle, he would sell it for £120 if they allowed him to have it engraved. I think, considering he stayed here a whole month to paint it this might well content him! I long for the time when I can ask long prices for my work. Carter invited me warmly to come & see his studio. I did not discuss possible lessons with him—he is quite ancient & an animal painter & his one idea is the Royal Academy students. I think it really would be worth making a great effort to come up later for some lessons. Feb. & March would be the best time for me. … Mary has already engaged me to paint a portrait next summer—life size, full length, of her eldest girl, dressed from head to toe in scarlet, feeding her grey pigeons. … Ever your own *Laure*

P.S. What luck the *Morning Post* reviewer turned out to be one of those rather rare birds—a friend of the Colonel's. [Adrian had taken Uncle Sommy's novel *The Haunted Harp* there for review.]

The 'Bloody Sunday' Battle of Trafalgar Square took place on 13th November. The disturbances had started a month earlier, when meetings held in the square and intended to call attention to the distress caused by unemployment in the metropolis were mobbed by lawless 'roughs' intent on defying the police. On 8th November, with the approval of the home secretary (H Matthews), Gen Sir Charles Warren, Commissioner of Metropolitan Police, made an order prohibiting all meetings in the square until further notice. The protesters, some MPs, and members of the public thought this rule to be unconstitutional and not in the interests of the underlying problem—unemployment. Better 'the adoption of just legislation than the repression of public meetings' was one MP's recommendation. Adrian's cousin, Robert Cunninghame Graham, then a Liberal MP, was determined to be an active supporter at the meeting of the Federation of Radical Clubs which was to go ahead, as already planned, on the 13th in defiance of the Home Office ban.

WHITE'S, ST JAMES'   SUNDAY NIGHT, 13TH NOVEMBER

My Darling, Such a day as I have had. Yesterday I heard that Robert Graham had determined to lead the Procession & to force his way into Trafalgar Square. In vain I tried to find him. Today I lunched at the Wanderers Club at the corner of Waterloo Place opposite the Athenaeum, whence I saw one Column of the Mob crumpled up by the Police who were very savage in their use of truncheons. A great heap of men lay groaning on the pavement. This made me very anxious for Robert so I rushed out when the first person I met was the Colonel also on the same errand. We went to Scotland Yard where we were told that Robert was badly hurt & a prisoner. There was great confusion & they could not find out which Police Station he was at. Off we went & after having been to 3 found Robert at Bow St. There we saw him & found that his head had been cut open. He was all over blood but quite cheery. We immediately offered bail but he had not yet been charged so we rushed off here to get some one else. J.M.S. was delighted to come & we returned when I saw Robert again who asked me to go & see his wife Gabrielle at the Hotel Metropole. I found her very wild, having had no news, but having seen (from a balcony) Robert knocked down. We had been told to return at 10. so I took her & left her in the Cab. We then formerly offered bail which was refused. She was however allowed to see him & we were told we might send in pillows

& rugs. I had previously given him Cigarettes & ordered a dinner to be sent in to him so he was looking better. Then I took Gabrielle back & went on to Chester Square to see Mrs Bontine (Robert's mother) from whom I got some pillows & got some more from Gabrielle & took them to Bow St. Poor old Don Roberto, I am full of grief & anxiety about him for with his excitable nature & the family history I am full of anxiety lest his head should give way.

The Police have been most brutal & the whole riot has been caused by them. The streets have been cleared by Life Guards. The Foot Guards were posted in the Square. There never was a thought of riot until the Police charged savagely. The Hospitals are full but I hope not many bad cases. Matthews ought to be hung [*sic*] along with Warren [Home Secretary and Commissioner, Metropolitan Police, respectively]. Now I must go to bed for I am worn out & furious. In this Club just now they were calmly talking of firing on the People to cool their blood. It is too horrible. Your Adrian

Sunny Hill, Thorpe, Norwich 14th November
[with Geoffrey & Mary Buxton]

My dearest Adrian, What an extraordinary day's work! I was *so* angry this morning when I read the account in the papers of Mr Graham's arrest. How *could* he have anything to do with such disgraceful low things as riots & that disgusting mob. I think I should die of shame if I were his wife. Imagine finding one's *husband*, whom one loved & reverenced, locked up in a police cell with a broken head, dirty & bleeding. I could never forget it. I cannot see that any good cause is served by it. There is Hyde Park, & plenty of other places for meetings and if it is illegal for Matthews & Warren to have prohibited meetings in the Square, there are other weapons for a gentleman to use to get this grievance redressed besides fists & personal violence on those who, after all, are only obeying orders. I cannot tell you how *repulsive* all this sort of thing is to me.

What a mercy you were there dearest to do what was right & good—& to befriend poor Gabrielle—for she must sadly have needed you. No wonder you feel anxious about your cousin. I should think this sort of excitement the worst possible thing for him. If I were her I should simply *make* him leave London at once. ... What a *disgrace* to see any one one loved heading a London mob—& yelling & fighting. Pah! it makes me sick even to think of it ... I am sorry you have made yourself responsible for such a firebrand. Still of course for the honour of the family you had to stand by him. What fools men are, this does not mean you dearest! I hope I shall hear tomorrow how you got him out of the scrape. Goodbye my own darling Adrian, Ever your Quaker love, *Laure*

P.S.—and yet I have the blood of the fighting Troubridges in my veins— & if it were in a good cause would have written very differently.

GREAT ORMOND STREET HOSPITAL, BLOOMSBURY   14TH NOVEMBER

My dearest Love, This morning I took Mrs Bontine to the Court at 10, where we found my Mother & Gabrielle. Robert has just been released on bail at 4. He has been kept 24 hours in custody. I will send you a *Pall Mall Gazette* & you will see how shamefully the Police knocked him about. The case never came on till 3. when the Govt. feebly withdrew the heavy charge of conspiring to riot—& only charged him with assaulting the Police. Old Poland, prosecuting on behalf of the Treasury, stumbled most lamely through an indifferent tirade & after two Inspectors had given evidence the Magistrate agreed to adjourn & to accept bail. We had grapes in court with which I fed Robert who looked very well but ghastly in his Coat drenched with blood & his head tied up. Poor Gabrielle sat by me & cried softly. Oh! the relief to find we could get him out for we feared Govt. were going to refuse bail. Now I have a Com.ttee for which I have prepared nothing. As they come in 5 minutes I must skim through my papers though all the while I am thinking of Robert. Your Adrian

SUNNY HILL, THORPE, NORWICH   15TH NOVEMBER
[WITH GEOFFREY & MARY BUXTON]

Dearest Adrian, I had your letter when I woke this morning—& immediately held an Indignation Meeting in my own mind to protest against Mr Roberto's behaviour! I am not the least surprised that the police hustled him—they are only rough men—and had their order to keep people out of the Square on Sunday. If it is true as it says in the papers that Mr Graham headed a yelling mob of 200 who tried to break through the police lines I think it is a pity they withdrew the graver charge of inciting to riot, for it was perfectly true, & he ought to have had 6 months in prison '*pour décourager les autres*' [to deter others], & Mrs Besant [who was a Radical Club Delegate] penal servitude for life. I think he got off very easily. ... I hope you do not think he is a Martyr. I think he is an ass. I know this is too strong for a girl to write—but I feel so hard when I think of it all—and his poor little wife crying beside you in the Court.

Darling you must have let Great Ormond Street slide indeed for once! and on the sacred Monday morning too when you generally leave me at 7. to get back in good time. Did you find it a heap of ruins from neglect! … Perhaps his poor wife as she is a stranger did not realize the full disgrace. So his head is badly hurt. I suppose he went quite mad with excitement. Since I wrote this I have been reading the papers, & the *Pall Mall*. From Sir Ed. Reed's[114] letter Mr Graham was evidently badly treated—but all the same I think he is *tremendously* to blame. What is the good of a fracas with the Police who after all are only *servants*, & bound to obey their orders just as much as soldiers— or any other servants. It is the *authorities* Mr Graham ought to have fought, & as gentlemen fight—not with fists.

I have read both their letters. It is a pity they did not compare notes—as they flatly contradict each other about the way the Life Guards were received.[115] Of course she writes wildly—as a wife would, thinking her husband had been ill-used—but she could hardly expect a beautifully furnished drawing-room & every comfort to be prepared for his arrest. If people break the laws they cannot expect to find prison a bed of roses—and he was allowed food— cigarettes & other comforts—which would scarcely be the case with a common thief—though she says her husband was treated as such. … As to his challenge, if he goes on waging the war as on Sunday he is far more likely to end his days in prison than to succeed in reviving the family titles & honours which you once told me was the wish of his heart.

I did not mean to write you such a long letter but the subject warms one. … Darling, for my sake do not take any part in these things yourself—it would simply kill me. I should *never* forget it, and it would indeed put an end to all our chance of getting on in the world & the future so dear to our hearts. … Ever your own true *Laure*

P.S. Evening. On reading over this letter I think it is rather *dour*. I wish I could come with it just to kiss you. Your L.

The Times of 15th November published three letters concerning Robert. In the first, from Gabrielle, she complained that her husband had to wait five hours before he was charged and that he was refused bail so that he passed the night in the cells 'as if he had been a common street thief.' This drew an unsympathetic response in the next day's letters' column, to which Gabrielle explained in a further letter that what she was objecting to was the most unfounded charge of assaulting the police which led to the refusal of bail. The second letter, signed 'A Peaceful Citizen', wondered whether the authorities considered Robert's duties as a JP in three counties and a DL for

Dumbartonshire 'compatible with his new functions'. The third was from the colonel who had tried, unsuccessfully, to go bail for Robert. He wrote: '… I owe it to those with whom I am politically associated to explain that I did so solely because he is my nephew and had received several severe blows on the head, besides having the nail torn off one toe by a horse's foot, and not because I approved of his course of action.' The whole occasion took a lighter turn with a letter on a later page recounting how an enterprising bus from Charing Cross, en route for the west, started offering circular tours of the square instead at tuppence a head, and did a roaring trade, the writer himself staying on it for six trips and passing unscathed through the thickest of the fight!

WHITE'S, ST JAMES'   16TH NOVEMBER

My darling, Let us agree to differ on the question of Robert's action. While I regret it I do not feel the least reason to feel ashamed of him. Now let us drop the subject. There must be some way of arranging for your art lessons … perhaps Mrs Jopling may be able to suggest some Ark of rest for you during the course of lessons. … Yesterday & today I had a long meeting for discussing the plan of the new Hospital. … Goodnight, my own dear Love, Your Adrian

SUNNY HILL, THORPE, NORWICH   16TH NOVEMBER
[WITH GEOFFREY & MARY BUXTON]

My darling Adrian, … It is a pity the Colonel cannot resist rushing into print on every possible occasion. I wish he would subside for a year or two. After the Ordnance failure correspondence no one is likely to care much for his testimony or to adopt his drastic remedies. I don't suppose Sir C.W. [Warren] will be dictated to, even by the Colonel. I am glad to hear he believes in the truth of the old saying 'Blood is thicker than water'. I only wonder he has not acted up to it a little more in his role of *père de famille*. What a curious man he is.

As to women writing in the newspapers I simply hate it—& their letters are almost always illogical—& ungrammatical!! What a confession from me—but I do really mean it. Just one of the things that make women nice—& a comfort to men is that they *are* a bit unreasonable & prejudiced when they love & this is just what unfits them to write for an unsympathetic & critical public, don't you agree dearest? …

Last night Mary went to bed early—& I sat over the fire with Geoffrey talking till near Midnight—he said he *had* enjoyed it so—when we said Good night. I wish it had been you dearest—our talks seem so few & far between, alas. ... Ever your own *Laure*

17TH NOVEMBER

My own darling Adrian, I was so unhappy when I woke this morning and found no letter from you. I thought you were perhaps angry with me and would not write & I felt quite mizzy in my heart. ... You are quite right, we must agree not to think alike about this. I will not say anything more—only that I am very sorry if I said anything to really vex you ... so forgive me sweetheart. ... My portrait of Mary is rather like but so badly painted. I feel how much I want more teaching. ... Ever your own *Laure*

WHITE'S, ST JAMES'   19TH NOVEMBER

My dearest Love, ... I rushed off to dine with Lady Cole in Warwick Road (Earls Court). She takes in young ladies. Her terms are 3 guineas a week for a very nice bedroom next to a bathroom & for the sole use of a Downstairs sitting-room, food & attendance. I do not think it dear. She is a nice old lady, the mother of Jem's friend Cole, but she & his two elderly sisters are very quiet, dull & respectable. ... Your Adrian

SUNNY HILL, THORPE, NORWICH   SUNDAY, 20TH NOVEMBER
[WITH GEOFFREY & MARY BUXTON]

My dearest Adrian, ... How good of you to dine with those old people for my benefit. ... Warwick Road is quite the end of the world and would make my 2 days a week I mean to get at the National Gallery rather a pilgrimage. I suppose one *could* go from Earls Court Station to Charing X but it would be rather frightening going alone by the underground & still more so coming back late. Do you think this silly of me darling? I know it is not far from Mrs Jopling's studio of Queens Gate but I would prefer to be nearer civilization instead of the wild west. Otherwise it is just the sort of thing I want & eminently respectable!

I am doing a sketchy sort of miniature on ivory of Mary's two little daughters, Joan & Olive. I am not very pleased with it. I see miniature painting cannot be attacked boldly—but must be learnt with patience like everything else worth knowing. ... Ever your faraway loving *Laure*

52 GREEN STREET, PARK LANE   SUNDAY, 20TH NOVEMBER
[WITH JEM & ELSIE HOPE]

My own dearest, I have dined here and now Elsie & I have been spending the evening with Mad.me Blavatsky who is a most delightful old woman. Very clever & interesting. Jem is full of hope about the Brunswick Hotel scheme which seems really to be going on well & may start into life next week. As there is an awful fog I am going to sleep here. ... Goodnight my Darling, Your Adrian

CATTON HALL, NORWICH   22ND NOVEMBER
[WITH GURNEY & MINNA BUXTON]

My own darling Adrian, ... Tom is here. He had such an *awfully* narrow escape out shooting last week. He was shot in the face by young Reggie Marsham, peppered all one side and one shot went in three quarters of an inch deep *just* one eighth of an inch below his eyeball, the Doctor told him it had lodged low down behind the eyeball. Of course it cannot be taken out. He has several in his cheek and one through his upper lip, and in the leg too but he does not seem to care a bit. ... Amy & I go to Ufford—to Mrs Brooke and her son—on the 26th. Goodnight, Your own true *Laure*

P.S. Isn't it *most* disappointing my 'Mermaid' drawings are *not* in the Christmas number of the *English Illustrated* yet Mr C.C. told me they would be? [They were not published until the Xmas issue, No 99 vol. IX, in 1891.]

WHITE'S, ST JAMES   22ND NOVEMBER

Dearest, All day I have been between my office & Bow St. When Robert's case came on it was again put off till Tuesday next [29th]. The Police are lying themselves into a hole I fancy, as they now admit that he had his hat in one hand while Burns [John Burns, Socialist labour organizer] held his other arm. This makes their story of his rushing about with clenched fists rather an odd one. Besides they do nothing but contradict one another. Such a gathering in Court, Charlie Graham looking very handsome, my Mother brought by the Colonel who is *still* on duty commanding Special Constables[116] at Bethnal Green. Fancy what joy for him but I think he regrets that there is no row down there. ... I think you would love Charlie & Robert if you met them. They are both so very nice & I am glad we have been brought together again for I care for so few people but when I do they never can do wrong in my eyes. Your A.

Hunstanton 24th November

My darling Adrian, ... The ball at Sandringham is on the 2nd. Tom met the Prince [of Wales] not long ago. He came up to Tom & said, 'I am so glad to hear your sister is married!' Tom said, 'no sir—it is a mistake, she is not married yet.' The Prince seemed so surprised & said he was certainly told so the other day. I wonder if he could have heard it through Kutch Behar [*sic*]. [If Adrian had been given the job in India, they would have married straight away.] ... I hope we shall be together Sunday week at Ufford. I am very *intrigué* to see the Brookie ménage. ... Ever your *Laure*

Great Ormond Street Hospital, Bloomsbury 25th November

My own dear *Laure*, Yesterday I dined with Mrs Schiff, we had an excellent dinner. Baron Stöeckl of the Russian Embassy, who is a friend of mine, was there. They kept one talking & laughing so that when we all left it was 1.30 instead of 11.30 as we all thought. Stoeckel looked at my hand & said that I had one absorbing long affair which governed my whole life which was rather nice. Everyone laughed & I said nothing. He showed me such a queer photograph of himself when we were both babies together at Washington. We are the same age & were born in the same month in America where his father was Minister. He says our fate is closely linked & that we shall both die a violent death. He is enormous & very good natured, devoted to your sex & always in love with some one different each time I meet him. I like him & he is so jolly always. ...

My Wednesday Com.ttee was so wonderfully pleasant. Every one in good humour & full of thanks to me for having got the needful money. ... The awful Mrs Hewatt who Elsie would have to stay at Green St has gone & Jem displays his ferocious joy over it. I very much fear that Elsie is trying his temper too far & she is evidently worrying him to the very verge of his endurance. Such a pity. If Sir Peter dies I expect Jem will just go off abroad & leave her to weep alone for some time & it will be mostly her own fault. ... I am going to snatch a hasty chop & then go to Dr Sturges for a meeting to draw up the Prospectus for my new hobby our Medical School here ... Darling, I kiss you in my soul's thought, your lover A.

Ufford Place, Woodbridge, Suffolk Sunday, 27th November
[with Mrs Francis C. Brooke]

My own darling Adrian, ... When we got *inside* the house here we were perfectly enchanted. It is full of really lovely things. It was only two days ago that the rooms were really arranged [and redecorated after Mr Brooke senior's death in 1886]. It is all done in such perfect taste. He has put down very pretty parquet floors all over the house on the ground floor. This chiefly for the sake of the books because it make less dust. Of course *the* feature of the house is the books—they are simply wonderful. I should think almost unique in a country house. There are thirty thousand of them lovely old editions, many unique—& almost priceless, & very old rare editions in the most beautiful bindings. Mr Brooke is very proud of them & is beginning to learn what he possesses. They are very little classed as they are mostly arranged in size to suit the shelves.

Last night I was thinking of you at the Greek Play—& I hope you wanted me a little at Cambridge. I *am* so glad the Hospital people seem to appreciate you more now. I wish they would propose a rise after 2 years hard work. … I do hope Mrs Brooke will ask you down here & that you will come. Ever your own *Laure*

6 Panton Street, Cambridge   Sunday, 27th November
[with Aunt Annie Cunninghame Graham]

My dearest Heart, … They were so sorry you were not here too, *ma Laure*. Yesterday we had such a nice little dinner when Charlie [Orde] arrived. He made himself quite at home with Aunt A. directly who liked him very much. About 9. we started for the Greek Play & came in for the middle of the first Act. At the back of the stage was a Greek façade … & 4 very handsome men—Guards in armour, in the middle there was a small Altar about which stood Oedipus & Jocasta, & on a lower level stood the Chorus of old men. … At first I own it was dull & I dozed off once or twice. But as the Play went on the awful horror of the situation took hold of me … this human being so utterly overwhelmed by the fates roused one to the very bottom of one's nature & when he bursts in with his sightless bleeding eye balls I felt that I should have to scream, the tension became so great. Jocasta was acted by a very powerful man who was really graceful in his passionate gestures though it *was* difficult to imagine him a woman. But then there were two hand maidens, one of whom made such a lovely girl, dark with beautiful arms & a lovely neck … I would hardly believe they were really two undergrads. The last scene when Oedipus bids farewell to his little daughters (two girls who are Laura's pupils) was quite heart rending & the Audience sniffled audibly. I had the most terrifying dreams all night. …

After dinner here tonight we took Charlie to meet the Clarkes. There was a Miss Cust there who sat in a corner talking to some man. I only saw her legs of which she happened to give me a very liberal view. Fortunately they were quite pretty in neat black stockings with a view of lace & pink ribbon about the knee. Really, some people seem to forget that others have eyes. ... I did so long for your sweet face to be here too. Goodbye my own, Your Adrian

UFFORD PLACE, WOODBRIDGE, SUFFOLK   29TH NOVEMBER
[WITH MRS FRANCIS C. BROOKE]

My darling Adrian, The Greek Play must have been *thrilling*. He must have been a wonderful actor to move you so without the help of words. I wish we had seen it together. Jimmy St Leger arrived yesterday & is quite a success here—a little toned down for Mrs Brooke's sake—& he makes us all laugh with his stories & vagaries. Brookie has quite forgotten his stiffness—Mrs Brooke says she does not know what has come over him he is so frivolous—& makes up to *me* dreadfully!! even calls me *darling*!! which offends me awfully. Of course it is all in fun—he is very chaffy, & so *chatty* & easy, and though he chaffs would never say anything that was not nice. I think he & Amy would suit capitally & I can plainly see his mother wishes very much they might take a fancy to each other—but it would be so unlike the Troubridge family if such a thing came off smoothly. ... Goodbye Sweetheart, Ever your Laura

P.S. After tea Mrs Brooke had a long talk with me in her room. It made me rather unhappy for she so strongly urged our marriage—but of course she has no idea what living on £500 a year would mean. It is I think *just* impossible, & a little more would be *just* possible—a hundred or two would make all the difference. I think we must have patience yet.

---

113 *10th Nov* Samuel John Carter RA, the animal artist who exhibited in London 1855/92.

114 *15th Nov* Sir Edward Reed, a Lord of Treasury (1886), and MP for Cardiff (1880/95).

115 *15th Nov* It is not surprising that Robert and Gabrielle Cunninghame Graham's letters gave differing versions of the reception given to the life guards detailed to clear Trafalgar Square during the 'Bloody Sunday' riot of 13th November. The first newspaper reports claimed, wrongfully, that the mob—including those with 'broken heads'—*cheered* the troops on. Robert, being in the thick of the fracas, would have known that the mob *hissed* the soldiers, and that it was a group of 'loungers by the Union Club and the Grand Hotel' who *cheered* them, as the newspapers later reported.

116 *22nd Nov* Col Hope was one of the many volunteer officers sworn in as special constables during the Trafalgar Square riots of November 1887.

DECEMBER 1887

At his next appearance in Bow Street on 30th November, Robert Cunninghame Graham was committed for trial at the Central Criminal Court after a spirited defence by Asquith (later prime minister but then a Liberal MP). The defence witnesses, including Sir Edward Reed, were impeccable and described how it was the police who attacked the defenceless Robert rather than the other way round. *The Times* of 1st December gave several columns to reporting the case and Asquith's skilful revealing of Warren's prohibition notice against public meetings in Trafalgar Square not being officially authorised, as well as his pointing out of the ambiguity in the prosecution claim that Trafalgar Square was private Crown property—in which case the police should not have been there executing their duty as *police constables*.

Great Ormond Street Hospital, Bloomsbury   1st December

My own Darling, … Yesterday was most interesting. The scene in Court funny beyond words & the result satisfactory. … I had to draw up my Charity Organization Society Appeal as well as my Medical School Prospectus, besides a lot of work for the Building Com.ttee—without counting Robert & Bow St. I am so sorry you had no letters for 2 days but I really could not manage one & even now I am writing against time for I have Com.ttee at 5. & another 2 Com.ttees tomorrow. Last night I worked on here till 10.30 to catch up my work which had fallen a bit behind … I have been on the rush since Tuesday. Goodbye my *Laure*, Your Adrian

Ufford Place, Woodbridge, Suffolk   Sunday, 4th December
[with Mrs Francis C. Brooke]

Dearest Adrian, … Amy & I went out to lunch with the Lowthers—we set off at a quarter to one walking to Campsey Ashe, lost our way & did not arrive till 3. Such a bore. We walked back, starting at 4. & had a sort of escapade coming home—we missed the way & walked 11 miles altogether in the darkness & fog & had sort of tightrope bridges to cross over rivers—and all sorts of adventures. We missed Jimmy & Mr Brooke who had come to meet us & did not get home till near 6. …

I should think it very hard to get people to subscribe to the *working* expenses of a charity but I hope the Appeal will stir them up. It is *very* good of you dearest to give so much of your precious time to the C.O.S. Appeal for of course there can not be any time left for looking after your own interests, &

nothing is heard of them. In ten years time I suppose we shall still be waiting patiently for each other … when our poor hearts have ceased to beat with love for each other—& our spirits flown where there is no marrying or giving in marriage. Goodbye my darling, Ever your *Laure*

Great Ormond Street Hospital, Bloomsbury   5th December

Dearest, On Saturday I went to fetch my sister at Kings X & after an early dinner at Green St we all went off to the French Play *L'Ami Fritz* where we had 4 capital Stalls in the front row. I went round behind the scenes & complimented Febvre (to whom I took a message from Laura) and little Jane May & we talked away till the Prompter was heard, he telling me the first news of the new French President 'Carnot'. Mad.me May is a dear little woman not a 1st rate Actress but with a good deal of charm. Yesterday Jem & Elsie & I went off to spend the evening with Mad.me Blavatsky. My sweet there was a sting in the end of your letter which has hurt me a good deal, for it suggests that I do not really care about getting some better thing which would make our marriage possible. If I left my time free I should only fret out my heart without any result. For after all what chance have I lost or what can I do except go about with a label 'To be hired'? … Your A.

7th December

My Darling, … I feel so ashamed of my little shabby notes but just now I am not up to my work let alone writing to you. I cannot throw off this cold which oppresses my head. … I quite dread the pain of another Xmas party which will bring back the Knocklofty days so vividly, & of meeting Ernest [due to arrive home just before Christmas]. If we could only have met before I should have asked you to let this Christmas go by without our meeting at Runcton. Only I have not the power to go on without seeing you again. … Your A.

P.S. I am so infinitely tired with myself & everything here that I just can't write.

White's, St James'   9th December

My darling *Laure*, Tomorrow I am going to take up my quarters at Green St when I hope to get rid of my cold which is still very heavy on me. Tonight Jem & I went to look for the Colonel after dinner & found him bossing the Promenade Concerts at Her Majesty's. The Col. offered to present us to Florence St John who he declared was the emblem of purity & innocence. We heard this with much delight & as we both know her we declined with thanks.

Fancy the Col. turned into an Empresario [*sic*] & making money apparently??
… Your Adrian

Ufford Place, Woodbridge, Suffolk   9th December
[with Mrs Francis C Brooke]

My Adrian darling, … After all we do not go to Hopton till Monday as Mr
Cullum has asked Amy & I to Hardwick for Sunday. I hope this will not vex
you dearest. I could not well have refused to go without making a sort of
breach with Amy. I believe Lady Lindsey & Lilah Bertie are there—& if so it
will probably be most correct. … I can see Mr Brooke does not quite like our
going there. Gerry Cullum's nieces live there entirely now & it was from the
eldest Miss Robertson the invitation came. … Ever your own *Laure*

White's, St James'   9th December

My Darling, I hope you will enjoy your visit to Hardwick though I wish that
I could be there to take care of my Sweet Love. Of course I don't really mind
you going though I don't care for the 'set'. … Darling *Laure* I wish that I
could be with you in our little house somewhere. Goodbye, Your Adrian

Hardwick House, Bury St Edmunds   12th December
[with Gerry Cullum & his nieces]

My own Darling Adrian, The party here is most respectable, indeed somewhat
heavy. The house contains a great many lovely & interesting things, pictures,
china & furniture—mixed with some very ugly objects of the taste of 5 to 20
years ago. It snowed all yesterday so I was not able to see the garden which is
the feature of the place. Mr Cullum is *very* civil to me, he took me in to dinner
on Saturday & yesterday morning took me all about the house showing me
the old pictures & things which he knows all about. …

   Amy & I had rather an adventure coming back from church & got in so
late. Mr Cullum drove us to church with Miss Blake, an old frump, about 3
miles off. Amy & I said we wished to walk home—she thought she knew the
way! so we set off but in about a quarter of an hour a heavy snowstorm came
on and it became *quite* dark—a thick fog—so we could only just see the track
left by the carriage wheels on the morning's snow & followed these most
patiently. After walking many miles & getting very tired we found the
Hardwick carriage drawn up in front of a perfectly strange house about 2
miles from Hardwick where Mr Cullum had gone to call. Amy thought she

knew the way home from there so we set off again, too wet through to get into the carriage & wait as the coachman suggested. Of course we missed the way again!! At one time it seemed perfectly hopeless—in a dark lane in deep snow but at *last* we got home at near 7, having started at 4. We sat in our bedrooms very warm & comfy, having tea, and Jimmy St Leger who is also staying here came knocking on our door every few minutes to *beg* us to come down as it was so dull without us!

The rest of the party here are Gerard Lowther (very old friend) & his sister. He has grown up *hugely* fat & rather dull but haunts me as of yore, much to the disgust of Maud Robertson who is trying to *snare* him I think. She is simply impossible to me, so vulgar & actressy & *covered* with paint. The sister is a good honest simple soul. Then there is old Miss Blake, 2 other men & a hugely fat American called Macaulay. Mr Cullum picked him up somewhere—he is supposed to be very clever but has not yet spoken!! Nothing could be nicer & more civil than Mr Cullum is both to Amy & myself, though at times his conversation is certainly broad—but never in tête-à-tête. It is when he is laughing & being funny with Jimmy etc. that he goes too far & says things which one can only entirely *ignore*—it is such a pity.

We had a tour de valse last night & some polkas. Saturday night I had my fortune told by old Miss Blake from cards. She knew nothing about me—or our engagement. Darling I went to bed quite happy after her predictions. The very first card I cut was the luckiest card in the whole pack, then *the* love card, then a card which told I was in someone's thoughts. Then came the card showing a love match, then the love card again—much to the amusement of the lookers on, then a wedding ring—& new frocks. ... She told me many curious things about the past ... she said I should marry the man I loved, and would be envied by a fair woman who knew him & me. This made me laugh darling, you will guess who I thought of. There was much more & some oddly true. I suppose it was all great nonsense. ... Ever your loving *Laure*

WHITE'S, ST JAMES'   17TH DECEMBER

My darling, The interview with the Clairvoyant took place yesterday. He could tell me nothing but that he saw a Cabman handing them [Laura's lost 'Jaw Crackers' drawings] to a short dark man who framed them & sold them as pictures. He said, 'they are gone into different houses'. He described two of the pictures accurately enough, valued them at a £100 & gave the number. His trance lasted for over an hour & it was a very curious experience indeed. When we meet I shall tell you what more he said. I am going to try another one, a woman this time.

After dinner in Green St Jem & Elsie set upon me & did all they could to persuade me that it was my duty to make you come straight up to Green St & be married in Xmas week even though I had only a lodging to take you to. We sat till past 1. talking over this & they put it on my conscience to make you this offer now at once. Dear *Laure*, even a hired lodging with you would be Paradise to me. I cannot think of any possible privation which the daily sight of you would not more than amply repay me for. But I feel this is more than I have a right to ask. For how could I hope to make up to you for the misery of such a life to you & for the open war with all our relations which this would entail. I for my part am eager to throw every scruple, every consideration, every friend & relation in the world to the winds in order to marry you tomorrow. … Finally what I mean you to understand is that nothing weighs with me except your happiness. If you are ready to face the music & to come to me & feel that I can make up to you for what you must lose, then God helping me I am ready. … I feel that Jem is right & that we ought not to wait on, losing our youth & freshness for the sake of what people may do or say because we decide to rough it together. … Can I trust your love to read this & to agree or disagree without feeling bitter towards me? Well I risk it & hope that you will recollect how dearly I love you with all my heart & soul, my own true love. Your Adrian

HOPTON ST MARGARET, GREAT YARMOUTH   19TH DECEMBER
[WITH AUNT MAGGIE ORDE]

My own darling Adrian, I only received your letter this morning—and it made my heart beat so loud I thought Amy who was beside me must have heard. Darling what you propose we had best talk over when we meet in a few days' time. Christmas week—spent as Jem proposes is of course out of the question! we have yet a *little* patience left—to wait for each other, don't you think so darling? and to begin life putting all our friends & relations against us— knowing as I should that *we* were in the wrong—would be more painful to me than I can say. If after we have talked together next week—*seriously*, we agree to marry on your Great O St appointment, & you really think I could make up to you for the poverty we should endure—we will at all events wait till Easter or the summer, & if we make this decision *we will abide by it—advienne que pourra* [come what may]. I am not afraid of poverty with you—and if we ourselves decide to take this step I do not fancy we should meet with much opposition.

One thing *only* I am firm about. I cannot marry you dearest until you are free from debts ... if we settle to do this we must at all events *start clear*. Is there any chance of the Brunswick Hotel scheme bringing in the small sum that is necessary? The family pictures you told me you would not attempt to sell—so I feel it is useless to allude to them again. Is there no chance of your salary at Great O. St being raised? Even another £50 would make our income up to a certain £500—independently of what I might earn. After all, after 2 years & a half it would not be very unusual to have a rise. I feel I cannot write all I think but would rather wait and talk with you ... but in all my heart & mind there is not *one* thought of bitterness—or regret for the past—I love you far too truly for this. I feel for you so—it is so *difficult* when one's inclinations and one's better judgements are at war—to choose the right path. ... I do feel very brave about the future & when I weigh what we should have to deny ourselves as small comforts, pretty frocks, & a few smart visits & play parties—in the balance against the happiness of even a very tiny, quiet, little *home* together—my heart cries for you. ...

After all we shall not meet until *Saturday*. There is only *one* person I would put off our meeting on the Friday at Runcton for—and that is Ernest. He arrives on the *Himalaya* in England on Thursday and writes that he wishes to come to Hunstanton on Friday—for one night—to see us all alone together first. Amy & I have arranged to leave here Friday morning (after the dance) to be in readiness to receive him. I hope you will go to Runcton all the same on Friday. *I* nearly always arrive first at our trysting place—it would be so nice to find *you* waiting for me on the Lynn platform, a quarter to 3. on Saturday. I am so sorry to disappoint you about Friday—I can not tell you how I am longing to see him again after these three years' absence, so please forgive your *Laure*. It was strange and interesting about the Clairvoyant. It interests me *deeply*. If only *one* of the drawings could be traced we might get on the track of the original thief. My book *Child Elves* came this morning. It is so prettily got up. ... Goodbye darling, ever your own true love *Laure*

20TH DECEMBER

Darling Adrian, I am so sorely tempted to throw everything to the winds & do as J. & E. propose, but I know it is best to wait at all events until those wretched bills are paid off. ... Somehow I feel next year will see us husband & wife. Adieu dear A. I trust my letter was not cold or disappointing. It was so hard to say 'no' to what you & they proposed. Ever your *Laure*

GREAT ORMOND STREET HOSPITAL, BLOOMSBURY   20TH DECEMBER

Darling, I quite understand & feel for your letter. ... Of course you want to be with Ernest on the Friday. Tell me where to find Ernest in London on the Thursday night as I long to feed him at White's. ... I am going to dine with Murray the Publisher's son who is on my Com.ttee & was one of the bitterest against me last year. What an odd change time brings except to us. ... My tender love, Goodbye, Your Adrian

At Runcton, King's Lynn
[with Uncle Sommy & Aunt Kitty Gurney]

24th December ... A most cheery dinner, all talking & laughing, danced a little to improve the floor—& Uncle Sommy read from the 'Runcton Annual'. Puny's [Reginald Gurney] skit of Uncle Sommy's *The Haunted Harp* called *The Jaunty Ape* is very clever. ...

25th December ... Found a whole plateful of presents & a lovely little pearl & diamond tortoise brooch from Adrian. I gave him a pin of our initials intertwined in diamonds. ...

26th December ... Afternoon worked at my fancy dress, putting ribbons on my shoulder knots & tambourine. Everyone in fancy dress, Adrian in white as a French Chef. After dinner 56 people came & we had a most cheery little dance—the best I ever saw here. Kept it up late, supper in the library. ...

27th December ... Had a series of *Tableaux Vivants*—a résumé of the last ones at Hunstanton. I wore my Schéhérazade dress & Adrian appeared as the Sultan. He looked so handsome. Afterwards a supper. ...

28th December ... A guitar & song concert in the schoolroom, Ernest, Uncle Sommy & Amy all playing. ...

30th December... Adrian could not stay for the ball in Lynn tonight—his visit seems to have passed away so quickly—but did not regret our decision—so said goodbye again bravely.

GREAT ORMOND STREET HOSPITAL, BLOOMSBURY   30TH DECEMBER

My Darling Love, ... When I got here there was a Meeting of the Architects, Lucas & Murray going on—they were astonished that I had come back & pleased. Then I had an interview with a tearful & very incoherent lady whose sister had left us a legacy the residue of her fortune. The tearful one explained that she was Executor & was ruined so wanted us to give up all or some of the money. I had to take refuge behind our lawyers to whom I am to take the Tearful one on Monday. Then I had to see 3 of our Doctors, each with a new grief against Miss Wood. ... To Uncle Sommy my thanks for all his kindness— dear good man, his friendship is another of the good things I owe to you my darling wife. Goodbye, Your Adrian

JANUARY 1888

7 Carteret Street, Queen Anne's Gate, Westminster

3RD JANUARY

My own dear Love, This evening I fairly broke down about 8. & left a lot of my letters unopened. Such a deluge of Subs: all being paid at once. Our dinner last night at the Guthries was rather funny. Barely enough to go round of each dish. But such Claret Lafite 58. Laura & Aunt Annie both seemed jolly. Old Guthrie made me stop & smoke with him but was evidently relieved when he saw that I had Cigarettes of my own. He lectured me on the sin of not saving money & said that I ought to lay by £150 a year out of my income which was, he declared, a large one for a bachelor. I said that if he would lend me £500 to marry on that I would try the plan. He laughed very grimly & said that for his part he did not see what right I had to marry at all & that beggars had no rights to anything. I just managed to keep my temper but saw there was no good in having a row.

There fades a little secret hope I had that he might help me. We parted quite good friends. He really is an awful screw & made me laugh to watch his eyes glisten as he described how even £10 a year put by would slowly grow & grow. It was, so he said, the most interesting thing in the world to watch money piling up year after year. Well I think I would prefer to be a beggar than love money as he does. ... Guthrie did ask if I had any chance of getting any other employment and that no doubt if I was really worth anything my Com.ttee would find me something better. Can't you see Lucas running about to do me a good turn? ... Your Adrian

Hunstanton

4TH JANUARY

My darling Adrian, ... Your conversation with Guthrie made me feel so indignant. What an unkind old screw he is. It must have been disgusting to hear him hold forth about £.s.d. and such an old man as he is [he was 63] to gloat over worldly goods—he ought to be paving the way to heaven for himself, with a few good generous deeds, and to give a helping hand to the son of his old friend[117] would not have been a bad beginning. It is evidently no good expecting anything from that quarter. ... Luckily hard words break no bones, especially from those we do not love. ... *Toujours ta Laure*

Great Ormond Street Hospital, Bloomsbury

5TH JANUARY

My own dear Heart, ... I stopped at Jem & Elsie's till 1 p.m. last night, my brain full of Jem & his affairs as I had to get his last words in writing. This morning I rushed down to see them off at Victoria. A huge bottle of milk for the baby which Elsie would pack in a hold-all broke & all their rugs, most of the Boxes & the Platform swam in milk to Jem's intense wrath. I did laugh so & at Jem's face when he had to pay £3 for excess luggage. Now they are gone & I feel lonely & sad as it was comforting to think of Green St as being always open to one. ... Goodnight my own true love, Your Adrian

7TH JANUARY

My own dear Love, ... Cole & I had a necessary explanation about some of Jem's work. It is not Jem's fault if Cole & I do not fight like cat & dog before all is over. ... After dinner last night (I never saw a bit of fish go so far) we, that is Aunt Annie, Laura, myself & Mrs Guthrie's sister went off to the Lyceum [*A Winter's Tale*]. The first two Acts were as dull as ditch water but as Perdita Mary Anderson dances quite beautifully in one long white garment which does as well as tights & shows off a pretty pair of legs to admiration. Her figure if there be no sustaining girdle is pretty. But as an Actress she is poorer than ever. A Mr. C. Collette acted Autolycus very wonderfully well. ... Your Adrian

WHITE'S, ST JAMES' SUNDAY, 8TH JANUARY

My Dearest, ... How do you think the top of a house would do for us? That is to say having a Doctor on the ground floor, we to have the rest of the house. Of course there would be his brass plate but we should be quite private in one part & would not be bothered I think. It would enable us to have a much nicer house & pay less for it by halving the cost. ... Goodnight my own, Your Adrian

HUNSTANTON HALL, HUNSTANTON 6TH JANUARY
[WITH MR & MRS HAMON LE STRANGE]

My darling, You will little think tonight when you are quietly asleep that your *Laure* will be gaily dancing at a ball! The Le Stranges asked me to come with them to the Tenants' Ball at Sandringham tonight. Unfortunately I had no invitation but the old and tried Uncle Sommy wrote off to Sir Dighton [Probyn][118] for me—and this morning I had a telegram from Sir D. 'By all means come to the ball.' This is very Cinderella like, isn't it? If only *my* Prince was to be there—instead of Prince Tum [the Prince of Wales]. ... Roland invites me to stay here with him all next week when all his people go up to town so *we* should be tête-à-tête. Shall I accept! ... Oh I wish I was there to kiss you & make you smile again & forget all the worries. Ever your *Laure*

Hunstanton

My darling Adrian, ... What a queer idea about halving a house—I should not care a pin who lived on the ground floor if we had room enough, even if the front door was regularly crusted over with brass plates. *Only* dear heart, *not* in that hateful dreary *quartier*: Bloomsbury. It is all I ask—it would be horrible to me to be divided by a gulf of slums from all my friends & pictures & shops & the park. I should never dare to trot about by myself up there where one sees such horrid people. I should get fat & dull always living in the house! ... I am just off to the Boileaus at Ketteringham for the Fellowes' ball at Shottesham tomorrow and the Gurney Buxtons' on Thursday. Roland Le Strange goes to Ketteringham tomorrow. He is much improved, not so conceited & *masherish* as he used to be, but really nicer. I feel like his grandmother—& would not condescend to flirt with him. ... Ever your *Laure*

Great Ormond Street Hospital, Bloomsbury   9th January

My own Darling, ... On Wednesday I dine with Mrs Molesworth who wants very much to get her next book done by you. I am seriously thinking of selling the family pictures if I can prevent the Col. getting hold of the money. That is the difficulty you know, for he has a life interest in them. ... Your Adrian

The two principal portraits involved were by Raeburn of Adrian's great-grandparents, Charles Hope of Granton, the Lord President, and his wife Lady Charlotte née Hope (second daughter of the 2nd Earl of Hopetoun by his third wife). Eventually there proved to be some fifty-eight pictures in all, including a Hoppner. Due to some maladministration these pictures had never been assigned, as they should have been after the death of the colonel's mother in 1872, to the colonel for his life only and thereafter to Adrian. The story of their final ownership is too long even to outline here but it led to painful confrontations with the colonel from March 1888 until Adrian's death.

Ketteringham Park, Wymondham, Norfolk   10th January
[with Sir Francis & Lady Boileau]

My own darling Adrian, ... I wonder if you will really ever find out about the pictures. I cannot help thinking that if the Colonel *could* claim the money if they were sold, he would already have taken some steps to do this as soon as your brother Charlie could give his consent. I suppose any lawyer could tell you about this if he saw the will. Would not Ld Hopetoun buy the family portraits if you thought of selling them? I have not much faith in this plan being carried through for I know the whole thing is so distasteful to you.

This house is delightful—full of countless pictures, old oak, books, antiques, china—every sort of thing like a museum. The dining-room is an old stone banqueting hall, just like the one at Penshurst but not nearly so large. The walls are covered & massed with arms of all dates & nations, armour, flags, & coat of arms—arranged pell mell in huge sort of trophies. It is very effective, & the lower part of the walls are hung with tapestry. I have just been looking at some trinkets that rather fascinated me—a whole collection of old fashioned *posy* wedding rings—all with some quaint motto inside, vows of love & fidelity exchanged by loving hearts long since returned to dust. ...

Last night we amused ourselves playing tunes on some hand bells, then we had some dancing—wild lancers & polkas—in the midst of this while we were all breathless & laughing—a solemn butler came in & announced 'Prayers'. It was *so* startling. We all tried to become grave & filed off to the stone dining hall again. There were a long line of servants drawn up down one side, we formed up in line the other side, with our backs turned to the world, faces to the chairs, all standing. It struck me as being *so* ridiculous somehow. Then at a signal we all knelt & had about 5 or 6 minutes of devotion, then all dashed away to the billiard room & played pool!!

There is no party here, only Roland Le Strange & two other youthlets, Chenny & Katty [two of the 'Runcton Rectory' Gurneys, grand-daughters of the Boileaus], the Boileau daughter, one nice son, the youngest, Raymond a Sandhurst youth, and one *dreadful* creature Maurice, the second son who poor thing is half idiotic. He goes about with shambling gait—shaking his hands & his arms dangling by his sides, & laughing. He gives me the creeps but they are all so used to him they don't seem to mind. He makes the most inane remarks & laughs like a child at nothing. There is some little thing wrong in his brain for he can work hard, has the most *marvellous* memory—& has passed every exam he has been up for yet at Oxford with perfect ease. Yet anyone seeing him dancing last night would think he had just escaped from Earlswood. He rather frightens me, and last night in my lovely *pompous* room, full of dark old pictures with watching eyes, I could not help thinking of that *other* son, the eldest, who lives in some far corner of the house—a hopeless imbecile, a huge man of 6ft 2 [inches] very handsome so the Rec Gurneys say, with a long dark beard. He cannot even speak—it is so *awful* for his father— a very clever agreeable man. I can not imagine a greater trial than 2 such sons.

The Fellowes' ball at Shottesham is tonight. The Boileaus thought Sandringham a dull ball because there were very few people—& it was bristling with Royalties. The Gurney Buxtons' at Catton (the day after tomorrow) they say will be the best of these 2. Ever your own loving *Laure*

11TH JANUARY

My darling, ... I *did* so enjoy the ball last night. There were such lots of nice people there, a lovely floor—crowds of partners. It was such an awful night with a thick impenetrable fog. It is only 7 miles to Shottesham but we were ages getting there and were all *but* upset about 3 times. Katty & I and Sir Francis (who is inclined to become a middle aged admirer of mine) went in one carriage—and twice the coachman got off the road & we suddenly found ourselves at an impossible angle & let down the windows to prepare for a smash—with Sir Francis hanging out of the window swearing at the driver & Katty & I convulsed with laughter inside. We did not get home until nearly 5. & feel a little limp today. ... Ever your *petite Laure*

GREAT ORMOND STREET HOSPITAL, BLOOMSBURY 12TH JANUARY

My own dear Love, ... The Molesworth dinner last night was amusing. All young people, no chaperons at all. ... Mrs M. never said a word about her books which rather annoyed me for I had fully hoped to be able to write to make you an offer on her part. ... I am really going to try to sell the family Piccy's only the money will have to be invested & I shall have to borrow on it to pay off a little every year. However I do not feel confident of being able to sell as we shall have to apply for leave to the Court of Session at Edinburgh. Look at yesterday's *Times* & see Mrs Molesworth's letter about our Xmas Tree. I hope it may bring money. Your Adrian

This 'letter', which described the recent children's 'Xmas Tree' treat that took place every year in one of the long wards of the Great Ormond Street Hospital, was written with the aim of drawing sympathy from readers of *The Times* in the form of much needed contributions to the planned new wing.

KING STREET, KING'S LYNN 13TH JANUARY
[WITH GEORGE & EVA CRESSWELL]

My own darling Adrian, ... I have only come in here to rest for 2 hours on my way home, & I had to see Uncle Sommy at the Bank for a business talk. He talked of our marriage & advised our marrying soon. I told him if we had £600 & a clear start we thought of beginning & he entirely approved, & said with *you* it would not be imprudent for you were so careful, which pleased me. I see you do really mean business about the Pictures. I suppose the consent of the Court is only a form for it really cannot signify to anyone whether these Piccys that have been mouldering in a warehouse for near 20 years continue to moulder or are sold. I was so sleepy when we got home about 5.30 from the Gurney Buxton ball. I *did* enjoy myself, but really truly only because of the pleasure of dancing hard the whole evening. There were no *old* friends there & I did not frivol at all. I went in to supper both dances with the faithful Tardy. ... I was quite relieved to find that the Sandringham Tenants' ball last week was an acknowledged failure & everyone hated it & thought it dull with no men to dance with. I was afraid till *these* 2 balls *I* was getting so dull no one would ask me to dance. ... Take care of yourself dearest for the sake of your loving—wife—*Laure*

Sunday, 15th January

Darling Adrian, ... I am afraid Jem's schemes, about the Italian Exhib. Etc. have all fallen through ... and I fear that the affair of the Pictures is becoming vague & cloudy—& will presumably fade away in the fatal way that all the plans for our future have hitherto done. Could not you *really* take some steps about this matter dearest so that we might have something to talk of besides vague plans & castles in the air, for I suppose this time it rests with you whether anything is done or only thought of. ... Ever your *Laure*

Great Ormond Street Hospital, Bloomsbury   17th January

My dearest Sweetheart, All yesterday I was the prey of the Auditors. We cannot find 11/- [shillings] which is such a bore & a worry. I don't think you quite realize that I can do nothing about the Pictures till after April when Charlie comes of age & that the Judges are as likely as not to refuse permission. In any case there is the Col. who will have to be thought of. But I am going to put the matter into Hastie's hands. ... Gatty has an idea that a shop—to be worked by Jo & I—for the sale of Brass & Copper work, made by a wonderful man whom his brother found out at Antwerp, would pay. We should trade under the name of the Antwerp Worker in Metals, say 'Tubal Cain & Co.' ... Goodbye, your Adrian

HUNSTANTON   19TH JANUARY

My darling Adrian, ... This morning I had a letter from Griffith & Farran Mr Okeden. The *Mermaiden* book[119] he proposed last autumn is on again now & he is very anxious to see me about the illustrations—for which I am to get £40—as he says it is so far simpler than writing. ... Adieu, your *Laure*

GREAT ORMOND STREET HOSPITAL, BLOOMSBURY   19TH JANUARY

My own dear *Laure*, ... We had such a long Com.ttee yesterday with old Aberdare in the Chair. He was very civil & announced to the intense & open joy of the Doctors that Miss Wood has at last placed her resignation in his hands.[120] Poor woman it must have been a bitter pill to swallow. But the Drs would have forced the Com.ttee to ask her to go so it is a good job over. ... I think I am incapable of being happy or cheerful now when away from you. You have so grown into my inmost thoughts that without you life is too stale & unprofitable. ... If only I can scrape together some cash, but how to do this I do not see at present. It makes me quite mad to think that only £500 is between us & a happy life together.

Do you see Robert has got six weeks? Well that won't kill him. ... All today my clerk Whitford has been in the wicked hands of the Auditor. He looks, I am pleased to observe, like a plucked sparrow. ... I feel you are not at all happy about something. Of late there has been something in your dear letters which has made me feel you were rather dispirited & in a gloom. You will tell me, *ma Laure*, what this is. Goodbye, Your Adrian

The case at the Old Bailey ran for three days, when Robert Cunninghame Graham and John Burns were charged with nine counts, forming three main charges: being participators in a riot; taking part in an unlawful assemblage; and assault upon the police who were in the execution of their duty. The jury found them guilty of only the fifth count—being part of an unlawful assemblage, and on 18th January they were both sentenced to six weeks' imprisonment without hard labour. It seemed to have been accepted that the Federation of Radical Clubs' wish to hold a meeting in Trafalgar Square was *bone fide* and that it was the police who started the aggression and the lawless mob who prolonged the riot. In the end the case turned on the legality or otherwise of the temporary prohibition of public meetings in Trafalgar Square.

On the back of Adrian's letter of the 19th was Laura's pencilled list of her trousseau requirements and the cost:

	£.s.d.		£.s.d.
underclothes:		tailor made dress & jacket	10
8 of each, 10/- each	8	dark blue & white frock	5
6 white petticoats	4	2 morning summer frocks	5
10 nightgowns	8	jacket	5
shoes, boots, stockings		black evening dress	8
£5 each	15	other evening dress	5
dressing gown & jackets	5	going away dress	7
corsets	5	teagowns	5
hats & handkerchiefs	5		
	50		50

WHITE'S, ST JAMES'   21ST JANUARY

My dearest Life, ... I joined Charlie [Orde] at the Lyceum for *A Winter's Tale*. Again I felt very bored with the first two acts but loved the dancing scene. We went & had some supper at the Cavour next to the Alhambra. C. had never been there & loved it though the company was rather naughty but it amused him. He made me smile by saying that you would have been so amused if you had been with us & that you would have found material for several sketches among the company. ... The Brunswick Hotel scheme has not been given up & may yet be carried out though it certainly does not look promising just now. Cole returns to town on Tuesday from Marseilles where he was staying with Jem & Elsie before they left for Egypt. I want to have a talk with him on business about the Cartridges deal. ... Goodbye my sweet, Your Adrian

On the back of this letter was the following pencilled list:

Adrian's disappointments since our engagement

1. Appointment representing Siam in Paris.
2. Mrs Hubbard's idea—in Zanzibar.
3. Jem Hope's scheme about Algiers [managing an orange farm].
4. Lloyds office in London.

5. County Auditorship.
6. Assistant Auditor in London.
7. School Inspectorship.
8. Colonial appt. in Cyprus.
9. British Honduras.
10. Consulship from Sir J.F. [Sir James Fergusson, in Trinidad].
11. Silver mine in California.
12. Sec'ship to Kuch Behar [*sic*].
13. Sec'ship to some company.
14. Italian Exhib. secretaryship.
15. Secretary to Chelsea Hospital.
16. Mrs Amherst's Sec'ship to Knights of Malta.

GREAT ORMOND STREET HOSPITAL, BLOOMSBURY   23RD JANUARY

My own Love, … I had lunch at Greenwich yesterday with Henry Chamberlain & his wife. They are the people who live on £530 a year with 3 children!!! We had really a very good lunch & I stopped there talking away till 5. when I rushed off by train to see Mrs Molesworth who was as usual very nice. She again referred to you & said she wished so much to see you & talk over a book. … Goodnight my Love, Your Adrian

HUNSTANTON   JANUARY 25TH

My darling one, … I cannot help hoping you may have some sort of news to tell me on Saturday when we meet at Eva's. It would be comforting to know that there was *something* we might safely look forward to—instead of this endless uncertainty. Our engagement has lasted so long I feel it is becoming a *farce* to our friends & a *tragedy* to ourselves, and to fix even a remote date would make all the difference, don't you agree dearest? but don't be vexed. Ever your own true *Laure*

P.S. Forgive my writing rather impatiently today—I cannot help telling you what is in my mind.

26TH JANUARY

My darling one, We have just finished off our 'Christmas tree' with great éclat. There were 40 children from 3 to 12, so very little pleasure goes a long way. (We bought a lot of little dolls for the tree & dressed them—rather uncongenial work, but much to the improvement of the rather inferior dolls.)

They departed with their arms full of presents—after 3 shrill wavering cheers for the Miss Troubridges. There are no treats here for the poor children & these favoured ones *beam* with delight whenever we meet them. I am tired after this performance—spending most of the day up on the top of a ladder as neither Amy nor Vi *dared* mount. ... Adieu my own Adrian, ever your *Laure*

---

117 *4th Jan* For the Guthrie—Hope friendship, *see* p302 and footnote 98.

118 *6th Jan* Sir Dighton Probyn (1833-1924), then Comptroller and Treasurer of the Household to HRH the Prince of Wales.

119 *19th Jan The Story of the Mermaiden*—adapted from the German of Hans Andersen by E Ashe, illustrated by Laura Troubridge (Griffith, Farran, Okeden & Welsh, 1888).

120 *19th Jan* Mrs Wood's letter gave as her reason for resigning the sudden death of her younger brother from typhoid, leaving his eleven children almost unprovided for so that she was needed to help her sister-in-law with their education.

FEBRUARY 1888

At 30 Thurloe Square
[with Johnny & Rosy Birkbeck]

2nd February Had a most wonderful day with Ernest. We set off walking to Christies—there saw the picture of Great-Grandfather [Nelson's Admiral, Sir Thomas Troubridge 1st Bt] to be sold on Sat. Became madly keen to get it. Ernest contributed £20 to our £30, Tom 10, & Aunt Chatty [Troubridge] £5—£65 in all. ... Set off after lunch by underground to Griffith & Farran where I had a successful interview with Herbert Okeden. ...

4th February At 1.10 arrived at Christies for the great sale, felt thrilled with excitement. 20 lots had already been sold, our picture was lot 28. The excitement became intense—for Ernest & I. We had to try & look as if we were not interested. When the lot was put up I could hardly hear the auctioneer. I became quite breathless. Touchall was bidding for us. I felt *sure* we should lose it—& so we did, by just £10 & the picture was knocked down to one of the Tuckers[121] for £75. We were *so* disappointed. Adrian & I went off to lunch at the Grosvenor, and then went on a little house-hunting expedition—to see some flats at £150, £180, & £200 [a year] to see what could be had for the money. Then paid some calls—but everyone was out.

5th February After lunch here Adrian & I walked to Chelsea to see a little house—with a bathroom—we thought might suit us as the rent was tiny. ... Then to Mrs Molesworth. I liked her much & she offered me several introductions to publishers. ... I am to stay here till Tuesday.

HUNSTANTON   8TH FEBRUARY

My own darling, ... I have been wondering how your business interview is getting on, & much of the future we have planned. ... I have told the others about the little house we saw in Carlyle Square—and they quite *love* the idea. ... I feel all smiles when I think of us two possibly established there before the end of this year. I had a letter from Aunt Chatty [Troubridge], the old humbug now pretends she never meant that ugly net for my wedding present at all— but only a little passing gift, as she thought it would look so well over *light satin* on one of my trousseau gowns. She seems rather pleased that I should wish for a family relic. ... Do take care of yourself my *sweet* for the sake of your own wife, *Laure*

P.S. Imagine the Tuckers were prepared to bid up to £200 to buy in that picture of Admiral Troubridge—so our chance was nil.

Great Ormond Street Hospital, Bloomsbury   9th February

Ma Laure chérie, ... My old servant is quite prepared to camp in No 15 Carlyle Square with me if I do take the house. From tonight 100 Jermyn St. will find me. Leaving my Carteret Street lair & having to pack all my things up again was very horrid. ... It is too dreadful that each parting should hurt more & more. ... Today I am enraged that I love you so & if you were here I think I should have to bite your white neck hard. Oh! *ma Laure* I want you so. Goodnight, your Adrian

Hunstanton   10th February

My darling Adrian, ... Yesterday I had another long yarn from Aunt Chatty proposing Oh horror! to present me with a pair of gilt console tables with marble tops. She says they would look '*verry* handsome' in our drawing room. Cannot you fancy what white elephants they would be to us dearest! I do so hate them too, don't you? The sort of thing that might look well in a large room furnished in the empire style, but not in our little house. They are not even a family relic as she means to buy them.

I hope sending Cole to *Newcastle*—about the Cartridges—will be a more useful operation than it is generally supposed to be. I cannot help hoping you will *not* decide to play a waiting game. The Colonel is such a warning not to refuse small *certain* profits for remote great possibilities. Now you have Jem's business all in your own hands, so now is your best chance of making the £500 which you really want ... so do try & come to terms with some of these people ... for I think it may just make the difference to the happiness of our *whole lives* if our marriage can be arranged this summer—instead of dragging on for another year. The uncertainty is so wearing. I feel we might lose heart altogether ... . Dearest I should like to tell you how *dearly* I love you, and what you are to me. ... Farewell, ever your *Laure*

15th February

My own darling Adrian, ... Mrs Molesworth went to see Rosy [Birkbeck] & my drawings. Rosy said she liked them *very* much & was going to write to me.[122] ... Ever your *Laure*

GREAT ORMOND STREET HOSPITAL, BLOOMSBURY 15TH FEBRUARY

My own Darling, … J.M.S. is to be kicked out as Manager of the West End Branch of his Assurance Co. & I am going to try to succeed him if I can work Guthrie who is a Director. I do not know whether they intend to have another Manager or to abolish the Branch. … I have been out during lunch to see some poor wretches in Holborn who are going to be turned out of their hovels into the Street by the Met. Board of Works, nearly 1000 people living in 56 houses too horrible to describe. I have summoned a meeting of the Charity Organization Society about this & shall probably write to *The Times* & go to the Home Secretary as something will have to be done for these Costermongers. No one will take them in or give house room to their Barrows.

As to the business there is nothing going on at all. I cannot see the least chance of getting the £500. You see if I borrow it on a Life insurance paying back £50 a year the cost would be another £50 which swallows at once £100 of my tiny income. … The Guards performances at Chelsea Barracks are over. Howard Vyse told me last night that the girls [amateurs] who were dressed as the Ballet had no tights & had forgotten the numerous frillings of Lace Petty's worn on the Stage so when they danced forward they presented a more liberal view of their Garters than they at all imagined. Rather horrid to have had a wife among them. Your Adrian

WHITE'S, ST JAMES'   18TH FEBRUARY

My own dear Love, My cold is getting worse & worse … and J.M.S. tells me that his Company have arranged some plan to do without an Agent. When I asked old Guthrie to let me know if I had a chance of the vacancy he *was* so grumpy. … I shall hope to know very soon whether Armstrong's will buy the Cartridges or not. … Two of Jo's friends are coming up for election today, they will be pilled I fear. I think your getting the wedding ring in the Shrove Tuesday Pancake must have been a good omen for us. Your Adrian

HUNSTANTON   21ST FEBRUARY

My dearest, I have been a prey to secret anxiety about you as you wrote your cold was getting worse every minute & seemed so poorly—and London seems to have become a sort of Siberia. … A disappointment about my 'Queen of Hearts' series. Mr Okeden writes regretfully that Griffith & Farran have decided against it chiefly because there is no other book of the same kind & they always try to publish in sets. I mean to try elsewhere at once, probably Marcus Ward. … Ever your *Laure*

GREAT ORMOND STREET HOSPITAL, BLOOMSBURY 21ST FEBRUARY

My Darling, I have had a long interview with Arthur Ponsonby who has undertaken the negotiations with Armstrong. He takes my view of the Cartridge being a valuable property but that it must take time before we can make money out of it. Did I tell you that Robert [Cunninghame Graham] came to see me on Saturday—the day he was released from Pentonville. He looks a bit thin but fairly well. ... I am still being interviewed to death by women one uglier than another—who want to be Lady Supt. here. ... Your Adrian

HUNSTANTON   23RD FEBRUARY

Darling Adrian, You asked me about Alexander House where Daisy Orde is lodging while studying at Mrs Jopling's studio. The terms are very low, between £4 & £5 a month but the régime must be rather awful. Dinner at *5.30*! & all sorts of rules—almost like a school. 86 girls—all dreaders I believe, & men only allowed to be interviewed in the *Council* room! The studio lessons I long to have—& if we ever really settle in Carlyle Square I hope darling this autumn might see me at work with Mrs Jopling. ... Goodbye my own dearest, always your *Laure*

---

121 *4th Feb* Charles Comyns Tucker's late great uncle, Gen. Sir Charles Bulkeley Egerton, had married Charlotte, only daughter of Sir Thomas Troubridge 1st Bt and the young Troubridges' great aunt.

122 *15th Feb* It was in February of 1887 that Adrian had got Mrs Molesworth to write to her publishers [Hatchard] about Laura illustrating her next story but this had already been commissioned. As Hatchard had liked Laura's work he commissioned illustrations for *Daddy's Boy* in June so that it was not until the following year that Laura was to illustrate Mrs Molesworth's *The Old Pincushion* (Griffith, Farran, Okeden & Welsh, 1889). In her journal of the time she wrote: ' I was rather disappointed that it was not a fairy book and also that the publishers wanted the illustrations in wash instead of outline.' She did not illustrate any more Molesworth books but the author dedicated her *The Wood-Pigeons and Mary* (Macmillan, 1901) to Adrian and Laura's elder daughter, Jaqueline, and presented her with a handwritten 'fair copy' of the MSS on her twelfth birthday. It was quite usual for successful authors such as Mrs Molesworth to present their friends with copies of their MSS, written out in their own hand. This original MSS was sold at Sotheby's for £380 in 1988 by Laura's grandson, Felix Hope-Nicholson.

MARCH 1888

WHITE'S, ST JAMES'   3RD MARCH

My Darling, When I got down to Bitter-sea after dining at Victoria Station, I found things in a dreadful condition. Also I learnt that the Col. had sent for the 4 most valuable Pictures from Scotland. These have arrived & are in the possession of Stronsberg, a Jew lawyer of the worst character. Hastie [Adrian's solicitors] has at once served Stronsberg with a formal legal notice that I have a claim on the Pictures & that I refuse to consent to anything. I am quite wild with rage. There is an Action hanging over the Col's head for some enormous sum for that stupid Gun. No money seems to be left anywhere & I see before me the pleasant prospect of having to provide for the Battersea household for the rest of my days. I am now going to see if Guthrie will help me to settle something.

My idea is that the Col. must bolt to America or Australia & find work where he can. I am just savage. ... The poor Aunts—Cha and Annie—have so little they can hardly do more & how we are to find money for my Mother to live on beats me. She is perfectly miserable & has lost her head for good. What to do or to suggest is beyond my feeble wits. Goodbye, Your Adrian

HUNSTANTON   SUNDAY, 4TH MARCH

My own Darling Adrian, What a *dreadful* state of things. Your poor Mother. ... The Colonel really is a *bad man* for he must know well he has no right to the Pictures, and I hope you will fight him to the last gasp for them. What I think is this—if you get rid of the Col. (supposing he consented to go which is not probable) would not your Mother & sisters fall upon *you* to take his place and support them ... Unless the Graham aunts undertook to take your Mother & sisters, I should think the Colonel, incubus & trial as he is, had better remain for it is clearly *his* duty and no one else's to support them.

If you were *free* darling perhaps you might wish to devote the rest of your life to your Mother & sisters but as it is I cannot see that you have any choice left you. Surely your first duty is owed to your promised wife. If we had been engaged weeks or even months, instead of *years*, we might have agreed to part: but *now* I do not see why our hearts should be broken & the happiness of our two lives sacrificed to that Moloch, the Colonel. ...

If once you undertake to support your Mother & sisters our marriage becomes *utterly* and *entirely* impossible. In fact darling you have to choose between them & me—your wife to whom you are pledged—the love of your life as you have often told me. I have promised to love you 'till Death do us part'—and should leave you with a broken heart. Still, to support both them—

and me—would be beyond even your strength & courage—so this is what it amounts to. You know I would wait on for years, knowing that I am your first thought and care, and that all your life is spent in working on towards our marriage & making a little home possible for us—but if this were all claimed by your Mother and sisters at Battersea—there would be no room for me in your life darling—and we should *have* to part. I want you to remember this when you are making arrangements for the future—that is why I have written so clearly—though it pains me even to see it written.

I did feel so for you having to go & see Guthrie about such business. I hope he was nice for auld lang syne. You must long for some friend to talk it all over with. If Jem were only in England. ... What a worry it all is for you my poor darling lover. ... Ever your own true *Laure*

WHITE'S, ST JAMES   5TH MARCH

My dearest, The Col. is rabid with rage & made my Mother come to tell me that I must at once withdraw etc. & that he will neither see me nor write to me until I give in. This does not trouble me much. ... I loved your letter & agree with it. But I think I am bound to contribute something to my Mother's support, and I should propose to contribute the income from the money got from the sale of the Pictures. ... Guthrie I found was out so I could not have a talk with him. I have seen their Picture Dealer who would take the Pictures & value them for me. He says a good 'Reynolds' may be worth anything up to £5000 or it may only fetch £50. ...

I think of going to the Levee on Wednesday with Jo as if I delay going the Col. will probably be bankrupt which would rather prevent one's turning up anywhere. It will also show the Col. too that I do not take his threats to heart much. Goodbye my Love, Your Adrian

HUNSTANTON   16TH MARCH

My own darling, ... I am *very* glad you are to rescue your books & things from Battersea for I think they are the beginning of our little home. ... I have bought a book which will amuse you, called *From Kitchen to Garret*, all about house furnishing and house keeping—addressed to 'Edwin and Angelina'. ... I think it must be written by rather a strong minded female—as she says husbands can be *trained* to do this & that!! such an odd idea, it made us all laugh. And now we have laughed so over Edwin & Angelina in *Punch* this week. Have you seen it—'Nothing darling—only *darling*, darling—' do look at it. ...[123]

I am so glad you are looking at houses—it gives such an air of *vraisemblance* [likelihood] to our plans this summer. Do you think Cole will attend strictly to business in Paris—& not frivol off! [Adrian had sent him there 'to bring back the 2000 Cartridges at any cost'] ... Soon we shall be always together, & read no more this little word *Adieu*, Ever your *Laure*

WHITE'S, ST JAMES'   16TH MARCH

Dearest *Laure*, Mrs Napier has promised to take in my Mother & Jessie when necessary. [The youngest daughter, Madge, is still at boarding school and is usually taken care of in the holidays by the aunts]. The Col. wrote a most abusive letter to Hastie threatening to bring actions for libel against us, & saying that he would cut me out of what he had to leave. ... All this does tend to worry one to death as I have gone through it all before, he is repeating the same scenes of 10 years ago when he tried to borrow on my mother's Marriage Settlement. ... I feel the shame of meeting any of your people ... I try to think what may be best for us all but I have lost all confidence in my own judgement & remain just sullenly obstinate. ... Goodnight my dearest, Your Adrian

SUNDAY NIGHT, 18TH MARCH

My own true Love, ... I found several people out this afternoon & wound up by calling on Mrs Molesworth who urged me to throw everything to the winds & marry you at once. She is going to house hunt for us. ... There is a chance of the Col. being appointed Sec.y of a Railway Co. & I have managed to stir him up to go & see Guthrie about it as it is a new Branch line in Scotland for a Ry. of which G. is a Director. ... I have a very good letter from Ponsonby re the Cartridges. He has been at Newcastle & seems to think that Armstrong's will take them up. ... Goodbye dear Heart, Your Adrian

JO'S ROOMS, ROYAL INSURANCE OFFICE,   20TH MARCH
ST JAMES' ST

My own true Love, ... My Mother came & saw me today. The Col. is most hopeless, he won't speak to her now & accuses everybody of being in a plot to ruin him except his dear friend the Jew. If I write to the Trustee in Scotland I feel that the Col. would never consent to the Sale of the Pictures & we can do nothing without his Consent. Nor can he as he now admits do anything without mine. My Mother has seen Stronsberg who began about my outrageous conduct but she soon shut him up. He then laughed & said I was a clever fellow. But she could see that his aim was to increase the feud between the Col. & myself.

I have seen Ld Kinnaird [brother of Adrian's admirer Mrs Yorke Bevan] & made enquiries about the Scotch Railway which is in the hands of the Jew Stronsberg & of which he promises the Secretaryship to the Col. As it was, Kinnaird said it was a good scheme but in very dangerous hands. ... All this comes at a time when I ought to be full of Hospital business & I feel painfully that I am neglecting work which I am paid to do, for the sake of my own affairs. ... Your Adrian

HUNSTANTON   SUNDAY, 25TH MARCH

My darling Adrian, I am so very glad you are coming here on Maundy Thursday for we are engaged to Hopton on Tuesday in Easter Week so we shall only just have four days together. ... By the by, Amy & Vi met Lothar de B. [Bunsen] & his wife while staying at Catton with Samuel and Minna Buxton. Lothar told Vi you were quite the best 'best man' he had ever seen—& he should always recommend you! He was delighted to hear we thought of marrying this summer. He said that he found he did not spend a penny more now—living with his wife & child, than he did as a bachelor at Wisbech. He thought it was partly because he did not go about so much, being very happy at home. ... Goodbye dearest, ever your *Laure*

GREAT ORMOND STREET HOSPITAL, BLOOMSBURY   26TH MARCH

My dear *Laure*, ... We have had such a row in Com.ttee. Lucas & I, and what made the thing so annoying was that I really was to blame for having quite forgotten all about some work. But he really is a bully. ... With tender love to you dear heart, Your Adrian

HUNSTANTON   26TH MARCH

Darling Adrian, ... I heard from Mr Okeden, he says the author of the *Mermaiden* likes my drawings very much. This is good news. Tom came last night, very pleased with himself about his promotion to Captain [in the 60th Rifles]. He & Ernest are busy making a putting green in the garden in the rain, sinking jam pots at short intervals. This golf rage is a blessed resource. I *am* so glad you are coming tomorrow to see your—*Laure*

123 *16th Mar* 'Fond and Foolish' cartoon by George du Maurier of a young couple sitting on a park bench next to an old man (*Punch*, 17th March, 1888):

Edwin (suddenly after a long pause)	"Darling!"
Angelina	"Yes, Darling?"
Edwin	"Nothing, Darling. Only *Darling*, Darling"

Bilious Old Gentleman feels quite sick.

APRIL 1888

The correspondence for this month became ever more repetitive, with Laura constantly urging Adrian to do more serious house-hunting if they are to be married in August, to speed up his various business projects so that he could clear his debts, and to chase up developments on the sale of the pictures, while Adrian's replies were often of the shortest as he could scarcely keep up with his hospital work let alone look after his own interests. The following extracts are greatly shortened. Adrian did, however, write to the trustee for the Hope family pictures held in Scotland, David Boyle Hope—a hitherto unknown cousin, and received the following reply:

'I am grieved to hear about your father's proposed sale of the pictures, which is of course quite illegal and must be prevented. The worst of it is, and I am very sorry to have to say it to you, that he recently got me to send them up on the statement that they were wished by you to clothe the walls of some large rooms which you occupy. He first of all asked for the measurements by way of seeing how they would suit the rooms, and then he selected some. I have been keeping them in order to save the expense of storing them. I should say that under your grandmother's Will he is entitled to the custody of them though not to sell them. But probably I could get authority to obtain them back, on the ground of the attempt to sell them. I am writing by this post to Mr Stronsberg. I am going up to London on Thursday and could see you or your solicitors on Friday. ... I will bring the Will with me. ...'.

Great Ormond Street Hospital, Bloomsbury   4th April

My own dear Heart, ... Laura [his sister] came to see me & we had a long talk. She says that the Col. must settle £6000 on you & that the family consider our marriage more important than the equal division of money 30 years hence. So we are going to attack my Mother on the subject together. ... Ask Charlie [Orde] whether if we can get this £6000 settled he would consider that to be enough. I would undertake to insure for £5000 as soon as I could afford it. ... I have been to the City stirring up Cole who was full of hopes & really there seems a chance of things [the Cartridges amongst other projects] pulling through. ... Goodbye my own wife, Your Adrian

Hopton St Margaret, Great Yarmouth   4th April
[with Aunt Maggie Orde]

My Adrian, ... I heard a piece of news at the dance here last night—Charlie told me & we simply *died* with laughter. You remember I told you another event was expected at Thurloe Square next *June*. Well, the unfortunate Geoffrey Buxton invited Rosy & Johnny for *one* night to Sunny Hill for Easter Monday—and she vaguely presented Johnny with *another pair of twins* in the night!!!!!! Imagine what a bore for the Buxtons. The Birkbecks have only been married 4 years and a half—and this makes six children!! Too dreadful isn't it?[124] ... We did not appear till 12 this morning to a late breakfast. I think we beat the record. ...

Daisy has been telling me about a Miss Darroch who is working at Mrs Jopling's studio & who is engaged to be married to the youngest Coleridge son (I mean the Judge's). She is working very hard as they are to marry on *£400 a year*, and she is going to earn lots of money to help besides, just like I want to do. Daisy said they seemed awfully happy & did not think it at all a bad look out. He makes pocket money too—by writing songs for the banjo. ... Ever your own true *Laure*

Hunstanton   Sunday, 8th April

My dearest, ... I had a talk with Charlie about possible marriage settlements. He thinks £6000 very good indeed if you could manage this—& he thought it would be a mistake to engage to insure your life as well for any *given sum*. I told him I thought it likely that nothing could be arranged before our marriage if we marry this summer (I thought it better to prepare Charlie for the worst!). Of course he thought it a pity but not an insupportable bar to our marriage this year—as he had *complete & entire confidence* in *your* doing what was right—and making what settlement you could at the first possible opportunity. This shows me that Charlie knows & appreciates you darling—but whether Uncle Sommy (as my Guardian) would think the same I do not know. ...

I had a restful evening reading a sort of essay on the life of Sir Henry Raeburn lent me from Hopton. Very interesting, he was knighted by George the fourth at Hopetoun House, and it mentions that he painted 2 portraits of Sir Walter Scott, one of which I suppose is actually one of your pictures. ... I expect you will be very busy now till your Hospital Dinner is over on the 25th. ... Adieu, *toujours ta Laure*

GREAT ORMOND STREET HOSPITAL, BLOOMSBURY 13TH APRIL

My Dearest *Laure*, … Secretly I am very pleased that David Hope won't hear of the good family Pictures being sold but we should have to go to the Courts for permission to sell any of the others & then the money would have to be invested & the Col. would get the interest all his life. This would hardly help us much. As to the Col. giving up those Pictures which he has really stolen I doubt his doing so until David goes after him in a Police Court. It is a great anxiety to me, the more so as I feel David to be both weak & timid. …

My night at the Owl club with Jo was rather fun but left traces the next morning as we sat up late & certainly smoked too much as is the way at a 'Cock' party. I send you the programme of the Owl Club which has just been started behind what used to be the York. Oscar Wilde is on the Com.ttee & some of the Rooms are too beautifully done up. His taste when he has been consulted is excellent. We had all sorts of songs & people. A Conjuror who was very good, & Harry Conway, etc. A very Bohemian crew but vastly amusing after supper. Wallscourt was there & sat in my pocket most of the evening.

Last night Jo & I dined at the famous Ship & Turtle in the City & went on to Musk Lane to see some private theatricals where we found Lady Wally & the too faithful George Macdonald, Lady Harrington & the Lincoln Stanhopes [Midget Wallscourt's mother, brother & sister-in-law] & such a lot of people we knew. Lady Wally was looking ill & when I gave her my arm down stairs she trembled all over so that I was afraid she would tumble down. She said she felt ill & then told me she was going on to a Ball which seemed absurd. … Goodnight my own sweet *Laure*, Your Adrian

WHITE'S, ST JAMES' SUNDAY, 15TH APRIL

Darling, Last night I had a most refreshing Turkish Bath & found young Gibbs there. He was one of J.M.S's Directors & told me that their real reason for getting rid of him was the number of J.M.S's creditors who beset the office. But he told me that I should have no chance of getting the Managership at the L.A. Assurance as they are determined to have only a Clerk at the Branch. … This morning was so fine that I went & sat in the Park. It was crammed with all sorts, Bean St Aubyn I saw, Robert [Cunninghame Graham] turned up & we walked up & down to the evident horror of those who recognized him. He is so anxious to meet you. Dear old Robin. I am so fond of him, with all his eccentricities. … Sweetheart goodnight, it is getting late—Your Adrian

HUNSTANTON   SUNDAY, 15TH APRIL

My Adrian darling, ... Your 'Owley' Programme was good but I did not think much of the Prologue, the puns were rather feeble. They seem rather proud of their idea of turning night into day—rather dissipated old birds & awfully pleased with themselves because of it! Shall you often join their Tu-Whit Tu-Whoos—when we are married darling? Well if you do I shall not sit up for you—in our little home, wherever it is. ... I saw in the papers that the Goldsmids were back. I suppose the Friday parties will soon begin again & you will be constant to them—as of yore—so like last year—& the year before—and the year before————.

I wish I were in town & we were strolling in Kensington Gardens having the nice quiet talk we both long for. ... Ever your own true love, *Laure*

16TH APRIL

Darling Adrian, We hear today of an arrival at Caynham [Court]—Mabel [Uncle Sommy's daughter, married to Sir William Curtis] of a daughter born on the anniversary of their wedding day. ... What a lot of people you saw on Sunday dearest, you are so gay! like a flutterby—sipping honey, here there & everywhere. Now it is V.G.—now fat Augusta Webbe, now Mrs Cooper etc. etc. while I am tearing my *brown* hair with jealousy & despair, alone by the sad sea waves! ... Pray don't have *too* many Turkish Baths—for I read yesterday in your favourite paper *The Lady* they were very thinning—& I should have to look for you with a magnifying glass next time we meet. ... Ever your *Laure*

20TH APRIL

Darling Adrian, ... Tom's things (from his military posting) suddenly appeared—on an immense luggage van piled sky high—14 packages, some perfectly immense—& packing cases far too big to bring into the house. Ernest, Helen & I unpacked a lot of them—never looked over or thrown away. Some of the cases had been in a damp cellar for 4 years, so many pictures & books were falling to pieces. Several of the former were rather queer, we were filled with laughter at Tanner's righteous horrors at the sight of the very much undraped ladies—which we burnt for they were not even pretty. Ernest is very pleased at getting appointed to the *Sultan*. *She* (how very odd!) forms part of the Channel Squadron. He is not to have his four months Gunnery Course at Portsmouth on the *Excellent* after all.

There is a bad account of Mabel Curtis today—who has suddenly become very ill indeed. Uncle Sommy was telegraphed for—Aunt Kitty is still there. … It would be *too* sad if she were to die—when she is so happy. … Always your *Laure*

White's, St James' 24th April

My own Dearest, Even now I have not got all the Speakers necessary for tomorrow's Dinner & I am in despair. As to money I have done pretty well for I have got £2600. Tonight I am rather happy as I have got a cheque for £25 the result of a speculation into which I put J.G. [Julian Goldsmid] who has made a large sum. … Lucas came back on Monday in such a bad temper. He left me really boiling with rage. Not one word of thanks, nothing but abuse showered on my head & we had such a real row in Com.ttee. It leaves one so sore all over to be at the mercy of such a man. Anything at such times seems better than enduring this degradation. Tonight I have been at the House of Commons trying to get someone to speak but it was no good. Now I have written to beg Oscar Wilde to speak once more. I am quite desperate. Dear old Jo is coming tomorrow & so is J.M.S. which is good of them. I do hope you have better news of Mabel … . Your Adrian

Hunstanton 26th April

My darling Adrian, We are all in such sorrow today. The news came of poor little Mabel's death. … It is dreadful to think of poor Willie—who adored her so—and even would not believe she was in any danger last week. Poor Limpet is heartbroken—she was always Limpet's dearest friend. I hope her little child will live. … Uncle Sommy & all of them will feel it most bitterly. … Ever your *Laure*

Great Ormond Street Hospital, Bloomsbury 27th April

My Darling, What very sad news. I am really so sorry for Curtis. It must be such an awful break up of his life poor fellow. It is sad for you all … and Helen must be very miserable though I always think that for the girl herself it must be the happiest as nothing can mar the one year of wedded happiness. Death must have a bitter sweet flavour about it under such circumstances. Well she is probably happy now if she can still see him as I believe the dead can & do. … Your Adrian

White's, St James'   Sunday, 29th April

My own dearest Love, ... Poor Mabel's death is so very sad yet I cannot help envying her, for she had the cream of life & was taken away before it had time to turn sour. ... At 7. this afternoon I attended the new Matron's first Chapel service. It was a pleasant rest & I did so pray for a little faith & hope. To have so strongly the aching longing for the comfort of religious belief & to have no faith is a trial very hard to bear. One cannot delude oneself into an abiding hope if all within is barren. Poor Mabel, she knows now what does exist beyond that so impenetrable veil between the living and the——? At dinner at Mrs Napier's last night I found my Mother & Jessie. My Mother was a bit more cheerful & certainly there seems a vast improvement in Jessie which is a comfort. ...

Sweetheart I think my love for you has eaten up all & that I really care for nothing but you. Everything says—*Laure, Laure, Laure*—to me for days before we meet & when I leave you I am only the shadow, the real I has tarried behind. My dearest Love, goodnight, Your Adrian

Hunstanton   30th April

My own darling Adrian, I am thinking so much of them all at Caynham & Runcton this afternoon. The funeral of someone beloved must be such a deep & bitter agony to live through. It would be *despair* if one had not a strong hope & belief in a life of happiness & peace beyond the grave, and in God's love and mercy to us poor mortals.

Darling Adrian I think in many ways I—as your chosen wife will bring you happiness—but in some ways you will find me wanting. I have not that firm strength & religious belief founded on a thorough knowledge of theology & arguments, that would perhaps have helped you, and that many good clever women might have. I believe in God—in Christ and in a heaven for us, through God's mercy—if we try to do right according to our lights & trust in God & do not fall into the fatal sin of indifference about God & religion—but I am afraid I have this faith more as a child might because I was brought up in it & because I *feel* it is true, more than as the result of deep thought, & could bring no recognized arguments to support me—only what I might find in my heart. Prayer alone I should think would bring you peace & comfort darling, and I do trust we shall not try & live without any thought of God—& of the future in our lives—that when the terrible parting comes to us that has come to Willie & Mabs so soon—we may have a strong abiding faith that we shall meet again when 'God shall wipe away all tears from our eyes—and there shall be no more death neither sorrow nor crying, neither shall there be any more pain for the former things are passed away.'

Goodbye darling—only till our happy meeting on Saturday, ever your *Laure*

---

124 *4th Apr* Laura did not then know that Johnny and Rosy Birkbeck's twins, born while staying with the Geoffrey Buxtons, lived only for a short time. Their first pair of twins in 1885 were stillborn, then they had a son and a daughter, born respectively in 1886 and 1887.

MAY 1888

The affairs of the hospital absorbed all Adrian's time and much to Laura's disgust he was now having to take on the extra burden of paying the weekly wages of all the porters, etc. on a Saturday which meant he would not arrive for their longed-for weekend with the Cresswells until late on the Saturday afternoon and would still have to leave on the Monday morning.

Hunstanton   3rd May

Darling Adrian, … You seem to have become a perfect *slave* to that hateful Hospital, working morning, noon, & night. … You never answer *anything* I say in my letters—or tell me of yourself, or the things I really want to know about. … Everything seems to fade away in disappointment, even Jem's business—that promised so well at Xmas—& was to do so much for us. What has become of it all! I often feel in despair for nothing *ever* seems to be carried through or finished. I don't believe even that wretched Picture affair is done with yet. … I don't think we have ever been so parted as this year—and there seems not the slightest whisper of our marriage this summer. Even Ernest has ceased to mention the subject. …

For God's sake don't write & say you have a bad cold and cannot come— I think to sit over the boudoir fire at the Cresswells & snuffle, with me to talk & even to laugh with all Sunday would be very good for it. Goodbye dearest, I wish you would try & forget the Hospital sometimes and think of me instead when you are writing. Ever your weary loving *Laure*

White's, St James'   8th May

My own Darling, Since I left your Sweet self I have been tearing about on Cartridge & other business. … Jo is here and his flow of talk continues unabated & makes it difficult to write. He has three brand new quarrels on, which he is graphically describing. Last night I dined with poor Freddy Bateman & Jo. F.B. is a pitiable sight, dying fast of consumption & still talking of what he means to do when he gets better. His brother Lee seems to have been behaving abominably to him. Lee has entirely got the poor old father under his thumb & is making things very unpleasant for his brother. Goodnight, Your Adrian

Great Ormond Street Hospital, Bloomsbury   9th May

My own dearest Love, … I left here at 5. sharp & walked down to see the Simeons in their tiny house in Elisabeth St. It is a corner over a shop which has one or two bits of furniture in the window. You go straight upstairs to a room at the back, the 'Studio' which is their drawing-room, a few more steps land you at 2 little rooms, one the Eating-room & the other a snuggery for smoking. Upstairs again these 2 little rooms become their bed & dressing-room, and higher up their Nursery & Maids room. They have 2 maids & a Nurse as she has had a baby which they are very proud of. I could not help wondering as I looked at her where the baby had got its nourishment from for she belongs to the strictly skinny order of beauty. The little house was a woeful delusion. I don't think you could endure it. Her great idea is that we ought to marry first & look for what would suit us from the safe position of furnished Apartments. They spent a lot on the drains [an essential detail in those days] but there is no possible Bathroom. They rent the house from the Shop at £120 which includes all taxes. This is cheap enough … but there is a dingy squalor about the whole place which would give you a fit of the blues in a day. …

I had to come back here to work and I am writing while Miss Hicks (the new Matron) is getting the books ready. Then we shall tackle the House Keeping. Fancy us sitting in judgement over the Butcher & Greengrocer. One thing I fear will not weigh with us & that is the piety of our tradesmen. Miss Wood always laid great stress on the true christianity of the butcher. … I cannot make out whether I have had any dinner tonight or whether I walked back from the Simeons so I think I will have a cup of Coffee & a cigarette on the chance. … This *is* a long dull yarn *ma Laure*—goodnight dear Heart, Your Adrian

WHITE'S, ST JAMES'   11TH MAY

My own Darling, I am in the thick of the negotiations about the Cartridges which I hope to finish next week. This will provide me with the money & I can then write & ask you to order your wedding gown for August. I am going to deal direct with the Company. One of the Directors has been here to see me today. They offer £6000, I ask £10,000 but will end by taking £8000. … It is so brave of you not to mind the idea of lodgings. The idea of being really in a position to face Matrimony in August quite drives me wild with delight. … Goodbye, Your Adrian

12TH MAY

My dearest, Such a surprise today. Jem has come back. I rushed down to find him in the City. He was in a very queer mood but finally we made it up & he approved of all I had done. I should like to have finished the affair of the

Cartridges alone. He is unfitted for the part I am playing & I fear may wreck my game. However he seems inclined to leave me alone to Act. ... Dear Heart, where can we get officially made one. C. [Charlie Orde] never said one word about Hopton when I said that Runcton was now out of the question. [Uncle Sommy & Aunt Kitty were going abroad for several months to get over their daughter Mabel's death.] We shall end by going to the Registrar at Lynn I think. Goodbye, Your Adrian

GREAT ORMOND STREET HOSPITAL, BLOOMSBURY   16TH MAY

My Sweet, Jem went to see the Directors yesterday instead of me. He reports well & they are to make a firm offer at once for our rights. Jem & Elsie & I dined together at the Café Royal last night. He went off to his Club & she took me to hers where we sat talking till 12. Her great idea seems to be that you should come up to stop with them at a hotel, be married from there & go down for our Honeymoon to the Boat (the *Crocodile*, now moored at Pangbourne) while they are in Scotland. Does this smile to you my own? ... Jem is rather furious about the office being kept on & I cannot make him see that it was necessary. It is a pity. ... Your Adrian

HUNSTANTON   17TH MAY

My Adrian darling, ... It must be rather nice having Jem & E. home again, though a bore to have to give up the helm to Jem. I felt he would not be able to keep out of the affair. ... It is nice of them to want to marry us off—& if the Hopton idea falls through we may be very glad of this alternative. I think the house boat—in lovely weather—would be rather perfect for a short time. Well, we will talk it over when we meet at Hopton on Whit Saturday. Mind you get first to our trysting place. Ever your own *Laure*

GREAT ORMOND STREET HOSPITAL, BLOOMSBURY   24TH MAY

My dearest *Laure*, ... Jem has been at once kind & so tiresome over this business. They insisted on me going down with them to the *Crocodile* at Pangbourne so off I went though not a bit prepared for it. ... Jem & E. were both so kind to me & so cross to each other. It was quite saddening. Really I fear that were she mine with all her money I should beat her. They tell me in their vague way that they will leave the Boat before the 1st August & then add that we could not get down there before the 15th which is too absurd. ... Jem has agreed to give me £500 if the Cartridges pull through & this may happen any moment now. The day I get the money we will settle the date for our wedding. [Adrian had hoped at one time to make £1000 out of the deal.] He says we ought to be married in London as being so much cheaper but surely a very quiet wedding at Hopton would not be costly. ... I long for the time when you & I would occupy the Stern Cabin. Goodbye, Your Adrian

26TH MAY

My own dear Love, ... My Aunts intend to give up Cambridge & go abroad to Italy & Laura has made up her mind to chuck her school & go with them. I am proposing that they should lend me their Goods, Chattels etc. & I will take a flat at once to store them, we to use them. What say you? Shall we take the faithful Jeannie too [their Swiss cook]? Goodbye, Your Adrian

GREAT ORMOND STREET HOSPITAL, BLOOMSBURY   28TH MAY

My sweet *Laure*, ... Yesterday I lunched with the Webbes where I found only the girls as their father & mother were gone to water cure themselves at Malvern. Augusta told me such a funny little story of her adventures with a Latch Key given to her as she was going to a Ball. For fear of losing the Key she dropped it down the valley of her figure. When she got home at 2 in the morning and the footman asked for the Key, though she could feel it where it was she could not reach it up so she had to try the footman's plan of jumping up & down on the door step. This had no effect so finally they had to wake up the house. She made me promise not to tell any one but of course you are my other self. ...

I have still got such a horrid cold which makes me so stupid & dull. I ought to go to Lady North's Ball tonight as there will be many people one should see there. Every night this week I have a Ball to which I am more or less bound to go for a short time so I shall order the funeral for Monday I think. ... My sister has written to me: 'My heart is nearly broken saying goodbye to the school life I loved, & the independence & all that was so pleasant here.' ... Somehow or another our wedding is bound to take place on the 2nd of August. I will not think of any other possibility. Can you get asked to Abbey Lodge for one night—so that I may take you straight to see the few suitable places [to rent] I have discovered. Your Adrian

THICKTHORN, NR NORWICH   29TH MAY
[WITH UNCLE HAY & AUNT MINNIE GURNEY]

My own darling, ... I had Elsie's note about our wedding and proposing lending us the boat. I vote we accept the boat without mentioning going abroad *yet* at all events as it *must* depend on £.s.d. but oh I do so long for it, the fun and the thorough change with you dearest. We could leave it vague how long we should remain on the boat. ... Tom has got off going to Gibraltar after all.

I have told my old friend here, Apie [Helen Gurney of Keswick] that we shall probably marry this summer—& as far a I can see everyone thinks us perfectly right to cut the knot in this way—not that it would make any real difference if they did not think so here, only you know I like to feel this. You should have heard Doonie [Julian Orde] on Sunday night at Hopton on the subject of marriage. As usual everyone at Hopton was sleeping quite early—& Doonie who was very wide awake & I—talked in the open doorway of my bed room for nearly 2 hours. He said it was impossible to realize beforehand the happiness of being married to the one you loved. There was nothing in the world like it— & it was worth any amount of so called sacrifice. He said: 'If I had only £200 or even £100 a year, and Alice was willing I would marry tomorrow—knowing as I do the joy of always being together.' They seem to have had from £500 to £600 out in America to live on, but rather fluctuating. He really is charming—& reminds of Ernest—he has much the same sort of cheery presence & kindliness—and is far more of a man than when he went out 3 years ago. He has all Charlie's sympatheticness with far more *savoir faire* & *grit* to use a yankee expression. I am sure you would have taken a great fancy to him. ... He told me it was too dreadful to be parted from his wife & babies & he did not think he could stand it for a whole week while they were visiting her family. He said it was surprising how far money would go for two people if managed together. At dinner on Sunday Doonie held forth tremendously about American politics and laws. They seem a good deal more corrupt even than we are at home. ...

I long to come up & help to decide about flats, even if I come up for the day which would give me from 1. to 5. in town. ... Aunt Maggie said all should be done for our marriage just as I wanted & whenever I wished. The clouds seem to have passed away. No time for more, ever your *Laure*

HUNSTANTON   31ST MAY

Darling Adrian, ... It is curious how Laura clings to that school life of hard monotonous work. To me, a winter in Italy seems *Paradise* compared to that Cambridge life. I am longing to hear more about that wonderful abode in High St Kensington [the upper part of a house for £70 a year]. We might live there as cheaply as in lodgings. Amy has found some wonderful rooms kept by a very nice woman who is ex-housekeeper to the Sam Hoares, a very good cook (French) & cleanliness, honesty & respectability in one, but they are a long way from most places though not bad for Gt O. St. by underground only 5 stations—No 7 Hereford Road, Westbourne Grove, close to Whiteleys. She has a set of rooms to let after July—drawing-room, dining-room, two good bedrooms upstairs, & a maids room on ground floor. They are small, but airy and light. In the same house lodges an ex-lady's maid of the Hoares who has just set up as a dressmaker. This would be rather convenient as she could *tweak* up my old frocks. Amy saw the housekeeper about terms. She said she could *do* for us entirely, *board and lodging* and *everything* for £5.5 [shillings] a week. ...

Yesterday I had some time in Lynn & went to see Uncle Sommy. I told him if you got a certain sum of money we meant to marry this summer. He was very kind but *so* grave about it. He said 'I do not think it difficult for you to live on £450 a year—(he would not count my earnings at all)—I think it simply impossible.' He advised our waiting till you had £600 a year. It is a good thing others should not know exactly what we have but of course Uncle Sommy knows exactly how we stand. He said he would not oppose—or forbid our marriage—but told me simply that he would never allow any of his own daughters to marry on such a small income and so he felt the same about me. I did not argue the point—I said very little, but I felt very cast down and sad. ... I think he saw that we had made up our minds and he said he would certainly write to your father & if possible get him to arrange something when he heard from you asking him to do so. So you see his opposition is entirely passive— and takes more the form of a warning as to our imprudence & a shifting of all responsibility on to our two selves—and when I am with you darling I feel well able to bear my share of it. ... Goodbye Sweetheart, ever your *Laure*

JUNE 1888

For most of this month Adrian was in a frenzy of competing for the job of Secretary to the Reform Club, and pursuing the elusive cartridge deal without his profit from which he and Laura would be unable to marry on their chosen date, 2nd August. Besides these aims he had to find somewhere for them to set up house, however temporary the accommodation, without committing himself financially until the last moment, added to which Laura could not find anyone to stay with for a night or two in London so that she could look at such flats as he had found.

White's, St James'   Sunday Night, 3rd June

My Dearest, I heard yesterday that the Secretaryship of the Reform Club worth £500 a year was vacant so I rushed off to lunch with the Goldsmids that I might get his opinion & support (he was for 9 years on the Com.ttee himself). … Some little Bird who told you about seeing me at the Coopers' Ball must have been Laura Gurney I fancy. She made herself so very ridiculous, looking round & saying that none of her Set were there & that she could not think who the people were. I introduced several partners to her but she was so patronizing that I did not dance more than one with her myself. I danced a good deal with May Parnell who leant back so on my arm that it has been stiff ever since. She is no light weight to pull round when she begins dancing badly. My Balls have got me some money & visitors for my Hospital which is one good result at any rate. … Your Adrian

6th June

My Dearest, … Today I went to the Reform & saw the Vice Chairman & some of the Com.ttee. It is only £400 to begin with but they would raise it to £500 at the end of the first year if I was satisfactory. Then Jo & I went to the 'Daneries' [Anglo-Danish Exhibition] when after the usual wait Amy & Vi arrived from Abbey Lodge. We tobogganed & switchbacked after seeing the *Tableaux*. Again & again I have heard the report about Tom succeeding 'Babbles' [Alwyn H.F. Greville, the Equerry to Prince Eddy][125] & they say that is the reason why he did not go to Gibraltar. Goodnight, Your Adrian

Hunstanton   7th June

Darling Adrian, I have had such a dose of the country. I never remember before feeling it all so utterly dull but now the monotony of it all seems to get on my nerves. Helen is so quiet to live with, & always seems in a sort of dream. She is never very gay & now poor child she is still grieving so for her friend Mabs. Still all day yesterday I worked—so I am quite certain I have 2 selves, one drawing away & quite keen about the design, the other self fretting & sad—& looking out all the time for a letter which never came. My 'Mermaidens' go at least to the publishers today. ... Dearest there are only 3 weeks more in which to decide if our marriage can be this summer or not, for we must know by the beginning of July—or there would not be time to have the *banns* asked, & £20 would be wasted on a licence. Besides I couldn't have time to get any frocks. ... Ever your tried *Laure*

SUNDAY, 10TH JUNE

My own dearest Adrian, ... It is curious about Tom and 'Babbles'. If true he has never told us anything about it. It would be a good thing for him I suppose, and yet it does not seem likely because he has never been the least in the Marlborough House set—nor has the Prince taken him up at all that I know of, though we know he is great pals with the Queen!

Mr Okeden (Griffiths & Farran) wrote to me by return of post. He said he was *so* pleased with my illustrations & he thought I must really have been a mermaid myself before—or at the time of the flood! He makes no criticisms at all, and I am to have 25 guineas instead of pounds (for the 38 drawings) because I did a little mermaid swimming along for the cover of the book. ... Ever your own *Laure*

SUNDAY, 17TH JUNE

My darling Adrian, ... I think I could work up Aunt Bache to take me up to Storeys Hotel—*The Inn*—with her for a night or two. This happy thought occurred to me in church this morning. I know she is always so glad of an excuse to dash up to London. ... How *blessed* for the poor Emperor [Frederick III of Germany, married to the Princess Royal, Queen Victoria's eldest daughter] to be at rest at last after his long martyrdom. Do you remember how splendid he looked at the Jubilee Procession last year? It is wonderful & so touching to read of his goodness & heroism to the last. I see that a general mourning is ordered for 14 days for the Emperor. I am glad there should be this to show the great sympathy everyone in England feels for the German Royal family. Ever your *Laure*

WHITE'S, ST JAMES'   19TH JUNE

My Darling, When I got to the Reform I found 4 other Candidates, Jo among them. After a long wait during which poor Jo got so painfully nervous that I could hear him snort as he breathed, I was taken in to see the Sub-Com.ttee who were most civil & very nice. I told them I was engaged to be married & asked if it was necessary to live in the club though I offered to keep my bedroom there & come & occupy it now & then. This they said was quite sufficient though they acknowledged that they would prefer a resident Secretary —I think this settles my chance. I feel sure that my want of experience of Club management will prevent my getting it. Well, if they only take Jo I shall be happy. Lucas was most civil & gave me a flourishing letter [testimonial] this morning. Old Aberdare was very the reverse but finally gave me a very shabby note. ... I do not now think I have much chance though the old boys I saw were very jolly & I found myself telling them stories & making them laugh instead of answering long questions about my fitness.

I wrote & offered £80 for No 78 Brompton Rd & got an answer saying that they would take £100. 3 months ago they were asking £115. The upper part consists of a little Hall. Downstairs there is a good Kitchen & a nice light room next to it looking on the back which is a paved yard. Upstairs (not a bad stair-case) there is a Drawing-Room to the front, a small Dining-Room & a queer long room that would do for your Studio. Here is the plan [rough sketch alongside]. Up again the bedroom is to the front with Bathroom over the queer room & Dressing-Room over the Dining-Room. On the top floor there are four rooms. But of course the look out is on a timber yard & the Brompton Rd is noisy. The front door too is round the corner & looks mean. Still it is wonderfully cheap & there are speaking tubes all over the house. The Bathroom is really wonderfully nice & would charm you. But the whole house is dirty & very ugly. What decoration there is is hideous beyond words. ... Your Adrian

On this letter Laura had written years later: 'It was our first home, we lived there nearly 4 years & were very happy there.'

HUNSTANTON   22ND JUNE

My darling Adrian, ... I have just been reading in the *Globe* about the fiasco of the late Secretary of the Reform who seems to have been let off easily poor wretch with 6 months in prison. By the by I see he was a married man—which has perhaps prejudiced the Committee! I am simply longing for you to have the Secretaryship. We seem to have been living in constant anxiety lately about something or another—for ever so long. ... Somehow I cannot help feeling if you had secured the little Brompton Road house & we have Aunt Annie's furniture we should soon find ourselves living there. Would the landlord do the repairs to the house & clean it now—or should we have to? If the latter do look over it very carefully. Is the Kitchen range up to the mark? Are you learned in such matters—for I am afraid I am not. ... Ever your own *Laure*

SCULTHORPE RECTORY, NR FAKENHAM   26TH JUNE
[WITH UNCLE HERB & AUNT BACHE JONES]

My own darling Adrian, Aunt Bache & Uncle Herb are so kind & delightful about everything, taking the keenest interest in our marriage. She only says occasionally, 'You know my girly you will have to be *very* economical'! ... That dreadful old fossil Marsh dined here last night. [Laura had earlier described him in her Journal as: 'a most unattractive old thing—tra la, with a caricature of a face'.] Helen & I were so amused at his lover like devotion to Aunt Bache. He said at dinner in fervid tones—gazing at her with his ancient ferret like eyes—'Oh Mrs Jones—*how* I should like to go to Palestine with you!'

We nearly died of if, imagining them eloping to the Holy Land together. Yesterday she wore a simple white dress—white from head to foot—it was rather wonderful. ... Your ever true *Laure*

GREAT ORMOND STREET HOSPITAL, BLOOMSBURY   27TH JUNE

My Dearest, I have just got a letter from the Reform to tell me that I am not elected. So that is over. ... But I shall keep thinking of August & its possibilities. ... Your Adrian

29TH JUNE

Dearest *Laure*, The Cartridge affair is settled. Jem goes to sign this afternoon when he gets a cheque for £1000 down & afterwards £3000 in shares. This is less than we had hoped. Had he got £6000 I was to have £500. On the same scale I can only hope for £380. However this is better than nothing. ... Will you read the enclosed letter from Uncle Sommy and a copy of my answer. Goodnight my own dear Love, Your Adrian

Sommy Gurney had written a formal letter to Colonel Hope urging him to make a settlement on Laura and also persuaded his co-guardian and brother-in-law, the Rev Herb Jones, to go to London in the hope of arranging an interview with the colonel himself. Uncle Sommy's formal letter to Adrian with his wishes for their happiness also set out his objections to the imprudent step of marrying on so limited an income: 'particularly as £300 of that income is precarious—and without a Settlement. ... This is my opinion, which perhaps I have no right to give, as you are both quite old enough to judge for yourselves ...'. Adrian's personal income amounted to £150 a year. To this letter he replied:

> '... I quite admit that to marry on £300 a year is imprudent still I do not think my income more precarious than that of a professional man while I have strong hopes of getting something better. I hope to start free from debt & with all furniture etc. The cost of living in London is chiefly what you choose to make it. ... We both feel the constant separation so very much that we are prepared to give up a good deal in order to be at last together after our 4 years of waiting. ...'.

WHITE'S, ST JAMES'   30TH JUNE

My own sweet Love, Yesterday my sister & I dined at the Guthries & went on to 'the Italianeries' where I bought a very pretty Iron hanging Candle Lamp which I know you will like. This morning Laura & I lunched at the Grosvenor. To us entered dear old Roberto & we had a merry time together going off to see Milly Graham's[126] picture at the New Gallery which is as lovely as the picture is hideous. I never thought [George] Richmond could produce such a daub. We agreed that the Sitter must be a soulless Doll which she is I believe. There is the fatal stamp of Marlborough House about her face & figure. ... I have written to Jem saying that he is the only thing now stopping the way to our marriage. ... Your Adrian

---

125 *6th June* Alwyn Henry Fulke 'Babbles' Greville, second son of the 4th Earl of Warwick, was equerry-in-waiting to Prince Eddy, Duke of Clarence (1884/88), and extra equerry to the Prince of Wales (1885/1901) and continued so after his accession (1901/10).

126 *30th June* Mildred 'Milly' Emily Barbara Bagot, daughter of the Rev C W Bagot, Vicar of Sandringham, married (1882) Commander Charles Cunninghame Graham RN, Don Roberto's younger brother. She was a close friend of the Prince of Wales and his circle. Her husband became, successively, groom-in-waiting to King Edward and to King George (1908-17).

JULY 1888

Hunstanton   Sunday, 1st July

Darling Adrian, … When I got home from Scully, Tanner told me with many regrets that her sisters have refused to give up their shop & farm…so we must now look out for some other treasures. … I was so glad you sent me those letters. Of course Uncle Sommy has a right to his opinion—& I think middle aged people even the nicest of them are always rather *sordid* (about money). You wrote a very good letter. I showed them both to Uncle Herb—I hope you don't mind—he liked your letter so much. I am glad you stuck up for your income—it is really absurd to call it *precarious* any more than other people's. … Ever your faraway lonely *Petite Laure*

Great Ormond Street Hospital, Bloomsbury   2nd July

My dearest, To both Jem & Elsie I have written explaining that all I want now is Cash for as Jem will get so much less he will only hand me over Shares which I shall want to sell or raise money upon. Tomorrow I shall try and settle about the house in Brompton Road. From Uncle Sommy I hear that my father has written first an evasive reply in which he burst into his affairs about Guns. … It is not for want of love that I feel I cannot come to you unless everything is fixed but from the very excess of love which so totally upsets me when I come away, & to be married in August will I foresee require all our determination & strength. Your Adrian

Hunstanton   3rd July

Darling Adrian, … I think you were not quite fair about the Col's letter. Of course he talks about his Guns, the breath of nostrils, because he really is a monomaniac on the subject—& I don't suppose he could write to his tailor or candlestick maker without mentioning them. All he does is to ask for an interview, and honestly I was relieved to hear he had written by return & civilly. I told Uncle Sommy how much I wished he could manage an interview—he said he would probably be in town next week and he has written again very strongly to your father so something may come of it. Meanwhile I was very glad to hear he had evolved an idea by which you might make a kind of Settlement which would satisfy my relations—and at the same time *not* depend on the Col's consent & signature. I agree with Uncle S. your mother would never give her consent to your being cut out of your father's will— even if he had such an evil design. …

It was such a wild night with torrents of rain. I wondered if the 2nd of

August would be as bad & what it would be like for instance on the Thames——but I suppose all would be snug in the Cabin. ... I am sorry to hear this complication about the Cartridge affair—I think it rather horrid of Jem who has every mortal thing he wants and knows how very very important this £.s.d. is to you. ... Dearest I want you to tell me by return of post if possible really & truly if it is safe for me to write and tell some of my friends that our marriage is on the 2nd of August. I want to write to Hopton too definitely, & it has been proposed that *you* should make yourself of the Parish of Hopton which would solve all difficulties. I could only do so by staying with the Ordes for 3 weeks. Uncle Sommy says all *you* would have to do would be to take a lodging in Hopton, a room in a cottage at a shilling a week would do, & place some belonging of yours there, as a portmanteau, & this would be sufficient. Then my banns would be asked here & yours at Hopton. What do you think of this scheme? Ever your *Laure*

An unexpected two weeks' stay was offered to Laura, first a few days with the Jem Hopes—and Adrian—on the *Crocodile* at Henley, then in London with various friends, including a few days with Amy and their maid, Tanner, as guests of Aunt Bache at Storeys Hotel, and ending up with Rosy Birkbeck in Thurloe Square. Despite five lots of packing and unpacking, this break did much to solve the communication difficulties over the Brompton Road house and its furnishings, the ordering of Laura's trousseau, and all the myriad other wedding details.

At Storeys Hotel, Dover St [with Aunt Bache Jones]

14th July... Chose my boxes at the Stores, two nice new trunks. ... After lunch flew off to the Silver Fête at the Anglo-Danish exhib—Adrian & I had a Jubilee cab, like a mad brougham in which we were the cynosure of all eyes—rather a bore. Dined at the 'Daneries' & Adrian & I spent a blissful evening, sitting on the terrace listening to the lovely band—& murmuring together till past 11. The fireworks & lamps were lovely. It reminded us of another fête in those same gardens just 4 years ago.

At 30 Thurloe Square, South Kensington [with Rosy Birkbeck]

18th July Amy & Helen went off at 8. to the Paddington Baths to see the St Aubyns swim— & to breakfast with them afterwards. I ordered a mackintosh ... then on to Osborne, the dressmaker, where I fitted on 5 frocks (£25 on account)—one my wedding gown—most lovely. She makes a neat glove fitting frock for about £4.10 [shillings].

HUNSTANTON   21ST JULY

Darling Adrian, I am going to write you a very practical letter. I enclose a list of the furniture I possess, besides this we have your two rooms full from Great Ormond Street. Then I have Aunt Annie's letter making us a present of their spare-room furniture and kitchen things—and her proposed loan of all the marqueterie. I think the only things left to get are—*le grand lit* [the master bed] & a wardrobe & dressing table for my room, & things for the servants' rooms. Here is [their future housekeeper] Mrs Panton's list of *their* requirements for each room: Japanned bedstead, palliasse, mattress, bolster & pillow, dressing table, toilet glass & ware, chair & washing stand, dhurries for bedside—all from Maples—at not more than £4.5 [shillings]. You have in any case to buy stair carpets & felt for the rooms, & all the carpets and curtains. ... The less furniture I have in my studio the better for my work. ... If we want a *sofa* & are not given one I am sure we can rig up something, a frame work & some soft cushions. ...

I found the whole place here flooded with presents—and yet another pair of silver candlesticks from yet another Dowager Countess, old Lady Harrington (Midget's mother), rather sweet of her. I was just going to write & thank the *other* one when I had another look at the card—rather lucky! ... Ever your own *Laure*

List of my things – July, 1888 L.T.

6 dining room chairs
1 large arm chair
1 small arm chair
1 round dining room table
1 large table for studio or
    housekeeper's room
1 small gilt table
1 tea table
1 Japanese writing table
2 corner cupboards
1 small oak cabinet
1 Japanese cabinet
1 large Japanese screen
1 fire screen glass & white enamel
1 glass cupboard for books or
    china

1 cream jug & sugar basin
tea set – breakfast set – coffee set
    – & finger glasses
Pictures, brackets, & ever so many
    odds & ends
4 or 5 looking glasses for drawing
    room, & 4 clocks

Plate

4 pair silver candlesticks
4 salt cellars
2 pair sugar tongs
1 sugar sifter spoon
6 apostle tea spoons
1 tea caddy

WHITE'S, ST JAMES'   21ST JULY

My own Darling Love, Jem & Elsie came back today & wired for me urgently. I went there when they gave me from her father Sir Peter £100 and from his son James another £100. Really I feel off my head as this removes all the terrible burden of anxiety. I have tried to thank them but am quite overcome with their kindness towards me. … Your Adrian

P.S. How gladly I shall sleep tonight. What a good old man he is.

HUNSTANTON   SUNDAY, 22ND JULY

Darling Adrian, How *very* kind and generous of old Sir Peter and Mr Coats. I cannot tell you how thankful I am that it frees your mind from anxiety. I knew you had many cares just now darling—by your restless nights you told me of. Now we may believe in the great happiness that is coming to us at last—the happiness of being together—till death do us part. …

Aunt Maggie wrote and formally invited the Col. & your mother to the wedding—and they have formally declined—so the right thing has been done—on both sides! … I should like you to send me as you proposed your silver tea pot & things as we are going to show the presents here—and it may as well be a good show. I think they will be quite safe for I constantly get presents of silver by parcels post or by rail *registered*. I would bring them to Hopton with my others, such a lot now. ...

I hope *now* you will order a nice warm pretty comfy smoking suit for yourself dearest. Don't have black—it would be so gloomy—for a bridegroom & not match me at all. Will you have a dark red, a deep *sang-de-boeuf*—or Indian red colour of soft stuff—with facings & cords of red *silk* to match. Would not this be nice? It would be becoming to *me*—as a background when we are together!! You ought to get something nice for yourself now you can afford it. ... Ever your own *Laure*

25TH JULY

My own darling Adrian, ... Your presents are lovely—they came this morning & have a little table to themselves near mine. ... After all the St Levans have sent me plate—it is rather disappointing as they have chosen *another* pair of silver candlesticks, the 5th I have had. I think we might quietly change them when we get back to town. ... Will you tell me where that maid I have engaged for the house boat is to meet Mr and Mrs A.H. at Paddington in the afternoon of the 3rd of August ... and to be very *terre-à-terre* [down to earth]. I think we had better take down some dinner with us—cold chickens or something—& ham for it would be difficult to arrange dinner directly we get down to the *Crocodile*. I thought we might go to the Fortnum & Masons or to the more humble [Army & Navy] Stores on the 3rd & get some *gobbits* for the boat. I want to let her know in good time—for I feel I shall forget all about everything but happiness at Hopton! Adieu darling darling, soon to be your own wife— *Laure*

WHITE'S, ST JAMES'   26TH JULY

My own *Laure*, I have taken rooms at a quiet hotel and ordered a little feast for just us two on the 2nd August. This day week just fancy being able to snap our fingers at the Chaperons & to do what we like. A telegram has just come from Jem & Elsie saying that Leo [their manservant] will be left on board. We now only want a cook & can do without the Lock Keeper's daughter or the maid you have arranged with, whichever you like. Good night, Your Adrian

HUNSTANTON   27TH JULY

Darling Adrian, ... I am inclined to keep the maid I engaged in London as I know her—& she is rather elderly & *engaged* so we imagine will not flirt with

Leo! I am very glad we are to keep him for he will valet you & he waits so well & is used to the ways of the boat. ... I imagine you arriving at Yarmouth today with Jo. I have had 7 presents today—including yet more antique teaspoons from Sir F. & Lady Boileau, such pretty ones with a little dancing Venus on the top instead of an apostle. ... Adieu my darling, Ever your *Laure*

Great Ormond Street Hospital, Bloomsbury   27th July

My Darling, In an hour I shall be off to Yarmouth. My Mother & Charlie are here & lunch with me. The Colonel has finally agreed to sign & Hasties' Clerks are in mad haste engrossing the deeds which must be signed on Wednesday [1st]. I really cannot write Sweet Love so goodbye, Your Adrian

Hunstanton   28th July

Darling Adrian, The presents are all on view this afternoon in the dining-room with their cards of names. They look so lovely, the house is full of people, Hunstonians buzzing in and out to see them. They seem so delighted & all have their congratulations for me. So many good wishes & it is rather embarrassing many people don't know us apart and congratulate the wrong sister—but that is a detail. My wedding gown is also on view—and spread out in the drawing room—so they come on and see it after the presents. Some of them are *too funny* with their remarks, we have been in fits of laughter. ... I had such a delightful letter from Ernest this morning—who alas cannot possibly come to our wedding. It is strange to think this is the last week of my life here. Adieu my darling, Your own *Laure*

P.S. I have put all your presents together darling, & your photograph in the midst. One old lady said—'I am sure you must love him Miss—why I could love him myself!' Lots more presents today.

Charlie Orde was now the banker at Barclays in Great Yarmouth so the Bank House was at his disposal and Adrian spent his last bachelor days there.

Bank House, Yarmouth   Sunday, 29th July

It was rather lonely here all alone the first night but yesterday Mrs Orde came & lunched with E. [the eldest daughter], & then I had to hurry off to meet Jo [who is to be best man]. After dinner as it was cold we lit a fire & smoked round it till bed-time. Today we drove over to Hopton to hear the Banns read. It was so curious to hear Muller mumble out your name & mine. It felt so real then, with everyone staring hard at me. Were you at the Old Church & did you hear the Banns too? *Please do not forget* that you must bring with you a certificate signed by Waller of the Banns having been read. Unless you do there can be no wedding on Thursday, so *REMEMBER*.

I drove Jo over to Hopton in such a nice Dog cart. After Church we had a very jolly lunch & then Golf & then I had a lesson on the Sandilo[127] given me by Betty. I quite love Julian who was there. There are parcels at Hopton for you which we all looked at longingly. ... This is positively the last letter but one which I shall ever write to the Laura Troubridge whom I have loved so well all these years. Do you think I shall love Laura Hope as well? My Darling I count the minutes until I see you again. Goodbye, Your Adrian

P.S. E. & Betty are delighted with their moonstone [bridesmaids'] Bracelets.

HUNSTANTON   30TH JULY

Darling Adrian, Tomorrow at 5 o'clock we expect to get to Yarmouth, Vauxhall Station. I have been very busy the whole day long—with all the others—packing our presents to bring to Hopton & putting away things about the house because of The Castle being let for the next month. ... I feel so tired darling—oh how *happy* we shall be at Pangbourne. I am sending you your mother's letter to me. ... I feel full of vague happiness, just like I used to feel at Knocklofty. Adieu my own dearest. Goodbye—goodbye—goodbye to Laura *Troubridge*

P.S. Tom *is* coming to give me away.

Mrs Hope's pencilled note to Laura enclosed her wedding present, and that of Jessie, together with the daughters' little notes:

'Dearest Laura, Will you accept the enclosed sachet, as a link with the past. It was one of the wedding presents of my dear Grannie M. Dundas when she married Mr Speirs in the end of the last century [Archibald Speirs of Elderslie in 1794]. It still looks bridal & I like to think of it in your hands. Jessie is afraid you will think her tidy old fashioned. It has given her such pleasure doing it for you. I do hope the "rain of love" may cease by Thursday. ...

'It's a bore about Fulham [the offer of Little Mulgrave House there for part of the honeymoon by Lady Napier & Ettrick's daughter-in-law Emily, wife of the 4th son Mark]. Mark's notions I suppose are too *grand seigneur*, he thought the place ought to be full fig for the bridal pair. Goodbye my new dear daughter, Your loving—M.J. Hope'

Mrs Hope's mother was née Speirs and this family heirloom, a cream satin sachet embroidered with *'Gage de mon éstime'* [A token of my esteem] in steel beads, still exists in its bridal state. Inside is a little cream satin roll-up needlecase with the original needles unused. This may be Jessie's tidy. These two daughters were by now aged eighteen and fourteen, and their diminutive notes showed how fond they were of Laura. The elder, Jessie, wrote:

> 'My dear Sister, I hope you will be very happy in your new life with Adie. I had nothing to give you so I worked this tidy for you. Madge is going to make some shades for your seven lamps. ...'.

Madge followed with her note but made no mention of the shades:

> 'I hope you will be *very, very* happy & will have everything you want to make you happy & merry & wise & gay, like Sunday's bairn. I wish I could give you anything like Jessie could, but I can't do that sort of thing & could not do anything else in time, and I can only send you my best wishes and love. Jessie would have written you a longer letter only her eyes were so sore, so she asked me to tell you in my letter that she could not as she doesn't like to make excuses for herself. ...'.

BANK HOUSE, YARMOUTH   30TH JULY

My Darling, At last our long letter writing time is ended. I can hardly believe that never again shall I write to the same L.T. at Hunstanton. It seems too wonderful to be true. Last night we were kept up very late by Julian who talked so amusingly. Now Jo & I are going over to play tennis at Hopton & to dine there. ... Every morning 'I arise from dreams of thee' darling love so soon now to be with me, Your Adrian

On the 31st Laura finally left Hunstanton and 'the dear little house' with her sisters, to be met by Adrian and Jo. The next two days were largely spent in opening more presents and arranging them to be on view in the drawing-room at Hopton, and writing still more thank-you letters. Tom (Troubridge) arrived the day before the wedding and was 'very nice & jolly' and Amy, whose thirty-second birthday it was, 'plays delightfully' in the evening.

---

127 *29th July* Sandilo. This object remains unidentified but was probably a game or a musical instrument. If any reader knows what a sandilo is, the editor would be most grateful to have the information. *The Editor, The Tite Street Press, 11 Winchester Court, Vicarage Gate, London W8 4AB*

LAURA'S JOURNAL

OUR WEDDING DAY

2ND AUGUST 1888

At Hopton, Yarmouth
[with Aunt Maggie Orde]

2nd August, 1888 – Our wedding day—and such a lovely bright day of sunshine. … down pretty early, all busy making the bridesmaids bouquets of roses, & decorating the wedding cake till 1 o'clock lunch. Then off to dress, in my bridal white satin, orange flowers & veil. Tom took me to the church. My bridesmaids all in the porch, Adrian already there. Uncle Herb did the service beautifully that united us at last. Felt in a strange kind of dream—but very happy, I could not realize the parting. About 50 people, little Dodsie [Wright] as my page, & nearly all people I loved present. We left at 5. & got up to London about 11 o'clock.

Laura's journal recounted blissfully happy days during the three weeks they spent on board the *Crocodile* house boat at Pangbourne, and on occasions they came up to London to complete arrangements concerning the 'half house' in Brompton Road. Laura sounded only one teasing note at the end of the first week: 'Went to Pangbourne to see the Exhibition but it was shut, bought some fruit & came home to lunch. Adrian sulky! would only eat salad!' By the evening all was well and it was 'a heavenly idle life …'.

EDITOR'S POSTSCRIPT

What of the future, did Adrian and Laura live happily ever after? The answer is yes and no. It was not until three years into their marriage, in 1892, that Laura really made her name as a pastel portraitist when she spent several weeks on the Isle of Wight with her great aunt, Lady Cochrane, whose daughter, Minnie, was lady-in-waiting to HRH Princess Beatrice of Battenberg. After seeing her portrait of Minnie Cochrane and other examples of her work, Queen Victoria asked Laura to paint portraits of her daughter, Beatrice, and several of her grandchildren. Laura's account of this extraordinary two months' visit was included as an 'Epilogue' at the end of her early journals, *Life Amongst the Troubridges – Journals of a Young Victorian 1873-1884* (published in 1966, reprinted 1999).

Later in the same year Adrian and Laura bought their final home—More House, No 34 (since renumbered as 52) Tite Street, Chelsea. They both loved the house, and the large studio was perfect for Laura whose career as an artist increasingly contributed to the family income. They remained in love all their married life and had two much-loved daughters, Jaqueline—my mother—born in 1889, and Esmé, born in 1897.

Adrian failed to extricate himself from the Great Ormond Street Hospital and indeed came to find it a rewarding challenge, although Laura never came to terms with its demands on his time and energy. Adrian's health deteriorated and every winter he suffered terribly from colds and flu so that he often went abroad on his own to recuperate with his Aunt Annie Cunninghame Graham and his sister Laura [by then married to Tom Allen], both of whom still doted on him. Laura remained at home as they could not both afford to go away together.

Ill-health apart, their life would have been idyllic but for the mad colonel. The business of the ownership of the Hope family portraits dragged on year after year. Col Hope took out no less than eight lawsuits against Adrian (four in Scotland and four in England), lost them all and lived in a permanent state of bankruptcy. Adrian battled on to get possession of the portraits, in order to sell some of them for his mother's benefit, but she eventually sided with her husband and neither of them were on speaking terms with Adrian. The legal expenses crippled them both and the worry exacerbated Adrian's ill-health.

The devastating blow fell in 1904 after less than sixteen years of marriage when Adrian died suddenly after an operation, dangerous in those days, for appendicitis. Laura was inconsolable, and within the year she lost her younger child, Esmé, from diphtheria. Not only did her world fall to pieces, but her financial situation was far from easy so that she had to rent out More House and move to smaller temporary homes. It took nearly ten years before she and Jaqueline could afford to return there, in 1915. Shortly after this, Jaqueline married Hedley Nicholson, and they took the surname Hope-Nicholson. They all three remained at More House, and Laura finally died there in 1929, happy to have known her three small grandchildren.

Laura did make a brave new life for herself, and kept up her journals as well as a voluminous correspondence with her innumerable uncles, aunts, brothers and sisters, nephews and nieces—all of which is neatly stored in the family archives—waiting its turn to form the basis of another book continuing the Hope family saga.

BIOGRAPHICAL NOTES

THE HOPE FAMILY (LINLITHGOW BRANCH)

Lt-Col William Hope VC (1843-1909) and Margaret Jane née Cunninghame Graham (d 1909)

Crimean War hero, awarded VC as twenty-one-year old lieutenant in 1855. After brief period in the Diplomatic Service abroad became an unsuccessful entrepreneur in the field of experimental agriculture and later designer of guns. Did not inherit the legal talents of his father (John Hope) or grandfather (Charles Hope, Lord Granton), respectively Lord Justice Clerk and Lord President of the Scottish Court of Session. His wife was a daughter of Robert C Cunninghame Graham of Gartmore and aunt to the writer, traveller and rebellious politician 'Don Roberto' Cunninghame Graham. Their six children, listed below in order of age, had a difficult and often unhappy upbringing.

Adrian Hope (1858-1904)

After basic schooling, educated by private tutors (frequently alcoholic) while helping his father in his agricultural farming enterprises. First worked in Bank of England, then to regain his health went to Ceylon (Sri Lanka) as Private Secretary to the Governor for three years. Returned to London in 1884, worked gratis for Poor Law Auditors until appointed Secretary to Great Ormond St Hospital for Sick Children, where he became highly successful as fund-raiser. Married Laura Troubridge (1888), had two daughters, Jaqueline (1889-1972) and Esmé (1897-1905). He died at forty-six after operation for appendicitis.

Laura Hope (1859-1936)

As a result of her parents' impecunious life, she was largely brought up abroad by her maternal aunt, Annie Cunninghame Graham. Spent brief period teaching French and German in a Cambridge school. In 1888 again lived abroad with her aunt, mostly in Italy, where she met her future husband, T W Allen, Greek scholar and Fellow of Queen's

College, Oxford. They married (1894), returned to live in Oxford and had a daughter, Charlotte, who in her turn wrote a lively journal when she was thirteen years old: *A Year in the Life of an Oxford Schoolgirl— Charlotte Allen's Private Journal for 1910* (not yet published). Laura became a passionate Christian Scientist.

John Hope (1864-97)

Unsuccessful 'soldier of fortune' as a trooper in Bechuanaland Border Police. After a visit to see his family in England in 1897, he shot himself in despair in an Amsterdam hotel room with less than £2 to his name.

Charles Hope (1867-1947)

Won scholarships at school and university, went to South Africa to make his fortune, became a noted educationist and founded schools modelled on British public school system. Married (1896) Alice Wilmot and had four sons and three daughters.

Jessie Hope (1870-1920)

For many years an invalid with a bad hip. Later lived with her married sister Laura Allen and their aunt, Annie Cunninghame Graham, in Oxford. Became a successful historical novelist under the pseudonym 'Graham Hope', and an active supporter of the Women's Unionist & Tariff Reform Association for which she was organising secretary for four years.

Madge Hope (1873-1947)

Only daughter to be sent away to boarding school. Soon became independent, married (1893) Francis Napier, ophthalmic surgeon, whose mother, Hon Mrs William Napier née Lloyd, was aunt to Constance Lloyd, wife of Oscar Wilde. They went to live in South Africa, had three sons and Madge scandalised the family by leaving her husband for another man.

THE TROUBRIDGE FAMILY

Col Sir Thomas St Vincent Hope Cochrane Troubridge CB, 3rd Bt (1815-67) and Louisa née Gurney (1830-67)

Crimean War hero, losing one leg and the other foot at battle of Inkerman in 1854. Afterwards ADC to Queen Victoria and head of Army Clothing Department. His grandfather, Admiral Sir Thomas Troubridge 1st Bt, was one of Nelson's favourite captains. Louisa was a daughter of Daniel Gurney (youngest of the Gurneys of Earlham and brother of Elizabeth Fry) and Lady Harriet Hay, daughter of 17th Earl of Errol. Their six children had a very happy but all too brief childhood with their parents who died within weeks of each other in 1867 when the oldest child was aged eleven and the youngest not yet two. They were then brought up by their widowed grandfather Daniel Gurney (1791-1881) at North Runcton Hall, King's Lynn, Norfolk.

Laura Troubridge's thumbnail sketches of her siblings from her journal of 1885 are given in *italics* at the start of the following biographical notes:

Amy Troubridge (1856-1932)

> *'A great love of music, of talking, and the powers of pleasing & charming when she wishes to do so.'*

Lively, popular but not a great beauty. Fell in love with the wrong people (those destined to marry money—or never to marry). Talented pianist and composer of music for Laura's amateur theatrical productions.

Laura Troubridge (1858-1929)

Also lively, popular, and with a very attractive personality. Became successful pastel portrait painter and children's book illustrator, her earnings contributing greatly to the family income after her marriage to Adrian Hope (1888). Had two daughters, Jaqueline (1889-1972) and

Esmé (1897-1905). Wrote and produced many short plays for her children and friends to act for charity and amusement. Was devastated by the early death of her husband in 1904 after an operation for appendicitis, followed by the death of Esmé from diphtheria within a year. Lived to see her surviving daughter, Jaqueline, married to Hedley Nicholson (1916) who assumed surname of Hope-Nicholson, and for a few years to enjoy the company of her three grandchildren: Lauretta (b 1919), Felix (1921-90) and Marie-Jaqueline (b 1922).

Violet 'Vi' Troubridge (1859-1931)

> '*Different in most ways to the two above, & so fitting in—like a mosaic—into each other's lives. Quiet & unemotional, a devourer of books but a neglecter of drawing—alas a buried talent.*'

The beauty of the family. Enjoyed a very social life in Norfolk although intensely shy, even in her own home. Married (1893) her first cousin Walter Gurney of Runcton (elder son of the young Troubridges' guardian, Sir Somerville 'Uncle Sommy' Gurney). Had one son and two daughters.

Sir Thomas 'Tom' Troubridge FSA, 4th Bt (1860-1938)

> '*Lieutenant in the 60th Rifles—popular, with many real friends notwithstanding a very empty purse. Singer of songs, raconteur & liked by women as well as men, & sporting.*'

Ten years in army, then partner on Stock Exchange. Despite family objections, only partly due to lack of money on both sides, married (1893) his first cousin Laura 'Queenie' Gurney, daughter of Charles Gurney and Alice Prinsep. Had one son and two daughters. Tom became a noted antiquarian and Queenie a novelist and author of the best-selling *The Book of Etiquette—the complete standard work of reference on social usages* (1926).

Admiral Sir Ernest Troubridge KCMG, CB, CMG, MVO (1862-1926)

> *'Lieutenant in the Royal Navy—half way to China on board* Agamemnon *(1885). Loved by everyone who knows him.'*

Served in RN all his life. Married (1st, 1891) Edith Duffus (d 1900) and had one son, two daughters; (2nd, 1908) Una Taylor and had one daughter. Separated in 1919 when Una went to live with the lesbian 'John' Radclyffe Hall (author of the notorious *The Well of Loneliness*, banned soon after it was first published in 1928). Ernest was adored by his sisters and had immense charm. He consulted Laura on the upbringing of his two elder daughters who could not abide their stepmother—and Laura often took charge of his youngest daughter, Andrea. Awarded Royal Humane Society's silver medal (1888) for saving life of a sailor fallen overboard. Made scapegoat for 'failing to pursue the enemy' in the battle cruiser *Goeben* in 1914. Requested a court martial after the official inquest and was there honourably acquitted but it ruined his naval career at sea. Later he served abroad with distinction on numerous diplomatic missions.

Helen 'Limpet' Troubridge (1866-1958)

> *'The baby of this family. She is 19! Alas time flies—alas.'*

Very attractive but suffered from—and perhaps enjoyed—being treated as the baby long after she was grown-up. Led a very social life in Norfolk but was not to marry until much later. Although a competent water-colour artist, she lacked the drive or will to develop her talents in this direction. After two sisters were married she and Amy shared a flat in London until Helen's marriage in 1917 to Capt John Brabant Bate RAMC (T) and West African Medical Staff. After his death in 1937, she developed greatly and was appreciated for her wit in old age. She made her final home with Laura's daughter and grandson, Jaqueline and Felix Hope-Nicholson, at More House—the studio house in Tite Street, Chelsea, that Adrian and Laura had bought in 1892.

INDEX

Numerals in **heavy** type refer to illustration sections between pages 132/133 and 324/325, and in Roman numerals to extended caption information in 'About the Illustrations' on pages xvii-xxii. AH refers to Adrian Hope and LT to Laura Troubridge.

Certain subjects are grouped under the following categories: AMATEUR THEATRICALS; BALLS/DANCES; BANDS; BOOKS; CHARADES/DRESSING-UP/TABLEAUX VIVANTS; CLUBS; FASHION/COSTUME COMMENTS; GAMES; LT ARTWORK/BOOK ILLUSTRATIONS; PUBLICATIONS; RESTAURANTS; SHOPS; THEATRE VISITS.

A

Abbey Lodge, Regent's Park, London *see* Bunsen (de)

Aberdare, Harry Bruce, 1st Lord 134-36, 236, 410, 446

Abergavenny, William, 1st Marquess of and Lady née Caroline Johnstone 121

Acton, John, 1st Lord 133, 139fn52

ADC, Cambridge *Henry IV* 275

Admiralty 266

Agamemnon —'the *Ag/Hag*' (ship) 78, 194, 364

Albert Exhibition Palace, Battersea Park, London *see* EXHIBITIONS/GALLERIES

Alexander, Maj Gen Sir Claud 1st Bt and Lady née Eliza Speirs 234

Alexander House lodgings, London 419

Alexandra (flagship) 355

AMATEUR THEATRICALS

  Beauty and the Beast 73

  A Comical Countess by W Brough 63, 64, 65-66, 68

  at Downton Castle 255

  Engaged by W S Gilbert 72-76, 77

  Guards, at Chelsea Barracks 418

The Happy Pair by S Theyre Smith 220, 215, 227, 230, 231, 282-83, 286

  at Middleton Towers 286

Our Wife 206

The Parvenu 346, 348, 352

  at Runcton, Xmas 1886 281, 282

Statue Gallery 206

Sweethearts by W S Gilbert 51, 54, 58, 60, 61, 63-66, 68

To Oblige Benson 206

Turn Him Out by Thomas J Williams 225, 227-28, 230, 231

Variety Entertainment/tableaux, Hunstanton 372-77

Amherst, William Tyssen (later 1st Lord Amherst of Hackney) and Margaret née Mitford 59, 82-83, 94fn30, 248, 319, 344

  Alice photographs AH/LT as profiles on coin 83

  Mary (later Baroness Amherst, m. Ld William Cecil)

  Hackney Hospital Bazaar and *In a Good Cause* album **17**, 116, 121-25, 127, 130fn49, 165

  Wilde's poem decorated by LT **17**, 122-25, 127, 165

amor vincit omnia (AH/LT's motto) 25, 33fn3

anatomy, LT studies 258

Anderson, Mary in *Romeo & Juliet* 76, 91 in *A Winter's Tale* 405

Annie, Aunt *see* Cunninghame Graham, Annie

anti-Jewish comments xxv, 38, 101-02, 422

Apsley House, Hyde Park Corner, London *see* Wellington, Duke of

Arab motto 132

Archdale, Alice *see* Orde, Julian

ALSO PUBLISHED BY THE TITE STREET PRESS

LIFE AMONGST THE TROUBRIDGES

Journals of a Young Victorian in Norfolk,

with forays to London

1873-1884

by Laura Troubridge

Edited by her daughter Jaqueline Hope-Nicholson

LIFE AMONGST THE TROUBRIDGES

It was the journals of Grandfather Daniel Gurney's sisters, one of them Elizabeth Fry, which first fired fifteen-year-old Laura Troubridge to keep her own journals from 1873. The father of the six Troubridge children was Colonel Sir Thomas St Vincent Troubridge, a hero of the Crimean War who became an ADC to Queen Victoria and who died a few weeks after his young wife in 1867. The six orphans then went to live at Runcton in Norfolk with their grandfather. He was very old-fashioned and had changed nothing since the death of his wife, Lady Harriet Gurney, in the 1830s.

In Laura Troubridge's journals and memoirs we have an inimitable, authentic eye-witness account of family life in Victorian England with vivid portraits of all their relations, governesses and tutors. She describes picnics and excursions, staying in country houses, visits to London and finally her engagement. Already she was designing decorative tiles, Christmas cards and illustrating children's books. Later, as Laura Hope, she became well-known as a pastelist and painted Queen Victoria's grandchildren at Osborne.

The journals and memoirs are edited by her daughter, Jaqueline Hope-Nicholson and illustrated by the author's own drawings and by family photographs.

… The trivia of these cheerful lives is something of a gold mine for the historian of trivia, and so is Laura Troubridge's language, the easy slangy teenage talk of a period in which the natural speech of the upper classes is hard to come by. … (The Times Literary Supplement, 26.1.67)

First published 1966; revised reprint 1999 by Tite Street Press, with 12pp of illustrations
£12.95
Available from Gazelle Book Services, Falcon House, Queen Square, Lancaster La1 1RN Tel 01524 68765